SERVICES LIBERALIZATION IN ASEAN

SERVICES LIBERALIZATION IN ASEAN

Foreign Direct Investment in Logistics

Edited by Tham Siew Yean and Sanchita Basu Das

ISEAS YUSOF ISHAK INSTITUTE

First published in Singapore in 2018 by
ISEAS Publishing
30 Heng Mui Keng Terrace
Singapore 119614

E-mail: publish@iseas.edu.sg
Website: bookshop.iseas.edu.sg

*The responsibility for facts and opinions in this publication rests exclusively with the authors
and their interpretations do not necessarily reflect the views or the policy of the publisher or
its supporters.*

ISEAS Library Cataloguing-in-Publication Data

Services Liberalization in ASEAN : Foreign Direct Investment in Logistics / edited by
　Tham Siew Yean and Sanchita Basu Das.
　1.　Business logistics—Southeast Asia.
　2.　Transportation—Southeast Asia.
　3.　Investments, Foreign—Southeast Asia.
　I.　Tham, Siew Yean.
　II.　Basu Das, Sanchita.
HD38.5 S49　　　　　　　　　　　　　　2018

ISBN 978-981-4786-18-8 (soft cover)
ISBN 978-981-4786-25-6 (E-book PDF)

Typeset by International Typesetters Pte Ltd
Printed in Singapore by Markono Print Media Pte Ltd

CONTENTS

LIST OF TABLES

LIST OF FIGURES

FOREWORD

ASEAN turns fifty this year. And there is cause for celebration. For a group of countries that are so economically, politically and culturally varied, it has achieved much over the five decades. To appreciate the strides made by this regional grouping one has to explore ASEAN's economic journey from modest goals of a preferential trade agreement (PTA) in the 1970s through the establishment of the ASEAN Free Trade Area (AFTA) in the 1990s, the AEC Blueprint 2015 (AEC 2015) and AEC Blueprint 2025 (AEC 2025).

The ASEAN story reflects the grouping's step-by-step confidence building approach towards integration. This served the members well, allowing for domestic adjustments even as it deepened its regional commitments, moving from voluntary liberalization under the PTA, through the rules-based ASEAN Trade in Goods Agreement (ATIGA) and services liberalization under the ASEAN Framework Agreement on Services (AFAS), and laying the foundation for an integrated investment region through the ASEAN Comprehensive Investment Agreement (ACIA). The latter three agreements are core to both the AEC 2015 and AEC 2025 as the region looks to deepening economic integration not just among the ASEAN Member States (AMS) but also with its Dialogue Partners.

ASEAN has been successful in the removal of tariffs for intra-ASEAN trade in goods; done significant work on services liberalization; and has managed some measure of streamlining of investment rules. Much work has also been done on Mutual Recognition Agreements and Standards and Conformance.

Even as ASEAN revels in its achievement, much more needs to be done. Key to ASEAN economic integration is trade facilitation. Meaningful market access for both goods and services requires that ASEAN move forward with work on Non-Tariff Measures, domestic regulations as well as continued infrastructure and human capital development. These measures are outlined in the AEC Blueprint 2025, which has the following features: (i) A Highly Integrated and Cohesive Economy; (ii) A Competitive, Innovative, and Dynamic ASEAN; (iii) An ASEAN with Enhanced Connectivity and Deeper Sectoral Cooperation; (iv) A Resilient, Inclusive, People-Oriented, and People-Centered ASEAN; and (v) A Global ASEAN.

Complementing AEC 2025 is the Master Plan on ASEAN Connectivity 2025 (MPAC 2025). The focus of MPAC 2025 is on (i) sustainable infrastructure; (ii) digital innovation; (iii) seamless logistics; (iv) regulatory excellence; and (v) people mobility. It builds on the work done thus far to improve connectivity in the region and recognizes that much remains to be done to realize the vision of a seamlessly connected ASEAN.

Both these Blueprints highlight that it is difficult to realize economic integration, innovative and inclusive growth, and have its industries weave into global value chains (GVCs), without paying attention to both physical and institutional connectivity. Physical connectivity is a prerequisite for economic development. Trade facilitation in the form of tariff elimination and reduction in logistics costs, efficient physical connectivity of roads, rail and ports, is necessary.

However, physical connectivity must be complemented by institutional connectivity, i.e., higher trade and investment facilitation which allows for transfer of knowledge and attraction of higher level skills, and the liberalization and strengthening of GVC-supporting services such as finance, telecommunication, transport, distribution, and professional services. It is the combination of physical and institutional connectivity which would enhance ASEAN's competitiveness, and draw quality Foreign Direct Investments (FDI) needed for the region's sustained economic growth.

The AEC 2025 and MPAC 2025 stress the importance of the services sector and measures to reduce services trade restrictiveness as these have a positive indirect impact on the manufacturing sectors that use services as intermediate inputs in production. This implies ensuring the development of seamless logistics in the region through strengthening ASEAN competitiveness. Therein lies the challenge. It is in this context that this publication is relevant.

Given the complexity of the services sector it is appropriate that this publication has focused on logistics as it is not only one of the twelve priority integration sectors for ASEAN, but it also encompasses key aspects of the manufacturing supply chain. Echoing MPAC 2025, the authors reiterate that an effective logistics sector enhances efficiencies in supply-chain movements, reduces trade costs and facilitates trade across countries.

Using the OECD Regulatory Restrictiveness Index, the World Economic Forum's (WEF) Human Capital Index, the WEF's Global Competitiveness Reports, the World Bank's Ease of Doing Business reports, the World Bank's Logistics Performance Index (LPI), and analyses of ASEAN's services commitments in AFAS and WTO GATS, the authors highlight the variation in performance and commitments across the region. The country chapters identify in detail the challenges for each AMS and dive deeper into measures that may be taken to address them.

The authors have aggregated the issues, provided substantial analyses of the challenges, and put forward recommendations that ASEAN, collectively, and each AMS, may take towards achieving the goals set out in AEC 2025 and MPAC 2025.

Policymakers in each AMS should find the individual case studies useful as they work to overcome the challenges in liberalizing and facilitating an FDI-enabling environment for the services sector in general, and the logistic sector, specifically.

Tan Sri Rebecca Fatima Sta Maria
Senior Policy Fellow
Economic Research Institute for ASEAN and East Asia (ERIA)
(and former Secretary-General,
Ministry of International Trade and Industry, Malaysia)

22 May 2017

PREFACE

A frequent question raised in discussions on Free Trade Agreements (FTAs) is the impact of liberalization in services on inflows of Foreign Direct Investment (FDI). Policymakers are concerned if liberalization has encouraged FDI inflows while researchers are keen to test the same relationship. Likewise, the public is curious as to whether FTAs are as useful as touted. Yet the relationship between liberalization and inflows of FDI is not as straightforward for services as in the case of manufacturing. This is because the services sector is frequently highly regulated due to information asymmetries between producers and consumers. Domestic regulations therefore play an important role in protecting domestic consumers but these regulations can at the same time hinder the entry of both domestic and foreign service providers. While liberalization is important, it is not sufficient and any attempt at investigating the impact of liberalization on inflows of FDI has to take into consideration the FDI enabling environment in a country.

Given this, we are motivated to undertake a study that can illuminate the academics, policymakers and businesses on liberalization issues in the services sector for the ten member countries in ASEAN. We decided to focus on FDI liberalization in services as commercial presence is considered as the most important mode of trade in services. Given the heterogeneity of the services sector, we chose to focus on the logistics industry as a case study as the industry plays a key role in the movement of goods, services and people across ASEAN.

The main objective of this book is, thus, to compare international and domestic policy measures for attracting FDI and its impact on inflows of FDI in the services sector in the ten ASEAN member countries. This has implications for ASEAN's economic cooperation, in general, and for the logistics sector integration, in particular.

To meet the objective, we gathered experts from ten Southeast Asian countries. We conducted one closed-door workshop and one public conference at ISEAS – Yusof Ishak Institute, Singapore to discuss the content of the chapters and gather feedback and comments from participants. The meetings were conducted in June 2016 and November 2016, respectively.

The book begins with an overview chapter that covers the literature on FDI in services sector, together with an analytical framework that is subsequently used in the country chapters and discussions on the logistics industry. The overview chapter also provides a preview of the subsequent country-chapters and outlines key findings and policy recommendations. It is then followed by ten country chapters written by experts on the services and logistics sector.

We hope this book will help stakeholders of ASEAN member countries and other interested parties in understanding the current state of services liberalization and facilitation measures in order to attract FDI. It will help readers to develop an understanding of the logistics sector in the region and the key factors that make it difficult to provide a seamless movement of goods and services across ASEAN member countries' borders. We hope the policy recommendations can provide food for thought for policymakers in the region.

ACKNOWLEDGEMENTS

This book would not have made it without the kind support from many within the ISEAS – Yusof Ishak Institute, Singapore. We sincerely thank ISEAS Director, Mr Tan Chin Tiong, for his unwavering support from the start to the completion of this book project. His trust in us, as coordinators of the project and subsequently as the editors of the book, has spurred us to do our very best. We also thank Dr Ooi Kee Beng, former Deputy Director of ISEAS, for his kind suggestions and advice over the course of the project.

Our heartfelt thanks to the authors, who made time for us to write the country chapters and also to attend the two meetings at ISEAS, Singapore, during the course of the project. Their frank and balanced opinion and willingness to share ideas and experiences have helped to improve the initial drafts greatly. In particular, we thank Dr Gilberto M. Llanto, President, Philippine Institute for Development Studies (PIDS) and Associate Professor Dr Ruth Banomyong of Thammasat University for sharing their insights with us at the two meetings of the initial draft chapters. We genuinely thank all authors for their patience and perseverance to work on their chapters during the review and the editorial process. It is their combined efforts that have enabled this book to be completed on time.

We are grateful, too, to Dr Francis Hutchinson, Coordinator of the Regional Economic Studies Programme, and to Dr Tang Siew Mun, Head of the ASEAN Studies Centre, both divisions based at ISEAS, for overseeing our work from inception to its final delivery. Both of them have always given us encouragement whenever we encounter unexpected difficulties during the year long duration of this project. Special thanks goes to Dr Francis Hutchinson, Dr Cassey Lee and Dr Siwage Dharma Negara of ISEAS, and Associate Professors Dr Toh Mun Heng and Dr Teofilo C. Daquila of the National University of Singapore, for moderating sessions during the two meetings of the project and also for their useful comments. We thank all the attendees during the meetings at ISEAS for their feedback on our papers and presentations.

We are grateful to Mr Ng Kok Kiong, Head of ISEAS Publishing, and his team for their meticulous work and to Mr Ang Swee Loh and his administrative and finance staff for their dedication in performing their tasks related to the project.

Our sincere thanks also extend to Ms Pham Thi Phuong Thao, Research Officer at the ASEAN Studies Centre for her diligent and excellent assistance and other support during the final stage of the project.

We earnestly thank Tan Sri Dr Rebecca Fatima Sta Maria, Senior Policy Fellow at Economic Research Institute for ASEAN and East Asia (ERIA) and former Secretary-General, Ministry of International Trade and Industry, Malaysia, for giving an insightful foreword for this volume. Tan Sri Rebecca was also an ASEAN SEOM Leader and had served as an eminent member for ASEAN's High Level Task Force for Economic Integration.

We are thankful to all who have helped us with the project to make it a success. Any shortcomings during the course of the study or in this publication are entirely our own.

Tham Siew Yean and Sanchita Basu Das
The Editors

ABBREVIATIONS

10MP	Tenth Malaysia Plan
11MP	Eleven Malaysia Plan
2PLs	Second Party Logistics
3PLs	Third Party Logistics
AANZFTA	ASEAN–Australia–New Zealand Free Trade Area
ACFTA	ASEAN–China Free Trade Agreement
ADB	Asian Development Bank
AEC	ASEAN Economic Community
AFAS	ASEAN Framework Agreement on Services
AFC	Asian Financial Crisis
AFFA	ASEAN Freight Forwarders Association
AMSs	ASEAN Member States
ASPBI	Annual Survey of Philippine Business and Industry
ASW	ASEAN Single Window
ATIGA	ASEAN Trade in Goods Agreement
ATISA	ASEAN Trade in Services Agreement
BCC	Brunei Competition Commission
BDNSW	Brunei Darussalam National Single Window
BEDB	Brunei Economic Development Board
BIMP-EAGA	Brunei Darussalam–Indonesia–Malaysia–Philippines East ASEAN Growth Area
BOI	Board of Investment
BOO	Build-Own-Operate
BOT	Build-Operate-Transfer
BRUFA	Brunei Freight Forwarders Association
CAAP	Civil Aviation Authority of the Philippines
CAGR	Compound Annual Growth Rate
CAMFFA	Cambodia Freight Forwarders Association
CAPEX	Capital Expenditure
CBTA	Cross-Border Transport Agreement

CDG	Capability Development Grant
CFE	Committee on the Future Economy
CLM	Cambodia, Lao PDR and Myanmar
CLMV	Cambodia, Lao PDR, Myanmar and Vietnam
CO	Certificate of Origin
CPC	Central Product Classification
CPPM	Customs-Private Sector Partnership Mechanism
CSEZB	Cambodian Special Economic Zone Board
DDA	Doha Development Agenda
DICA	Directorate of Investment and Company Administration
DOS	Department of Statistics
DOTC	Department of Transportation and Communication
DOTr	Department of Transportation
DPWH	Department of Public Works and Highways
DTAs	Double Taxation Agreements
DTIS	Diagnostic Trade Integration Study
DVA	Domestic Value Added
ECER	East Coast Economic Region
EDB	Economic Development Board
EPU	Economic Planning Unit
EU	European Union
EVFTA	EU–Vietnam FTA
EWEC	East–West Economic Corridor
FAST	FDI Action and Support Centre
FBA	Foreign Business Act
FBL	Foreign Business License
FDI	Foreign Direct Investment
FESR	Framework for Economic and Social Reforms
FIC	Foreign Investment Committee
FIL	Foreign Investment Law
FIMC	Foreign Investment Management Committee
FTAs	Free Trade Agreements
GAFA	Gross Additions to Fixed Assets
GATS	General Agreement of Trade in Services
GDCE	General Department of Customs and Excise
GDL	Goods Drivers Licence
GDP	Gross Domestic Product
GFC	Global Financial Crisis
GLCs	Government-Linked Companies
GMS	Greater Mekong Sub-region

GMS-CBTA	Greater Mekong Sub-region Cross Border Transport Agreement
GRP	Good Regulatory Practices
GSA	General Sales Agent
GSO	General Statistics Office
GSP	Generalized System of Preferences
GVA	Gross Value Added
GVCs	Global Value Chains
IAI	Initiative of ASEAN Integration
ICD	Inland Container Depot
ICT	Information, Communication and Technology
IDA	Infocomm Development Authority of Singapore
IE	International Enterprise
IILS	International Integrated Logistics Services
ILO	International Labour Organization
ILS	Integrated Logistics Services
IMP	Industrial Master Plan
INSW	Indonesia National Single Window
IO	Input-Output
IP	Intellectual Property
IPA	Investment Promotion Authority
IPD	Investment Promotion Department
ISIC	International Standard Industrial Classification
ITA	International Trade Administration
ITM	Industry Transformation Map
JETRO	Japan External Trade Organisation
JICA	Japanese International Cooperation Agency
KAMSAB	Kampuchea Shipping Agency and Brokers
KII	Key Informant Interview
LIFFA	Lao International Freight Forwarder Association
LPI	Logistics Performance Index
LRTA	Light Rail Transit Authority
LSPs	Logistics Service Providers
LTFRB	Land Transportation Franchising and Regulatory Board
MFN	Most Favoured Nation
MIAA	Manila International Airport Authority
MIC	Myanmar Investment Commission
MIDA	Malaysian Investment Development Authority
MIFFA	Myanmar International Freight Forwarders' Association
MLC	Malaysian Logistics Council

MNCs	Multinational Companies
MNP	Movement of Natural Persons
MoC	Ministry of Commerce
MoIC	Ministry of Industry and Commerce
MoPWT	Ministry of Public Works and Transport
MoTC	Ministry of Transport and Communications
MPAC	Master Plan on ASEAN Connectivity
MPC	Malaysia Productivity Corporation
MPI	Ministry of Planning and Investment
MRAs	Mutual Recognition Agreements
MSC	Multimedia Super Corridor
MSIC	Malaysia Standard Industrial Classification
MSMEs	Micro, Small and Medium Enterprises
NCC	National Competitiveness Council
NEDA	National Economic and Development Authority
NEM	New Economic Model
NESDB	National Economic and Social Development Board
NLA	National Logistics Association
NLD	National League for Democracy
NLMP	National Logistics Master Plan
NPDIR	National Policy on the Development and Implementation of Regulations
NSA	National Single Window
NSEC	North-South Economic Corridor
OECD	Organisation for Economic Co-operation and Development
OFDI	Outward Foreign Direct Investment
OLI	Ownership, Location and Internalization
PIC	Productivity and Innovation Credit
PIS	Priority Integration Sector
PISFA	Philippine International Seafreight Forwarders Association
PNR	Philippine National Railways
PPAP	Phnom Penh Autonomous Port
PPP	Public–Private Partnership
PSIC	Philippine Standard Industrial Classification
RCEP	Regional Comprehensive Economic Partnership
RIA	Regulatory Impact Analysis
RILS	Roadmap for the Integration of Logistics
RORO	Roll-on Roll-off

RTAs	Regional Trade Agreements
RURB	Reducing Unnecessary Regulatory Burdens
SEEs	State Economic Enterprises
SEF	Services Export Fund
SEOM	Senior Economic Officials Meeting
SEZA	Special Economic Zone Authority
SEZs	Special Economic Zones
SISLOGNAS	Development of the National Logistics System (Sistem Logistik Nasional)
SLA	Singapore Logistics Association
SMEs	Small and Medium Enterprises
SOEs	State-owned Enterprises
STRI	Services Trade Restrictiveness Index
TBP	Temporary Border Pass
TDSP	Trade Development Support Program
TFCP	Trade Facilitation and Competitiveness Project
TISA	Trade in Services Agreement
TiVA	Trade in Value Added
TPP	Trans-Pacific Partnership
TPPA	Trans Pacific Partnership Agreement
TVET	Technical Vocational Education and Training
UMFCCI	Union of Myanmar Federation of Chambers of Commerce and Industry
UNCTAD	United Nations Conference on Trade and Development
UNESCAP	United Nations Economic and Social Commission for Asia and the Pacific
UNIDO	United Nations Industrial Development Organization
VAT	Value Added Taxes
VLA	Vietnam Logistics Association
WDA	Workforce Development Agency
WGI	Worldwide Governance Indicators
WSQ	Workforce Skills Qualification
WTO	World Trade Organization

ABOUT THE CONTRIBUTORS

Titik Anas is Managing Director at Presisi Indonesia and a Lecturer in the Faculty of Economics and Business of Padjadjaran University, Indonesia. She received her PhD from the Australian National University, Australia. She can be contacted at tanas@presisi-indonesia.com.

Ruth Banomyong is currently an Associate Professor at the Department of International Business, Logistics and Transport Management at the Faculty of Commerce & Accountancy (a.k.a Thammasat Business School), Thammasat University in Thailand. He has a PhD in International Logistics from Cardiff University. He can be contacted at ruth@banomyong.com.

Vannarith Chheang is a Visiting Fellow at ISEAS – Yusof Ishak Institute, Consultant at the Nippon Foundation, and Chairman of the Advisory Board at the Cambodian Institute for Strategic Studies (CISS). He has a PhD in Asia Pacific Studies from the Ritsumeikan Asia Pacific University, Japan. He can be contacted at chheangcam@gmail.com.

Sanchita Basu Das is Fellow and Lead Researcher (Economic Affairs) at the ISEAS – Yusof Ishak Institute. She holds a Masters in Economics from University of Delhi, India, and Masters in Business Administration from National University of Singapore. She is currently pursuing her PhD from the Nanyang Technological University, Singapore. She can be contacted at sanchita@iseas.edu.sg and sanchitabasu@yahoo.com.

Min Ye Paing Hein is Executive Director of Myanmar Development Institute and member of the Development Assistance Coordination Unit (DACU) of the government of the Union of Myanmar. He received his PhD from the University of Wisconsin-Madison. He can be reached at myhein@wisc.edu.

Gilberto M. Llanto is President of the Philippine Institute for Development Studies. He was formerly Undersecretary (Deputy Minister) of the National Economic and Development Authority, and President of the Philippine Economic Society. He is Regional Coordinator of the East Asian Development Network. He has a PhD in Economics from the School of Economics, University of the Philippines. He can be reached at gllanto@mail.pids.gov.ph and gmllanto@gmail.com.

Nguyen Anh Thu is a Lecturer at the University of Economics and Business, Vietnam National University and presently is the Vice Rector of the University. She has a PhD in Economics (International Development) from Yokohama National University, Japan. She can be contacted at thuna@vnu.edu.vn.

Nguyen Thi Minh Phuong is a Lecturer at the University of Economics and Business, Vietnam National University. She has a M.A. degree in International Economics from the Berlin School of Economics and Law. She can be contacted at phuongntm.ueb@vnu.edu.vn.

Phanhpakit Onphanhdala is Deputy Director of Laos-Japan Human Resource Development Institute, National University of Laos. He has a PhD in Economics from Kobe University, Japan. He can be contacted at o.phanhpakit@gmail.com.

Nur Afni Panjaitan is Junior Economist at Presisi Indonesia, and a graduate student in the Faculty of Economics and Business of Padjadjaran University, Indonesia. She can be contacted at npanjaitan@presisi-indonesia.com.

Vanvisa Philavong is a Visiting Research Fellow at Faculty of Economics and Business Management, National University of Laos. She holds a M.S. in Economics from National University of Laos. She can be contacted at visa0373@gmail.com.

Tham Siew Yean is a Senior Fellow at ISEAS – Yusof Ishak Institute and an Adjunct Professor at the Institute of Malaysian and International Studies (IKMAS), Universiti Kebangsaan Malaysia. She has a PhD in Economics from the University of Rochester, United States. She can be contacted at siew_yean@iseas.edu.sg and tham@ukm.edu.my.

Vu Thanh Huong is a Lecturer at the University of Economics and Business, Vietnam National University, Hanoi. She has a Master in Natural Resource Economics from University of Queensland, Australia. She can be contacted at huongvt@vnu.edu.vn.

Evelyn Peiqi Ooi Widjaja is a Senior Research Analyst at TRPC Pte. Ltd. and was a former research associate at ISEAS – Yusof Ishak Institute. She has a Masters in Education specializing in International Education Policy from Harvard Graduate School of Education. She can be contacted at peo526@mail.harvard.edu.

1

INTRODUCTION

Tham Siew Yean and
Sanchita Basu Das

INTRODUCTION

In the last two decades, the services sector has gained increasing importance in terms of its contribution to a country's Gross Domestic Product (GDP) and employment. Its share in total GDP for the Organisation for Economic Co-operation and Development (OECD) countries has grown from 70 per cent in mid-1990s to 75 per cent more recently, while its share for the countries in East Asia and Pacific has moved up from 37 per cent to 48 per cent over the same period. It further accounts for about 70 and 47 per cent respectively of total employment in the OECD countries and East Asia and Pacific region respectively (World Bank 2016).

The increasing importance of the services sector is driven by production fragmentation or outsourcing activities. While production fragmentation entails goods to be produced in multiple countries, outsourcing happens when multinational corporations (MNCs) focus on functions that they have comparative advantage while other functions are subcontracted to other firms. The resulting spatial or functional fragmentation is connected through service links such as transportation, ICT, distribution services, financial intermediation services and others (Jones and Kierzkowski 2005). Consequently, the competitiveness of manufacturing firms in an increasingly globalized world is determined to a large extent by the cost effectiveness and reliability of these service links.

In turn, the changing nature of manufacturing production has led to an increasing importance of trade in services as opposed to the earlier significance of trade in goods (Grossman and Rossi-Hansberg 2008). Trade in services now accounts for more than a fifth of global trade volumes (Saez et al. 2015). For the past two decades, trade in services has grown faster than merchandise trade, reaching over US$9 trillion for the first time in 2013 and constituting 11.9 per cent of the world GDP (UNESCAP 2015). It has also increased in recent years *vis-à-vis* trade in goods as the latter has been affected by the slowdown in growth in the developed world after the global financial crisis while economic recovery is retarded by the crash in commodity and oil prices in 2015.

In the case of countries of Southeast Asia (or ASEAN countries), inflows of foreign direct investment (FDI) have enabled some to participate in the fragmentation of production and the emergence of regional networks (Athukorala 2013). The services sector assumes increasing importance as it enables these ASEAN countries to plug into the production networks more efficiently. The sector accounts for more than 40 per cent and 50 per cent, respectively, of total value added and total employment in ASEAN (ASEAN Secretariat and the World Bank 2015). Although trade in services has grown over the years, it is still less significant than the world average. The sector, however, draws a significant share of FDI inflows in the region (ASEAN Secretariat 2015*a*).

The growth performance of the services sector varies across the member countries in ASEAN due to differences in policies and institutions, extent of commitment at regional or multilateral levels and willingness to comply with services sector liberalization commitments. For example, although the ASEAN countries aspire to deepen services sector integration within the region to enhance the contribution of services to economic development and growth (ASEAN Secretariat 2015*a*), services liberalization has progressed much more slowly compared to goods liberalization. Limited liberalization ambition and the pervasiveness of regulatory barriers have contributed to the slow progress in the liberalization of services in ASEAN (ASEAN Secretariat and the World Bank 2015).

Therefore, there is a need to examine the development of the services sector, including the liberalization efforts for this sector in ASEAN. This book will focus on FDI in the services sector, as of the four main modes of trade in services, commercial presence is the most important, constituting an estimated 55–60 per cent of total trade in services (Saez et al. 2015). Moreover, the shift from trade in goods to trade in tasks (or services) has led to increasing interest in the "trade-investment-services" nexus as regional production networks has taken over as the driver of international trade (Baldwin 2011). Liberalization commitments in the General Agreement on Trade in Services (GATS) commitments under the World Trade Organisation (WTO) and the ASEAN Framework Agreement on Services (AFAS) under the ASEAN Economic Community (AEC) will be discussed since all ten ASEAN member countries are also WTO members. However, while liberalization measures can contribute to FDI inflows, empirical evidence also indicates that economic fundamentals such as market size, macroeconomic stability, and fiscal incentives also play a significant role (Banga 2003). A holistic assessment of the impact of liberalization measures will therefore need to take into consideration domestic policies, covering institutions and regulations, which are necessary for improving the enabling environment for FDI.

The main objective of this book is to compare international and domestic policy measures, including institutional and regulatory reforms for attracting FDI and its impact on inflows of FDI in the services sector in the ten ASEAN countries. Specifically, each country study will:

1. Compare the liberalization of FDI in services at the regional and multilateral levels with domestic policies, including the promotion of FDI through incentives, institutional and regulatory reforms;
2. Examine its impact on inflows of FDI;
3. Identify challenges in the liberalization and promotion of FDI and provide suggestions for policy changes based on these challenges.

Given the heterogeneous nature of the services sector, this book will focus on the logistics industry as a case study as the industry plays a key role in the movement of goods, services and people across the ASEAN region. Logistics was also one of the twelve priority integration sectors in ASEAN.[1]

Following the introductory remark, this chapter is organized as follows. It provides a literature review on the determinants of FDI, including in the services sector in Section 2. The analytical framework is presented in Section 3 while the importance of FDI in services liberalization with reference to WTO and ASEAN are discussed in Section 4. Section 5 discusses the logistics sector in ASEAN. Subsequently, the chapter highlights the key findings of the study and also the individual country experience (Section 6). It concludes by giving policy recommendations, both for ASEAN as a region, and its member countries, with respect to their respective services sector liberalization and development of their logistics sector (Section 7).

LITERATURE REVIEW ON DETERMINANTS OF FDI

Theoretically, numerous models have been postulated to explain the determinants of FDI.[2] These can range from the standard movement of capital in neoclassical models to Dunning's eclectic model as well as other models that seek to explain capital mobility in terms of the types of capital. In this volume, we choose to adopt Dunning's eclectic paradigm, based on ownership, location and internalization (OLI) advantages as it is by far the most influential framework for empirical investigation on the determinants of FDI, despite its limitations some of which were accepted by Dunning (2001) himself. To overcome these limitations, the framework has been extended to accommodate for example, institutional theory, as proposed by Dunning (2006), in the choice of variables to represent locational advantages. In particular, it is the locational advantages that are of interest to host economies in ASEAN, as it includes country specific advantages such as the availability of factor endowments (for example, natural resources and geographical factors) as well as public intervention in the allocation of resources (Dunning 1977). In particular, the incorporation of policy variables which is also suggested by UNCTAD (2009), is of special interest based on the third objective of this book. The Dunning framework thus provides us with the flexibility to analyse the policy issues that are explored in this book.

There is a voluminous empirical literature on the determinants of FDI flows, with different results due in part to the different methodologies used. According to Singh and Jun (1995), these empirical studies can be divided into three approaches: micro-oriented econometric study, survey data analysis, and aggregate econometric analysis. Since our book deals with country studies based on aggregate data, we focus specifically on the empirical evidence at the aggregate level, which can be cross country studies or country specific in nature. Singh and Jun's (1995) summary and Blonigen's review of the empirical literature a decade later in 2005, indicates that there is no broad consensus on the major determinants of FDI as the overall empirical evidence is mixed in terms of causal direction as well as the magnitudes of estimates obtained in the regression studies that have proliferated to examine this issue. This in turn can be attributed, in part, to data problems as reliable and accurate data on FDI flows and its determinants, especially for developing countries, are difficult to come by. For example, Blonigen (2005) acknowledges while the quality of institutions is likely to be an important determinant, especially for developing countries, it is difficult to obtain accurate measurements of institutions so that the magnitude of this variable's impact on the determinants of FDI is difficult to capture in econometric studies. This is further compounded by comparability issues since cross country studies essentially pool together data from countries that are structurally diverse and at different stages of economic development. Moreover, although theoretically there are many variables that can affect inflows of FDI based on Dunning's locational advantages, they may not all be simultaneously relevant since the relevance of each depends on home and host country characteristics as well as the type of FDI being analyzed. This is clearly shown in Asiedu (2002)'s study, where some standard variables tested for driving foreign capital to developing countries, such as infrastructure development and openness to trade, did not have the same impact for sub-Saharan Africa. It would appear that context is important in examining the impact of different variables as determinants of FDI in a particular host economy.

In the case of the services industry, can the same FDI theories and their determinants be applied given services' unique characteristics such as invisibility, intangibility, perishability and the need for geographical proximity or the simultaneity of production and consumption?[3] Dunning (1989) argues that the distinction between goods and services is a false one. This is because most goods purchased are supposed to offer certain services (like the food we eat) and, in general, all goods embody non-factor services and services may also require physical goods. The two main differences are found in services' direct association of production and consumption as opposed to separate activities for goods and the issue of ownership i.e. transaction of goods imply change of ownership, whereas for services, only part of the price is for ownership (like airplane and air tickets). Thus, Dunning's eclectic theory is also currently used to explain FDI in services whilst generally most of the determinants in manufacturing also apply for services so that no special FDI theory for international service firms is deemed necessary (Yin et al. 2014).

ANALYTICAL FRAMEWORK

The analytical framework used in this book is based on the locational advantages of host economies which encompasses the natural and created resources of a country. The latter refers specifically to the FDI enabling environment that can be provided by a judicious use of appropriate government policies. It includes political and macroeconomic stabilities as fundamental conditions for drawing in both foreign and domestic investors; institutions; and physical, ICT as well as social infrastructure (Sun 2002; Australian Department of Foreign Affairs and Trade 2016).

In particular, institutions or "rules of the game" have become increasingly important as good governance increases the productivity prospects of a country, which in turn benefits foreign investors while poor institutions can increase costs as in the case of corruption (Bénassy-Quéré et al. 2005). Moreover, FDI represents sunk costs and poor institutions heighten the risks of policy reversals while weak enforcement of laws increases uncertainty for investors. In the case of services, regulations play an important role as shown by Dee (2009) as these may intentionally or unintentionally deter the entry of foreign and domestic suppliers. Regulatory restrictions and uncertainty can thus serve as FDI barriers while clear, transparent, consistent policies, which are timely, implemented and enforced, reduces regulatory ambiguity thereby reducing investment costs.

Investments in physical, ICT and social infrastructure mitigate the limitations of natural resource endowments, especially the lack of it and facilitates the movement of goods, services and people. This volume is especially interested in investments in infrastructure that can facilitate trade and reduce the trade costs of a country. ICT investment expedites the movement of goods and services, particularly exports from small and medium enterprises (SMEs) by providing an avenue for a direct link with customers, including from outside the country, thereby reducing the need for establishing a physical presence (Kotnik and Hagsten 2012). Human capital is one of the most important investments in social infrastructure, especially for moving up the global value chain (GVC) when the quality of education and talents play a critical role in industrial upgrading as well as in the shift to a service-oriented economy as aspired by some of the ASEAN member countries.

Using the above framework, we now provide a brief overview of the FDI enabling environment in ASEAN member countries.

Institutions

Institutions are defined as the rules of the game in a society or more formally as humanly devised constraints that shape human interactions (North 1990). The quality of institutions in a country at the macro level is usually proxied by the four main indicators shown in Table 1.1, namely political stability, corruption, rule of law and the ease of doing business. Singapore is the best performer in all the proxies used for measuring institutional quality, while Cambodia, Laos and Myanmar are ranked the worst. This leads to significant differences in each member country's approach to logistics integration as both liberalization and facilitation measures may require changes in the rules and regulations of a country.

TABLE 1.1
Ranking of ASEAN Countries for Political Stability, Perceived Level of Corruption, and Rule of Law, 2014 or 2015

	Political Stability and Absence of Violence/ Terrorism: Percentile Rank (2014)	Transparency International Corruption Perceptions Rank (2015)	Rule of Law: Percentile Rank (2014)	World Bank's Ease of Doing Business Rank (2015)
Brunei	95.1	n.a.	70.2	84
Cambodia	44.7	150	17.3	127
Indonesia	31.1	88	41.8	109
Laos	61.2	139	26.9	134
Malaysia	58.7	54	75.0	18
Myanmar	11.7	147	8.7	167
Philippines	22.8	95	43.3	103
Singapore	92.2	8	95.2	1
Thailand	16.5	76	51.4	49
Vietnam	46.1	112	44.7	90

Source: World Governance Indicators, World Bank (for data on Political Stability and Rule of Law); World Bank, Doing Business; Transparency International (for the Corruption Perception Index).

Since this book is concerned about FDI, we use the OECD FDI Regulatory Restrictiveness Index[4] to ascertain the restrictiveness of FDI rules in each ASEAN member country, in terms of equity limitations, screening or approval mechanisms, restrictions on the employment of foreigners as key personnel and operational restrictions such as on branching, capital repatriation or on land ownership. Figure 1.1 shows only two ASEAN member countries are below the OECD average for the year 2015 while the rest are above the same average, implying there is considerable room for further FDI liberalization and improvement in the FDI enabling environment in most ASEAN member countries.

FIGURE 1.1
OECD Regulatory Restrictiveness Index, 2015

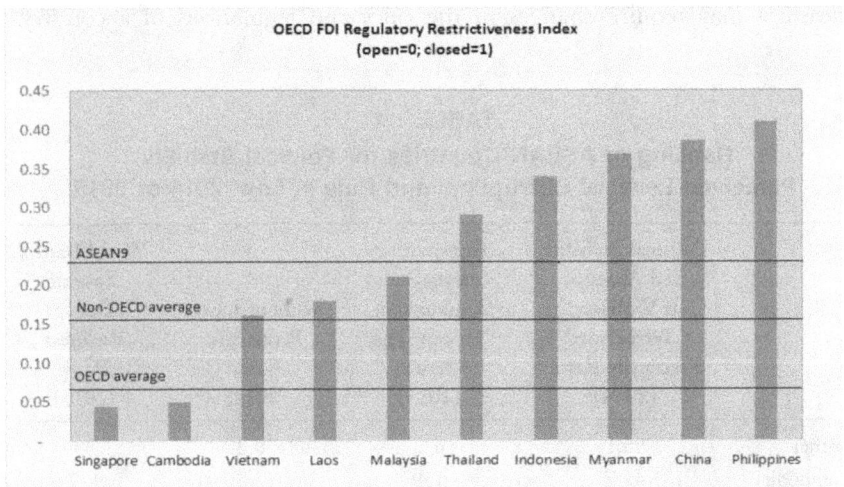

Note: ASEAN 9 refers to the average scores of the nine ASEAN member states covered. It excludes Brunei Darussalam which is not covered. Data for Lao PDR, Vietnam, Cambodia, Singapore and Thailand are preliminary.
Source: OECD FDI Regulatory Restrictiveness Index, OECD. Stat as of end 2015.

Infrastructure

Table 1.2 presents a comprehensive summary of the infrastructure competitiveness of ASEAN member countries, published by the World Economic Forum. Apart from Singapore, Malaysia and Thailand, most ASEAN member countries suffer from poor infrastructure quality. Poor infrastructure leads to high transportation costs, which is a key component of logistics expenses.

TABLE 1.2

Infrastructure Competitiveness by Sector, 2015

Country	Quality of Roads	Quality of Railroad Infrastructure	Quality of Port Infrastructure	Quality of Air Transport Infrastructure	Quality of Electricity Supply	Mobile Subscriptions
Brunei	n.a.	n.a.	n.a.	n.a.	n.a.	n.a.
Cambodia	3.3	1.6	3.7	3.7	3.1	155.1
Indonesia	3.7	3.6	3.8	4.4	4.1	126.2
Laos	3.6	n.a	2.2	3.8	4.7	67
Malaysia	5.7	5.1	5.6	5.7	5.8	148.8
Myanmar	2.3	1.8	2.6	2.6	2.7	49.5
Philippines	3.3	2.2	3.2	3.7	4.0	111.2
Singapore	6.2	5.7	6.7	6.8	6.7	158.1
Thailand	4.4	2.4	4.5	5.1	5.2	144.4
Vietnam	3.3	3.2	3.9	4.2	4.1	147.1

Notes: Index 1 (extremely underdeveloped) to 7 (extensive and efficient) for the Quality of Roads, Railroad, Port and Air Transport Infrastructures. Index 1 (extremely unreliable) to 7 (extremely reliable) for the Quality of Electricity; Number of mobile-cellular telephone subscriptions per 100 population for Mobile Subscriptions.
Source: *The Global Competitiveness Report 2015–2016*, World Economic Forum.

Human Capital

The differences in human capital across ASEAN countries have been pointed out as another impediment in ASEAN's efforts to integrate its logistics sector (see Table 1.3) (Tongzon 2011). In Indonesia, Cambodia, Laos, Myanmar and Vietnam, a shortage of trained professionals and the lack of on-the-job training in SMEs reduce the competitiveness of the logistics industry, resulting in the stalling of liberalization in some of these countries.

TABLE 1.3
Human Capital Index, 2015 Ranking, ASEAN

Country	Rank	Score
Singapore	24	78.15
Philippines	46	71.24
Malaysia	52	70.24
Thailand	57	68.78
Vietnam	59	68.48
Indonesia	69	66.99
Cambodia	97	58.55
Lao PDR	105	56.16
Myanmar	112	52.97
Brunei	n.a.	n.a.

Notes: The Human Capital Index is a proxy tool to gauge the extent of knowledge and skills embodied in individuals that enable them to create economic value in a country. It captures the complexity of education, employment and workforce dynamics. The ranking is among 130 countries. The Index assesses Learning and Employment outcomes on a scale of 0 (worst) to 100 (best).
Source: Human Capital Report, World Economic Forum

ASEAN COMMITMENTS IN SERVICES LIBERALIZATION IN GATS AND AFAS

WTO Commitments in Services

Under WTO, ASEAN countries liberalized their services trade through the General Agreement of Trade in Services (GATS) that came into effect as part of the Uruguay Round in January 1995. The GATS rules provided a comprehensive legal framework covering 161 services activities across twelve sectors — telecom, maritime, finance, energy, business, education, environment and distribution services.[5] The main aim was to establish a legal framework to cover rules and practices of services trade. As many services in a country are subject to domestic regulations, the agenda for liberalization under GATS was not too ambitious. Much flexibility was provided to countries in choosing the services sector that they wish to liberalize or to maintain limitations in specific subsectors (Chanda 2002). Moreover, GATS' "request and offer" approach of negotiation, i.e. WTO members choose the sectors that they wish to offer binding commitments in response to requests from other WTO members, lack clear liberalization targets. This, in turn, has not been successful in encouraging "offers" to liberalize the sectors that the member countries wish to protect from the foreign competition in WTO (Nikomborirak and Jitdumrong 2013).

In particular, GATS is built on three main elements — provisions, commitments and sectoral annexes. The main GATS provisions include Most-Favoured Nation Treatment, i.e. countries cannot discriminate among the WTO members in terms of their treatment of foreign services and services suppliers,[6] and transparency.[7] Commitments under GATS are undertaken in a mode-wise approach — mode 1 (cross-border supply), mode 2 (consumption abroad), mode 3 (commercial presence) and mode 4 (movement of natural persons). Sectoral or issue-wise annexes spell out the sectoral commitments and procedural and implementation issues in various areas as well as a timeframe for future discussion.

Table 1.4 summarizes the country-wise structure of commitments for ASEAN member countries. Of the 161 service activities, two countries in ASEAN have committed forty sectors or less, another three countries have committed sixty-one to 100 and the rest of the five countries have committed 101 and more. There is also substantial variation in the commitments across sectors. While business services and tourism cover multiple subsectors and have several scheduled commitments, public services such as health, communication (telecom), transport and education, are either not scheduled by many ASEAN member countries or, if scheduled, have partial commitments and are subject to domestic regulations. This implies that public goods type of sectors where there are social and economic considerations and where there is regulatory mediation and government undertakings tend to have relatively fewer commitments.

TABLE 1.4

Structure of Commitments by ASEAN Members in GATS

Sectors Committed	ASEAN Country	Sectors Committed	ASEAN Country
20 or less	Myanmar	81–100	Indonesia, Laos
21–40	Brunei	101–120	Cambodia, Philippines, Thailand
41–60		121 and more	Malaysia, Vietnam
61–80	Singapore		

Note: The GATS commitments of individual ASEAN member countries are counted at their year of accession.
Source: Authors' compilation from <https://www.wto.org/english/tratop_e/serv_e/serv_commitments_e.htm>.

Nevertheless, the depth of the commitments is relatively low with limitations on market access and national treatment. There are two indices developed by the World Bank to observe the extent of services trade liberalization among ASEAN member countries. First is the GATS Commitment Index, where 0 implies least liberal and 100 the most. Cambodia and Vietnam have the highest scores as these are the countries that are late entrants to the WTO and had to undertake far-reaching commitments as part of their accession to the WTO. Brunei and Myanmar have made least concession in the GATS, reflecting their highly protected services sector. The rest of the countries fall between the two extremes, with Indonesia at the lowest at 9.52 and Malaysia at the highest at 25.4. Second, is the Services Trade Restrictiveness Index (STRI), where 0 implies completely open, 25 relates to virtually open with minor restrictions, 50 implies major restrictions, 75 means virtually closed with limited opportunity to enter and operate and 100 depicts completely closed. Under STRI, Myanmar is highly protective of its services sector, whilst Cambodia and Vietnam, are more liberal for the same reason as mentioned above (see Table 1.5).

Key reasons for modest liberalization lie in the political economy of the ASEAN countries, regulatory restrictions in individual services as well as financial and human-resource capacity of individual countries to undertake domestic reforms. For most of the public utility and financial services in ASEAN member countries, entry is subject to certain limits on new licenses and the licensing procedure is not very

TABLE 1.5
Extent of Liberalization under GATS Commitment

Countries	Bru	Cam	Indon	Laos	Mal	Mya	Php	Sgp	Tha	Viet
GATS Commitment Index	4.35	40.08	9.52	n.a	25.4	4.94	14.08	22.66	19.73	30.15
STRI of GATS Commitment	89.3	24.1	78.2	76.0	76.0	100.0	78.7	60.4	80.4	38.3

Note: Bru: Brunei; Cam: Cambodia; Indon: Indonesia; Mal: Malaysia; Mya: Myanmar; Php: Philippines; Sgp: Singapore; Tha: Thailand; Viet: Vietnam.
Source: Nikomborirak and Jitdumrong (2013) and the ASEAN Secretariat and the World Bank (2015).

transparent. According to the ASEAN Services Integration Report (ASEAN Secretariat and the World Bank 2015, p. 53),

> in several ASEAN countries, licenses and foreign equity ownership are decided on a case-by-case basis, subject to requirements or approvals that involve several regulators and ministries. Some countries in certain sectors have no regulation at all, especially the lower-income countries in the region and pertaining to the supply of services through the cross-border and consumption abroad modes. In general, the high level of discretion and the absence of regulation create a less predictable policy environment and makes it difficult to accurately define and assess the policy regime.

Following the Uruguay Round, several new rounds of service sector negotiations were undertaken in end-2001, under the Doha Development Agenda (DDA). Two key objectives were stated under the Doha Round: (a) to update and undertake reform in the current GATS rules and principles and (b) to open up more of the services sectors to foreign competition. The WTO services negotiations for DDA have been going on for more than ten years now and it is unlikely to be concluded. Negotiating format, Mode-4 commitments on Movement of Natural Persons and rules and regulations were cited as common causes for the prolonged negotiations (Cooper 2011). Given the stalemate in DDA, a subset of WTO members, undertook a plurilateral arrangement, namely the Trade in Services Agreement (TISA). The objective is to "improve on the GATS and negotiate a higher-standard agreement on services among like-minded WTO members" (Stephenson 2015). TISA negotiations, that have started in early 2013, involve twenty-five participants (including the EU twenty-eight nations in total), though there are no ASEAN members.

ASEAN Framework Agreement on Services

ASEAN's desire to liberalize services trade was institutionalized by the signing of AFAS in 1995. Thereafter, in the 2007 AEC Blueprint, a free flow of services is mentioned under the first pillar of "single market and production base". Broadly, the aim under services liberalization is

(a) to eliminate "substantially all existing discriminatory measures and market access limitations amongst member States"; and (b) to prohibit "new or more discriminatory measures and market access limitations" (ASEAN Framework Agreement on Services 1995). This may be achieved through greater certainty in ASEAN member countries' services regime, Mutual Recognition Agreements (MRAs) of specific professions and negotiation of trade in services agreements with FTA partners (ASEAN Secretariat 2015a).

Specifically, services sector liberalization in ASEAN stipulates the following: removing restrictions on trade in services by 2010 for four priority services sector (air transport, e-ASEAN, healthcare and tourism); by 2013 for logistics and by 2015 for all other services sector (such as construction, distribution, maritime transport, education, environmental services). In 2004, the ASEAN-X formula was also adopted, where negotiations can be undertaken if there are at least three members involved. Since the fifth package, signed in 2006, it was decided that an AFAS package would include all commitments made by ASEAN countries under WTO, earlier AFAS packages commitments and new commitments for each new round of negotiations.

Studies have shown that AFAS commitments have improved considerably over the years (Dee 2015). The ninth package shows the most number of sectors covered in the commitments to date (see Table 1.6). The commitments included: no restrictions for cross-border supply (mode 1) and consumption abroad (mode 2), except for certain regulatory reasons; foreign equity participation should not be less than 51 per cent by 2008 and 70 per cent by 2010 for the four priority services sector; 49 per cent by 2008, 51 per cent by 2010 and 70 per cent by 2013 for logistics services; and 49 per cent by 2008, 51 per cent by 2010 and 70 per cent by 2015 for other services sectors (mode 3) and to progressively remove other market access restrictions by 2015. ASEAN member states have also committed themselves to MRAs for certain professionals (mode 4): the countries committed to complete negotiation of MRA for architectural, accountancy, surveyor and medical professionals by 2008, dental professional by 2009 and others by 2015. This enables the qualification of a service provider recognized by a regulatory authority in their home country to be mutually recognized by other ASEAN countries.

TABLE 1.6.
Number of Services Subsectors Covered in
AFAS Packages of Commitments

	7th	8th	9th
AFAS Targets	80	80	104
Brunei	5	79	92
Cambodia	74	87	94
Indonesia	83	86	97
Lao PDR	74	80	92
Malaysia	81	96	101
Myanmar	66	79	90
Philippines	95	98	99
Singapore	78	84	101
Thailand	93	104	108
Vietnam	84	88	99

Source: CIMB ASEAN Research Institute (CARI) (2016).

Nevertheless, liberalization commitments under AFAS remained limited and modest compared to countries' applied policies (see Table 1.7). The STRI, where 0 implies completely open and 100 depicts completely closed, shows that Indonesia and Vietnam have domestic policies that are at par with AFAS commitments, whereas for countries like Cambodia, Myanmar and Singapore, their unilateral liberalization policies are more open than their respective AFAS commitments.

With regard to implementation, ASEAN member countries have met most of the mode 1 and mode 2 commitments. For mode 3, all ASEAN member countries, except Singapore, have fallen behind the liberalization targets for foreign equity participation. Restrictions in national economies in terms of equity and land holdings and licensing requirements continue to act as a barrier to services sector trade. As AFAS commitments do not touch on domestic regulation that is pervasive in services, these are likely to continue to restrict trade in this sector (Chia and Plummer 2015).

For MRAs (mode 4), they have been signed for eight professionals – engineering (2005), nursing (2006), architectural (2007), surveying qualification (2007), accountancy (2009), medical and dental practitioners (2009), tourism professional (2009). There are different ways of cooperation under these MRAs: the ones under engineering and architecture provide

TABLE 1.7
Restrictiveness of AFAS Commitments and Applied Policies

Countries	Bru	Cam	Indon	Laos	Mal	Mya	Php	Sgp	Tha	Viet
STRI of AFAS Commitment	65.2	18.5	49.5	55.3	54.2	42.8	55.0	30.5	58.5	36.4
Restrictiveness of Applied Policies	n.a.	10.0	48.3	44.6	42.3	26.4	48.6	10.8	43.8	36.0

Notes: Bru: Brunei; Cam: Cambodia; Indon: Indonesia; Mal: Malaysia; Mya: Myanmar; Php: Philippines; Sgp: Singapore; Tha: Thailand; Viet: Vietnam.
Source: ASEAN Secretariat and the World Bank (2015).

recognition of qualifications for registered ASEAN professionals, MRAs for nursing, medical and dental practitioners aim to exchange information and best practices on the licensing of healthcare practitioners, MRAs on accountancy and surveying services provide a framework of broad principles to advance bilateral and multilateral negotiations among the ASEAN members states and MRA on tourism professionals facilitates mobility of skilled workforce by exchanging information and providing capacity building exercises (ASEAN Secretariat 2015*a*).

In general, MRAs do not contain any liberalization commitments but try to facilitate mobility of professionals between member states on a voluntary basis, thereby generating flexibilities. As MRAs are not supposed to override local laws and are applicable only in accordance with the host countries' prevailing regulations, behind-the-border barriers to trade may emerge from local laws and regulations. For example, in Thailand, the Alien Employment Act remains in force and this requires a work permit for all foreigners working in the country. The country has yet to align its domestic legislation to regional agreements on MRAs. Hence, MRAs cannot be equated with market access and effective intra-ASEAN mobility of skilled labour (Nikomborirak and Jitdumrong 2013).

In summary, services sector liberalization under the AEC 2015 blueprint does not support the development of a free flow of services as aspired. This is because liberalization in mode 3 envisions only 70 per cent of ASEAN equity shares, while liberalization of mode 4 is confined to the movement of some professionals but there are still many flexibilities and exceptions.

CASE OF LOGISTICS SERVICES IN ASEAN

Defining Logistics Services

Logistics services facilitate the movement of goods and services within and across borders from producers to producers/consumers. A seamless logistics sector enhances efficiencies in supply-chain movements, reduces trade costs and facilitates trade across countries. The US Coalition of Services Industries defines logistics services sector as "the process of planning, implementing, managing and controlling the flow and storage of goods, services and related information from the point of origin to the point of consumption" (Sugie et al. 2015, p. 8). In the WTO Services Sectoral Classification List,[8] logistics services mostly appear under "Transport Services" and covers auxiliary services attached to all modes of transport (such as cargo handling services, storage and warehouse services and freight transport agency services). This WTO classification is based on the United Nations Provisional Central Products Classification (CPC Prov.), and it is used by countries to schedule commitments under the GATS and other trade agreements, following the GATS approach.

However, the definition of logistics services has moved beyond the narrow description of handling and transport/distribution of goods. It has evolved, depending on a country's development stage, and can encompass activities that facilitate economic transactions in connection with production and trade such as warehousing, storage, communication, and infrastructure. Figure 1.2 describes the full range of logistics services activities, divided over stages of development. To increase efficiency, each of these components has to be further supported by the appropriate institutions.

FIGURE 1.2
Logistics Service Activities[1]

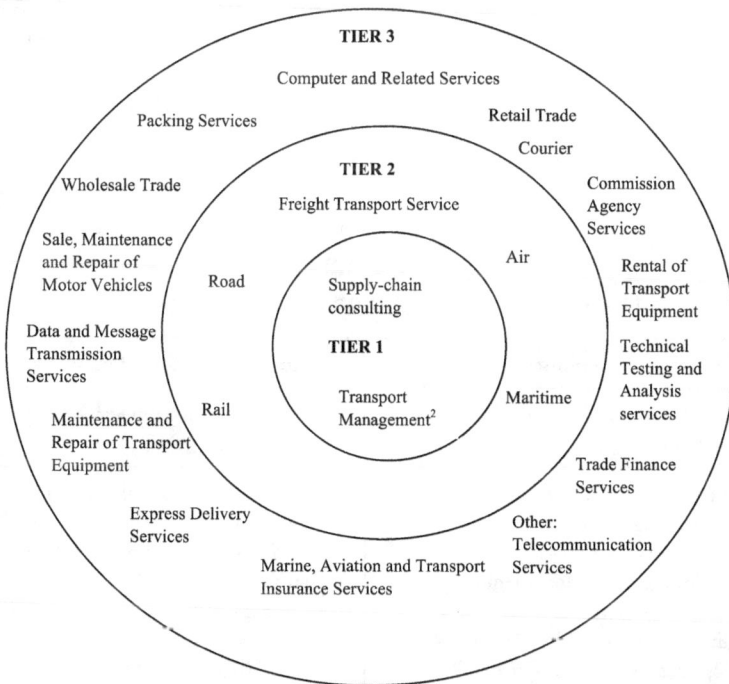

Notes: [1] These activities are based on USTR's definition of logistic services. Where applicable, the figure lists activities using the WTO's services Sectoral Classification List as a guide.
[2] Transport management services include storage and warehousing, cargo handling, transport agency services and customs brokerage.
Source: United States International Trade Commission (2005).

Case of Logistics Integration in ASEAN

In view of its importance, the logistics sector was declared a priority sector in 2004 and the ASEAN Secretariat subsequently commissioned a study to develop a roadmap for its development in 2006 (Banomyong, Cook and Kent 2008). The study used survey findings to identify the core strengths and weaknesses in this sector. The survey findings and stakeholder consultations were then used to formulate the roadmap for logistics integration, which was later endorsed in 2008.

The objectives of the Roadmap for the Integration of Logistics (RILS) are two-fold: (i) it aims to create an ASEAN single market by 2015 by strengthening ASEAN economic integration through liberalization and facilitation measures in the area of logistics services; and (ii) to support the establishment and enhance the competitiveness of an ASEAN production base through the creation of an integrated ASEAN logistics environment.[9] The liberalization and facilitation measures in the Roadmap and their respective implementation mechanisms are summarized in Table 1.8. While liberalization is to be implemented in AFAS commitments, facilitation measures are to be implemented through the ASEAN Strategic Transport Plan since transportation is a major component in this sector.

TABLE 1.8
Roadmap for the Integration of Logistics (RILS)

	Components	Implementation Mechanism
1.	Liberalization of nine logistics services subsectors	ASEAN Framework Agreement on Services (AFAS)
2.	Four key facilitation measures: • Enhancing competitiveness of ASEAN logistics service providers through trade (including documentation simplification; • Expanding capability of ASEAN logistics service providers; • Human resource development; • Enhancing multimodal transport infrastructure and investment	• Measures are implemented and monitored through the action plans of ASEAN sectoral bodies in Services, Transport and Trade/Customs; • Measures have been aligned with the ASEAN Strategic Transport Plan (2011–2015).[10]

Source: Tham (2016).

The aim in the liberalization measures is aligned with services liberalization in AFAS that targeted the completion of negotiations for ten packages by 2015, with stipulated targets over the different modes of delivery, as shown in Table 1.9.

TABLE 1.9
Liberalization Targets in Logistics

Modes	Description	Targets for Logistics by AFAS 10 in 2015
1	Cross border supply	None
2	Consumption abroad	None
3	Commercial presence	To allow foreign equity of up to 70 per cent; with no limitations on national treatment
4	Movement of natural persons	Superseded by ASEAN Agreement on the Movement of Natural Persons, 2011

Source: Tham (2016).

Unlike the liberalization measures, facilitation measures are numerous (thirty-three in total), wide ranging with open-ended timelines for twenty-six of them.[11] The plan thus envisages liberalization to move ahead of the facilitation measures which are deemed to be more long-term in nature.

Logistics Performance in ASEAN Member Countries

There are challenges in the liberalization and facilitation goals in logistics integration in ASEAN as reflected in the disparate performance in logistics in the ten ASEAN member countries in Figure 1.3, based on the World Bank's Logistics Performance Index (LPI).[12] In the figure, Singapore is ranked fifth among 160 countries in terms of its logistics performance and this is followed by Malaysia, Thailand and Vietnam. At the other end of the spectrum, Lao PDR is ranked 152. This disparate performance can be traced to great disparities in all six components of the LPI, namely infrastructure; customs; international shipments; tracking and tracing; logistics quality; and timeliness (see Figure 1.4). This disparity implies that logistics integration in ASEAN is not going to be easy task as explained in each of the country chapters that provides details on the challenges encountered in the integration process.

FIGURE 1.3

Ranking in Logistics Performance of ASEAN Member States, 2016

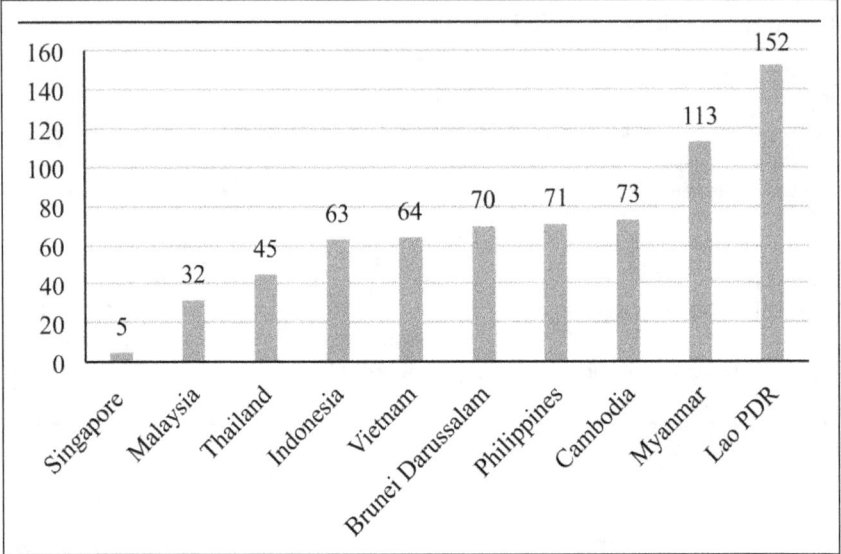

Source: World Bank, Logistics Performance Index 2016.

FIGURE 1.4

Logistics Performance in ASEAN Member States, 2016

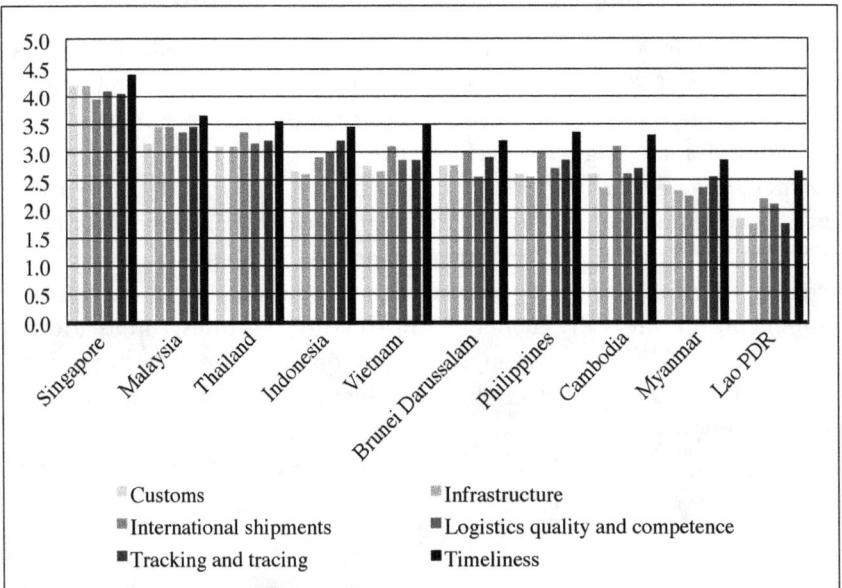

Source: World Bank, Logistics Performance Index 2016.

KEY FINDINGS AND OVERVIEW OF COUNTRY CHAPTERS

Using transportation and storage to represent the logistics sector, the contribution of logistics to the ASEAN member state's GDP in 2015, ranged from 3–7 per cent for the older ASEAN-5 countries (Indonesia, Malaysia, the Philippines, Singapore and Thailand) and Vietnam (see Table 1.10). Data for the Cambodia, Lao PDR and Myanmar (CLM countries) appear to be bigger because of definitional differences as communication is included in their industry classification. More importantly, the contribution of logistics to GDP from 2010 to 2015 for most of the ASEAN countries has remained more or less the same or fallen slightly, with the exception of Indonesia. Brunei's contraction is exceptional as it is due to the negative impact of the fall in oil prices on its economic growth. The country's logistics sector, which serves primarily the main output produced and exported, namely oil and gas, also contracted accordingly and with it, the contribution of this sector to the country's GDP.

TABLE 1.10
Contribution of Logistics Sector to National GDP of ASEAN Countries

(in US$ million)	Brunei[a]		Cambodia[b]		Indonesia	
	2010	2015	2010	2015	2010	2015
GDP	13,707	12,930	11,242	18,050	755,094	861,934
Transport and Storage	218	165	469	686	26,993	43,240
Share to GDP (%)	1.59	1.27	4.17	3.80	3.57	5.02
	Laos[b]		Malaysia		Myanmar[b]	
	2010	2015	2010	2015	2012[c]	2015
GDP	7,128	12,369	255,017	296,283	59,731	62,601
Transport and Storage	312	432	9,003	10,211	9,230	7,508
Share to GDP (%)	4.38	3.49	3.53	3.44	15.45	11.99
	Philippines[d]		Singapore		Thailand	
	2010	2015	2010	2015	2010	2015
GDP	199,591	292,451	236,422	292,739	340,924	395,168
Transport and Storage	12,995	18,813	18,645	20,311	19,162	22,773
Share to GDP (%)	6.51	6.43	7.89	6.94	5.62	5.76
	Vietnam					
	2010	2015				
GDP	115,932	193,599				
Transport & Storage	3,334	5,280				
Share to GDP (%)	2.88	2.73				

Notes: a – the Brunei figures of transport and storage is only for transport;
　　　　b – the Cambodia, Myanmar and Laos figures for transport and storage pertain to transport and communication;
　　　　c – 2010 figures are not available for Myanmar; and
　　　　d – Philippines transport and storage data is for transport, storage and communication.
Source: Authors' compilation from CEIC Database.

Each country chapter examines the research questions raised in this book, with the logistics sector as a case study for identifying the challenges in liberalizing and facilitating an FDI-enabling environment for this sector. However, since all ten countries are at different stages of development in their service sector, including logistics, the emphasis in each country chapter differs accordingly. The chapters are organized as ASEAN-5 countries (Indonesia, Malaysia, the Philippines, Singapore and Thailand), Vietnam, followed by Brunei, Cambodia, Laos and Myanmar.

Chapter 2 by Titik Anas and Nur Afni Panjaitan shows that Indonesia's services sector, including logistics, is relatively small. It has been estimated that Indonesia suffers from relatively high logistics costs at 27 per cent of GDP, compared to 8 per cent in the case of Singapore, 13 per cent for Malaysia and 20 per cent for Thailand. The largest part of the logistics costs is transportation costs. The government has, however, shifted from state dominance to increasingly more participation from the private sector in the development of the logistics sector. A number of necessary institutions are established to develop the sector. In 2012, Indonesia launched the Blueprint for the Development of the National Logistics System to provide an integrated framework and action plans to develop the country's logistics system. Concurrently, a number of laws were amended in the late 2000s.

But, Indonesia's logistics sector continues to be restrictive and its performance remains poor. The changes in laws in the reform process are important but are insufficient. According to the OECD Services Trade Restrictiveness Index (STRI 2015), almost all subsectors of the logistics remain less open to trade *vis-à-vis* the OECD average. Besides a restricted foreign investment policy, Indonesia's logistics sector continues to face constraints from domestic regulations in freight forwarding, warehousing, cargo handling in sea and air-ports. An improvement in the performance of the sector will require follow-up, including reforming the laws to be more investment friendly, implementing regulations and improving the existing infrastructure. Pursuing reforms will take time and it has to be consistent until there is an improvement in the performance of the logistics sector. For infrastructure, although the government is undertaking many initiatives to address the challenges, such as building maritime highways and an integrated freight sea transport, the huge investment required (estimated at US$55.4 billion between 2015 and 2019) can make this a daunting task.

Tham Siew Yean in Chapter 3 on Malaysia finds that the country has not met all the AFAS targets for the logistics sector. Continuous efforts are being made to improve the FDI enabling environment by improving the ease of doing business and by establishing good regulatory practices (GRP), based on international best practices. In 2015, the National Logistics and Facilitation Master Plan was launched with the goal of improving the performance of this sector by addressing its main current challenges, such as regulatory as well as infrastructural bottlenecks. The Ministry of Transport is placed in charge of the implementation, with a clear governance structure and a council to monitor its implementation in order to address the inherent fragmentation in this sector. These new initiatives hold great promise in terms of enhancing the future FDI environment. Nonetheless, FDI in this sector is relatively small, though growing. It is unlikely that the current liberalization commitments have contributed to these inflows as these commitments are limited and licenses are still needed for the regulated sectors.

There are still several outstanding challenges for Malaysia. First, there is a need to rationalize some subsectors where there are a large number of firms, mainly SMEs, as this implies the use of a price strategy rather than strategies that promote exports through service differentiation, innovation and standards compliance. Second, regulatory reviews have to lead towards regulatory de-bottling in terms of actual legal and regulatory amendments that will improve the governance of this sector. Adopting good regulatory practices alone, without effective changes in regulations is not enough to lower the cost of compliance for both domestic and foreign investors. Third, identifying existing barriers to entry to foreign participation will ensure that liberalization commitments will not be offset by domestic regulations or practices that deter entry.

The logistics services comprise an important part of the service economy, which has been a major growth driver of the Philippine economy (Chapter 4). According to the author, Gilberto M. Llanto, the Philippines stands to gain if it can successfully attract FDI that will bring in capital, technology, innovations, and management expertise to improve the logistics sector. The Philippine Development Plan 2011–2016 proposed the development of a National Logistics Master Plan (NLMP) that can integrate seamlessly multimodel transport system and logistics in the country. A single bureau, called the Bureau of Multimodal Transport and Logistics, is established for the registration and accreditation processes for land, air, and maritime transportation. Under regulatory reform, there is an enactment of the Anti-Red Tape Act so as to promote transparency in government transactions. The government has also created a National Competitiveness Council (NCC) that is tasked with overseeing efforts to reduce the cost of doing business in the country. With regard to liberalization, the Philippines is currently implementing the ninth package of commitments under the AFAS. In general, 100 per cent of foreign equity participation is allowed for repair of vessels, domestic and international freight forwarding, and others such as packaging and crating. However, the subsectors that are considered to be public utilities are limited by the Philippines Constitution to a maximum foreign equity participation of 40 per cent.

The author has listed several outstanding challenges to attract FDI flows into the Philippines logistics sector. These are mainly, removing constitutional and legal restrictions to FDI inflows; complementing liberalization with the establishment of market-enhancing domestic policies and regulations and making significant investments in hard infrastructure, with emphasis on transport and logistics.

In Chapter 5, Sanchita Basu Das and Evelyn Widjaja observe that Singapore is a staunch follower of multilateral (WTO GATS) and regional trade (AFAS) liberalism. Its services sector is regarded as more open to inward FDI, when compared to the manufacturing sector or to the other economies in ASEAN. Importantly, Singapore's applied policies are more liberal than its AFAS and WTO commitments. Efforts are made to provide an enabling environment, in terms of institution, infrastructure and human capital, to attract FDI. However, the country suffers from its small size and an equally small educated workforce.

In the case of the logistics sector, there are many plans to increase the competitiveness of this sector, including a roadmap to increase the long-term productivity of the logistics and transportation industry. The city-state is looking at increased automation in the sector with initiatives like the "Mobileye" and "Software-as-a-System (SaaS) Total Logistics Information System". Some of the more recent initiatives include developing a Logistics Skills Framework and revamping the goods delivery system. Singapore has made significant liberalizations commitments both at the WTO and the ASEAN levels. It has no investment restrictions in most of the subsectors. As a result of various measures, FDI stocks in Singapore's transport and storage sector has gone up from S$17.6 billion to S$37.4 billion during 2005–14. Of the components, while FDI stock in water transport and supporting services grew by 7 per cent per annum, the same grew by 14 per cent for warehousing, post and courier services. Nonetheless, the authors list several challenges in the development of the logistics services sector. Businesses are facing rising operating costs due to high rental and manpower costs. The city-state's port faces strong competition from neighbouring countries, particularly from Malaysia, Indonesia and Sri Lanka. A major challenge for Singapore also originates from other ASEAN countries' reluctance to deepen cooperation in the logistics sector, particularly with regard to the smooth cross-border movement of goods. This is especially because Singapore considers itself a headquarter economy, while the rest of ASEAN is its immediate hinterland.

Thailand in Chapter 6 by Ruth Banomyong, also has not been able to meet its liberalization commitments under AFAS for the logistics sector. The author identifies the Foreign Business Act (FBA), 1999 to be the main stumbling block in the liberalization of the foreign equity share. Although operationally, the use of Thai nominee partners imply that the Act does not pose a problem for a foreign logistics provider to establish a commercial presence in the country, it is better to amend the Act in the interest of transparency. However, changing the law will take time as there is a general lack of political will to change its content. There is also a lack of a unified perspective from the different domestic institutions handling the logistics sector due to the complex scope of activities offered by logistics service providers (LSPs). Thus, there can be conflicts in terms of priorities for the development of this sector as for example between investment promotion and the development of local LSPs. Thai LSPs are by nature opposed to liberalization as they consider themselves at a disadvantage while investment promotion favours liberalization in the interest of foreign investors.

The competitiveness of local LSPs is considered important by the Thai Government in their national logistics development plan. However, the implementation of the plan has mostly focused on achieving quantitative targets such as the number of Thai LSPs going abroad (even if it is just for an event) rather than on the establishment of a successful commercial presence in a foreign country. However, if the perspective of the cargo owners and users of logistics services is taken into account, liberalization will further enhance competition in the logistics services market and enable users of logistics services to have access to efficient and effective logistics services. The Thai government should therefore choose between supporting local LSPs or local traders, manufacturers, or importers and exporters. The benefit of supporting local LSPs is minimal on the country.

According to Nguyen Anh Thu, Vu Thanh Huong and Nguyen Thi Minh Phuong, Vietnam (Chapter 7) has made great efforts to improve its services liberalization in terms of both the number of subsectors and the depth of commitments. The regulatory framework related to the services sector is increasingly more transparent and open to ASEAN service suppliers, enabling them to have better access to Vietnam's service market. Investment liberalization can be seen in the revisions of investment laws, making these changes the most important policy changes in the country. The main motivation is to create a more liberal, transparent and non-discriminatory investment environment for all investors. Significantly, the liberalization commitments in WTO and AFAS are embedded in the new investment laws. However, the main constraint lies in the cumbersome bureaucratic measures for establishing foreign presence.

Vietnam's logistics services sector is still relatively under-developed. A major drawback in developing the sector arises from the country's state of infrastructure and related issues such as road safety, road and bridge quality. It is difficult to develop a multimodal transportation system if there is poor connection between infrastructure and production centres. Another issue is a lack of qualified human resource in the sector as it is only the professional level that is evaluated above average according to the logistics providers. Soft skills, foreign language skills and information technology qualifications remain inadequate. Additionally, the regulations and procedures relating to the entry and operation in logistics sector are still quite complicated. The institutions involve many ministries and state agencies. As a result, both domestic and foreign investors in logistics sector bear high cost and low competitiveness. The legal framework on logistics operation also lack transparency and consistency. Thus, the legal framework relating to logistics needs to be reviewed and updated to ensure transparency, consistency and compliance with new commitments.

Tham Siew Yean, in Chapter 8, highlights the importance of diversification strategies and enhancing the role of the private sector in the wake of the drop in oil prices in oil-dependent Brunei. Attracting FDI is an important part of its diversification strategy as evidenced by the on-going efforts to improve the ease of doing business, FDI promotion and regulatory changes such as the enactment of the Competition Order in 2015. But since the country is competing against other countries in the region for FDI, its liberalization efforts and reforms may be inadequate to overcome its inherent domestic disadvantages in terms of domestic market size and the size of its workforce. Therefore, despite the regulatory changes, inflows in FDI fell sharply after 2012 and it is still concentrated in the mining sector. Liberalization in terms of commitments has been improving but it is still far short of the bold liberalization efforts in some of its neighbouring countries. Improvements in bureaucracy and transparency continue to be needed.

Since the size of Brunei's domestic economy cannot provide adequate economies of scale, FDI cannot be focused on the domestic economy alone and needs to be outward-oriented. Using FDI to join GVCs especially in the non-oil and gas sector, will help to alleviate the broader issue of scale that is needed for the diversification of Brunei's economy. Improving the private sector's role will require appropriate policies for assisting local SMEs to attain scale through internationalization strategies. Finally, improving connectivity with its immediate neighbours and the region is another way of addressing the scale problem.

In Chapter 9, Vannarith Chheang observes that Cambodia, similar to other ASEAN countries, is largely committed to all modes of liberalization (except for mode 4) under the GATS process. Currently, it is implementing and enacting several domestic policies to facilitate the development of its service sector (such as Special Economic Zones and e-commerce laws). Specific to the logistics sector, the country lacks a reliable network of transportation, telecommunications, and warehousing, pushing up the export costs 33 per cent higher than that of Thailand and 30 per cent higher than that of Vietnam. Its LSPs mainly offer domestic services, with limited service range and low quality, except for one or two that offer a wide range of services in transport, brokerage, and warehousing. The final users of logistics services, i.e. traders and manufacturers, are not aware of the benefits of efficient logistics services. While Cambodia is engaging multilateral agencies and countries like China and Japan to develop its transport infrastructure, it is also working on institutional and legal frameworks to support infrastructure development. Given the logistics sector commitments under GATS and AFAS, FDI in the sector is in high demand, accounting for 41 per cent of total accumulated FDI between 2011 and 2015.

However, there are many challenges in Cambodia's services sector, in general, and the logistics sector, in particular. Some of these are overlapping institutional arrangements, lack of coordination among government agencies, lack of government officials with the expertise on logistics, lack of data and operation standards. Corruption among government officials is also a dominant factor stalling the development of the sector. The private sector is not yet interested to invest in the sector due to high risks and low return. The sector also suffers from a shortage of working professionals with an understanding of the logistics sector.

In case of Laos (Chapter 10), Phanhpakit Onphanhdala and Vanvisa Philavong highlight the importance of the logistics sector as it can connect a landlocked Laos to the rest of the region. Under AFAS, there is no limitation on market access and national treatment in modes 1, 2 and 3 on maritime, inland waterway and rail transport services. For road transportation, Laos allows 100 per cent foreign equity participation in domestic freight transportation, while restrictions prevail on cross-border services.

However, several challenges exist in Laos' logistics sector. Based on feedback from key informants, the authors identify three main issues such as the lack of a comprehensive logistics system, too many procedures and documentation, and high costs. From a survey of joint-venture freight companies, the challenges observed are — insufficient and old trucks, lack of qualified professionals in freight forwarding business, absence of necessary equipment for loading and unloading in logistics business and inadequate skills in private sector to market their services. There are other concerns too, like trucks returning with empty load, road conditions and changes in fuel price, that plague the industry from further development. The chapter also gives an example of the development of a dry port and the country's plans to improve its logistics system in the future. There are two crucial components for dry port operations that Laos is exploring: providing management of a logistics hub (including cross dock warehousing) and establishing a single custom declaration. The development of dry ports will facilitate the country's aspired shift from being a landlocked to a landlinked country.

Min Ye Paing Hein and Ruth Banomyong, in Chapter 11, find that there are two interlocking layers of challenges — governance of FDI and governance of the services and logistic sector — in Myanmar's development strategy. There are various issues of agency in the governance of the services sector and it is manifested as an issue of coordination given the vast differences in information and incentives amongst multiple principals (focal agencies) and agents (implementing agencies) in terms of negotiation and implementation of agreements. However, at the local level, "thinness" of the presence of government agencies in regulating and monitoring economic activities at the border leads to a limited agency of the state in the governance of the services and logistics sectors.

The collective action problem due to the presence of multiple principals and agents in a fragmented policy space created by the first challenge will require extra efforts at coordination. The government has launched a National Transport Masterplan and it is also in the process of developing a National Logistics Masterplan, with the Ministry of Transport and Communication as the lead agency. But these Masterplans need to be coordinated and linked with the overall national strategic priorities. The government's role is to provide LSPs with an institutional, regulatory, and operational environment that can stimulate and guarantee the level of service needed for the efficient movement and storage of goods, services, and information. It also points to the need for a broader reform of public administrative issues as well as a conflict-sensitive development agenda. Therefore, the authors argue that the reform of governance and policy environment in FDI and general investment climate is the first priority in promoting the role of logistics and infrastructure in the national development agenda. It is also important to put facilitating FDI in logistics within the context of broader regulatory and policy reforms that can create an enabling ecosystem for logistics sector.

Three common issues have emerged from the ten countries in terms of the main challenges encountered for the development of the logistics sector at the country and ASEAN level. These are: (i) definition of the sector and its comparability across countries; (ii) the inherent complexities in governance, planning and coordination within this sector due to the many subsectors involved; and (iii) overcoming domestic constraints in the liberalization commitments of a country.

First, in terms of definition, the country-level studies show that most of them do not have a precise definition for this sector despite prioritizing its development (see Table 1.11). Data-wise, there is no such sector in the International Standard Industrial Classification of All Economic Activities (ISIC) industry codes commonly used for industrial classification. This implies there is no common definition for this sector in ASEAN. Operationally, transportation and storage is usually taken as a proxy of this sector in most countries.

TABLE 1.11
Definition/Understanding of Logistics Services in
ASEAN Member Countries

Countries	Logistics Definition/Understanding
Brunei	No official definition. Transport and storage can be used as a proxy.
Cambodia	No official definition. Logistics, is generally understood as a combination of four main subsectors namely transportation infrastructure (land, rail, maritime, air), logistics service providers (such as trucking, warehousing, freight forwarding, shipping, materials handling, inventory, packaging, courier and postal services), institutional framework relating to logistics (such as custom clearances and border reforms), and logistics users (such as traders and manufacturers).
Indonesia	It is defined as parts of the supply chain activity that involves handling of goods, information and money through procurement, warehousing, transportation, distribution and delivery services from point of origin to point of destination. It comprises of business activities ranging from transport and storage, post and couriers, and distribution.
Laos	Defines as a system management chain that plans, controls, stores, packs, loads, transports and provides efficient and effective service and information of moving goods between origin to destination in order to meet customers' requirement. Since there are no ports, maritime transportation is not relevant.
Malaysia	A broad conceptual definition but there is no operational definition in terms of specific subsectors in the main policy documents in Malaysia. Data used for this sector usually covers land and water transport, warehousing and support activities and postal and courier activities (or Malaysian Standard Industrial Classification 2008 (MSIC 2008)).
Myanmar	There is no widely accepted official definition of logistics in Myanmar.
Philippines	No official definition. The Annual Survey of Philippine Business and Industry (ASPBI) divides the logistics industry in the Philippines in three subgroups – Storage and Warehousing, Sea and Coastal Water Transport and Inland Water Transport, since there is no logistics industry in the ASPBI.
Singapore	No official definition. Authors use activities as described under the SSIC 2015 industry classification – transporting, freight forwarding, warehousing, and some supporting activities.
Thailand	No common definition within the country. Domestic definition used can vary from one ministry to another.
Vietnam	Logistics services is defined as a commercial activity that is broadly classified into three main subsectors: principal logistics services; transport-related logistics services and other related logistics services.

Source: Authors' compilation from the country studies.

Second, the governance structure in this sector is inherently complex. Almost all the country studies indicate this as a critical challenge encountered in the development of the logistics sector as there are multiple institutions and agencies involved. Each of these institutions and agencies has different regulations and procedures, leading to regulatory bottlenecks. As in the case of most services, information asymmetries require consumer protection through licensing requirements that may intentionally or unintentionally restrict the entry of domestic and foreign investors.

Likewise, policy planning and implementation is organized according to the terms of reference of the specific institutions and agencies that are involved. For example, the Ministry of Transportation merely focuses on the four main modes of transport such as air, maritime, roads and rails while the Customs Department has to handle cross-border issues. Organizationally, there is a tendency to work in silos, rather than across institutions and agencies, leading to the fragmentation observed in this industry for almost all the countries in this study. Moving towards integrating all the different activities requires coordination efforts across all ministries and agencies involved in the development of logistics, where a small city-state like Singapore may be better placed to do so.

Third, liberalization is an on-going process in all the ten countries as the targeted 70 per cent equity cap has yet to be met for all the targeted subsectors in the Roadmap. Similarly, domestic reforms in terms of changes in regulations is also very much work-in-progress, with some countries encountering more challenges in the reform process, compared to others as it may require changes in laws such as in the case of Thailand and the Philippines. Even a small-country like Singapore is constantly exploring ways to keep its industry abreast with global changes, including increasing use of technology to raise productivity and hence its competitiveness.

POLICY RECOMMENDATIONS

We summarize here the recommendations made by the ten country chapters in this book. The policy recommendations are provided at two-levels — country and ASEAN level.

Country-level

a. *Continuing and Sustaining Domestic Regulatory Reform*: The two necessary domestic changes suggested in all country papers, with the exception of Singapore, are continuing with domestic regulatory reforms and better coordination. Country papers acknowledge that while domestic regulatory reforms have started, there are still outdated, overlapping laws as well as many regulations governing the logistics industry. However, national level regulatory reforms so far tend to use a piecemeal approach for most of the countries, and the suggestions imply a continuation of this piecemeal approach. Malaysia has started implementing regulatory reform for the whole government by adopting GRP while Singapore has always emphasized functional policy changes that are cross-cutting rather than sectoral in their focus. The Philippines is also making a shift towards the adoption of GRP.

b. *Improving Coordination*: Better coordination also includes the need for a more holistic and comprehensive understanding of the logistics sector. Some of the country papers have suggested the need for a cross-cutting advisory body or council as an implementation mechanism for overseeing the development of the sector as an integrated whole, with the use of Master Plan.

c. *Enhancing Competitiveness of Local SMEs*: Local SMEs tend to concentrate in segments of the logistics industry that are non-asset based, such as freight forwarding, while bigger players, including state-owned enterprises (SOEs), are found in the asset-based segments that require high fixed costs, such as transportation infrastructure or warehousing. Competition is stiff in the SME dominated segments as they provide a limited range of logistics services and frequently serve as outsourced providers for the multinational logistics providers in some of the countries. Intense competitive pressures and less capability on the part of local logistics suppliers compared to foreign logistics suppliers have led to SMEs pressing for less liberalization as they fear even more competitive pressures will emerge with further liberalization. Policy measures recommended include assisting these domestic providers to grow bigger and to expand their range of services so that they can compete with the foreign providers. The Thai country paper made an exceptional call for more liberalization despite facing the same domestic challenges as the government needs to consider the perspective of logistics users who need to have lower logistics costs in order to compete.

d. *Investing in Infrastructure Development*: More investment needed in infrastructure is highlighted especially for Indonesia, the Philippines, and the Cambodia, Lao PDR, Myanmar and Vietnam (CLMV) countries. In particular, Cambodia and Lao PDR are focussing on the development of dry ports and logistics parks. These countries also recognize the need to use public–private partnerships (PPPs) and FDI to complement government expenditure in infrastructure development in view of fiscal constraints.

e. *Improving Customs Clearance:* Since customs clearance is also a concern, some country papers suggest the need to improve their national single windows by making it more functional and more connected to more government agencies. The use of single windows will not only reduce delays at ports but will also assist in reducing corruption encountered in some of these countries.

f. *Improving Data Collection*: All the country papers show that data are scarce for the services sector, and especially for logistics. Collecting better data at each country level will enhance policy formulation for the country and the region.

ASEAN-wide

a. *Agree on a Common Working Definition for Logistics*: As indicated, it is not possible to compare and monitor the development of logistics without a common definition of the subsectors to be included in logistics.

b. *Continue to Improve Liberalization Commitments in the ASEAN Trade in Services Agreement (ATISA)*: It is important to implement the ASEAN Economic Community 2025 Consolidated Strategic Action Plan, endorsed in February 2017, for ATISA (ASEAN Secretariat 2015*b*).

c. *Facilitating Domestic Regulatory Reform*: The important role of domestic regulations in creating a more attractive environment for FDI is also recognized in the AEC 2025 Consolidated Strategic Action Plan in ATISA and under Good Governance (ASEAN Secretariat 2015*b*). However, domestic regulatory reform is not just about adopting best practices alone. Rules and regulations related to investment in the services sector must be made readily available in English language for ASEAN investors. Changes undertaken must be made readily available in a timely fashion.

d. *Accelerate the Activation and Operation of the ASEAN Single Window*: The ASEAN Connectivity Master Plan for 2025 has already listed this as a priority initiative. Again, implementation is vital.

e. *Capacity Building*: ASEAN countries suffer from uneven implementation of liberalization and facilitation measures under the AEC Blueprint and regional connectivity plans. A key reason for this is lack of human resources in government agencies, especially in the less developed countries. ASEAN, under its Initiative of ASEAN Integration (IAI) scheme, can develop a capacity building programme where the advanced ASEAN members can impart logistics training and skills to less developed economies.

f. *Harmonizing Data Collection*: The basic data needed for understanding the services sector, including its FDI data and definitions used for subsectors like logistics can be harmonized so that each country will collect the same set of basic data. This includes basic data like a common price deflator for this sector to make meaningful analysis over time.

g. Finally, to conclude, in the case of logistics, enhancing cooperation and coordination across different Implementing Bodies and Working Groups in ASEAN is important as the sector is spread across several bodies at the regional-level. These include Coordinating Committee in Services, Customs Coordinating Committee, Senior Transport Officials Meeting, Customs Procedures and Trade Facilitation Working Group, Telecommunication Senior Officials Meeting, ASEAN Single Window Steering Committee, ASEAN Freight Forwarders Association, Coordinating Committee on Investment and others. Although the Senior Economic Officials Meeting (SEOM) is the overall coordinating and monitoring body for integration of logistics services in ASEAN, it is neither responsible for the extent of information flow across these agencies nor is it accountable for coordination at the national level. In general, efficient coordination at the regional level is a reflection of better coordination at national-level and vice-versa. It is quite possible that there is a disconnect between national- and regional-level in logistics planning and implementation. It is also possible that the people responsible for national and regional plans are different and hence there is a lack of coherence and consistency, thereby affecting coordination. Going forward, efficient coordination between regional bodies that takes into account better coordination of national agencies is necessary for ASEAN logistics cooperation. This will not only help to link together all the many and different initiatives across services development, transportation, governance and connectivity plans but it can also accelerate logistics integration in ASEAN.

Notes

1. "2007 ASEAN Sectoral Integration Protocol for the Logistics Services Sector", Signed by Economic Ministers in Makati City, the Philippines on 24 August 2007, available at <http://cil.nus.edu.sg/rp/pdf/2007%20ASEAN%20 Sectoral%20Integration%20Protocol%20for%20the%20Logistics%20 Services%20Sector-pdf.pdf>).
2. See Faeth (2009) for a detailed explanation of the different models.
3. But there are some exceptions too such as consultants' reports (tangible), movies (visible) and many services require physical assets (that can be classified as goods) and vice versa (UNCTAD 2004).
4. The OECD FDI Regulatory Restrictiveness Index covers only statutory measures discriminating against foreign investors (e.g. foreign equity limits, screening & approval procedures, restriction on key foreign personnel, and other operational measures). Other important aspects of an investment climate (e.g. the implementation of regulations and state monopolies among other) are not considered. All 34 OECD countries and 25 non-OECD countries are covered, including all G20 members. Larger values imply more restrictive FDI rules in a country.
5. GATS cover both horizontal and sectoral commitments.
6. Note that Most Favoured Nation (MFN) exemption can be accorded to a country for ten years if they can fulfil certain rules for such exemption.
7. The other GATS provisions are domestic regulations, monopolies and exclusive service supplier, emergency safeguard measures, balance of payment safeguard, government procurement, general exceptions and subsidies.
8. World Trade Organisation, Services Sectoral Classification List (MTN. GNS/W/120).
9. The Roadmap can be downloaded from <http://www.asean.org/storage/images/ archive/20883.pdf> (accessed 1 September 2016).
10. See <http://asean.org/wp-content/uploads/images/archive/documents/BAP%20 2011-2015.pdf> (accessed 1 September 2016. The Brunei Action Plan charts the course for transportation development in ASEAN in land, rail, air and sea. Since transportation is a big component in logistics, the facilitation measures in RILS aligned with the facilitation measures in the Brunei Action Plan.
11. For example, the timeline for strengthening intra-ASEAN maritime and shipping transport services has "on-going" in its timeline with no binding deadline, while the timeline for the transportation facilitation agreements merely states that it is to begin in 2008 and there are no binding deadlines as well.
12. The LPI is a multi-dimensional assessment of logistics performance and an international benchmarking tool focusing specifially on measuring the trade

and transport facilitation friendliness of a country. The LPI summarizes the performance of countries through six dimensions that capture the most important aspects of the logistics environment, namely, customs (efficiency of the customs clearance process); infrastructure (quality of trade and transport-related infrastructure); international shipments (ease of arranging competitively priced shipments); logistics quality (competence and quality of logistics services); tracking and tracing (or the ability to track and trace consignments); as well as timeliness (or the frequency with which shipments reach the consignee within the scheduled or expected time) (Arvis et al. 2014).

References

Arvis, Jean-François, Daniel Saslavsky, Lauri Ojala, Ben Shepherd, Christina Busch, and Anasuya Raj. *Connecting to Compete 2014: Trade Logistics in the Global Economy — The Logistics Performance Index and Its Indicators*. Washington, D.C.: The World Bank, 2014.

ASEAN. *ASEAN Framework Agreement on Services*. Bangkok: ASEAN, 1995. Available at <http://investasean.asean.org/files/upload/Doc%2008%20-%20 AFAS.pdf>.

ASEAN Secretariat. *ASEAN Integration Report 2015*. Jakarta: ASEAN Secretariat, 2015*a*. Available at <http://asean.org/asean-integration-report-2015-4/> (accessed 2 February 2016).

———. *ASEAN Economic Community Blueprint 2025*. Jakarta: ASEAN Secretariat, 2015*b*. Available at <http://www.asean.org/storage/2016/03/AECBP_2025r_FINAL.pdf> (accessed 2 February 2016).

ASEAN Secretariat and the World Bank. *ASEAN Services Integration Report*. Jakarta: ASEAN Secretariat; Washington D.C.: World Bank, 2015. Available at <http://documents.worldbank.org/curated/en/759841468178459585/pdf/100637-Revised-WP-PUBLIC-Box393257B-ASEAN-Report-web.pdf> (accessed 2 February 2016).

Asiedu, Elizabeth. "On the Determinants of Foreign Direct Investment to Developing Countries: Is Africa Different?". *World Development* 30, no. 1 (2002): 107–19.

Athukorala, Prema-Chandra. "Global Production Sharing and Trade Patterns in East Asia". *Working Papers in Trade and Development*. Working Paper no. 2013/10. Arndt-Corden Department of Economics, Crawford School of Public Policy, ANU College of Asia and the Pacific, 2013.

Australian Department of Foreign Affairs and Trade. "Improving the Investment Climate for Global Value Chain Development". Paper presented at the Public–Private Dialogue on Improving the Investment Climate for Global Value Chain Development, Shangri-la Hotel, Kuala Lumpur, 28–29 April 2016.

Baldwin, Richard. "21st Century Regionalism: Filling the Gap between 21st Century Trade and 20th Century Trade Rules". *Staff Working Paper ERSD-2011-08*. Geneva: World Trade Organisation, 2011. Available at <https://www.wto.org/english/res_e/reser_e/ersd201108_e.pdf> (accessed 2 February 2016).

Banga, Rashmi. "Impact of Government Policies and Investment Agreements on FDI Inflows". Working Paper no. 116, Indian Council for Research on International Economic Relations (ICRIER). New Delhi: ICRIER, 2003.

Banomyong, Ruth, Peter Cook and Paul Kent. "Formulating Regional Logistics Development Policy: The Case of ASEAN". *International Journal of Logistics Research and Applications* 11, no. 5 (2008): 359–79.

Bénassy-Quéré, Agnès, Maylis Coupet, and Thierry Mayer. "Institutional Determinants of Foreign Direct Investment". *CEPII, Working Paper No 2005-05*. Available at <http://www.cepii.fr/PDF_PUB/wp/2005/wp2005-05.pdf> (accessed 16 May 2016).

Blonigen, Bruce A. "A Review of the Empirical Literature of FDI Determinants". *Atlantic Economic Journal* 33 (2005): 383–403.

Chanda, Rupa. "GATS and Its Implications for Developing Countries: Key Issues and Concerns". DESA Discussion Paper no. 25. Geneva: United Nations, 2002.

Chia Siow Yue and Michael G. Plummer. *ASEAN Economic Cooperation and Integration: Progress, Challenges and Future Directions*. UK: Cambridge University Press, 2015.

CIMB ASEAN Research Institute (CARI). "Liberalization of the Trade in Services". *AEC Blueprint 2025 Analysis*, vol. 1, paper 3. Jakarta: CARI, March 2016.

Cooper, William H. "Trade in Services: The Doha Development Agenda Negotiations and U.S. Goals". Cornell University ILR School, Digital Commons @ILR, 2011. Available at <http://digitalcommons.ilr.cornell.edu/cgi/viewcontent.cgi?article=1816&context=key_workplace>.

Dee, Philippa. "Services Liberalization toward the ASEAN Economic Community". In *Deepening East Asian Economic Integration*, edited by Jenny Corbett and So Umezaki. ERIA Research Project Report 2008-1, pp. 58–96. Jakarta: Economic Research Institute for ASEAN and East Asia, 2009. Available at <http://www.eria.org/publications/research_project_reports/images/pdf/y2008/no1/DEI-Ch02.pdf> (accessed 16 May 2016).

———. "Monitoring the Implementation of Services Trade Reform towards an ASEAN Economic Community". *ERIA Discussion Paper Series*, ERIA-DP-2015-44. Jakarta: Economic Research Institute for ASEAN and East Asia, May 2015.

Dunning, John H. "Trade, Location of Economic Activity and the MNE: A Search for an Eclectic Approach". In *The International Allocation of Economic Activity*, edited by Bertil Ohlin, Per-Ove Hesselborn, and Per Magnus Wijkman. London: Macmillan, 1977. (The first statement of the

OLI approach, later refined and extended in many books and papers by the author and his collaborators.)

———. "Multinational Enterprises and the Growth of Services: Some Conceptual and Theoretical Issues". *Service Industry Journal* 9, no. 1 (1989): 5–39.

———. "The Eclectic (OLI) Paradigm of International Production: Past, Present and Future". *International Journal of the Economics of Business* 8, no. 2 (2001): 173–90.

———. "Towards a New Paradigm of Development: Implications for the Determinants of International Business". *Transnational Corporations* 15, no. 1 (2006): 173–227.

Faeth, Isabel. "Determinants of Foreign Direct Investment: A Tale of Nine Theoretical Models". *Journal of Economic Surveys* 23, no. 1 (2009): 165–96.

Grossman, Gene M. and Esteban Rossi-Hansberg. "Trading Tasks: A Simple Theory of Offshoring". *American Economic Review* 98, no. 5 (2008): 1978–97.

Jones, Ronald W. and Henryk Kierzkowski. "International Fragmentation and the New Economic Geography". *The North American Journal of Economics and Finance* 16 (2005): 1–10.

Kotnik, Particia and Eva Hagsten. "ICT Use and Exports", 2012. Available at <http://is.jrc.ec.europa.eu/pages/ISG/innovation/documents/ICTexports_pk_seville.pdf> (accessed 16 May 2016).

Nikomborirak, Deunden and Supunnavadee Jitdumrong. "ASEAN Trade in Services". In *ASEAN Economic Community: A Work in Progress*, edited by Sanchita Basu Das, Jayant Menon, Rodolfo Severino and Omkar Lal Shrestha, pp. 95–140. Singapore: Institute of Southeast Asian Studies, 2013.

North, Douglass C. *Institutions, Institutional Change and Economic Performance*. Cambridge: Cambridge University Press, 1990.

Saez, Sebastian, Daria Taglioni, Erik van der Marel, Claire H. Hollweg and Veronika Zavacka. *Valuing Services in Trade: A Toolkit for Competitiveness Diagnostics*. Washington, D.C: The World Bank, 2015.

Singh, Harinder and Kwang W. Jun. "Some New Evidence on Determinants of Foreign Direct Investment in Developing Countries". *Policy Research Working Paper 1531*. Washington D.C.: The World Bank, 1995.

Stephenson, Sherry. "Overview of the TISA Negotiations". Training Workshop on Trade in Services Negotiations for AU-CFTA Negotiators, 2015. Available at <http://unctad.org/meetings/en/Presentation/ditc-ted-Nairobi-24082015-USAID-stephenson-2.pdf>.

Sugie, Kazuhiro, Massimo Geloso Grosso, Hildegunn Kyvik Nordås, Sébastien Miroudot, Frederic Gonzales, and Dorothée Rouzet. "Services Trade Restrictiveness Index (STRI): Logistics Services". OECD Trade Policy Papers, no. 183. Paris: OECD Publishing, 2015.

Sun, Xiaolun. "How to Promote FDI? The Regulatory and Institutional Environment for Attracting FDI". Paper prepared by the Foreign Investment Advisory Service for the Capacity Development Workshops and Global Forum on

Reinventing Government on Globalization, Role of the State and Enabling Environment, sponsored by the United Nations Marrakech, Morocco, 10–13 December 2002. Available at <http://unpan1.un.org/intradoc/groups/public/documents/UN/UNPAN006349.pdf> (accessed 16 May 2016).

Tham Siew Yean. "Examining ASEAN's Logistics Sector Integration". PowerPoint presentation at ASEAN Roundtable 2016. Singapore: ISEAS – Yusof Ishak Institute, 2016.

Tongzon, Jose. "Liberalisation of Logistics Services: The Case of ASEAN". *International Journal of Logistics Research and Applications* 14, no. 1 (2011): 11–34.

United Nations Conference on Trade and Development (UNCTAD). *World Investment Report 2004: The Shift to Services*. Geneva: UNCTAD, 2004. Available at <http://unctad.org/en/Docs/wir2004_en.pdf> (accessed 25 April 2017).

———. "The Role of International Investment Agreements in Attracting Foreign Direct Investment to Developing Countries". UNCTAD Series on International Investment Policies for Development, Geneva: UNCTAD, 2009. Available at <http://unctad.org/en/Docs/diaeia20095_en.pdf> (accessed 25 April 2017).

United Nations Economic and Social Commission for Asia and the Pacific (UNESCAP). *Asia Pacific Trade and Investment Report 2015*. Bangkok: UNESCAP, 2015.

United States International Trade Commission (USITC). *Logistics Services: An Overview of the Global Market and Potential Effects of Removing Trade Impediments*. Investigation no. 332-463, USITC Publication 3770. Washington, D.C.: USITC, 2005.

World Bank. World Development Indicator [online]. Washington, D.C.: World Bank, 2016.

———. *Logistics Performance Index*. Washington, D.C.: World Bank, 2016.

Yin, Feng, Mingque Ye and Lingli Xu. "Location Determinants of Foreign Direct Investment in Services: Evidence from Chinese Provincial-level Data". *Asia Research Centre Working Paper 64*. London: London School of Economics & Political Science, 2014.

2

REFORMING INDONESIA'S LOGISTICS SECTOR

Titik Anas and Nur Afni Panjaitan

INTRODUCTION

Indonesia's services sector is relatively small at 42 per cent of Gross Domestic Product (GDP), compared to an ASEAN average of 47.3 per cent and a world average of 68.3 per cent in 2014. The share of services to GDP increased marginally from 40.6 per cent in 2011 to 42 per cent in 2014. Services trade as a share of total trade is also relatively low at about 6.4 per cent in 2014 compared to the world average of 13 per cent. Furthermore, compared to the manufacturing sector, policies governing the services sector are relatively more restrictive, as for example in the case of Indonesia's foreign direct investment (FDI) policy.

The logistics sector is no exception to the above pattern in Indonesia's services performance. The contribution and performance of this sector is below that of Singapore, Malaysia and Thailand. The World Bank's Logistics Performance Index (LPI) indicated that Indonesia's logistics performance ranked the 63rd out of 160 countries, while Singapore ranked the 5th, Malaysia the 32nd and Thailand the 45th (World Bank 2016).

Given its current performance, improving the logistics sector's efficiency is among the main priorities of the current government. The immediate challenge for Indonesia is to make the sector more efficient so that logistics cost can be reduced, remove barriers to entry as well as to improve the quality of logistics infrastructure. The logistics cost for international and domestic freight in Indonesia in relatively high compared to its peers in the region. World Bank (2012) reported the typical charge for a forty-foot dry container or a semi-trailer (total freight including agent fees and other charges) in 2012 was only US$178 in Singapore while it costs around US$415 in Indonesia. Therefore, the logistics costs for exporting and importing in Indonesia are more expensive than a neighbouring high labour cost country like Singapore.

Domestic logistics cost in Indonesia, especially inter-island, is also higher than international export–import costs. The cost of sending a 100-kilogram package from Jakarta to Tanjung Pinang, in Kepulauan Riau Province of Indonesia, using Jalur Nugraha Ekakurir's (JNE) cheapest service is IDR2.5 million (about US$260). On the other hand, JNE charges only IDR1.2 million (about US$130) for a package of the same weight sent from Jakarta to Singapore, a distance farther than the route from Jakarta to Riau Islands.

The poor performance of Indonesia's logistics sector, as reflected in its relatively higher cost, can be attributed to several inter-related factors, such as domestic imbalances in demand and supply. This is, in turn, partly due to incompatible policies compared to the dynamic changes in this sector (Anas et al. 2012).

In the early 1990s, Indonesia's government did not have a coherent set of policies to develop the sector. To improve the performance of the sector, it developed a Blueprint for the Development of the National Logistics System (Sistem Logistik Nasional, thus, SISLOGNAS) and issued it as Presidential Regulation no. 26/2012. The objective of the blueprint is to provide an integrated plan to develop the logistics system. Prior to this, a number of regulatory reforms were undertaken, including amendment of laws, such as the law on railway (2007), shipping (2008), air transport (2009), road transport (2009), postal (2009) and electronic information and transaction (2008).

Interestingly, although the laws governing the sector have been amended, the logistics sector remains relatively closed. Both the Organisation for Economic Co-operation and Development (OECD) Services Trade Restrictiveness Index (STRI) and the FDI Restrictiveness Index indicates that this sector continues to be restrictive. How did changes in regulations affect Indonesia's logistics sector performance? What additional changes are required to improve the performance of Indonesia's logistics sector so that the economy can function more efficiently? This chapter aims to address these two issues, especially on the role of FDI in improving the performance of the logistics sector. The chapter is organized as follows: the next section discusses the services sector in Indonesia, its performance and regulations. Section 3 provides an overview of the logistics sector. Section 4 discusses policy measures in the logistics sector followed with a discussion on the outstanding challenges and policy suggestions. Section 6 concludes this chapter.

SERVICES SECTOR IN INDONESIA

Services contributes a significant portion of world GDP, increasing from 64.3 per cent in 2000 to about 68.3 per cent in 2014 (see Figure 2.1). The share of services in GDP is significantly higher for the high-income countries, compared to the low and middle-income group of countries, for the entire period shown in Figure 2.1. For Indonesia, as a middle income country, the share of services in its GDP is relatively lower than the average for the low and middle income group. It is in fact lower than the ASEAN average of 47.3 per cent in 2014, although there was a modest increase from 38 per cent in 2000 to 42 per cent in 2014.

FIGURE 2.1
Services in GDP, 2000–14 (%)

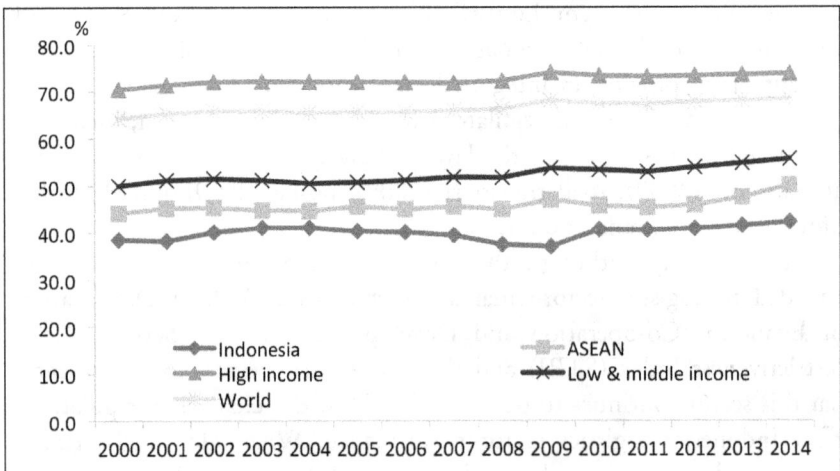

Source: World Development Indicators, World Bank, available at <http://data.worldbank.org/data-catalog/world-development-indicators>.

Services share in total employment had increased gradually from 35 per cent in 1994 to 38.7 per cent in 2004 and to 44.8 per cent in 2014 (ILO 2015). However, Indonesia's share is still lower than the world average of 49.0 per cent. Compared to other countries in ASEAN, the contribution of services to total employment in Indonesia is lower than the respective shares in Brunei Darussalam (80.8 per cent), Singapore (70.6 per cent), Malaysia (60.3 per cent), and the Philippines (53.6 per cent) (see Figure 2.2).

FIGURE 2.2
Share of Total Employment in Services, 2014 (%)

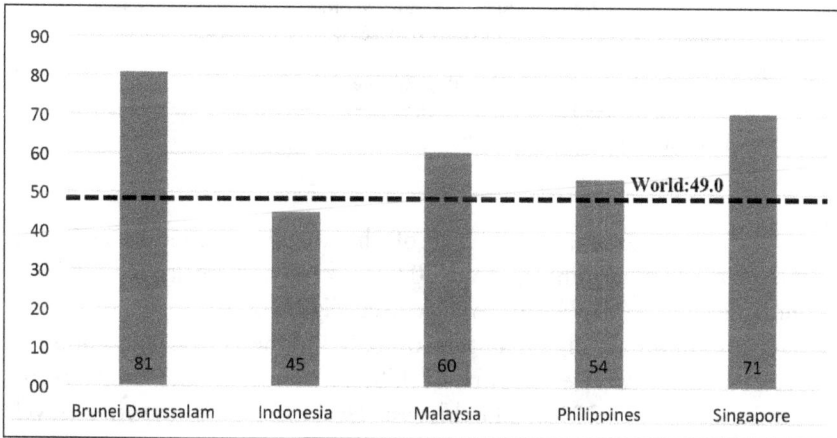

Source: ILO (2015).

The relative importance of the services sector in Indonesia's economy can also be shown using the Indonesia's Input–Output (IO) tables. The 2005 and 2010 IO tables indicated that the services sector accounted about 33 per cent and 30.7 per cent respectively, of total intermediate input, with wholesale and retail trade and transport providing the largest services input to the manufacturing sector. Based on 2010 IO table, wholesale and retail trade services is the largest intermediate services input, providing for about 8.2 per cent of total intermediate inputs used in the economy. Transportation is the second largest services input, contributing about 4.2 per cent of total intermediate input used in the economy.

Trade in services, as briefly discussed earlier, is relatively low for Indonesia. On average, services trade constituted about 15.3 per cent of total trade for the period 2005–15, compared to the world average of 20.9 per cent (see Figure 2.3). Services export is particularly small, about

FIGURE 2.3
Average Share of Services in International Trade, 2005–15

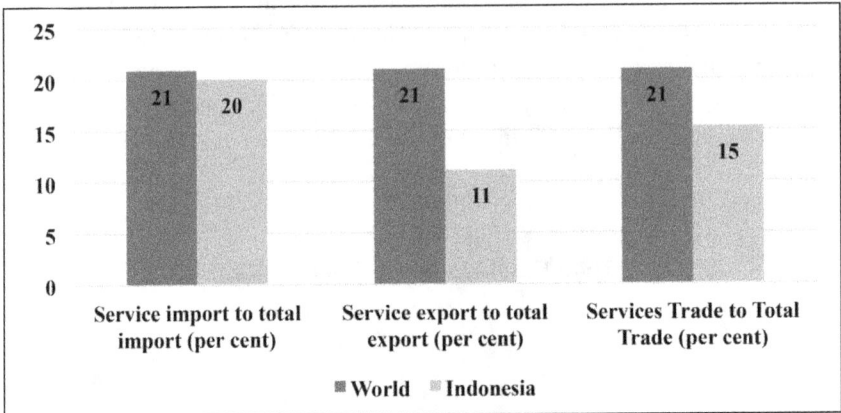

Source: UNCTAD Statistics.

11.1 per cent of total exports, half of the world average. In contrast, imports of services accounted about 20.0 per cent of total imports, which is almost similar to the world average (see Figure 2.3).

It is important to highlight that overall; Indonesia is a net importer of services, with services export of US$22.2 billion and imports of US$30.5 billion for 2015. The biggest services export was the travel sector, about US$10.8 billion, followed by other business services (US$4.9 billion) and transport (US$3.5 billion). Import is dominated by transport services (US$9.6 billion), followed by other business services (US$7.5 billion), and travel (US$7.3 billion) (see Table 2.1). Except for travel and personal, cultural and recreational services, Indonesia was a net importer of services.

How restrictive are the policies for the services sector? The OECD STRI[1] indicates that Indonesia's policy regulating the services sector is still relatively restrictive. The STRI scores for twenty-two services sectors covered in the OECD STRI index are higher than the average (see Figure 2.4). Logistics customs brokerage, architecture, and engineering services are the three sectors with the lowest scores (most open), although these are still above the sample average. Legal services, motion pictures, and air transport (covering establishments only) scored the highest, implying these are the most restrictive service sectors in Indonesia.

TABLE 2.1
Export and Import of Services: Indonesia, 2005 and 2015

	Value (US$ million)			Share (per cent)	
	2005	2015	Changes (per cent)	2005	2015
Exports					
Manufacturing services on physical inputs	447.5	355.6	−20.5	3.3	1.6
Maintenance and repair service	44.0	118.3	168.9	0.3	0.5
Transport	2,842.0	3,479.4	22.4	21.0	15.7
Travel	4,521.9	10,761.0	138.0	33.5	48.4
Construction	484.1	378.3	−21.9	3.6	1.7
Insurance and pension services	14.8	26.5	79.5	0.1	0.1
Financial services	465.2	263.6	−43.3	3.4	1.2
Charge for the use of intellectual property	263.3	54.5	−79.3	1.9	0.2
Telecommunication, computers and information	1,145.6	1,045.6	−8.7	8.5	4.7
Other business services	2,875.6	4,998.6	73.8	21.3	22.5
Personal, cultural, and recreation service	57.0	115.0	101.6	0.4	0.5
Government goods and services	355.1	631.8	77.9	2.6	2.8
Total services export	13,516.0	22,228.1	64.5	100.0	100.0
Imports					
Manufacturing services on physical inputs	–	–	–	–	–
Maintenance and repair service	148.0	359.5	142.9	0.7	1.2
Transport	7,450.8	9,601.8	28.9	33.3	31.5
Travel	3,584.3	7,292.2	103.5	16.0	23.9
Construction	725.5	452.5	−37.6	3.2	1.5
Insurance and pension services	338.3	942.6	178.7	1.5	3.1
Financial services	723.7	744.4	2.9	3.2	2.4
Charge for the use of intellectual property	960.9	1,652.7	72.0	4.3	5.4
Telecommunication, computers and information	1,055.5	1,791.2	69.7	4.7	5.9
Other business services	7,016.5	7,462.6	6.4	31.3	24.4
Personal, cultural, and recreation service	165.7	66.8	−59.7	0.7	0.2
Government goods and services	212.4	162.8	−23.4	0.9	0.5
Total services import	22,381.4	30,529.1	36.4	100.0	100.0
Net Export	**−8,865.4**	**−8,301.0**			

Source: Bank Indonesia (2017).

FIGURE 2.4

**OECD Services Trade Restrictiveness Index (STRI)
by Sector and Policy Area: Indonesia, 2015**

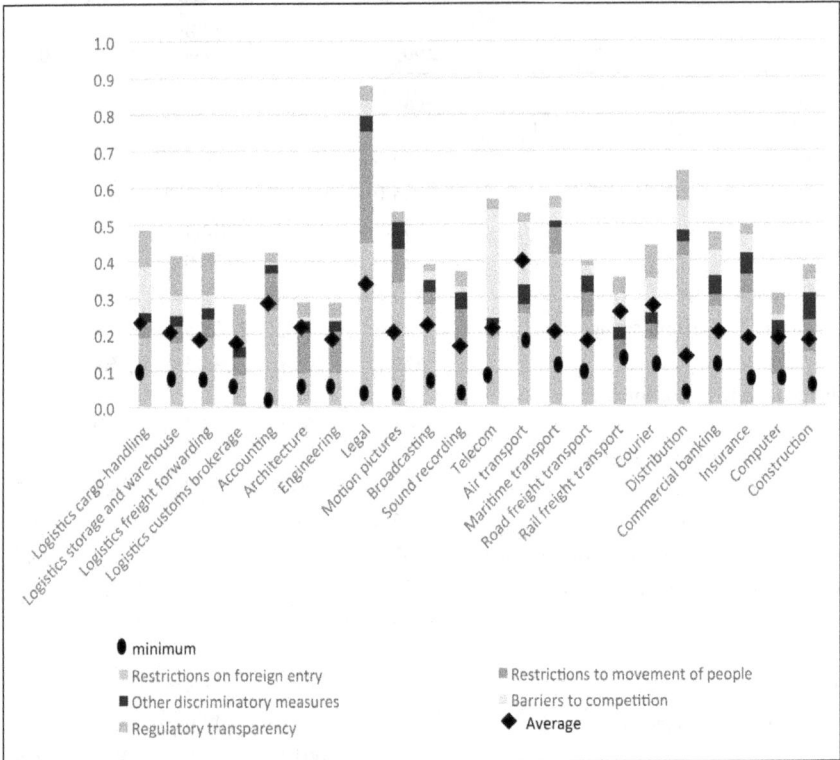

With regards to FDI policy, the OECD FDI restrictiveness index shows the evolution of Indonesia's FDI policies since 1997. The index suggests that Indonesia has always been more open for foreign investment in the manufacturing sector relative to services. The results differed greatly within the services sector (see Figure 2.5). Some services subsectors have become increasingly more open to FDI over time, particularly in the hotels and restaurants sector. In contrast, communications and distribution have become more restrictive from 1997 to 2014. Real estate services, on the other hand, are completely closed throughout the observed period.

FIGURE 2.5

Evolution of Indonesia's Services FDI Regulatory Restrictiveness

(1 = completely closed, 0 = completely open)

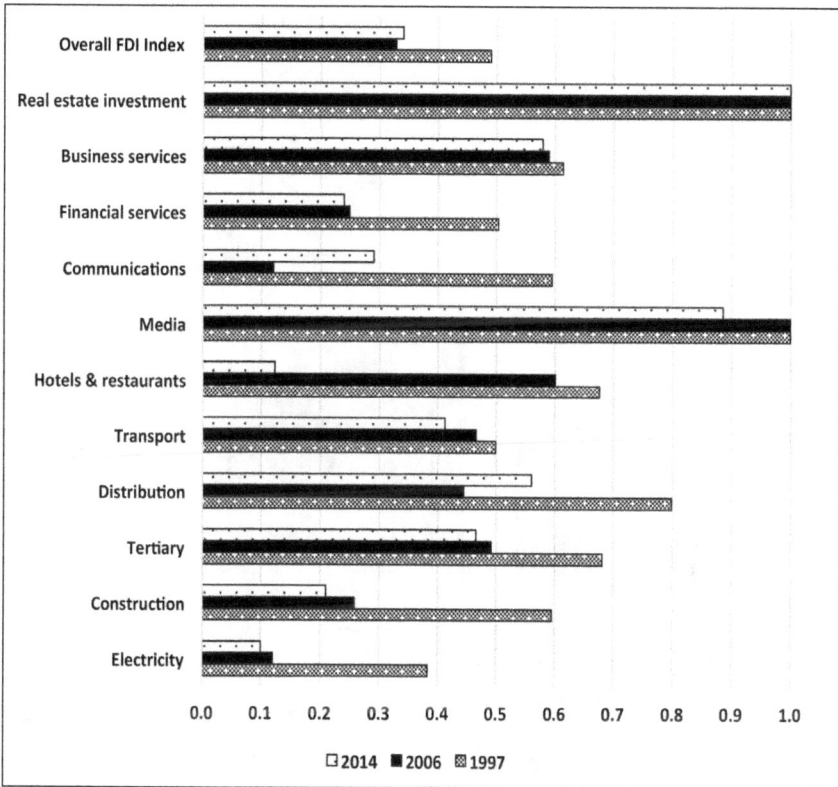

Source: OECD (2014).

FDI in services sector, in value terms, is relatively smaller compared to other sectors. Based on the number of projects, the services sector receives the largest number of FDI realized projects (see Figure 2.6). In 2010, this number was 1,515 and it increased by more than five times, to 8,270 projects in 2015. The manufacturing sector is the second largest recipient in terms of number of projects, increasing from 1,091 to 7,184 projects respectively, from 2010 to 2015. However, in terms of value, manufacturing remains the largest recipient of FDI in 2015, with an investment amounting to US$11.8 billion while the services sector accounted for only US$8.2 billion.

FIGURE 2.6
Indonesia's Direct Investment Projects (Left) and
Indonesia's Direct Investment Value (Right)

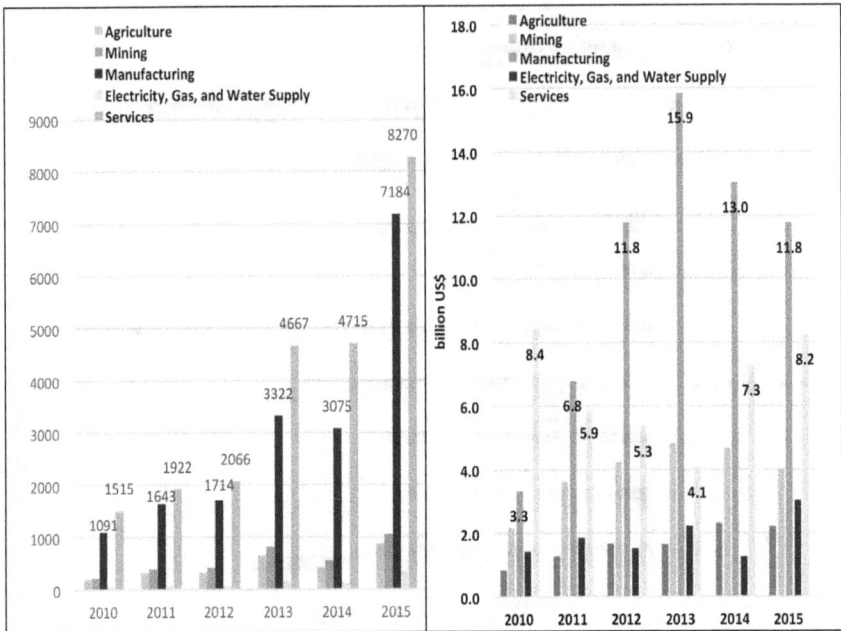

Source: Indonesia Investment Coordinating Board (2016).

OVERVIEW OF THE LOGISTICS INDUSTRY
IN INDONESIA

In 2012, the government formulated a blueprint of the national logistics system (SISLOGNAS). Based on SISLOGNAS, the logistics sector in Indonesia is defined as parts of the supply chain that involves handling of flows of goods, information and money through procurement, warehousing, transportation, distribution and delivery services from point of origin, to point of destination (Government of Indonesia 2012, p. 4). It comprises business activities ranging from transport and storage, post and couriers, and distribution. The sectors follow the regulations from a large number of government institutions including the Ministry of Trade, Ministry of Transport, Ministry of Information and Technology and the Custom Office of Ministry of Finance.

Drawing from GDP sectoral data, it seems that the logistics sector contributed significantly to Indonesia's GDP. Based on the value added of wholesale and retail, transportation and communication sectors in GDP, the contribution increased slightly from 21 per cent in 2000 to 27 per cent in 2014 (see Table 2.2). Within the logistics sector, wholesale and retail contributed the most of value added though its share has decreased over the years. The share of wholesale and retail is about 74 per cent in 2000 but this dropped to 58 per cent in 2014. The transportation subsectors showed a similar pattern as the share declined from 19 per cent to 15 per cent in the same period. In contrast, the communication subsector showed a positive trend where its contribution increased from 7 to 27 per cent from 2000 to 2014.

TABLE 2.2
Contribution to GDP, 2000–14 (%)

Sectors	2000	2005	2010	2011	2012	2013*	2014**
Share of Logistics to GDP	21	22	25	26	27	27	27
Wholesale and Retail share to Logistics	74	69	60	60	60	59	58
Transportation share to Logistics	19	19	16	15	15	15	15
Communication share to Logistics	7	12	24	25	25	26	27

Notes: * Preliminary; ** Very Preliminary
Source: Badan Pusat Statistik (2016).

Domestic value added (DVA) content in Indonesia's logistics sector is high. Table 2.3 shows the OECD's Trade in Value Added (TIVA) computation of DVA content of gross export for this sector, which was about 94.3 per cent for wholesale and retail trade and repair, 92 per cent for transport and storage, and 95 per cent for post and telecommunication in 1995. The contribution of DVA in gross exports decreased slightly for wholesale and retail trade and repair to 93.2 per cent but it decreased significantly for transport and storage, to 81.7 per cent in 2011. In contrast, DVA share in post and telecommuncation's gross exports increased to 95.9 per cent in 2011.

Bahagia, Sandee and Meeuws (2013) indicated Indonesia's relatively high logistics cost,[2] which at 27 per cent of GDP, was higher than other ASEAN countries such as Singapore (8 per cent), Malaysia (13 per cent), Thailand (20 per cent), and Vietnam (25 per cent) (see Figure 2.7). The largest share in Indonesia's logistics costs is transportation costs, which was almost half of the total logistics costs (see Figure 2.8). In 2011, the

TABLE 2.3
Indonesia in Logistics Global Value Chain (%)

Indicators	Wholesale and Retail Trade, Repair		Transport and Storage		Post and Telecommunication	
	1995	2011	1995	2011	1995	2011
Domestic value added (DVA) share of gross exports	94.3	93.2	92.1	81.7	95.0	95.9
Foreign value added share of gross exports	5.7	6.8	7.9	18.3	5.0	4.1

Source: OECD (2015*b*).

FIGURE 2.7
Logistics Cost (% of GDP)

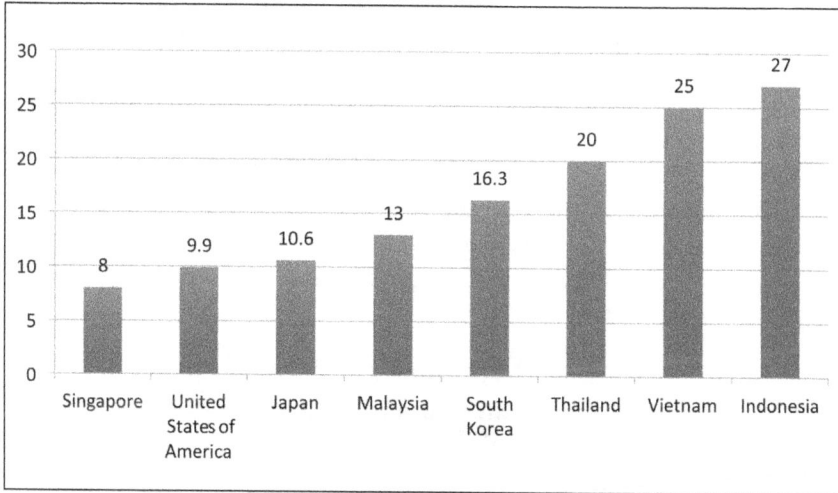

Source: Bahagia, Sandee and Meeuws (2013).

FIGURE 2.8
Share of Transportation in Indonesia's Logistics Cost

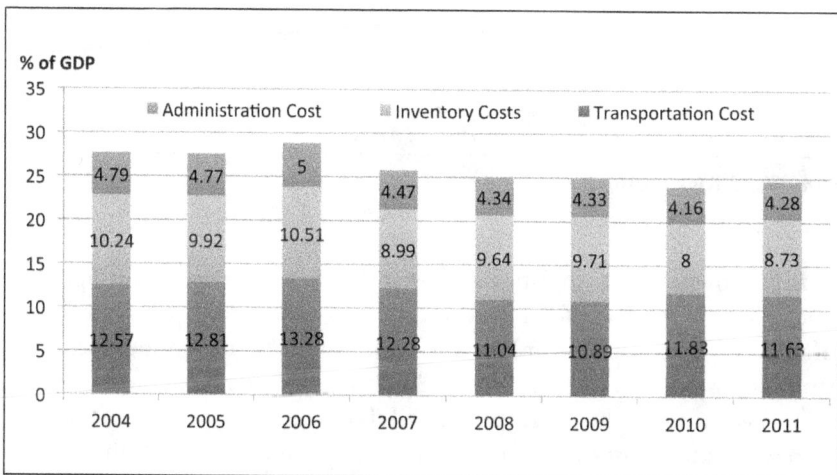

Source: Bahagia, Sandee and Meeuws (2013).

logistics cost was about 24.6 per cent of GDP, where 11.6 per cent is transportation cost, 8.7 per cent is inventory cost, and 4.3 per cent is administration cost. Figure 2.8 also shows that the cost declined from 27.6 per cent in 2004 to 24.0 per cent in 2010, but it increased to 24.6 per cent in 2011.

The overall performance of Indonesia's logistics sector can be described using the World Bank's logistic performance index. Figure 2.9 displays Indonesia's LPI in 2016. In 2016, the overall LPI index is 2.98. Based on subcomponents of the indicator, timeliness has the highest score, which is 3.5, followed by tracking and tracing (3.2). On the other hand, infrastructure and customs performance have a score of below 3.

FIGURE 2.9
Indonesia's Logistics Performance Index, 2016

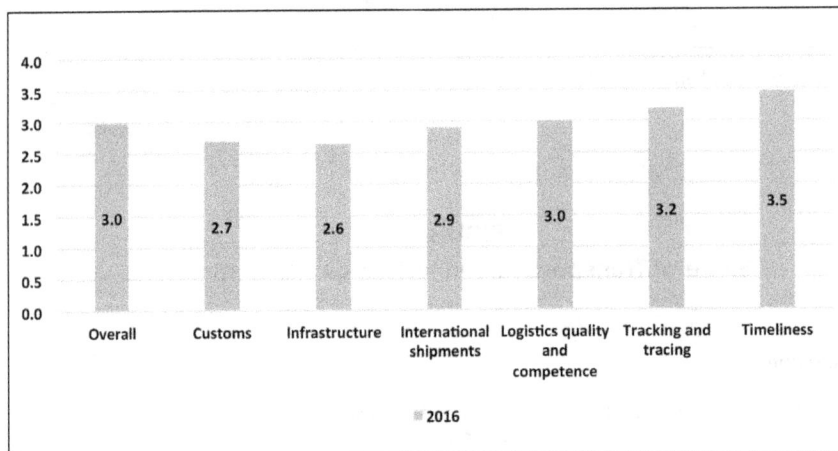

Source: World Bank (2016).

FDI flows to the logistics sector was small and is declining (see Table 2.4). In 2015, FDI in logistics sector (trade and repair, transport, storage and communication) was US$3.9 billion (or 13 per cent of Indonesia's total FDI) which was a drop from US$5.8 billion in 2010. In contrast, during the same period, FDI to all other sectors increased. Given that the logistics sector is quite capital intensive and there is a need to upgrade its infrastructure and facilities, a more open FDI regime to attract investment in the sector is necessary.

TABLE 2.4
FDI for Logistics Sectors (US$ million)

Sectors	2010		2011		2012		2013		2014		2015	
	No. of Projects	Value	No. of Projects	Value	No. of Projects	Value	No. of Projects	Value	No. of Projects	Value	No. of Projects	Value
Trade and Repair	735	774	899	826	983	484	2,233	606	2,339	867	3,705	625
Transport, Storage and Communication	87	5,072	86	3,799	93	2,808	198	1,450	228	3,001	493	3,290
Logistics	**822**	**5,846**	**985**	**4,625**	**1,076**	**3,292**	**2,431**	**2,056**	**2,567**	**3,868**	**4,198**	**3,915**
Share Logistics to Total (per cent)	**26.7**	**36.1**	**22.7**	**23.7**	**23.5**	**13.4**	**25.3**	**7.2**	**28.9**	**13.6**	**23.7**	**13.4**
Indonesia Total FDI	**3,076**	**16,215**	**4,342**	**19,475**	**4,579**	**24,565**	**9,612**	**28,618**	**8,885**	**28,530**	**17,738**	**29,276**

Notes:
1. Excluding Oil & Gas, Banking, Non-Bank Financial Institutions, Insurance, Leasing, Investments which licenses issued by technical/sectoral agency, Portfolio as well as Household Investments.
2. Data received by BKPM until 31 December 2015.
3. Excluding Oil & Gas, Banking, Non-Bank Financial Institutions, Insurance, Leasing, Investments which licenses issued by technical/sectoral agency, Portfolio as well as Household Investments.
4. Data received by BKPM until 31 December 2015.
Total of projects in the period of January–December 2015 is the latest position of report during the year 2015.
Source: Indonesia Investment Coordinating Board (2016).

POLICY MEASURES FOR THE DEVELOPMENT OF
THE LOGISTICS INDUSTRY

Domestic Regulations

In Indonesia, the largest subsector of logistics is transport services which is dominated by state-owned enterprises as historically the development of these sectors is government-led. Airports, seaports, airlines, shipping and the manufacture of ships and aircrafts are still state-dominated sectors. However, state-dominance in the logistics sectors has gradually declined in sea transport services and more rapidly in air transport. State dominance declined as the government allowed private sector participation in the transport sector while in the past, the laws regulating the sea and airport transportation sectors clearly stated that these are to be provided by the government. A number of legislations have been amended to allow private participation. These include among others, law on rail transport (2007), shipping (2008), air transport (2009), road transport (2009) and postal (2009). The introduction of competition law in the country added to the good governance of the sector.

The following section discusses the main policy changes in various subsectors of logistics services.

a) *Rail Transport*

In the 1990s, rail transportation operation was the monopoly of state-owned enterprise, PT. Kereta Api Indonesia (PT KAI), while infrastructure was provided and managed by the government via PT. Kereta Api Indonesia (PT KAI).[3] In 2007, the government deregulated the sector to allow regional government and private participation in the sector. The new law is expected to provide rooms for improvement and expansion of the railway networks and services. The Law no. 13/1992 was replaced with the enactment of Law no. 23/2007 regarding rail transportation. The Law no. 23/2007 provided for private participation in railway services as the law states that general railway operator business is open for all business entity that have business license, developing license, and operational license (Chapter 24, Article 1 of Law no. 23/2007).

The government has also opened the sector to foreign investors. Based on the latest negative list of investment as in Government Regulation no. 44/2016, rail transportation with industrial code of 49111, 49112, 49121 and 49129 are not listed as sectors closed or open with restrictions. Consequently, the sector is open for 100 per cent foreign investment.

In the earlier version of negative list of investment, only construction of large scale railway networks was open for foreign investment, with a maximum foreign equtiy in the company of 67 per cent.

Subsequent to these changes, there are a number of joint ventures companies building and operating railway networks in Indonesia. A subsidiary of a Russian Railway company is operating in Kalimantan to build and operate railway network. A joint venture company, based on a consortium of Indonesia's state-owned enterprises with China Railway International, PT KCIC is also building and will operate a fast train network connecting Bandung and Jakarta.[4]

b) *Road Transport*

Road transportion in Indonesia is highly regulated. According to Law no. 22/2009 on Traffic and Road Transport, the government is responsible for road infrastructure development and maintenance. Based on the same law, road transport operators have to obtain a license to operate (Chapter 173 of the Law no. 22/2009). The law did not state any restrictions for foreign investment. However, based on the negative investment list, often referred as DNI (Daftar Negatif Investasi), foreign investment is capped at 49 per cent for most of the road transport's business segments.[5] Regulatory segments of logistics services, such as the management of weighbridge and infrastructure provision, including road transport terminals are closed to foreign investors. Minimum tariffs are often determined by the transport association, such as the minimum economy taxi fare which is set by the road transport organization (Organisasi Pengusaha Angkutan Darat (Organda) 2016).[6]

A new business model of road transport has emerged in Indonesia in 2015 with Go-jek, Uber and Grab in the market of passengers transport.[7] Go-jek later in 2016 also started to offer logistics services, e.g. goods delivery and moving services. This new business model basically bypassed the FDI equity limits of foreign investment in road transport. It has also led to policy disputes between taxi companies supported by the road transport organization (Organda) and application-based transportation. The taxi companies and Organda argued that the application-based transport is illegal as they did not have transport licenses as required by transport law. After a series of demonstrations and consultations, the Ministry of Transportation and Ministry of Communication decided that application-based transport providers need to form cooperatives so that they can get the required transporation license, based on Law no. 22/2009.[8]

c) *Maritime and Inland Marine Transport*

Similar to rail transportation, maritime transportation was also dominated by state-owned enterprises. Subsequently, Law no. 17/2008 removed the monopoly power of the Indonesian Port Corporation (Pelindo) as the sole port service provider. The law, furthermore, separates the regulatory from operational functions of seaports services. The law mantains the *cabotage* right that the maritime transportation services must be supplied by Indonesian flagships (Chapter 8, Articles 1 and 2).

The law, however, does not specify equity limits for FDI in the sector. Based on the 2016 negative investment list, foreign investment is allowed up to 67 per cent in maritime passengers and freight transportation for non-ASEAN investors and 70 per cent for ASEAN investors. For ports facilities, ferry services, river and lake passengers and freight transportation, inland water, river and lake transportation, foreign equity limit is 49 per cent. Services related to regulatory function and small scale shipping are closed to foreign investment. The relatively more open FDI regime is expected to attract foreign investment in the sector. However, concerns remains regarding regulatory restrictions to establish shipping company in Indonesia.

Air Transport

Similar to railway and sea transportation, air transport was also controlled by the state, as stated in Law no. 15/1992 regarding Air Transportation. Article 31 of the law stipulated that the government regulated the use of facilities and services at airports, which also provided the basis of the power to regulate prices. In 2001, however, the Minister for Transport eased entry requirements to set up airlines companies by issuing Decree No. 11/2001, allowing new scheduled airlines to obtain a license to operate but limited to only two aircrafts (previously the requirement had been five aircraft). In 2009 Indonesia enacted a new air transport law, Law no. 1/2009, replacing Law no. 15/1992 which was considered as incompatible with the development of the sector. The new air transport law also has provisions on investments, tariffs and licensing. Foreign investment for scheduled airlines is capped at 49 per cent (Article 108 of Law no. 1/2009).

The new air transport law of 2009 continues to limit foreign equity in the commercial airline business. It is, however, not clear about foreign investment in other subsectors. The current negative list of investment includes foreign equity limits on air transport (see Table 2.5). The foreign equity limit for supporting services, including computer-based reservation system, passenger and cargo ground handling, and aircraft leasing is 67 per cent. Similarly, foreign equity in freight forwarding services, airport support

TABLE 2.5

Foreign Equity Limits in Indonesia's Logistics Sector

Maritime	Telecommunication and navigation aid services are closed to foreign investment.
	Maritime passenger and freight transportation for which foreign ownership is limited to 67 per cent except for companies from ASEAN which may have 70 per cent ownership in international maritime passenger transportation.
	Vessel traffic information systems is closed to foreign investment.
	Foreign capital ownership is limited to 49 per cent for harbour waste reception facilities.
	Foreign capital ownership is limited to 49 per cent for harbour facilities.
	Small-scale shipping is closed to foreign investment.
	Ferry services for which foreign ownership is limited to 49 per cent.
Inland Marine	Foreign capital ownership is limited to 49 per cent in river and lake passenger and freight transportation.
	Foreign capital ownership is limited to 49 per cent in international ferry services.
	Foreign capital ownership is limited to 49 per cent in provision and operation of inland water or river and lake harbour.
Air Transport	Foreign capital ownership is limited to 49 per cent for general scheduled and non-scheduled domestic air transport services provided that an Indonesian holds the largest single share.
	Foreign capital ownership is limited to 49 per cent for scheduled international air transport services provided that an Indonesian holds the largest share.
	Foreign capital ownership is limited to 67 per cent for supporting services, include computer-based reservation system, passenger and cargo ground handling, and aircraft leasing.
	Foreign capital ownership is limited to 49 per cent for airport services.
	Foreign capital ownership is limited to 67 per cent for air expedition freight forwarding services.
	Foreign capital ownership is limited to 67 per cent for airport support services.
	Foreign capital ownership is limited to 67 per cent for general airline sales agent.

TABLE 2.5 (continued)

Services	
Services Auxiliary to All Forms of Transport	The cargo condition survey service is closed to foreign investment.
	The survey of land, sea, and air transportation facilities is closed to foreign investment.
	Foreign capital ownership is limited to 67 per cent for supporting business in terminals.
	Foreign capital ownership is limited to 67 per cent for freight forwarding services.
	Foreign capital ownership is limited to 67 per cent for warehousing.
	Foreign capital ownership is limited to 49 per cent for multimode transportation.
	The management of weighbridges is closed to foreign investment.
	Rental land transportation without operator is closed to foreign investment.
	Foreign capital ownership is limited to 49 per cent for services of motor vehicle periodic testing.
	The management of terminal for passenger land transport is closed to foreign investment.
Road Transport	Foreign capital ownership is limited to 49 per cent for scheduled and non-scheduled routes passenger transportation.
	Foreign capital ownership is limited to 49 per cent for freight transportation.
	Foreign capital ownership is limited to 49 per cent in cargo terminals.
	Foreign capital ownership is limited to 49 per cent in transport management service suppliers.
Other Transport	Foreign investment in vessel salvage and under water works services need special license from Ministry of Transportation.
Postal services	Foreign capital ownership is limited to 49 per cent in postal services.
Distribution Services	Commission agent service is closed to foreign investment.
	Retail and wholesale trade of alcoholic beverages or liquor require alcoholic beverage trading business license.

Source: Government of Indonesia (2016).

services and general airlines sales agencies is capped at 67 per cent. The subsectors, which are closed to foreign investment, are cargo condition survey services and survey of air transport facilities.

Postal

Postal services was previously a government monopoly and closed to all types of private investment. Law no. 38/2009 states that postal services can be operated by Indonesian business entities (Chapter 4, Article 1). Foreign postal company may operate in Indonesia through joint ventures but the equity should be majority owned by local entity (Chapter 12). However, according to Magiera (2011), there are a few other requirements that applies for foreign postal operators in order for them to operate in Indonesia, including: (a) work closely with the domestic postal operator; (b) through a joint venture with a majority share owned by domestic postal operator; (c) domestic postal operator who will cooperate should not be owned by a citizen or a foreign business entity affiliated to domestic postal operator; (d) operator of foreign mail and its affiliates can only cooperate with the domestic postal operator; and (e) organizing cooperation with foreign postal mail providers in the country are limited to areas of operation in the capital of a province that has airports and/or seaports.

Competition Law

Apart from sectoral laws discussed earlier, competition law is also relevant to logistics sector. In 1999, Indonesia's parliament enacted Law no. 5/1999 concerning the Prohibition of Monopolistic Practices and Unfair Business Competition. The law made a few exceptions to small businesses and cooperatives. To implement the law, an independent Competition Commission (Komisi Pengawas Persaingan Usaha/KPPU) was established. The role of the Competition Commission is to investigate and decide on anti-competitive conducts among firms in Indonesia and anti-competitive regulations. Often times, monopolistic practices and unfair business competition is embedded in government regulations, e.g. Minister for Transport no. 25/1997 grants the authority to set price for economy class airfare in scheduled passenger air transport to the airlines association, thereby paving the way for non-competitive prices to be used. For cases like this, the role of the Competition Commission is to determine that the regulation has violated Law no. 5/1999 before it can request the relevant Minister to revoke the regulation. In this case, the relevant Minister of Transport revoked the non-competitive regulation which allowed airfares to float since 2002.

d) *National Logistics System (Sistem Logistik Nasional/ SISLOGNAS)*

Indonesia launched the Blueprint for the Development of the National Logistics System (Sistem Logistik Nasional, thus, SISLOGNAS) in Presidential Regulation no. 26/2012 in March 2012. The blueprint provides an integrated framework and action plans to develop Indonesia's logistics system. It was developed to support the implementation of Indonesia's Master Plan for Economic Development.

While the definition and coverage of the sector was settled by SISLOGNAS, at present, the responsibility of managing Indonesia's logistics system falls under different ministries. Table 2.6 lists all relevant ministries responsible for the logistics sector, in which distribution services are under the authority of the Ministry of Trade, while transportation is under the Ministry of Transport, infrastructure management are under Ministry of State Owned Enterprises, custom under Ministry of Finance and product specific issues handled in different technical ministries. As a result of these multi-ministries and authorities, complexities and coordination problems are frequently encountered in issuance of licenses and goods clearance.

Table 2.6
List of Trade Logistics Related Responsibility and Their Respective Ministries

No.	Area of Responsibility	Ministry
1	Distribution, Storage and Marketing	Trade
2	Strategic Commodity and Export–Import	Trade, Industry, Agriculture Energy and Mineral Resources
3	Transportation	Transport
4	Company Establishment and Investment	Investment Coordinating Board
5	Design and Development of Infrastructure	Public Works
6	Telecommunication, Mail and Courier	Information and Communication
7	Infrastructure Management and Logistics Service Provider	State Owned Enterprises
8	Customs, Insurance Tax and Banking	Finance

Source: Government of Indonesia (2012).

How restrictive is the sector? The OECD STRI 2015 included ten logistics subsectors. All ten subsectors are less trade friendly than the average OECD STRI sample. Among the subsectors, air transport, freight forwarding, and cargo handling are the most restrictive sectors with a respective index of 0.64, 0.57, and 0.50. The breakdown of the index showed that the relatively high STRI in logistics are mostly contributed by restrictions on foreign entry, barriers to competition and issues with regulatory transparency. In term of restrictions on foreign entry, freight forwarding (0.353), air transport (0.334), maritime transport (0.272), and road freight transport (0.227) are relatively restrictive. For barriers to competition indicator, air transport, cargo handling, rail freight transport, and courier are relatively more restrictive sectors with indexes of 0.211, 0.195, 0.132, and 0.128, respectively. In terms of regulatory transparency, custom brokerage (0.111), courier (0.1), and freight forwarding (0.092) are relatively restrictive.

FIGURE 2.10
Overall STRI for Logistics Sectors, 2015

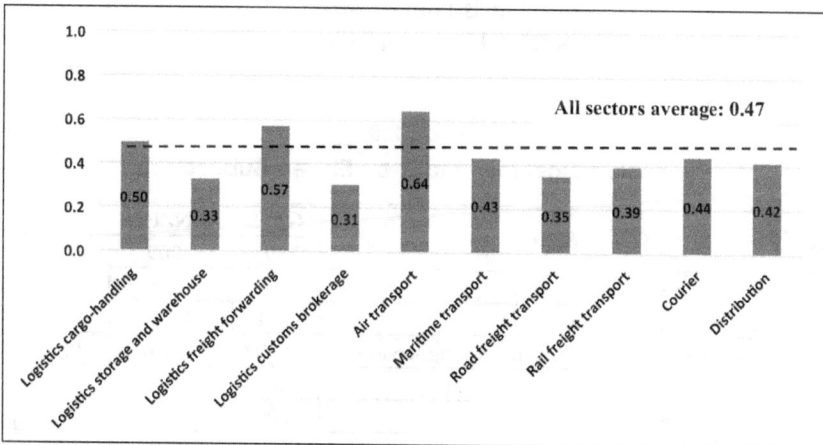

Source: OECD (2015a).

Liberalization Measures: Multilateral and Regional

In terms of services liberalization under multilateral and regional trade arrangement, it has been observed that from GATS (General Agreement of Trade in Services) (multilateral) to AFAS (ASEAN Framework Agreement on Services) 9, the coverage of committed sectors have increased (see Table 2.7). The level of openness has also increased as required by the ASEAN Economic Community (AEC) Blueprint.

TABLE 2.7
Coverage of Sectors in AFAS 8 and AFAS 9

	AFAS 8	AFAS 9
Brunei Darussalam	79	92
Cambodia	87	94
Indonesia	**86**	**97**
Laos	89	92
Malaysia	96	100
Myanmar	79	90
Philippines	98	99
Singapore	84	101
Thailand	104	108
Vietnam	88	99

Source: Ministry of Trade, 2017 (unpublished).

Fukunaga and Ishido (2015) calculated the Hoekman Index, which shows the level of policy restrictiveness, for eleven services sectors under GATS, AANZFTA (ASEAN–Australia–New Zealand Free Trade Area), and AFAS 8 (see Table 2.8). The index ranges from 0 to 1, where 0 is unbound, 0.5 is restricted (but the commitment is bound) while 1.0 is interpreted as fully liberalized. Table 2.8 shows that Hoekman Index for GATS commitments is

TABLE 2.8
Indonesia's Hoekman Index by Eleven Subsectors

No.	Sector	GATS 1995	AANZFTA 2009	AFAS 8 2012
1	Business services	0.07	0.14	0.26
2	Communication services	0.31	0.31	0.31
3	Construction and related engineering services	0.40	0.50	0.50
4	Distribution services	0.00	0.00	0.10
5	Educational services	0.00	0.25	0.40
6	Environmental services	0.00	0.00	0.25
7	Financial services	0.09	0.21	0.21
8	Health-related and social services	0.00	0.00	0.00
9	Tourism and travel-related services	0.06	0.25	0.25
10	Recreational, cultural, and sporting services	0.00	0.00	0.15
11	Transport services	0.03	0.07	0.29
	Simple average of 1–11	0.09	0.16	0.27

Note: Aggregation from the 154 subsectors directly to eleven subsectors has been made. Where there is ambiguity of commitments (especially "other sectors" usually at the end of the subsector at issue), reconciliation is made among the agreements. Fully liberalized = 1.0; Limited (but bound) = 0.5; Unbound = 0.0
Source: Fukunaga and Ishido (2015).

relatively low, average 0.09, with some unbound sectors. Construction and related engineering services as well as communication servcies are relatively more open than other subsectors. AANZFTA is more open than GATS, with an average Hoekman Index of 0.16. Again, construction and related engineering services as well as communication services are relatively more open than other sectors. AFAS 8 is the most advanced commitments for Indonesia with average Hoekman Index of 0.27. Apart from construction and communication services, more sectors are opening up, including education and transportation.

Although its AFAS 9 commitments are the most advanced compared to other regional Free Trade Agreement (FTA) and multilateral FTA commitments, among ASEAN members, Indonesia is relatively behind in implementing its ASEAN services liberalization commitments. Based on the AEC Blueprint, Indonesia should have already achieved the 70 per cent cap of foreign equity participation in its services sectors by 2013.[9] However, the existing regulations regarding foreign equity participation limits it to less than 70 per cent. Moreover, Indonesia has yet to ratify even AFAS 8.

Indonesia's commitment in transport services for the ninth package of AFAS is shown in Table 2.9. Overall, foreign investment in the logistics sector is relatively restricted and foreign equity is mostly limited below 70 per cent; 60 per cent for international passenger and freight transport, which is below the 2016 negative investment list where foreign equity limit is capped at 67 per cent. Foreign equity limit in the transportation of petroleum and natural gas is limited to 30 per cent. While railway transportation is not listed in Indonesia's negative list of investment, the sector is listed in AFAS 9 with 49 to 70 per cent foreign equity limit, depending on subsectors within railway transportation.

Apart from a relatively restricted foreign investment policy, the sector also faces constraints from domestic regulations such as in freight forwarding, warehousing, cargo handling in ports, and cargo handling in airports (World Bank 2016). In terms of freight forwarding, high capital requirements (Rp 25 billion equivalent to US$2 millions),[10] is required together with recommendation letter from association, and unrealistic staff conditions for establishing a new freight forward business entity. For warehousing, manufacturing companies are not permitted by law to outsource warehouse activities as it is considered as core-business, and unclear regulation on stock reporting is also an issue.

As in the case of freight forwarding, cargo handling in ports also face a higher capital requiment which is about Rp 1 trillion (equivalent to US$80 millions),[11] while they also face price setting, profit control policy, and license renewal issues. They are also forced to use port-labour union even when the

TABLE 2.9

Foreign Equity Limits in Transport Services Committed in the Ninth Package of AFAS

Maritime	Foreign companies from ASEAN must form a joint venture with foreign equity limited to 60 per cent for international passenger and freight transport.
	Foreign companies from ASEAN must form a joint venture with foreign equity limited to 51 per cent for maintenance and repair of vessels and are only allowed to operate in East Java and Eastern part of Indonesia.
	Foreign companies from ASEAN must form a joint venture with foreign equity limited to 51 per cent for pushing and towing services.
	Foreign companies from ASEAN must form a joint venture with foreign equity limited to 49 per cent for vessel salvage and refloating services.
Inland Marine	Foreign companies from ASEAN must form a joint venture with foreign equity limited to 60 per cent for passenger and freight transport.
	Foreign companies from ASEAN must form a joint venture with foreign equity limited to 51 per cent for maintenance and repair of vessels and are only allowed to operate in East Java and Eastern part of Indonesia.
	Foreign companies from ASEAN must form a joint venture with foreign equity limited to 51 per cent for pushing and towing services and other supporting services.
	Foreign companies from ASEAN must form a joint venture with foreign equity limited to 49 per cent for passenger transport, except for interurban passenger transport in which foreign equity may up to 51 per cent.
	Foreign companies from ASEAN must form a joint venture with foreign equity limited to 49 per cent for passenger transport, except for transportation of frozen food in which foreign equity of 70 per cent.
Rail Transport	Foreign companies from ASEAN must form a joint venture with foreign equity limited to 51 per cent for pushing and towing services and other supporting services.
	Foreign companies from ASEAN must form a joint venture with foreign equity limited to 49 per cent for maintenance and repair of rail transport equipment, except if the cooperation is formed with PT. INKA (state owned company) in which foreign equity may up to 51 per cent.

Services Auxiliary to All Forms of Transport	Foreign companies from ASEAN must form a joint venture with foreign equity limited to 70 per cent for maritime cargo handling and are only allowed to operate in Bitung, Kupang, Ambon, and Sorong, while foreign equity may up to 60 per cent in other areas.
	Foreign companies from ASEAN must form a joint venture with foreign equity limited to 49 per cent for storage and warehousing services outside port area.
	Foreign companies from ASEAN must form a joint venture with foreign equity limited to 49 per cent for maritime freight forwarding services.
	Foreign companies from ASEAN must form a joint venture with foreign equity limited to 49 per cent for freight transportation.
Road Transport	Foreign companies from ASEAN must form a joint venture with foreign equity limited to 49 per cent for supporting services for road transport terminal.
	Foreign companies from ASEAN must form a joint venture with foreign equity limited to 49 per cent for maintenance and repair of road transport equipment.
Pipeline Transport	Foreign companies from ASEAN must form a joint venture with foreign equity limited to 30 per cent for transportation of petroleum and natural gas.
Distribution	Foreign companies from ASEAN must form a joint venture with foreign equity limited to 51 per cent for wholesale trade services above 5,000 square metre.
	Foreign companies from ASEAN must form a joint venture with foreign equity limited to 51 per cent for direct selling (multi-level marketing).

Source: ASEAN Secretariat (2015).

workers are not able to operate modern operating equipment, as well as to use rupiah, although USD is the common industry practice.

For cargo handling in airports, establishing a new business is also restricted by high capital requirements for ground handling companies and regulated agents, price control policy for ground handling companies and regulated agents, incorrect interpretation of regulated agents, and unpractical technical requirements for regulated agents.

RECENT REFORMS, OUTSTANDING CHALLENGES AND RECOMMENDATIONS

Recent Reforms

In recognition of the importance of reforms, the goverment has launched fourteen economic policy packages. In the ninth package of economic reform, the government proposed four programmes, specifically for the logistics sector. These are: (1) harmonization of tariffs to encourage efficient postal services; (2) unification of port payment services using electronic gateway (Single Billing); (3) electronic integrated port services; (4) utilization of rupiah as payment currencies in port.[12]

The government has considered harmonization of postal tariffs as a necessary condition for a more efficient postal service. In the past, based on the Ministry of Information and Communication Regulation no. 32/2014, tariffs of private commercial postal service should be set higher than tariff of postal services provided by the government. This regulation was found to be a barrier for competition for commercial postal operators. Thus, the government requested the Ministry of Information and Communication to revise the regulation to harmonize tariff of commercial postal services.

The unification of port payment services using electronic gateway (Single Billing) is proposed as the payment of ports services was not integrated electronically. This has impacted the duration for processing transactions (20 per cent of lead time) at the port. The government aims to improve port service efficiency with the unification of electronic payments.

For electronic integrated port services, although Indonesia has already implemented the *National Single Window* (INSW) portal, handling 90 per cent of Indonesia's trade in sixteen ports and five airports nation-wide for a number of years, the portal has not yet been supported by integrated goods flow information system (intraportnet) such as a yard planning system, customs, delivery order, trucking company, and billing system. This has led to a higher goods lead time and it has also simultaniously increased dwelling time. Subsequently, the goverment has instructed the relevant agencies to improve electronically integrated port services. However, the result of this new instruction is to be seen.

In addition to the above-mentioned reform packages for the logistics sector, the government is also currently in the process of formulating the fifteenth package of reforms which also focuses on logistics. The emphasis of the reform is to reduce the dwelling time to two days and improve the performance of Indonesia *National Single Window* (INSW) portal.[13] In 2016, the dwell time at the largest port in Indonesia, the Tanjung Priok port was 3.2 to 3.4 days.[14]

Outstanding Challenges

Low quality infrastructure, high barriers to entry, and high costs are the remaining challenges for a more competitive and efficient logistics sector in Indonesia. As discussed in the previous section, although the logistics sector has been liberalized, it remains relatively closed compared to other sectors in the economy. The restrictions to foreign invesment and high barriers to entry, not only for foreign investors but also to private domestic investors have constrained the growth of the sector. This has resulted in less competition in the sector which may have led to higher prices and low incentives to improve the quality of logistics services.

Policy Recommendations

To address the infrastructure needs and to improve the performance of sea transport service, the goverment plans to develop a modern sea transport system, known as "maritime highways", an integrated freight sea transport within Indonesia. It also plans to develop twenty-four commercial ports, over 1,000 non-commercial ports and the procurement of vessels between 2015 and 2019 requiring US$55.4 billion. With this integrated programme and more seaports available, the logistics costs are expected to reduce from 23.5 per cent of the GDP in 2014 to 19.2 per cent in 2019 (Baan et al. 2015).

By 2016, the government had made progress in building transportation infrastructure, road, railway, ports and seaports.[15] Excessive infrastructure spending has resulted in a deficit fiscal budget which has led the economy into a budget crisis in 2016. As a result, the government needed to slash its budget in October 2016. To increase revenue, the government also launched the tax amnesty programme and received Rp 143 trillion (US$1.2 billion) repatriation from the tax amnesty programme as of

11 November 2016. For the remaining of infrastructure development, the government has targeted more private sector participation. From the plan of IDR 4,796.1 trillion infrastructure spending for 2015–19, 36.5 per cent is expected to come from the private sector.

The most important policy action is to address the financing needs of new infrastructure. Given the fiscal constraints, Public–Private Partnership (PPP) schemes and foreign investment (direct investment and portfolio investment) are the only sources for financing the logistics infrastructure. But, the analysis in the earlier sections indicate there are still considerable restrictions on foreign equity ownership as well as entry barriers in terms of conditions imposed on foreign investors. For example, although the government had opened up the railway transportation services for 100 per cent foreign equity in its negative list of investment, other logistics subsectors are still closed or limited to less than 100 per cent foreign equity ownership. New private participation schemes and the removal of investment restrictions in terms of equity restrictions and conditions, are needed. The negative list for foreign investment needs to be aligned with the infrastructure needs of the country and improvements in the transparency of regulations.

Improving the performance of the INSW is also crucial. The current INSW system has successfully connected fifteen ministries/institutions and eight license issuance agencies involved in goods clearance into the INSW system. However, its success is limited to certain pre-clearance and custom clearance. The current INSW system does not deal with licensing process within each of the institutions' work process as well as post clearance stage. Thus, improvements to the INSW, including completing pre-clearance, custom clearance and post clearance will significantly improve dwell time. One of the proposal to improve the system is for INSW to have single submission, single process and single decision making for goods clearance (INSW Portal Management 2016). This will require the relevant authorities to relinquish its authority to issue license/permit/clearance to INSW system administrator. This is consistent with the findings of Baan et al. (2015) that improvements in documents handling and information exchange across institution will reduce dwell time.

Finally, reforms efforts must be sustained and consistent. This will entail continuous reviews of laws and processes as exemplified in the recent reforms. Strengthening stakeholder consultations will help to enhance the reform process as these stakeholders have deeper insights on the problems encountered with different rules, regulations and processes in the conduct of their business.

CONCLUSION

Indonesia's logistics sector has shown a relatively poor performance compared to its peer in the region. High logistics cost and a long dwell time are the current challenges for Indonesia's logistics sectors that need to be addressed immediately to increase the sector's competitiveness and the efficiency of other sectors. The high cost and long dwell time are partly due to low quality of logistics infrastructure, high barriers to entry and regulatory impediments.

To improve performance, the government has amended a number of laws and drafted a blueprint for the development of the sector in 2012. Nevertheless, its investment policy remains relatively restrictive, except for a few sectors for ASEAN member states and the overall performance of the sector has not yet improved.

With the aim to increase connectivity within the country and efficiency of the logistics service in general, the government has expanded logistics infrastructure excessively and introduced a number of reforms to the sector in the series of reform policy packages issued in 2016. The aim is to reduce the logistics costs to 19.2 per cent in 2019. However, the first two years of expansion has contributed to a fiscal crisis and a need for alternative sources of funding for increasing infrastructure capacity by increasing private investment, including FDI. For the remaining of its term, the current government seeks to have more private investment and bond issuance for infrastructure expansion.

Noting that improvements in the logistic sector take time, the government has to be consistent in its reforms efforts. Policies and investment need to gear towards reducing cost and dwell time. In the short to medium term, given the archipelagic nature of Indonesia, the limited public funding available, the government needs to focus on the improvement of main ports and seaports and engage the private sector in PPP, reduce barriers to entry, including foreign equity limits and other conditions such as minimum capital requirements. Multilateral and regional agreements also play an important role, by exerting external pressures on the government to improve the efficiency of the sector. Improving the efficacy of the INSW and the ASEAN Single Window is also paramount to reduce dwell time.

APPENDIX 2.1
STRI Index for Logistics Sectors, 2015

Classification	Sector	STRI
Indicator STRI	Logistics cargo-handling	0.497
	Logistics storage and warehouse	0.329
	Logistics freight forwarding	0.572
	Logistics customs brokerage	0.307
	Air transport	0.642
	Maritime transport	0.433
	Road freight transport	0.350
	Rail freight transport	0.394
	Courier	0.441
	Distribution	0.417
Restrictions on foreign entry	Logistics cargo-handling	0.160
	Logistics storage and warehouse	0.060
	Logistics freight forwarding	0.353
	Logistics customs brokerage	0.078
	Air transport	0.334
	Maritime transport	0.272
	Road freight transport	0.227
	Rail freight transport	0.125
	Courier	0.149
	Distribution	0.207
Restrictions to movement of people	Logistics cargo-handling	0.045
	Logistics storage and warehouse	0.041
	Logistics freight forwarding	0.066
	Logistics customs brokerage	0.071
	Air transport	0.030
	Maritime transport	0.091
	Road freight transport	0.076
	Rail freight transport	0.057
	Courier	0.052
	Distribution	0.038

APPENDIX (*continued*)

Classification	Sector	STRI
Other discriminatory measures	Logistics cargo-handling	0.016
	Logistics storage and warehouse	0.016
	Logistics freight forwarding	0.018
	Logistics customs brokerage	0.021
	Air transport	0.044
	Maritime transport	0.006
	Road freight transport	0.018
	Rail freight transport	0.029
	Courier	0.012
	Distribution	0.037
Barriers to competition	Logistics cargo-handling	0.195
	Logistics storage and warehouse	0.127
	Logistics freight forwarding	0.042
	Logistics customs brokerage	0.025
	Air transport	0.211
	Maritime transport	0.038
	Road freight transport	0.014
	Rail freight transport	0.132
	Courier	0.128
	Distribution	0.081
Regulatory transparency	Logistics cargo-handling	0.081
	Logistics storage and warehouse	0.085
	Logistics freight forwarding	0.092
	Logistics customs brokerage	0.111
	Air transport	0.022
	Maritime transport	0.027
	Road freight transport	0.014
	Rail freight transport	0.051
	Courier	0.100
	Distribution	0.053

Source: OECD (2015*a*).

Notes

1. The Service Trade Restrictions Index (STRI) is calculated by OECD. The Index helps to identify which policy measures restrict trade. The STRI indices take a value from 0 to 1, where 0 is completely open and 1 is completely closed. They are calculated on the basis of information in the STRI database which reports regulations that are currently in force. The indices examine five dimensions of policies, which are restrictions on foreign entry, restrictions to movement of people, barriers to competition, regulatory transparency, and other discriminatory measures.

2. Bahagia, Sandee, and Meeuws (2013) explained that national logistics cost are not fully comparable among countries due to different calculation method (p. 19). National logistics cost of Indonesia consist of three components which are transportation, inventory, and administration cost. In calculating each component, South Korea's and the United States' logistics cost model are used. In addition South Africa's logistics cost model was also used to identify the business sectors due to the similarity between Indonesia and South Africa as natural resource producing countries (p. 20).

3. Law no. 13/1992 and Government Regulation no. 81/1998.

4. <http://www.republika.co.id/berita/ekonomi/makro/15/10/16/nwarda328-bangun-kereta-cepat-konsorsium-bumncina-dibentuk>.

5. <http://www.bkpm.go.id/id/prosedur-investasi/daftar-negatif-investasi>.

6. <http://organda.or.id/kppu-minta-pemerintah-hapus-tarif-batas-bawah-taksi-konvensional/>.

7. <http://theconversation.com/uber-and-gojek-just-the-start-of-disruptive-innovation-in-indonesia-43644>.

8. Ministry Decree No. 32/2016.

9. ASEAN Economic Community Blueprint stated that in 2013, foreign equity participation in four priority services sectors (air transport, e-ASEAN, healthcare and tourism) and logistics services should be allowed up to 70 per cent.

10. 1 USD = Rp 12,500

11. 1 USD = Rp 12,500

12. <http://www.bappenas.go.id/id/berita-dan-siaran-pers/paket-ekonomi-ix-pemerataan-infrastruktur-ketenagalistrikan-dan-stabilisasi-harga-daging-hingga-ke-desa/>.

13. <http://www.antaranews.com/berita/604888/pemerintah-siapkan-paket-kebijakan-ekonomi-mengenai-logistik>.

14. <http://www.thejakartapost.com/news/2016/09/18/tanjung-priok-port-sets-dwell-time-benchmark.html>.

15. <http://nasional.kompas.com/read/2016/08/16/14453101/ini.infrastruktur.yang.dibangun.selama.dua.tahun.jokowi-jk>.

References

Anas et al. "Towards Informed Regulatory Conversations and Improved Regulatory Regime in Indonesia: Logistics Sector and Trade Facilitation". ERIA Research Project 2012 Working Group "AEC Scorecard Phase III Project". Jakarta: Economic Research Institute for ASEAN and East Asia, 2012.

Anas, Titik and Christopher Findlay. "The Deregulation of Air Transport Service and Its Impact: Case of Indonesia". Singapore: Asia-Pacific Economic Cooperation Policy Support Unit, 2016.

Antaranews. "Pemerintah-Siapkan-Paket-Kebijakan-Ekonomi-Mengenai-Logistik", 4 January 2017. Available at <http://www.antaranews.com/berita/604888/pemerintah-siapkan-paket-kebijakan-ekonomi-mengenai-logistik>.

ASEAN Secretariat. "ASEAN Framework Agreement for Services - The Ninth[th] Package", 2015. Available at <http://asean.org/asean-economic-community/sectoral-bodies-under-the-purview-of-aem/services/agreements-declarations/>.

Asian Development Bank. *Indonesia: Transport Sector Assessment, Strategy, and Road Map*. Manila: Asian Development Bank, 2012. Available at <https://www.adb.org/sites/default/files/institutional-document/33652/files/ino-transport-assessment.pdf>.

Baan, Cas van der, Adhi Dipo, David Wignall, Dini Takola, Hafida Fahmiasari, Vincent Hinssen, Henry Sandee, and Rene Meeuws. *State of Logistics Indonesia 2015*. Washington, D.C.: World Bank, 2015. Available at <http://www.nestra.net/uncategorized/state-of-logistics-indonesia-2015/>.

Badan Pusat Statistik. "Produk Domestik Bruto (Lapangan Usaha)", 2016. Available at <https://www.bps.go.id/Subjek/view/id/11#subjekViewTab3|accordion-daftar-subjek1>.

Bahagia, Senator Nur, Henry Sandee, and Rene Meeuws. *State of Logistics Indonesia 2013*. Washington, D.C.: World Bank, 2013.

Badan Koordinasi Penanaman Modal (BKPM). "Daftar Negatif Investasi: DNI". Available at <http://www.bkpm.go.id/id/prosedur-investasi/daftar-negatif-investasi>.

Bank Indonesia. "Statistik Ekonomi dan Keuangan Indonesia (SEKI)", 2017. Available at <http://www.bi.go.id/id/statistik/seki/terkini/eksternal/Contents/Default.aspx> (accessed 4 February 2017).

Fukunaga, Yoshifumi and Hikari Ishido. "Values and Limitations of the ASEAN Agreement on the Movement of Natural Persons". ERIA Discussion Paper no. DP-2015-20. Economic Research Institute for ASEAN and East Asia, 2015.

Government of Indonesia. National Logistics Blueprint (Cetak Biru Pengembangan Sistem Logistik Nasional). Lampiran Peraturan Presiden Republik Indonesia Nomor 26 Tahun 2012.

———. Presidential Regulation no. 44/2016. Available at <http://www.bkpm.go.id/en/investment-procedures/negative-investment-list>.

Indonesia Investment Coordinating Board. Statistic of Foreign Direct Investment Realization based on Capital Investment Activity Report by Sector, 2016 [online]. Available at <http://www.bkpm.go.id/en/investing-in-indonesia/statistic> (accessed 21 February 2017).

INSW Portal Management. INSWMagz, 1st ed., 2016. Available at <http://www.
    insw.go.id/public/INSWMagz_Edisi_I_-_2016.pdf>.
International Labour Organization (ILO). *Key Indicators of the Labour Market
    (KILM) 2015.* Geneva: ILO, 2015.
Kompas. "Ini Infrastruktur yang Dibangun Selama Dua Tahun Jokowi-JK", 16 August
    2016. Available at <http://nasional.kompas.com/read/2016/08/16/14453101/
    ini.infrastruktur.yang.dibangun.selama.dua.tahun.jokowi-jk>.
Magiera, Stephen. "Indonesia's Investment Negative List: An Evaluation for
    Selected Services Sectors". *Bulletin of Indonesian Economic Studies* 47, no. 2
    (2011): 195–219.
Ministry of Trade. "Analisis SWOT Atas Perkembangan Terbaru Free Trade
    Agreements (FTA) Indonesia Di Bidang Jasa: AFAS9, ACFTA, AIFTA".
    Unpublished. Jakarta: Ministry of Trade of Indonesia, 2017.
Organda. "KPPU Minta Pemerintah Hapus Tarif Batas Bawah Taksi Konvensional",
    7 January 2016. Available at <http://organda.or.id/kppu-minta-pemerintah-
    hapus-tarif-batas-bawah-taksi-konvensional/>.
Organization for Economic Co-operation and Development (OECD). FDI
    Regulatory Restrictiveness Index, 2014 [online]. Available at <http://stats.
    oecd.org/Index.aspx?datasetcode=FDIINDEX#>.
————. Services Trade Restrictiveness Index, 2015*a* [online]. Available at <https://
    stats.oecd.org/Index.aspx?DataSetCode=STRI> (accessed 5 September 2016).
————. Trade In Value Added, 2015*b* [online]. Available at <https://stats.oecd.
    org/index.aspx?queryid=66237> (accessed 18 May 2016).
Republika. "Bangun Kereta Cepat, Konsorsium BUMN-Cina Dibentuk", 16 October
    2015. Available at <http://www.republika.co.id/berita/ekonomi/makro/15/10/16/
    nwarda328-bangun-kereta-cepat-konsorsium-bumncina-dibentuk>.
The Conversation. "Uber and Gojek Just the Start of Disruptive Innovation in
    Indonesia", 8 July 2015. Available at <http://theconversation.com/uber-and-
    gojek-just-the-start-of-disruptive-innovation-in-indonesia-43644>.
The Jakarta Post. "Tanjung Priok Port Sets Dwell Time Benchmark", 18 September
    2016. Available at <http://www.thejakartapost.com/news/2016/09/18/
    tanjung-priok-port-sets-dwell-time-benchmark.html>.
Tongzon, Jose. "The Challenge of Globalization for the Logistics Industry:
    Evidence from Indonesia". *Transportation Journal* 51, no. 1 (2012): 5–32
UNCTADstat. International Trade in Goods and Services [online]. Available
    at <http://unctadstat.unctad.org/wds/ReportFolders/reportFolders.aspx?sCS_
    ChosenLang=en> (accessed 14 February 2017).
World Bank. "Services, etc., Value Added (% of GDP)". World Development
    Indicators [online]. Washington, D.C.: World Bank, 1995–2014. Available
    at <http://data.worldbank.org/indicator/NV.SRV.TETC.ZS>.
————. *Logistics Performance Index 2012.* Washington, D.C.: World Bank,
    2012. Available at <http://siteresources.worldbank.org/TRADE/Resources/
    2390701336654966193/LPI_2012_final.pdf>.
————. *Logistics Performance Index 2016.* Washington, D.C.: World Bank, 2016.
    Available at <http://lpi.worldbank.org/> (accessed 10 October 2016).

3

FDI LIBERALIZATION IN MALAYSIA'S LOGISTICS SERVICES

Tham Siew Yean

INTRODUCTION

The use of a foreign direct investment (FDI)-led development strategy in Malaysia started in the early 1970s when the first Free Trade Zone was established to attract FDI for manufacturing development. With this early mover advantage, FDI flowed into labour-intensive manufacturing based on Malaysia's host country advantages at that time such as cheap labour, economic and political stability, relatively good infrastructure and supportive government policies. Malaysia became one of the top ten developing host economies by the early 1990s but its rapid manufacturing development led to the dissipation of its low wage advantage as wages rose swiftly in response to the excess demand for labour after full employment was attained.

In recognition of the loss in competitiveness in low wage manufacturing, the government promoted a manufacturing ++ strategy based on cluster development using services development as a means to move up the value chain in the Second Industrial Master Plan (IMP2) 1996–2005. Despite this, the advent of the Asian Financial Crisis (AFC) in 1997–98 stalled the implementation of IMP2 by redirecting the focus of government policies from industrial development towards managing the financial crisis and its aftermath. Nevertheless, the focus on service sector development continued to be prioritized in the Third Industrial Master Plan (IMP3) 2006–20, where the services sector was targeted as the next engine of growth. The development of services has shifted from its role as a facilitator for deepening manufacturing development to the development of selected services with the logistics sector as one of the targeted services. Reportedly, the government allocated RM3 billion for the development of this sector under the IMP3 with a target of 36 million TEU or 751 million tonnes of cargo to be handled by Malaysian ports by 2020 (MPC n.d.).

The emphasis on services development continued in the New Economic Model (NEM) that was launched in 2010 for re-energizing economic development. Likewise, it is also the focus of development in the Economic Transformation Plan (2010) and the Tenth Malaysia Plan (10MP) 2011–15, although the logistics sector was not included among the 12 targeted sectors in these plans. The continued push towards a service-led economy led to the unveiling of a Services Blueprint in 2015 for the development of this sector. In the Blueprint, however, the motivation to develop services is to facilitate the overall development of the country, including manufacturing, rather than selected services development.

At the same time, FDI has also gradually shifted from manufacturing to services as manufacturing is relatively open. The country is also no longer competitive for low labour cost manufacturing. Services, on the other hand, is relatively closed as there are still legacy monopolistic issues and an extensive presence of government-linked companies (GLCs). While the government has progressively opened up the services sector for FDI, substantial barriers remain as regulatory barriers continue to deter the entry of both domestic and foreign investment. FDI continues to be courted, especially since the 2008 Global Financial Crisis (GFC) as the government is increasingly fiscally constrained by its recurring annual fiscal deficit since the AFC. Consequently, there is a push for using more private investment, including FDI, for Malaysia's aspired shift up the global value chain.

Trade continues to be emphasized in the country's five-year plans. The Eleventh Malaysia Plan (11MP) 2016–20, for example, aims for 4.6 per cent average growth of gross exports over the next five years. Enhancing services exports is one of the key strategies in this Plan, with an improved Services Export Fund (SEF) to assist service firms to expand overseas (EPU 2015*a*). Free Trade Agreements (FTAs) are also used to improve the market access for Malaysia's exports. This makes the logistics sector an indispensable partner in Malaysia's current and immediate future development path.

Given the continued emphasis on FDI, services development and trade in Malaysia, the objectives of this chapter are two-fold: first, it seeks to examine key policy changes in the logistics sector, including FDI policies, and the impact of these changes on inflows of FDI in this sector. Second, it also aims to identify the outstanding challenges that can affect the future development of this sector. The chapter is divided into the following sections. A brief overview of the services sector is outlined in Section 2, following the introduction. Section 3 presents basic data on the logistics industry while the key policies in this sector are discussed in Section 4. Investment and trade data are reviewed in Section 5 while Section 6 identifies the outstanding challenges and provides some policy recommendations. The conclusion summarizes the key findings of this chapter.

DEVELOPMENT OF THE SERVICES SECTOR

Overview of the Services Sector

The services sector is the largest sector in the country, in terms of its contribution to Gross Domestic Product (GDP) and employment since 1960 (see Figures 3.1 and 3.2). The services sector was in fact the largest economic sector in 1960, contributing to 42 per cent of the GDP of Peninsular Malaysia, followed by agriculture at 31 per cent while manufacturing contributed only 9 per cent (Hirschman and Aghajanian 1980, p. 33). The increase in the share of manufacturing in GDP was accompanied by a decline in the share for agriculture. Manufacturing's share in GDP peaked at 31 per cent in 2000, with a clear decline since 2004.

Likewise, Malaysia's share of employment in services to total employment is higher than the share of employment in manufacturing for the period shown in Figure 3.2. The relatively higher share of employment in services is attributed to the labour-intensive nature of this sector in Malaysia. As in the case of the share of GDP, the increase in the share of employment in manufacturing is accompanied by a fall in

FIGURE 3.1
Share of Agriculture, Manufacturing and Services to GDP, 1960–2015

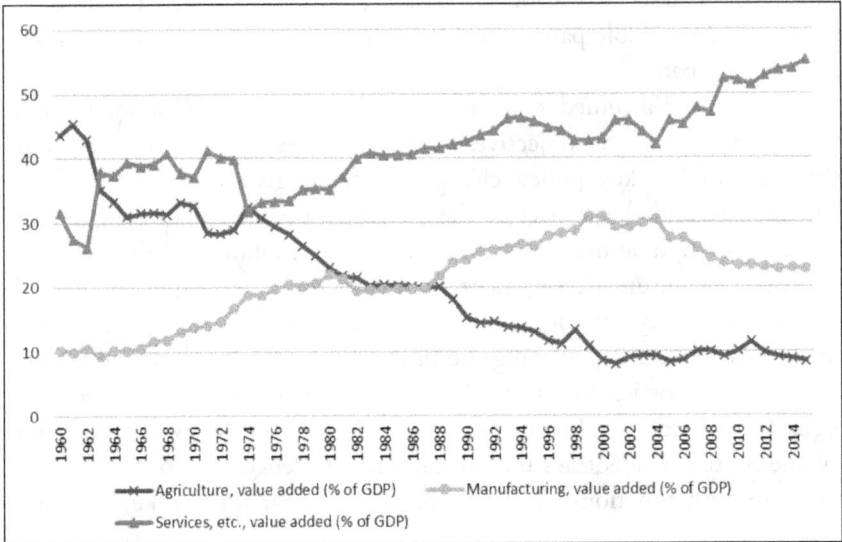

Source: World Development Indicators, World Bank.

FIGURE 3.2
Share of Employment in Agriculture, Manufacturing and Services, 1982–2014

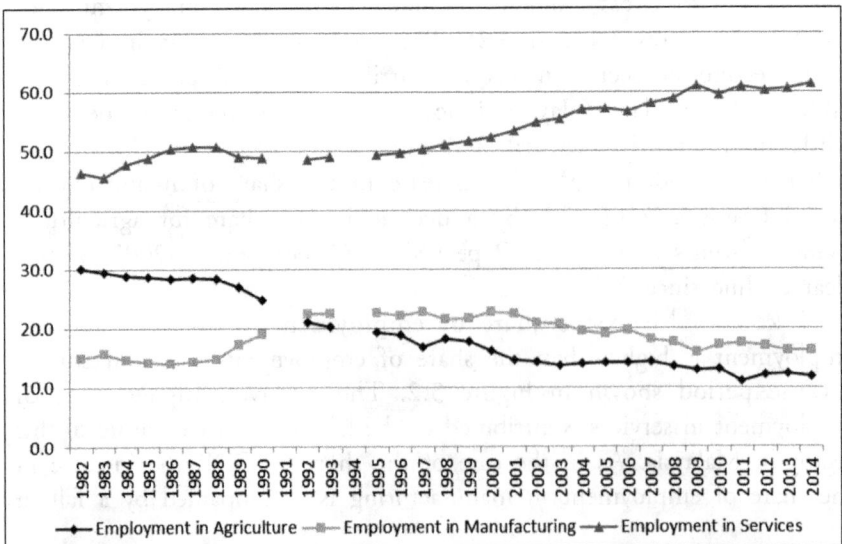

Source: Department of Statistics of Malaysia.

agriculture's share. The share of employment in manufacturing peaked at 22.8 per cent in 1997 and then fell slightly due to AFC before reaching the same share in 2000, after which it fell progressively while the share of services increased.

Since the share of services in GDP and employment is bigger than that of manufacturing for the entire period shown in these two figures, it is not possible to use changes in the relative shares of output and employment in manufacturing and services to identify a sectoral shift from manufacturing to services. Instead, there is a downward trend in the share of manufacturing output and employment since 2000, indicating a sectoral shift to services and the onset of a relative decline in the manufacturing sector that Rasiah (2011) identifies as deindustrialization. The decline in manufacturing, in turn, has led to the services sector to be targeted as the key driver of growth, as exemplified in the 11MP 2016–20 (EPU 2015*a*). Its share in GDP is expected to increase from 53.8 per cent in 2015 to 56.5 per cent by 2020.

FDI Policies in Services

In general, the Companies Act 1965 does not stipulate any equity conditions on Malaysian incorporated companies. However, services that need a license to operate will require compliance with the specific equity conditions of the particular subsector as for example in the case of private higher education and health services. The need to apply for approval constitutes a screening process, which is deemed necessary to protect the consumer due to the inherent information asymmetries in these sectors. But the percentage of foreign equity permitted varies from subsector to subsector and allows for discretionary decision-making, as shown in Table 3.1.

There are unilateral efforts made to liberalize services in order to attract more FDI, professional workers, technology and to strengthen the competitiveness of this sector. On 22 April 2009, the government had liberalized twenty-seven services subsectors, with no equity conditions imposed in health and social services, tourism services, transport services, business services and computer and related services. In 2012, the government further liberalized an additional seven broad services sectors (telecommunications, healthcare, professional services, environmental, distributive, education and courier services), consisting of eighteen subsectors to allow up to 100 per cent foreign equity participation in phases.

TABLE 3.1
Foreign Equity Limits in Selected Services, 2016

	Services Subsectors	Foreign Equity Allowed
1.	Telecommunications: Application service providers	100 per cent
2.	Telecommunications: Network facilities providers and network service providers	70 per cent, can be increased subject to discretionary approval
3.	Distribution Services: Department and specialty stores	100 per cent
4.	Distribution: Foreign owned large retailers (Hypermarkets) and locally incorporated direct selling companies	70 per cent; 30 per cent *Bumiputera* equity ownership
5.	Financial services	49–70 per cent, for domestic investment banks, insurance companies, Islamic banks, Islamic insurance operators; Above 70 per cent for insurance companies, on a case-by-case basis; Foreign banks can have up to four branches, subject to restrictions
6.	Audio-visual and broadcasting	Joint ventures with foreign equity capped at 30 per cent for cable and satellite platforms; No FDI restrictions for wholesale supply of pay TV programming; FDI in terrestrial broadcast networks is prohibited

Note: Bumiputera: referring to Malays and indigenous groups in the country.
Source: The International Trade Administration (ITA), US Department of Commerce, available at <https://www.export.gov/apex/article2?id=Malaysia-Licensing-Requirements> (accessed 23 March 2017).

Apart from the commitments at the multilateral level under the General Agreement of Trade in Services (GATS), and at the ASEAN and ASEAN+1 levels, the services sector is also offered for liberalization in the bilateral FTAs of Malaysia with Japan, Pakistan, New Zealand, India and Australia. The latest agreement, with the inclusion of services liberalization is the Trans-Pacific Partnership Agreement (TPPA) that was signed in February 2016.

Although Malaysia is generally open to FDI and promotes inbound FDI with fiscal incentives provided for selected sectors, the services sector is deemed to be less open to foreign investment. This is reflected in the FDI Restrictiveness Index computed by Thangevalu (2015). The index is created from six areas, namely, foreign ownership or market access, national treatment, screening and approval procedure, board of directors and management composition, movement of investors, and performance requirements.[1] For Malaysia, the score for services is less than manufacturing indicating that the services sector is more restricted compared to manufacturing (see Table 3.2). The score for services also shows that it is the third most restrictive services sector in ASEAN, after Thailand and Indonesia.

A focal point named the National Committee for Approval of Investments in the Services Sector, was also established at the Malaysian Investment Development Authority (MIDA) to receive and process applications of investments in the services sector, excluding investments in financial services, air travel, utilities, Economic Development Corridors, Multimedia Super Corridor (MSC) and Bionexus status companies and distributive trade.[2] MIDA also promotes and processes applications for incentives, besides facilitating companies looking for joint-venture partners and the implementation of investment projects.

FDI and International Trade

Figure 3.3 indicates that inward flows of FDI reached a peak in 1996 and registered sharp falls in 2001 during the dot.com crisis and the 2008 GFC. Although inflows have recovered after the GFC, there is another dip from 2012. Significantly, Malaysia has become a net capital exporter since 2007, although the most recent data available indicates a possible reversal of this trend in 2015.

The gap between the stock of inbound and outbound capital are closing over time (see Figure 3.4). By 2015, the stock of outbound capital has overtaken the stock of inbound capital. The stock of inward FDI is highest in manufacturing, followed by services from 2010 to 2013 (see Table 3.3). However, by 2014, the services sector has overtaken

TABLE 3.2
FDI Restrictiveness Index for Manufacturing and Services in ASEAN, 2015

Sectors	Brunei	Cambodia	Indonesia	Laos	Malaysia	Myanmar	Philippines	Singapore	Thailand	Vietnam
Manufacturing	0.569	0.686	0.536	0.597	0.618	0.563	0.640	0.669	0.637	0.588
Services	0.680	0.644	0.558	0.617	0.573	0.650	0.626	0.846	0.459	0.6276

Source: Thangevalu (2015).

FIGURE 3.3
Malaysia's Inward FDI and Outward FDI by Flows, 1980–2015
(US$ billion)

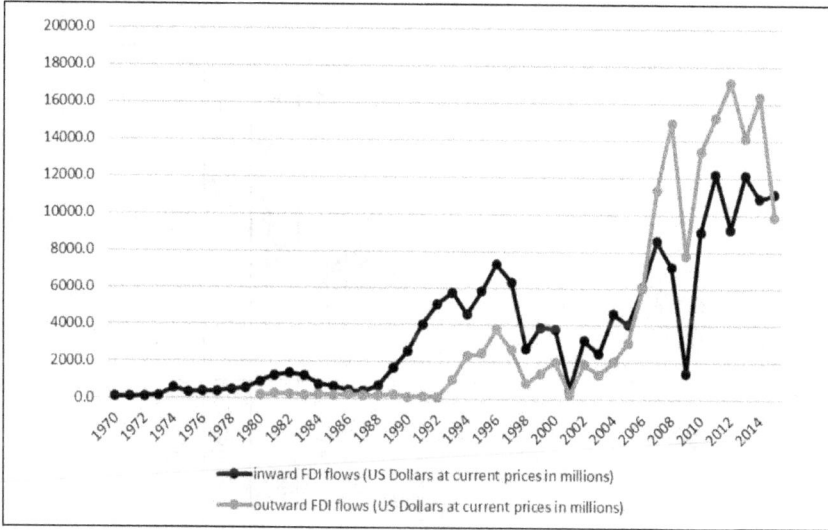

Source: UNCTADstat (2015).

FIGURE 3.4
Malaysia's Inward FDI and Outward FDI by Stocks, 1980–2015
(US$ billion)

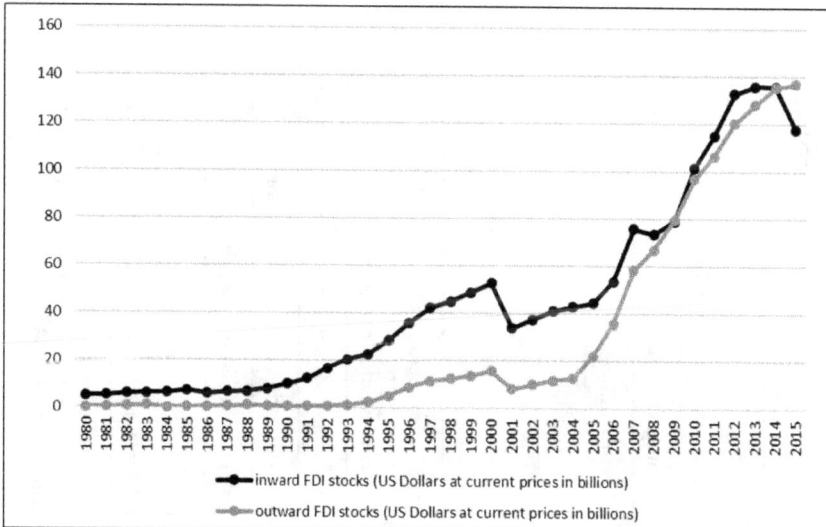

Source: UNCTADstat (2015).

TABLE 3.3
FDI Stock by Sector as at Year End, 2010–14 (RM million)

Sectors	2010	2011	2012	2013	2014
Agriculture, forestry and fishing	9,359	9,471	9,901	10,913	11,063
Mining and Quarrying	18,364	24,288	27,527	35,000	35,770
Manufacturing	146,755	173,276	187,622	203,428	204,071
Construction	1,370	1,390	1,610	2,788	3,420
Services	137,498	157,133	179,035	194,248	213,192
• Utilities	225	665	652	829	774
• Wholesale and retail trade	25,529	30,529	34,092	32,256	34,468
• Transportation and storage	3,300	3,036	2,824	3,988	3,986
• Accommodation and food service activities	3,090	3,235	3,935	4,334	4,422
• Information and communication	21,766	25,555	33,462	34,748	45,010
• Financial and insurance	73,895	81,384	87,344	94,824	97,955
• Real estate activities	5,888	7,481	7,130	10,997	13,584
• Professional, scientific and technical activities	1,348	1,472	1,657	1,915	1,773
• Other services	2,457	3,782	7,940	10,357	11,222

Source: DOS (2015).

manufacturing as the largest recipient of FDI stock. Within services, the top three recipients are financial and insurance, followed by information and communication, and wholesale and retail trade.

A key policy concern in the development of services is the export of services which remains relatively low compared to manufacturing (see Figure 3.5). The services sector has a trade deficit since 1960 except for a brief period from 2007 to 2010 when small surpluses were generated. Internationalizing services through exports is therefore one of the main strategy in the Services Sector Blueprint 2015. The 11MP continues this policy focus in its emphasis on enhancing the export capabilities of service firms (EPU 2015a). While the policies tend to emphasize direct service exports in targeted sectors such as tourism, private higher education and private health care, the World Bank (2016) has noted the need to improve the contribution of services to manufacturing exports through distribution services.

FIGURE 3.5
Exports of Malaysia, 1980–2015
(US$ billion)

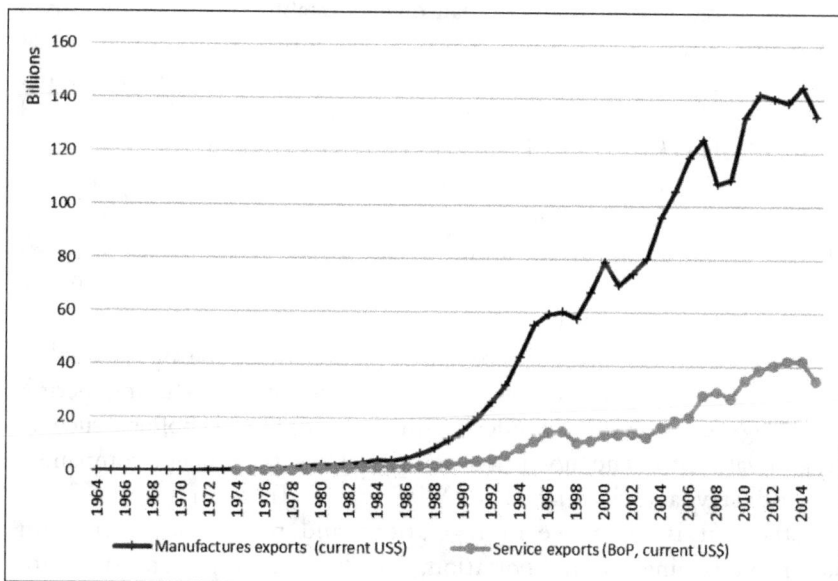

Source: World Development Indicators, World Bank.

CASE STUDY: FDI LIBERALIZATION IN
LOGISTICS SERVICES

According to UNESCAP (n.d., p. 8), "there is no universally agreed definition for logistics services, and the role may be interpreted in very different ways across the region". The ASEAN Roadmap for the Integration of Logistics Services covers "freight logistics and related activities"[3] while the sector is not defined in terms of specific subsectors in the main policy documents in Malaysia. Data used for this sector in this chapter covers land and water transport, warehousing and support activities and postal and courier activities based on Malaysia Standard Industrial Classification 2008 (MSIC 2008) for Divisions 49, 50, 52 and 53).[4]

Based on the above-mentioned classification, the sector's value added contributed up to 3.8 per cent of GDP in 2010 (see Table 3.4). In the same year, the number of establishments totalled 41,424. It is dominated mainly by Malaysian-owned establishments, mostly micro, small and medium establishments in land and water transport as well as warehousing and support activities.[5] Air transport and post and courier services show only combined data for the types of establishments since the Department of Statistics Act does not allow data with less than three establishments to be revealed. This implies that there are either less than three foreign or Malaysian-owned establishments in these two subsectors. Total employment stood at 312,962. The value added of this sector grew to RM37.2 billion in 2014, contributing to 3.4 per cent of GDP although total employment fell to 286,637. It should be noted that Economic Planning Unit (EPU) and the Economic Report from the Ministry of Finance report a slightly higher share for the contribution of logistics to GDP. Both agencies also acknowledge that the contribution of this sector has stagnated between 3.6 per cent to 3.7 per cent of GDP from 2005–14 (EPU 2015b; Ministry of Finance 2015).

Since there are several subsectors involved, regulatory control is complex as it involves several government agencies, including permit issuing agencies for cross border trading, multiple stakeholders such as local private listed and not listed companies, GLCs, foreign companies, and industry associations. The Ministry of Transport is the main ministry that is in charge of regulations and policy formulation for matters pertaining to transportation, which is an important subsector in logistics.

TABLE 3.4

Principal Statistics of Transportation and Storage Services, 2010 and 2014

Year 2010	Number and Type of Establishments		Value Added (RM'000)	Employment
	Foreign-owned	Malaysian-owned		
Land Transport	13	36,211	7,008,904	159,248
Water Transport	10	790	4,713,967	24,042
Sea Transport	10	401	4,554,416	20,793
Inland Water Transport	0	389	159,551	3,069
Air Transport		25	4,918,611	28,963
Passenger		16	3,590,284	27,261
Freight		9	1,328,327	1,702
Warehousing and support activities	61	3,296	13,511,180	80,704
Post and Courier Services		193	1,260,830	29,005
Total 2010	*41,424*		*31,413,492*	*312,962*
Year 2014			**(RM billion)**	
Land Transport	n.a.		17.2	109,812
Water Transport	n.a		4.8	24,248
Air Transport	n.a		8.6	32,293
Warehousing and support activities	n.a		15.7	90,591
Post and Courier	n.a		1.4	29,683
Total 2014	*n.a*		*37.2*	*286,637*

Note: n.a.: not available
Source: Department of Statistics (2010, unpublished) and DOS (2015 for 2014 data).

POLICY MEASURES FOR THE DEVELOPMENT OF THE LOGISTICS INDUSTRY

The main domestic measures undertaken to foster the development of a vibrant logistics sector include a Master Plan, housing this sector's development under a single Ministry (the Ministry of Transport) to overcome coordination problems, and promoting the development of this sector with incentives. Unilateral and regional liberalization measures such as FTAs are also used as part of the country's overall services liberalization strategy. FTAs are also used to expand market access for its domestic providers that are exporting or planning to export.

Domestic Policies for the Development of the Logistics Industry

The logistics sector was identified as a priority sector in IMP3 2006–20 based on a background study of the sector. In line with this Plan, a Malaysian Logistics Council (MLC) was formed in January 2007 to formulate actions plans and blueprints for activities to support this aspiration; as well as to provide leadership, coordinate, and monitor the implementation of programmes and activities in the different ministries that are involved in this Council.[6] A supply chain and logistics research and training body was also established under the supervision of the Council to undertake assigned research from the Council. The research centre is set up as a joint government and private sector entity, with the government providing most of the funding, while the private sector contributes to the funding, and may participate in research through the secondment of staff. Despite these plans, the MLC went into hiatus for three years before it was revived in December 2013 (*The Sun Daily*, 16 December 2013).

Later in November 2013, Prime Minister Najib announced that the government would formulate a Logistics Sector Master Plan to improve the performance of the country's logistics activities from its 29th ranking in the World Bank Logistics Performance Index Report 2012 in recognition of the importance of the logistics sector. The Logistics and Trade Facilitation Master Plan (2015–20) was subsequently launched in 2015. The Plan essentially provides "the strategic framework to resolve bottlenecks in the logistics sector and elevate Malaysia to become a regional player in the medium term" (Ministry of Transport 2015, p. 6).

It envisages five strategic shifts, executed through twenty-one action items that will facilitate Malaysia to become "The Preferred Logistics Gateway for Asia" by 2020 and beyond (Ministry of Transport 2015, p. 11). The Plan is divided into three phases: Phase 1 (2015–16) focuses on debottlenecking the sector using two strategic shifts, namely strengthening the institutional and regulatory framework and developing infrastructure and freight demand; Phase 2 (2016–19) concentrates on enhancing domestic growth through two strategic shifts, that is by improving the trade facilitation mechanism and strengthening technology and human capital; while Phase 3 (2020 and beyond) aims to create a regional footprint through the fifth shift which is to internationalize logistics services (see Table 3.5).

TABLE 3.5
Summary of the Logistics and
Trade Facilitation Master Plan, 2015–20

Strategies	Phases of Development
Strengthening Institutional and Regulatory Framework	*Phase 1 (2015–16): Debottlenecking the Sector*
Developing Infrastructure and Freight Demand	
Enhancing Trade Facilitation Mechanism	*Phase 2 (2016–19): Enhancing Domestic Growth*
Strengthening the capabilities of logistics service providers through technology and human capital	
Internationalizing Logistics Services	*Phase 3 (2020 and Beyond): Creating Regional Footprint*

Source: Summarized from Ministry of Transport (2015), p. 14.

The goals of the Plan are to increase the contribution of the transport and storage subsector to GDP from 3.6 per cent in 2013 to 4.3 per cent in 2020, or an estimated increase of RM22.2 billion (Liow 2016). The cargo volume is projected to grow 8 per cent annually to reach 880 million tonnes in 2020. It also aims to generate 146,000 new jobs by 2020, mostly in the high skilled category. The Masterplan also envisions that Malaysia's Logistics Performance Index (LPI) ranking will be in the top twenty position globally, by 2020.

A National Logistics Task Force was subsequently established to oversee the implementation of the Plan, chaired by the Minister of Transport and reporting directly to the Economic Council for Service Sector, which is in turn chaired by the Prime Minister. Its Secretariat is housed in the Ministry of Transport while members are senior officials from the relevant ministries as well as industry experts. The Task Force meets three times a year to assess the status in the implementation of this Plan with the five strategic shifts organized into cluster working groups reporting to them.

Updates on the progress towards implementation are released to the media regularly by the Minister of Transport. For example, the media statement released on 19 October 2016 provided a progress report on the status of implementation of the First Phase. As announced, the key achievements in the implementation of the Plan so far, are: the establishment of a national logistics data programme, a user guide for the warehousing business, a Malaysian ship registry, initiation of a new programme to meet human capital needs called MyLesen-GDL programme, that aims to attract potential job seekers to apply for a Goods Drivers Licence (GDL) and to become professional hauliers/lorry drivers, and the launching of Port Klang Net, a port single window that aims at establishing a port and trade focused community system by connecting key industry players under a common platform[7] (Liow 2016). Johor Port Authority has also initiated a similar initiative, named the Johor Net. In December 2016, it was announced that 85 per cent of the Action items under Phase 1 under the Masterplan have been completed (*Business Times*, 2 December 2016). But there is as yet no independent external assessment on the achievements thus far, and how these changes have translated into lowering logistics costs in Malaysia.

Regulatory Changes

The logistics sector is governed by a complex system of regulations that are also fragmented[8] due to the multi-sectoral nature of this sector, the large number of players, as well as different ministries and agencies involved, as explained in the earlier section. The goods handled also pose different risks to society and regulatory intervention is used to overcome informational asymmetries, security, safety, health and environmental concerns (MPC n.d.). Complex regulations, however, increase inefficiencies and compliance costs besides creating unnecessary and sometimes unintended barriers to trade.

Efforts are made to improve the ease of doing business and to modernize the business regulations of Malaysia in line with the government's policy to improve regulatory quality as stated in NEM and the Tenth Malaysian Plan (2011–15) (WTO 2014). Two key changes were made: first, a Special Task Force to Facilitate Business (PEMUDAH) was established in 2007 to improve the ease of doing business by addressing bureaucracy in business government dealings and to enhance the regulation of business. PEMUDAH's secretariat is housed within Malaysia Productivity Corporation (MPC).

Second, a Regulatory Department was established in MPC in 2010. The launching of a National Policy on the Development and Implementation of Regulations (NPDIR) in 2013 is a watershed in terms of policy development as it marks a significant change in the government's approach to regulatory reform — from deregulation to whole-of-government approach on good regulatory practices (GRP). The policy is applied to all federal government ministries, departments, statutory bodies, and regulatory commissions (WTO 2014). NPDIR published a handbook for best practice regulations, benchmarked against the Organization for Economic Co-operation and Development (OECD) guidelines, and it was launched together with the national policy document in 2013 (MPC 2013). This guide outlines the steps to be taken in developing new regulations that affect trade, investment and business, such as reviews and regulatory impact analysis. The goal is to ensure that any new regulation will not lead to disincentives to business, investment and trade.

The government also requested OECD to review its regulatory management system in 2013 and to provide support for implementing GRP. The review led to the launch of the OECD (2015) report for implementing GRP that aims to institutionalize GRP into government planning, its performance indicators and also decision-making process. MPC has conducted numerous outreach and training programmes towards this end and Malaysia is in the process of embedding GRP in the implementation of the 11MP.

MPC has also conducted a few pilot projects for the purpose of reducing unnecessary regulatory burdens (RURB)[9] and accelerating sectoral regulatory reform since 2015. A review of the logistics sector's regulations was conducted in 2015/16 and the report was uploaded for the public to review (MPC n.d.). The study seeks to identify the regulations that are burdensome for the logistics sector and to make recommendations for change. Outcomes from this review process has yet to be made public at the time of writing this chapter.

Overall, these changes do indicate that the government is making a concerted effort towards reforming regulations and improving the country's regulatory environment. Nevertheless, amending laws requires implementation from the different agencies involved and this will take time and effort from the different custodians of the relevant laws and regulations, even with diligent monitoring from the Ministry of Trade and Industry as the coordinating body. It remains to be seen how long it will take for the regulatory reviews to be translated into actual amendments that can overcome the regulatory bottlenecks that is needed to complement physical de-bottling efforts. But it is this last mile in regulatory changes that will determine whether the changes have been effective in improving the governance structure or whether it is just another form of isomorphic mimicry.[10]

Incentives for the Development of Logistics Industry

In view of the need to encourage local logistics services providers to assume a bigger role in providing integrated logistics services, the government has introduced the Integrated Logistics Services (ILS) incentive in 2002 to encourage logistics service providers to consolidate or integrate their activities and become Third Party Logistics Service Providers (3PLs) (MIDA n.d.). ILS incentives are granted to logistics companies that undertake warehousing, transportation, freight forwarding and other related value added services such as distribution and supply chain management undertaken on an integrated basis.

Subsequently, incentives are also given for International Integrated Logistics Services (IILS) and Cold Chain activities (MIDA n.d.). In contrast to ILS companies, an IILS Status company provides integrated and seamless logistics services (door-to-door) along the logistics value chain as a single entity on a regional or global scale. Qualified IILSs will be issued a Customs Agent Licence. A company that provides

Cold Chain activities such as cold room services and refrigerated trucks for perishable agriculture produce i.e. fruits, vegetables, flowers, ferns and meats and aquatic products, is eligible for either Pioneer Status or Investment Tax Allowance. The incentives available to companies within these three subsectors vary according to the company's capabilities and scope of investment.

According to the MIDA, as of 31 December 2014, a total of fifty-eight companies with investments valued at RM3.7 billion have been granted ILS incentives (MIDA 2014). Of these companies, nine were new projects and forty-nine were expansion projects. In 2014, eight companies were awarded IILS status in Malaysia, including Worldgate Express (M) Sdn Bhd — a Malaysian-owned company that provides logistics services to more than twenty countries.

Liberalization Measures: Unilateral, ASEAN Framework Agreement on Services (AFAS) and World Trade Organization (WTO)

Malaysia's Transport and Logistics commitments under AFAS and the WTO are shown in Table 3.6, based on the identified subsectors in the Roadmap for the Integration of Logistics Services. There are no commitments made for these subsectors under GATS in the Uruguay Round and the uncompleted Doha Round. In the case of AFAS 9, the commitments made for modes 1 and 2 are met but not for mode 3, as the agreed 70 per cent foreign equity ownership has yet to be complied, as at 2016. Some reasons given for the shortfall includes the fact that there are some unregulated sectors (CPC 876), while others fall under the jurisdiction of other ministries (e.g., courier services (CPC 7512) is supposed to be under telecommunications), and the existence of concession agreements that effectively excludes foreign participation (e.g., CPC 741).

In addition to commitments made in trade agreements, five subsectors under Transport and Logistics have been autonomously liberalized to allow foreign equity participation since 22 April 2009. These are Class C Freight Transportation; rental/leasing services of ships that excludes cabotage and offshore trades; rental of cargo vessels without crew (Bareboat Charter) for international shipping; maritime agency services; and vessel salvage and refloating services.

TABLE 3.6
Malaysia's Commitments in WTO and ASEAN for the Logistics Sector, as of 2016

Sector	CPC	GATS: UR		GATS (Doha Round Offers) (2006)		AFAS 9	
		Market Access (MA)	National Treatment (NT)	MA	NT	MA	NT
Packaging services	876	–	–	–	–	M1: N M2: N M3: Up to 51%	M1: N M2: N M3: N
Courier services	7512	–	–	–	–	M1: N M2: N M3: 51%	M1: N M2: N M3: N
Maritime freight transportation, excluding cabotage	7212	–*	–	–*	–	M1: N M2: N M3: 70% Limitations stipulating conditions for Malaysian registered vessels	M1: N M2: N M3: N
Rail freight transportation	7112	–	–	–	–	No commitment	
Road freight transportation	7123	–	–	–	–	M1: N M2: N M3: 70%	M1: N M2: N M3: N

Service	Code						
Maritime cargo handling services	741	—	—	—	—	M1: N M2: N M3: Up to 49%	M1: N M2: N M3: N
Storage and warehouse services: covering private bonded warehousing services only	742					M1: N M2: N M3: Up to 51%	M1: N M2: N M3: N
Maritime freight forwarding services only	748	—	—	—	—	M1: N M2: N M3: 70%	M1: N M2: N M3: N
Other auxiliary services	749	—	—	—	—	No commitment	

Notes: M1: mode 1; M2: mode 2; M3: mode 3; N: none
 * Although commitments were made in international maritime transportation services, it excluded CPC 7212.
Source: WTO and MITI.

FDI AND TRADE IN LOGISTICS INDUSTRY

Generally, the overall evidence on the impact of FTAs on FDI in ASEAN is rather sparse, with no secondary empirical evidence for Malaysia alone. The available evidence is mixed and mostly focused on total investment in manufacturing rather than services.[11]

For services, it is unlikely that services liberalization commitments alone are sufficient to draw in FDI as the commitments are limited (ASEAN Secretariat and the World Bank 2015), while the FDI commitments in some sectors are even less than what is practised (Tham 2016). In particular, the need for licenses to operate in the regulated sectors imply that foreign investors cannot enter based on the commitments alone.

Table 3.3 suggests that FDI in services favour other subsectors rather than transportation and storage. In 2014, the share of FDI in transport and storage amounts to a mere 1.9 per cent of total FDI stock in services (see Table 3.3). Table 3.7 shows that FDI is largest in water transport and warehousing and support facilitates, with a noticeable increase after the GFC.

Since logistic services are affected by infrastructure development, FDI in infrastructure, that is usually categorized under construction, can help to improve the logistic performance of a country, especially for developing countries with weak infrastructure. Table 3.7 indicates an increase in FDI in construction after 2013. This trend is likely to increase over the next few years due to the announced investment from China in Kuantan port, reportedly RM3 billion by the Guangxi Beibu Gulf International Port Group and IJM Corporation Berhad in the Kuantan Port expansion project.[12] The expansion of Kuantan port is also supported by the government through the provision of income tax exemptions and infrastructure provisions such as improvement of the access road between the port, the industrial park and the East Coast Expressway. More importantly, the proposed expansion will contribute to a quicker and direct route between the East Coast Economic Region (ECER) and ports in China's eastern region in addition to the rest of the world. Reportedly, it is only five sailing days from Qinzhou Port to Kuantan Port. The project is expected to be completed by 2017.[13]

Recent reports indicate that Malaysia is trying to tap on China's One Belt One Road initiative by wooing Chinese investment for two other ports, Melaka port and Port Klang, as these ports hold locational importance for China in the region.[14] This is in line with the strategy to build freight infrastructure efficiency and capacity as stated in the National Logistics and Trade Facilitation Master Plan. These strategic investments seek to use port investment with strategic partners that can also help to draw ships to the port. The development of Tanjung Pelepas in the south used a similar

TABLE 3.7
FDI Stock in Transportation and Storage, 2005–15 (RM million)

Subsectors	2005	2006	2007	2008	2009	2010	2011	2012	2013	2014ᶠ	2015ʳ
Land Transport	39.32	45.79	–64.42	40.96	80.34	21.86	80.98	79.47	141.86	153.26	138.75
Water Transport	685.20	657.92	251.46	1,642.49	1,819.75	1,776.69	1,222.78	1,108.00	1,438.61	1,029.33	865.00
Air Transport	555.43	—	—	—	81.04	382.35	360.69	361.43	963.36	714.84	539.18
Warehousing and Support Facilities	360.61	540.23	9,447.39	841.42	1,203.68	1,641.05	1,932.27	1,826.13	2,062.29	2,831.01	3,743.53
Post and Courier Services	549.34	1,030.32	1,574.53	–497.43	–447.18	–522.05	–560.37	–551.23	–617.64	–742.81	–822.93
Construction	n.a.	n.a.	n.a.	n.a.	n.a.	1,370	1,390	1,610	2,788	3,420	n.a.

Note: f: final; r: revised
Source: DOS (unpublished data) for transporation and storage and DOS (2015) for the construction sector.

strategy by forming an equity partnership with Maersk. Liberalization commitments are unlikely to matter in this kind of investment.

In terms of trade, there is a deficit in this sector as a whole but a small surplus is obtained for warehousing and storage, although the export values are small compared to water and air transport (see Tables 3.8 and 3.9). Since the deficit is tied to the underlying export structure, which is associated with multinational production, it will take time to reduce the deficit as it will require a transformation of the underlying production and export structure.

TABLE 3.8
Exports of Transportation and Storage, 2010–15 (RM million)

Component	2010	2011	2012	2013	2014	2015
Water Transport	7,774	7,190	6,079	5,945	6,320	6,416
Air Transport	7,061	7,283	6,528	7,503	7,979	7,798
Land Transport	358	445	607	694	722	838
off which: warehousing and storage	*110*	*183*	*300*	*349*	*378*	*466*
Post and Courier services	504	565	547	558	595	614
TOTAL	15,696	15,482	13,761	14,701	15,617	15,667

Source: DOS (unpublished data).

TABLE 3.9
Imports of Transportation and Storage, 2010–15 (RM million)

Component	2010	2011	2012	2013	2014	2015
Water Transport	18,407	20,592	21,797	23,042	24,354	24,849
Air Transport	10,105	10,042	9,761	11,284	12,990	11,651
Land Transport	3,910	3,624	3,570	3,648	3,776	3,793
off which: warehousing and storage	*415*	*236*	*302*	*212*	*272*	*228*
Post and Courier services	442	671	673	636	545	648
TOTAL	32,864	34,928	35,801	38,610	41,666	40,940

Source: DOS (unpublished data).

OUTSTANDING CHALLENGES AND POLICY SUGGESTIONS

While the National Logistics and Trade Facilitation Master Plan addresses many of the existing problems in the logistics industry, it is notably silent on the market structure and market fragmentation that prevails in this sector.

The market structure of this industry varies considerably from one subsector to another. While road haulage, warehousing, and freight forwarding have a large number of firms and face intense domestic competition, duopolistic and oligopolistic competition reigns in the other subsectors such as airport operators, ground handlers, and airlines that is dominated by GLCs. There are only two airport operators, one of which is private while the other airport operator (MAHB) has more than 70 per cent of its shares held by Khazanah National Bhd, a government investment holding company. Similarly, there are three main airlines, two of which are owned by the government (MAS and Firefly which is the Low Cost Carrier belonging to MAS) while the other Air Asia is privately owned. For ground handlers, one is owned by MAS while the other is privately owned. The presence of GLCs may deter liberalization efforts as some of these have to implement the national agenda in terms of redistributive requirements thereby leading to an inclination towards a more protectionist stance.

The large number of establishments as shown in Table 3.4 indicates a fragmented market in some segments of this sector such as land transport and warehousing and support activities (Gopal 2012). There are reportedly 1,091 members in the Federation of Malaysian Freight Forwarders, providing a broad and varied range of services.[15] A large number of small domestic players implies the use of price competition with providers focusing on a pricing strategy rather than service quality or breath of services provided (Gopal 2012). Yet the end goal of creating a regional footprint and internationalizing logistics services, especially through exports, requires a focus on the quality of service provided, innovation and compliance to international logistics standards (PwC n.d.). This will require a paradigm shift from a mere price strategy alone. Moreover, global trends project industry consolidation is needed for the industry to achieve the necessary economies of scale (PwC n.d.). Possible consolidations may include the provision of integrated services that combine several activities along the supply chain or the consolidation of several providers/services as for example, in the consolidation of multiple smaller warehouses into larger state-of-the-art facilities near population centres, ports and major intermodal facilities suitable for reaching consumers quickly, with the increasing use of e-commerce and its ensuing demand for rapid delivery. Small firms that characterize the nature of this industry as explained earlier will not be able to do this as they are likely to be constrained financially.

Since 2014, Malaysia has offered an incentive for mergers and acquisition for 100 per cent Malaysian owned Small and Medium Enterprises (SMEs) to merge into large entities for building domestic capacity.[16] This incentive comprises a flat tax rate of 20 per cent will be given on all taxable income for a period of five (5) years effective from the date of merger as well as exemption on stamp duty on the merger document. Beyond incentives, a more focused policy initiative may be needed to hasten the consolidation process by encouraging collaborations, joint ventures and other forms of partnerships, including between multinationals and SMEs as well. SMEs that wish to survive the consolidation process will have to focus on providing very niche and specialized services.

Second, apart from simplifying and streamlining regulations to reduce unnecessary burden, there is a need to follow through the reviews on existing regulations so that it will translate into amendments that will lead to regulatory "de-bottling". Again, this falls back to a careful monitoring of the implementation process of the suggestions for amendments from the regulatory reviews and coordinated efforts from all the related agencies in making the necessary amendments.

Third, there is little attention paid to FDI restrictions in this sector. In particular, the redistributive policies in the country confer *Bumiputera* privileges in the form of *Bumiputera* equity requirements. It is important to note that the repeal of the Foreign Investment Committee (FIC) Guidelines in 2009 does not mean that the *Bumiputera* equity participation rule[17] has been waived. *Bumiputera* equity participation continues to be enforced by the relevant ministries without needing approval from the FIC as before (Christopher & Lee Ong 2016).[18] Although this reduces the layers of bureaucracy that impede foreign equity participation in the country, these requirements may intentionally or unintentionally serve as entry barriers for foreign providers. Moreover, equity holdings for *Bumiputera* and for Malaysians differs from one segment of the logistics value chain to another. For example, public bonded warehouse must have at least 30 per cent *Bumiputera* equity participation whereas transportation companies for certain categories of licenses must have at least 51 per cent Malaysian equity (including 30 per cent *Bumiputera* equity) and up to 49 per cent foreign equity ownership is allowed.[19] In maritime trade, the cabotage policy continues to restrict domestic trade to Malaysia's own flagged vessels. Existing concession agreements especially in maritime cargo handling services imply that foreign participation is also restricted. Hence, identifying FDI restrictions and other entry barriers will complement liberalization measures offered in the FTAs as these liberalization measures can be constrained or offset by *Bumiputera* equity requirements and other entry barriers.

The goal to be a regional player will also require Malaysia to consider ASEAN's initiatives that can support the development of its logistics industry. The fact that Malaysians are already investing abroad, including in services, implies that pressing for greater liberalization in the service sector will benefit the country's investors in the region. Therefore, it is important to continue efforts to improve the liberalization commitments in AFAS and the planned ASEAN Trade in Services Agreement (ATISA) even though current liberalization measures fall short of what is aspired as explained in the introductory chapter.

Since Malaysia has already started on the path of GRP, it will be helpful for outward Malaysian investors to face less regulatory barriers in ASEAN. It is therefore in Malaysia's advantage to press for the implementation of better regulatory changes in the forthcoming ATISA and the AEC 2025 Consolidated Strategic Action Plan under Good Governance (ASEAN Secretariat 2017).

In particular, the Plan's measures to enhance trade facilitation by moving towards paperless trading will benefit potential exporters by pressing for its use in ASEAN. UNESCAP (2016)'s survey on the state of paperless trade in Asia Pacific 2015 indicates that Malaysia is well placed as its implementation is higher than both the regional and subregional average. Out of the seven paperless trade procedures surveyed, Malaysia has already implemented six. E-application for customs refund is the least implemented of the seven procedures. Hence, at the regional level, it will enhance internationalization efforts, for Malaysia to focus on cross border paperless trade through the ASEAN Single Window initiative. Moreover, the ASEAN 2025 Connectivity Master Plan (ASEAN Secretariat 2016) also supports improving trade facilitation through activating the ASEAN Single Window.

CONCLUSION

The main findings of this chapter indicate that Malaysia's commitments in the logistics sector fall short of the targets in AFAS for various reasons. In terms of the FDI environment, there are on-going efforts to improve the ease of doing business as well as to establish GRP based on OECD guidelines. These new initiatives will guide the formulation of new regulations in the future for the whole government. The National Logistics and Facilitation Master Plan, launched in 2015, aims to improve the performance of this sector by addressing its main current challenges. It also aims to internationalize this sector by creating a regional footprint. Efforts are made in implementation through key performance indicators, with the Ministry of Transport in charge, a clear governance structure and a council to monitor its implementation. These new initiatives hold great promise in terms of enhancing the future FDI environment. Nonetheless, FDI in this sector is relatively small, though growing. It is unlikely that the current liberalization commitments have contributed to these inflows as these commitments are limited and there is still the need to obtain licenses for the regulated sectors. Investment in logistics infrastructure such as ports are poised to increase with new investment from China at the Kuantan port and reportedly the possibility of more Chinese investment in Melaka port and Port Klang.

There are still outstanding challenges. First, there is a need to rationalize some subsectors where there are a large number of firms, mainly SMEs, as this implies the use of a price strategy rather than strategies that promote exports through service differentiation, innovation and standards compliance. Rationalization is also part of the global trend for this sector as it enables economies of scale to be reaped. Second, regulatory reviews have to lead towards regulatory de-bottling in terms of actual amendments that will improve the governance of this sector. Adopting GRP alone, without effective changes in regulations is not enough to lower the cost of compliance for both domestic and foreign investors. Third, identifying existing barriers to entry to foreign participation will also ensure that liberalization commitments will not be offset by domestic regulations or practices that deter entry.

At the ASEAN level, there are two main incentives for Malaysia to press for greater liberalization and removing regulatory barriers. First, the country has shifted from being a net capital importer to net capital exporter since 2007, though there is a recent reversal in the 2015 data. Second, it will improve market access for current and future exporters, which is in line with the ambition to export services, including logistics services. The regional market is important bearing in mind that the domestic market is limited by its size. In this regard, the ASEAN Single Window can facilitate cross border paperless trade in line with the goals for improving trade facilitation and future exports in the National Plan.

Notes

1. The higher the scores, the more open the FDI rules are.
2. See <http://www.mida.gov.my/home/services-sector/posts/> (accessed 1 November 2016).
3. See page 1 of Appendix 1 of document, from <http://asean.org/wp-content/ uploads/images/archive/20883.pdf> (accessed 3 November 2016).
4. Based on discussions with the Department of Statistics, Malaysia.
5. Data from the Economic Census conducted in 2010 on small and medium enterprises (SMEs) in Malaysia, indicate that there are 40,025 SMEs in transportation and storage subsector, of which 34,790 are micros, while 3,901 are small and 1,334 are medium. See <http://www.smecorp.gov.my/index. php/en/policies/2015-12-21-09-09-49/sme-statistics> (accessed 1 November 2016).
6. Members of the MLC were from the government, private sector as well academics.
7. The implementation of this initiative is to improve competitiveness of the port and logistics industry through increased efficiency and cost reduction.
8. Regulations are fragmented because each segment of logistics is governed by different licenses, such as for customs clearance agent, trucking, warehousing, handling dangerous goods and fire safety (MPC n.d.).
9. This includes among others, excessive coverage by a regulation, subject-specific regulations, prescriptive regulations, overly complex regulations, unwieldly license application, excessive time delays in obtaining responses and decisions from regulators, rules and enforcement of rules that creates inefficiencies, overlapping or conflicts in activities by different regulators and inconsistent application or interpretation of regulations by regulators (MPC n.d.).
10. MacDonald (2011) explains this term as building institutions and processes in weak states that *look* like those found in functional states. In other words, these reforms copy the reforms from other countries that have been successful in their reform efforts, but without their core underlying functionalities. Hence a state can have the same institutions and agencies but not the same level of functionality.
11. See for example, Thangavelu and Findlay (2011) for the evidence on the Asia-Pacific region and Verico (2012).

12. See East Coast Economic Region (ECER) website at <http://www.ecerdc. com.my/en/media_releases/mckip-receives-rm10-5-billion-of-new-investments-8500-job-opportunities-for-the-rakyat-in-ecer/> (accessed 1 November 2016).

13. See East Coast Economic Region (ECER) website at <http://www.ecerdc. com.my/en/media_releases/malaysia-china-kuantan-industrial-park-mckip-seals-investment-worth-rm1-58-billion-from-china-and-malaysia/> (accessed 1 November 2016).

14. See <http://www.scmp.com/news/asia/southeast-asia/article/1934839/china-malaysia-tout-new-port-alliance-reduce-customs> (accessed 1 November 2016) and <http://www.thestar.com.my/news/nation/2016/07/03/a-winwin-relationship-chinas-onebelt-oneroad-regional-economic-expansion-will-shower-abundant-trade/> (accessed 1 November 2016).

15. On the other hand, there are also large Multinational Companies (MNCs) operating in some of the subsectors. For example, in air freight, the large multinationals operating in the country reportedly have a large slice of the market share; with DHL Global Forwarding taking 26 per cent of the market, followed by Nippon Express (11 per cent), Baxglobal (9 per cent) and Shenker (4 per cent) in 2007 (Interview DHL in Tham 2007). MasKargo is the only domestic player that has a substantial market share in air freight.

16. See <http://www.smecorp.gov.my/index.php/en/resources/2015-12-21-11-03-46/entrepre-news/161-entrepre-news/tahun-2014/356-incentive-for-merger-and-acquisition-for-small-malaysian-services-providers>.

17. This is part of the redistributive strategy of the NEP that was implemented since 1971. Although the NEP has been officially replaced by other policies since 1990, the redistributive strategies continue to be practised till this day.

18. Thus, the removal of the FIC restrictions from the horizontal commitments in market access in the AFAS 9 package in 2016 does not imply any improvements in Malaysia's commitments. Instead, the FIC restrictions in market access in the horizontal commitments should have been removed immediately after the 2009 repeal of FIC Guidelines in order to align these commitments with domestic regulations.

19. See MIDA (n.d.) for logistics services.

References

ASEAN Secretariat. *Master Plan on ASEAN Connectivity 2025*. Jakarta: ASEAN Secretariat, 2016. Available at <http://asean.org/storage/2016/09/Master-Plan-on-ASEAN-Connectivity-20251.pdf> (accessed 27 March 2017).

―――. *ASEAN Economic Community 2025 Consolidated Strategic Action Plan*. Jakarta: ASEAN Secretariat, 2017. Available at <http://asean.org/storage/2017/02/Consolidated-Strategic-Action-Plan.pdf (accessed 27 March 2017).

ASEAN Secretariat and the World Bank. *ASEAN Service Integration Report.* Jakarta: ASEAN Secretariat, 2015.

Business Times. "First Phase of Logistics Masterplan Completed: Liow", 2 December 2016. Available at <http://www.nst.com.my/news/2016/12/193877/first-phase-logistics-masterplan-completed-liow> (accessed 15 December 2016).

Christopher & Lee Ong. *Doing Business in Malaysia.* Kuala Lumpur: Christopher & Lee Ong, 2016. Available at <http://www.christopherleeong.com/our-work/publications/doing-business-in-malaysia> (accessed 1 November 2016).

Department of Statistics (DOS). "Principal Statistics of Transportation and Storage Services". Unpublished data, 2010.

——. *Statistics on Foreign Direct Investment in Malaysia.* Putrajaya: DOS, 2015.

Economic Planning Unit (EPU). *Eleventh Malaysia Plan: 2016–2020 – Anchoring Growth on People.* Putrajaya: Malaysia National Printers Ltd., 2015*a.*

——. "Unleashing Growth of Logistics and Enhancing Trade Facilitation". Putrajaya: EPU, 2015*b.* Available at <http://epu.gov.my/sites/default/files/Strategy%20Paper%2014.pdf> (accessed 1 November 2016).

Gopal, R. "ETP Implications on Potential for Supply Chain and Logistics Sectors". PowerPoint Presentation at the Global Logistics & Cargo Symposium 2012, Kuala Lumpur. Available at <http://vietnamsupplychain.com/assets/upload/file/publication/1341934556089-2883.pdf> (accessed 15 December 2016).

Hirschman, Charles and Aghajanian Akbar. "Women's Labour Force Participation and Socio-Economic Development: The Case of Peninsular Malaysia, 1957–1970". *Journal of Southeast Asian Studies* 11, no. 1 (1980): 30–49.

International Trade Administration (ITA), US Department of Commerce. "Malaysia – Licensing Requirements for Professional Services", 2017. Available at <https://www.export.gov/apex/article2?id=Malaysia-Licensing-Requirements> (accessed 23 March 2017).

Liow Tiong Lai. "National Logistics and Trade Facilitation Masterplan". Media Statement on 19 October 2016. Available at <http://www.liowtionglai.com/national-logistics-and-trade-facilitation-masterplan/> (accessed 1 November 2016).

MacDonald, Lawrence. "One Size Doesn't Fit All: Lant Pritchett on Mimicry in Development", 14 March 2011. Available at <https://www.cgdev.org/blog/one-size-doesn%E2%80%99t-fit-all-lant-pritchett-mimicry-development> (accessed 23 March 2017).

Malaysian Investment Development Authority (MIDA). "Logistics in Services Sector", n.d. Available at <http://fwwcloud.com/demo/mida/v3/logistics-in-services-sector/posts/> (accessed 12 April 2017).

——. "Malaysia Investment Performance Report 2014", 2014. Available at <http://www.mida.gov.my/env3/uploads/PerformanceReport/2014/IPR2014> (accessed 12 April 2017).

Malaysia Productivity Corporation (MPC). "Reducing Unnecessary Burdens on Business: Logistics", n.d. Available at <http://www.mpc.gov.my/reducing-unnecessary-regulatory-burdens-rurb-2/> (accessed 1 November 2016).

———. *Best Practice Regulation Handbook*. Petaling Jaya: MPC, 2013.

Ministry of Finance. *Economic Report 2014/15*. Putrajaya: Ministry of Finance, 2015.

Ministry of Transport. "Logistics and Trade Facilitation Masterplan: 2015–2020". Putrajaya: Ministry of Transport, 2015. Available at <http://www.mot.gov.my/en/Penerbitan%20Rasmi/Executive%20Summary%20Logistics%20and%20Trade%20Facilitation%20Masterplan.pdf> (accessed 18 May 2016).

Organisation for Economic Co-operation and Development (OECD). *Implementing Good Regulatory Practice in Malaysia*. Paris: OECD, 2015.

PricewatershouseCoopers (PwC). "Transportation and Logistics 2030 Volume 3: Emerging Markets – New Hubs, New Spokes, New Industry Leaders?", n.d. Available at <http://www.pwc.com/gx/en/industries/transportation-logistics/tl2030/new-hubs_new-spokes_new-industry-leaders.html> (accessed 2 November 2016).

Rasiah, Rajah. "Is Malaysia Facing Negative Deindustrialization?". *Pacific Affairs* 84, no. 4 (2011): 715–36.

Tham Siew Yean. "The Remaining Barriers for the Liberalization of Trade in Services in ASEAN: Case of Malaysia". Final Research Report submitted to World Bank in 2007.

———. "The AEC and Domestic Challenges in Malaysia: Examining the Liberalization of Services in AFAS". In *Moving the AEC Beyond 2015: Managing Domestic Consensus for Community-Building*, edited by Tham Siew Yean and Sanchita Basu Das. Singapore: ISEAS – Yusof Ishak Institute, 2016.

Thangavelu, Shandre Mugan. "FDI Restrictiveness Index for ASEAN: Implementation of AEC Implementation Measures". ERIA Discussion Papers, ERIA-DP-2015-43. Jakarta: Economic Research Institute for ASEAN and East Asia, 2015.

Thangavelu, Shandre Mugan and Christopher Findlay. "The Impact of Free Trade Agreements on Foreign Direct Investment in the Asia-Pacific Region". In *ASEAN+1 FTAs and Global Value Chains in East Asia*, edited by Christopher Findlay. ERIA Research Project Report 2010–29. Jakarta: Economic Research Institute for ASEAN and East Asia, 2011, pp. 112–31.

The Star. "Malaysia to Become Preferred Gateway to Asia", 20 October 2016. Available at <http://annx.asianews.network/content/malaysia-become-preferred-gateway-asia-30850> (accessed 1 November 2016).

The Sun Daily. "Malaysian Logistics Council Makes a Comeback", 16 December 2013. Available at <http://www.thesundaily.my/news/906243> (accessed 18 May 2016).

UNCTADstat. "Investment", 2015. Available at <http://unctadstat.unctad.org> (accessed 4 September 2016).

United Nations Economic and Social Commission for Asia and the Pacific (UNESCAP). *Guide to Key Issues in Development of Logistics Policy*. Bangkok: UNESCAP, n.d. Available at <http://www.unescap.org/resources/guide-key-issues-development-logistics-policy> (accessed 18 May 2016).

————. "Towards an Enabling Environment for Paperless Trade". UNNExt Brief no. 18, February 2016. Bangkok: UNESCAP, 2016.

Verico, Kiki. "The Impact of Intra Regional Trade Agreement on FDI Inflows in Southeast Asia: Case of Indonesia, Malaysia and Thailand". MPRA Paper no. 42087, Munich University Library, 20 October 2012. Available at <http://mpra.ub.uni-muenchen.de/42087/> (accessed 1 November 2016).

World Bank. "Malaysia Economic Monitor: Leveraging Trade Agreements". Washington, D.C.: World Bank, 2016. Available at <http://documents. worldbank.org/curated/en/897661467211093280/pdf/106711-WP-P158456-PUBLIC.pdf> (accessed 1 November 2016).

World Trade Organization (WTO). *Trade Policy Review: Malaysia 2014*. Available at <https://www.wto.org/english/tratop_e/tpr_e/tp392_e.htm> (accessed 1 November 2016).

4

LOGISTICS SERVICES LIBERALIZATION IN THE PHILIPPINES

Gilberto M. Llanto[1]

INTRODUCTION

Services now account for a significant share of output and employment in the Philippines. It has become a major growth driver for the Philippine economy with rising growth rates in transportation, communication, storage, finance and IT-business process management. Together with a resurgent domestic manufacturing it is expected to continue to propel growth in the immediate term. The liberalization of the services sector will be important in order to bring in foreign direct investment (FDI) that will further strengthen its growth prospects. The logistics services comprise an important part of the service economy. This chapter examines the liberalization of the services sector, domestic regulatory reform and inflows of FDI to the logistics services. Liberalization is expected to lead to an infusion of capital, expertise, modern technology, and to expand market opportunities through FDI.

The chapter is structured as follows: after a brief introduction, Section 2 provides an overview of the services sector with a focus on maritime transport industry and freight forwarding services, which have the biggest share of the logistics industry. Data availability drives the discussion to these two components of the logistics sector. Section 3 reviews the policy measures for the development of the logistics services industry. The policy measures cover: (i) domestic policies and incentives, (ii) regulations, and (iii) unilateral, regional, as well as multilateral liberalization measures under ASEAN Framework Agreement on Services (AFAS) and General Agreement of Trade in Services (GATS). Section 4 discusses the overall enabling environment and inflows of FDI to the economy and, data permitting, the logistics sector. Section 5 identifies outstanding challenges and policy suggestions.

Gonzalez (2014) points out two aspects of the rise of services: first, because of improvements in information and communications technology (ICT), services have become more and more tradable, and second, domestically produced services serve as vital inputs to the production and trade of goods and services. Services are used and traded along with inputs into other economic activities, with both playing a key role in a country's competitiveness and participation in global value chains (GVCs) (Hollweg et al. 2014). The emerging picture shows a substantial share of services trade in global trade. ESCAP (2015) noted that despite the moderation in growth in the Asia Pacific, commercial services trade has increased substantially and more rapidly than merchandise trade. Even with the global slowdown, Asia-Pacific exports of services increased at a slightly faster rate at 5.1 per cent, compared with 4 per cent in the previous year. Import growth, at 6.1 per cent, was also slightly higher than in 2013. Presently, services trade is more than a fifth of global trade if measured in volumes, and 50 per cent of global trade if measured in value addition. Increasingly, a comparative advantage in tradable services will enable countries to export and also use them as a strategic driver of competitiveness in the global markets (Hollweg et al. 2014).

In today's global economy, services trade has assumed a lead role, given the changing nature of manufacturing production (Grossman and Rossi-Hansberg 2008). The profound transformations in manufacturing activities over the last few decades involve changes in structures, technologies, sectoral interlinkages and geographical boundaries. Manufacturing is framed as a system with complex interdependencies across a range of sectors that contribute a variety of components, materials, production systems and subsystems, producer services and product-related service systems (UNIDO 2013). Modern manufacturing uses a multitude of service providers such as telecom and travel service providers to connect workers in global production networks, logistics providers, and others, to produce their goods. Service-type activities like marketing and sales, and customer support form an integral part of what manufacturing companies do and provide (McKinsey Global Institute 2012).

In this regard, after years of negligible performance, manufacturing in the Philippines seems to be on a resurgent mode as policy reforms and improvements in governance in the last decade start to shape an environment conducive to investments and growth. The average growth rate of the manufacturing subsector from 2013 to 2015 is 8.1 per cent while the industry sector averaged at 6.3 per cent. Meanwhile, their average contribution to the Gross Domestic Product (GDP) during the same period was recorded at 22.7 and 33.2 per cent, respectively. A complementary thrust is the drive for more substantial investments in infrastructure, such as transport and logistics. However, continued growth whether in manufacturing, industry or services requires sustained investments, which implies lifting barriers to entry of FDI. This brings us to the main point of this chapter (and this volume): inflows of FDI in the services sector, particularly in logistics, would be necessary to continue and enhance a country's participation in regional and global value chains. This can happen with the right combination of liberalization measures, domestic policies, regulatory reform and sustained investments in physical and human capital. Liberalization is in the realm of first-order reforms that open up the markets to competition (Nye 2011) and that provide non-discriminatory treatment to any investor so that economies may be able to transition from limited-access to open-access societies (North, Wallis and Weingast 2009). However, it is equally critical to address regulatory restrictions that create barriers to entry and reduce efficiency and competition in the services sector. They will complement first-order efforts to create a competitive environment.

OVERVIEW OF THE SERVICES SECTOR

The services sector, in particular logistics services, provide the Philippines, an open archipelagic country, with an important link to the regional and global value chains. It fosters the connectivity with other countries, especially those of East Asia and ASEAN. Stronger external and inter-island connectivity will enable the economy to take advantage of trade, investment, and growth opportunities in this dynamic region, thereby fostering inclusive growth (Llanto 2016a). The logistics sector is at the cusp of transformation in the ASEAN region. The full implementation of the commitments in the AFAS and GATS will make ASEAN and the Philippines more competitive and innovative. Llanto and Navarro (2012) pointed out that the way forward involves continuing the market-oriented reforms in the Philippines, especially liberalization in trade in services.

For the past decades, the growth of the Philippine economy has been strongly anchored on the services sector, which has accounted for more than half of the GDP (see Figure 4.1). In 2015, it accounted for 57.3 per cent of the GDP, while the industry and agriculture sectors contributed 33.4 and 9.5 per cent, respectively. Its average growth in the past five years reached 6.3 per cent, which surpassed GDP growth at 5.9 per cent — an indication that, indeed, the services sector continues to be the main driver of the economy.

The sector's increasing share of value added in the economy may be attributed to the upward trend of the demand for services both as intermediate, final producer inputs and consumer services.

FIGURE 4.1

GDP Shares by Industry, 1998–2016

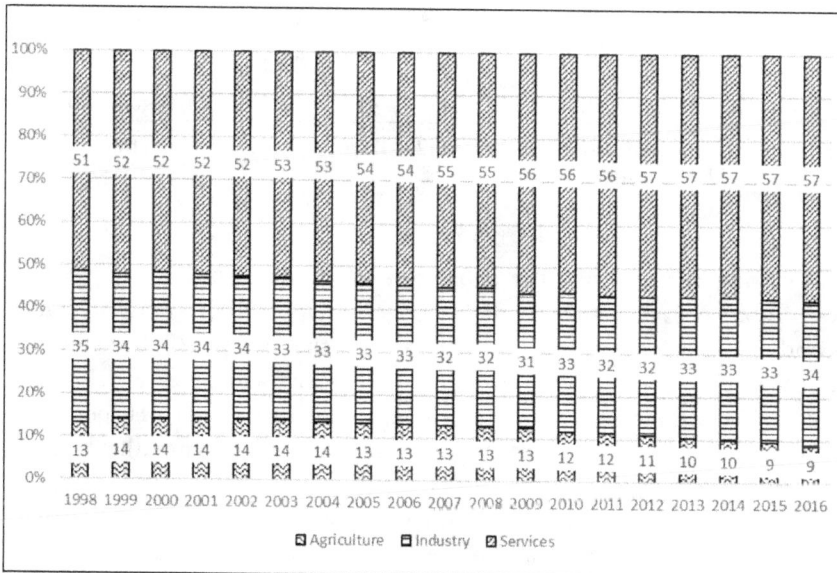

Source: Philippine Statistics Authority, *Philippine Statistical Yearbook* (various years).

Table 4.1 shows the average growth of value added and employment generated by the services sector in comparison to the other sectors including manufacturing under the industry sector. In terms of employment, it is apparent that in the 2000s, the services still dominate the jobs market in the Philippines with an average share of 50.2 per cent. However, in the period 2010 to 2014, the industry sector's growth rate surpassed that of services primarily because of the resurgence of the manufacturing sector, which is one of the government's current thrusts, and growth in other industry subsectors such as construction, and electricity, gas, and water (Serafica forthcoming).

TABLE 4.1
Value Added and Employment in the Philippines, 1980s to 2000s

	Value Added						Employment		
	Average Growth			Average Share			Average Share		
	80s	90s	20s	80s	90s	20s	80s	90s	20s
GDP	1.7	3	5.1	100	100	100	100	100	100
Agriculture	1.1	1.8	2.5	23.9	20.8	12.4	49.6	43.2	34.4
Industry	0.3	3	5.1	38	34.1	32.9	14.5	16	15.5
Manufacturing	0.9	2.5	4.9	26.3	24.3	23.2	9.9	10	11
Services	3.3	3.6	5.7	40.4	42.4	54.7	35.9	40.9	50.2

Source: Philippine Statistics Authority; Aldaba (2013); 2000s figures cover data from 2000 to 2015 (updated by the author).

Looking further into the subsectors of services, it can be gleaned from Table 4.2 that storage and services incidental to transport rank second in terms of annual growth rate in the period 2010 to 2014. Moreover, despite their relatively small gross value added (GVA) share to total services, their share in total services increased from 1.41 per cent in 2014 to 1.46 per cent in 2015. Retail trade contributes the highest share in terms of GVA at 23.23 per cent.

Moreover, transportation and storage sector accounted for 7 per cent of the total employment in the country, which is the second highest employer in the services sector next to wholesale and retail trade and repair of motor vehicles and motorcycles (see Table 4.3).

TABLE 4.2
Gross Value Added of the Services Sector

Industry	Growth per Annum 2010–14 (%)*	Share in Total Services, 2014 (%)	Share in Total Services, 2015 (%)
Real estate	12.29	5.09	4.81
Storage and services incidental to transport	**11.24**	**1.41**	**1.46**
Health and social work	8.9	2.86	2.92
Insurance	8.39	2.37	2.19
Renting of machinery & equipment and other business activities	8.33	10.28	8.61
Non-bank financial intermediation	7.29	4.45	4.11
Banking institutions	5.58	6.09	5.64
Activities auxiliary to financial intermediation	5.46	0.74	0.70
Recreational, cultural, and sporting activities	5.45	3.1	3.93
Water transport	5.42	0.34	0.40
Air transport	5.35	0.91	0.63
Land transport	5.34	3.54	2.88
Maintenance and repair of motor vehicles, motorcycles, personal and household goods	5.29	0.93	1.01
Sewage and refuse disposal sanitation and similar activities	5.09	0.07	0.07
Retail trade	4.85	24.13	23.23
Hotels and restaurants	4.82	2.94	3.12
Other service activities	4.6	0.96	0.91
Communication	3.35	4.61	8.05
Wholesale trade	3.04	5.91	5.11
Public administration	2.77	6.94	6.82
Education	1.84	6.27	7.02
Ownership of dwellings	1.46	6.06	6.38
Total services	4.97	100	100.00

Note: Using GVA at constant 2000 prices; data for 2015 was compiled by the author.
Source: Philippine Statistics Authority, available at <http://nap.psa.gov.ph/> (accessed 31 December 2015).

TABLE 4.3
Employment in the Services Sector, 2014

Industry	In thousands	Share of Total Employment (%)
Wholesale and retail trade; repair of motor vehicles and motorcycles	7,248	18.75
Transportation and storage	**2,686**	**6.95**
Accommodation and food service activities	1,694	4.38
Information and communication	352	0.91
Financial and insurance activities	491	1.27
Real estate activities	168	0.43
Professional, scientific and technical activities	209	0.54
Administrative and support service activities	1,085	2.81
Public administration and defense; compulsory social security	1,964	5.08
Education	1,254	3.24
Human health and social work activities	480	1.24
Arts, entertainment, and recreation	349	0.90
Other service activities	2,187	5.66
Total Services	20,167	52.18

Note: Based on ISIC Rev. 4 classification.
Source: ILOSTAT, available at <http://www.ilo.org/> (accessed 31 December 2015).

The transportation and storage subsector, which is an official classification under the 2009 Philippine Standard Industrial Classification (PSIC) Code, approximates the logistics sector since there is currently no specific sector classified as "logistics" in the statistics collection system. Table 4.4 provides a profile of the "logistics" sector, indicating that it is a key growth sector of the economy.

The 2013 ASPBI data showed a significant decline in the number of storage and warehousing, inland water transport establishments. There was a slight increase in the number of establishments in the sea and coastal water transport sector. It is noted that from 2010 to 2013, productivity, defined as sales per employee, in storage and warehousing rose from US$45,010 in 2010 to US$48,280; in the sea and coastal water transport from US$60,950 to US$69,330, and in inland water transport from US$13,090 in 2010 to US$36,580.

Overall, investments per establishment increased from 2010 to 2013 for all three logistics subsectors. The gross additions to fixed assets (GAFA)

TABLE 4.4

Annual Survey of Philippine Business and Industry: Transport, Storage and Communication (US$ thousand)

	2008	2009	2010	2013
Storage and Warehousing				
Number of Establishments	155	195	180	111
Total Employment	3,615	3,488	6,083	6,406
Sales	154,988.49	184,344.71	273,796.28	309,258.12
Sales/Employee	42.87	52.85	45.01	48.28
Cost	115,142.57	153,233.85	219,208.73	290,830.68
Sales/Cost	1.35	1.20	1.25	1.06
Gross Additions to Fixed Assets (GAFA)	8,472.72	6,553.52	2,720.77	44,849.83
GAFA/Establishment	54.66	33.61	126.23	404.05
Value Added	–	56,746.92	84,134.52	113,598.01
Sea and Coastal Water Transport				
Number of Establishments	105	139	147	153
Total Employment	12,286	14,266	17,630	15,505
Sales	926,294.53	858,744.04	1,074,579.70	1,074,908.94
Sales/Employee	75.39	60.20	60.95	69.33
Cost	678,966.75	661,141.36	788,129.01	882,954.19
Sales: Cost	1.36	1.30	1.36	1.22
Gross Additions to Fixed Assets (GAFA)	116,004.16	106,068.67	114,102.16	123,460.38
GAFA/Establishment	1,104.80	763.08	776.21	806.93
Value Added	–	294,534.35	429,053.02	416,424.18

TABLE 4.4 *(continued)*

	2008	2009	2010	2013
Inland Water Transport				
Number of Establishments	46	49	47	23
Total Employment	418	365	518	630
Sales	3,706.42	5,996.52	6,778.32	23,046.92
Sales/Employee	8.87	16.43	13.09	36.58
Cost	2,396.74	4,754.10	4,801.76	20,855.01
Sales: Cost	1.55	1.26	1.41	1.11
Gross Additions to Fixed Assets (GAFA)	1.03	–	82.11	311.43
GAFA/Establishment	0.02	–	1.75	13.54
Value Added	-	1,427.31	2,374.50	4,261.84

Note: The values were originally reported in Philippine peso. For the purposes of this study, they were converted into US dollars.
Source: Annual Survey of Philippine Business and Industry (ASPBI): Transport, Storage and Communication (various years), Philippine Statistics Authority.

per establishment in storage and warehousing tripled from US$126,230 to US$404,050 in 2010–13. Likewise, GAFA per establishment has also increased in sea and coastal water, and in inland transport. Value added had also increased to some extent in 2010–13 for storage and warehousing and inland water transport establishments. However, it is noticeable that the value added of the sea and coastal water transport has slightly declined to US$416.4 million in 2013 from US$429.1 million in 2010.

Meanwhile, it can also be seen from Table 4.4 that profitability, as measured by the sales to cost ratio, has decreased from 2010 to 2013 for all of the three subsectors. For storage and warehousing, the ratio went down by 15.2 per cent; for sea and coastal water transport, 10.3 per cent; and inland water transport by 21.3 per cent.

The major players in logistics services have maintained a bullish market forecast showing the dynamism of this sector. The 2015 Transport Intelligence Report (see Table 4.5) estimated that the market worth of

TABLE 4.5
Philippine Logistics Market Forecast

	2013 Market Size (US$ million)	Scenario	2020 Market Size (US$ million)	CAGR 2013–20 (%)
CONTRACT LOGISTICS	430	High	8,651	10.5
		Low	1,271	16.7
FREIGHT FORWARDING	377	High	1,011	15.1
		Low	690	9.0
Sea freight forwarding	168	High	540	18.1
		Low	347	10.9
Air freight forwarding	209	High	470	12.3
		Low	344	7.4
EXPRESS	802	High	3,317	22.5
		Low	1,944	13.5
International	133	High	458	19.2
		Low	287	11.5
Domestic	668	High	2,859	23.1
		Low	1,657	13.9
TOTAL	1,609	High	5,599	18.0
		Low	3,500	11.0

Note: CAGR – compound annual growth rate; the original figures in Euro were converted to US dollars. The 2016 average exchange rate that was used to convert the figures is US$0.9/EURO.
Source: Transport Intelligence (2015) as cited in the draft National Logistics Master Plan by the Department of Trade and Industry (2016).

the Philippine logistics business will range from around US$3.5 billion to US$5.6 billion by 2020. The Department of Trade and Industry's National Logistics Master Plan (NLMP) referring to the report noted that while the country's logistics market appears to be fragmented, it is supported nevertheless by strong cooperation between local service providers and integrated international logistics service providers.

Table 4.6 presents the results of the most recent survey conducted by the World Bank regarding the condition and obstacles faced by the Philippine logistics sector.[2] High levels of fees and charges, the poor quality of road and rail infrastructure, inefficiency of processes in customs especially those affecting exports, and problems with competent delivery of services are major challenges faced by the sector. However, survey respondents also observed some improvements in the logistics environment since 2013 such as customs and other official clearance procedures. The government has been working with the private sector, especially those located in the economic zones to address bottlenecks in logistics and regulatory processes.

TABLE 4.6
Domestic Logistics Performance Index,
Environment and Institutions, 2016

Level of Fees and Charges	Per Cent of Respondents Answering High/Very High
Port charges	100
Airport charges	83.33
Road transport rates	83.33
Rail transport rates	75
Warehousing/transloading charges	83.33
Agent fees	50
Quality of Infrastructure	**Per Cent of Respondents Answering Low/Very Low**
Ports	50.00
Airports	66.67
Roads	100
Rail	100
Warehousing/transloading facilities	66.67
Telecommunications and IT	66.67

TABLE 4.6   (*continued*)

Competence and Quality of Services	Per Cent of Respondents Answering High/Very High
Road	0
Rail	0
Air transport	20
Maritime transport	0
Warehousing/transloading and distribution	0
Freight forwarders	0
Customs agencies	0
Trade and transport associations	0
Consignees or shippers	0

Efficiency of Processes	Per Cent of Respondents Answering Often or Nearly Always
Clearance and delivery of imports	40
Clearance and delivery of exports	80
Transparency of customs clearance	40
Transparency of other border agencies	40
Provision of adequate and timely information on regulatory changes	40
Expedited customs clearance for traders with high compliance levels	40

Sources of Major Delays	Per Cent of Respondents Answering Often or Nearly Always
Compulsory warehousing/transloading	20
Pre-shipment inspection	0
Maritime trans-shipment	60
Criminal activities (e.g. stolen cargo)	40
Solicitation of informal payments	60

Changes in the Logistics Environment since 2013	Per Cent of Respondents Answering Improved or Much Improved
Customs clearance procedures	60
Other official clearance procedures	60
Trade and transport infrastructure	20
Telecommunications and IT infrastructure	40
Private logistics services	40
Regulations related to logistics	40
Solicitation of informal payments	20

TABLE 4.6 *(continued)*

Availability of Qualified Personnel	Per Cent of Respondents Indicating "Low" or "Very Low" Availability of Qualified Personnel for the Following Employee Groups in Their Country of Operation
Operative logistics staff	0
Administrative logistics staff	20
Logistics supervisors	20
Logistics managers	60

Soure: The World Bank, available at <http://lpi.worldbank.org/domestic/environment_institutions/2016/C/PHL>.

POLICY MEASURES FOR THE DEVELOPMENT OF LOGISTICS SERVICES

Policy measures for the development of the logistics services industry may be classified as follows: (i) domestic policies, (ii) regulatory reforms and (iii) unilateral liberalization measures and multilateral measures under GATS and AFAS. The first two measures address "behind-the-border" issues while the third lifts barriers to entry faced by foreign investors, and thus, creates a competitive environment and expands export opportunities.

Domestic Policies

A wave of policy reforms started in 1987 and has continued till the present time. These reforms covered water, power, telecommunications, domestic shipping, banking and finance, air transport, and retail trade. In the logistics sector, the deregulation of first and second class passage and freight rates in domestic shipping and the abolition of surcharges for insurance premiums took place. The air transport industry was deregulated accompanied by the elimination of restrictions on domestic routes and frequencies and control on rates and charges. In 2004, the Civil Aeronautics Board (now the Civil Aviation Authority of the Philippines) issued CAB Resolution no. 23 to deregulate the air charter industry. These reforms attracted major investments, mostly by domestic investors and service delivery improved to a great extent. However, those reform efforts were not sufficient to sustain investments in infrastructure in the absence of appropriate regulatory frameworks, a competitive environment, and a policy of non-discriminatory treatment of investors. Domestic reforms were neither deep nor comprehensive enough as exemplified by a "pocket open skies" policy for Clark and Subic through Executive Order no. 500 (series of 2007) instead of a total open skies policy. In the telecommunication sector, inefficient interconnection, low internet penetration, in fact the lowest in ASEAN, and the slowest interconnection speed in ASEAN are symptomatic of the lack of competition and ineffectual regulation. There is a need to combine domestic policy reforms with liberalization reforms that open the markets for competition and non-discriminatory treatment of foreign nationals who invest in the country.

The Philippine Development Plan 2011–16[3] tasked the Department of Trade and Industry with the development of a NLMP to guide the investments and development in the sector. The objective is to develop an integrated and seamless multi-model transport system and logistics that is critical for sustaining the economy's robust growth. The NLMP rests on four pillars: (i) major investments in expressways, international gateways (airports and ports), roads and bridges, (ii) enhancement of regulations and strengthening of regulatory capacities, (iii) upgrading institutional capacities, and (iv) formulation of appropriate policies for connectivity, resilience to climate change and countryside development. A High Level Inter-Agency Task Force on Logistics reporting to the President himself shall be created and led by the Department of Trade and Industry to oversee and coordinate the implementation of the NLMP. The NLMP is an important step to improve logistics performance of the Philippines, which in 2016 is ranked the 6th in ASEAN or the 71st out of 160 economies.

Another important reform being pursued by the Department of Transportation (DOTr) is the transfer of registration and accreditation processes for land, air, and maritime transport to a single bureau, which will be called the Bureau of Multimodal Transport and Logistics. This initiative, which has been included in the Philippine Multimodal Transportation and Logistics Industry Roadmap, was based on the ASEAN Framework Agreement on Multimodal Transport signed by the Department of Transportation and Communication (now called the Department of Transportation) in 2005.[4]

It is noted that some of the necessary logistics infrastructure are already in place such as the Subic and Batangas Port, Subic-Clark Tarlac Expressway, Southern Tagalog Arterial Road, Tarlac Pangasinan La Union Expressway. The main challenges to these infrastructure are the provision of proper maintenance and reforming regulatory frameworks to move them away from control toward a market-enhancing orientation.

For new infrastructure, the Public–Private Partnership (PPP) reports a number of huge transport and logistics projects in varying stages of completion, procurement, and contract signing (see Appendix 4.1). Through various reforms, the government was able to inject new life into the PPP programme. In the recent past, there seemed to be some wariness and distrust of both sides of the partnership because of problems with procurement through unsolicited bids and political intervention. The government's PPP Center[5] has recently announced the award of contracts with indicative project cost of around PHP189 billion (US$4.01 billion) to ten PPP projects covering expressways, modernization of public facilities, including airports and transport terminals (Llanto 2016a). There are more than forty more PPP projects in the pipeline in various stages of preparation for tendering, that is, procurement of transaction advisors, preparation of feasibility studies, finalization of project structure and review by the National Economic and Development Authority (NEDA) Investment Coordination Committee. With a substantial number of approved infrastructure projects in the pipeline, the government has increased the previous target infrastructure spending of 5 to 7 per cent of GDP over the term of the incumbent president. Infrastructure spending was estimated at around 2 per cent of GDP in 2014; it was at 1.24 per cent of GDP in 2006 (Llanto 2016a).

The provision of infrastructure, transport and logistics services basically falls under the responsibility of the Department of Transportation and the Department of Public Works and Highways. They are complemented by several government owned and controlled corporations such as the Light Rail Transport Authority, Philippine National Railways, and Philippine Ports Authority. The regulatory bodies, e.g., Toll Regulatory Board, Maritime Industry Authority, Civil Aviation Authority of the Philippines form part of the governance structure for transport and logistics. There is a need for policy coordination among these different governmental bodies for efficient logistics services provision. To address the issue of coordination, the government is proposing the creation of a government body on supply chain and logistics to coordinate and follow through on implementation and compliance to policies.[6]

Regulatory Reforms, 2010–16

The government has aimed at improving regulatory quality which is a significant factor in reducing the cost of doing business in the country (Llanto 2015; Llanto 2016*b*). The challenge faced by the Philippines is shown in Figure 4.2. An important development is the enactment of the Anti-Red Tape Act (Republic Act 9485) to promote transparency in government transactions by requiring each agency to simplify frontline service procedures, formulate service standards in every transaction, and make these standards known to the customer or client. Under this law, each government agency is enjoined to prominently display in its premises a Citizen's Charter that shows the specific services provided by the agency, and a step-by-step guide on how to avail of those services, and the standards on quality and timeliness to be expected from the agency (Llanto 2015, drawing on LGA–DILG 2008).

FIGURE 4.2

Regulatory Quality in ASEAN, 2008–13

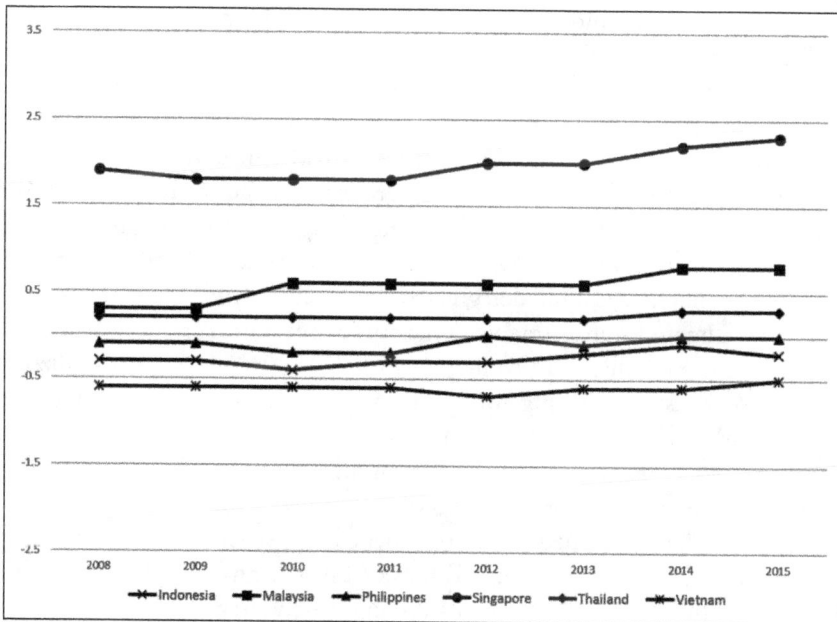

Source: World Bank's Worldwide Governance Indicators (WGI) project, available at <http://info.worldbank.org/governance/wgi/#home>.

The government likewise created a National Competitiveness Council (NCC) composed of government and private sector members that was tasked with monitoring and overseeing efforts to reduce the cost of doing business in the country. The NCC has recently inaugurated Project Repeal, basically patterned after the activities of Malaysia's PEMUDAH and National Policy on the Development and Implementation of Regulations, that will improve the Philippines' regulatory environment by revoking burdensome regulations.

Project Repeal will be implemented along side efforts to establish regulatory impact analysis (RIA) as a whole-of-government policy to improve the regulatory environment. Since 2012 the Philippines has been implementing three pilot RIA projects (Departments of Tourism and Labor and Employment, and the NEDA) with a view toward government-wide application.[7] The RIA pilot projects are implemented through a technical assistance programme of the Asian Development Bank called the Strengthening Institutions for an Improved Investment Climate with the Philippine Government.

Unilateral, AFAS and GATS Liberalization Measures

The Philippines has undertaken unilateral liberalization and deregulation of different sectors in the past decades. To foster investments in overseas shipping, Republic Act 7471 was enacted in 1992. It provides exemption from import duties and taxes imposed on importation of ocean going-vessels. Republic Act 9295 enacted in 2004 provides incentives to domestic shipping operators while Executive Order no. 170 (series of 2003) eliminated the payment of cargo handling charges and wharfage dues by users of roll-on roll-off (RORO) vessels. The Maritime Industry Authority has likewise liberalized and deregulated route entry and exit to foster a favourable climate for investments in maritime transport. A recently enacted law, the Foreign Ships Co-Loading Act of 2015 (RA 10668) liberalized shipping services by allowing foreign ships to transport cargo for import or export directly to and from any local port other than the Port of Manila. Serafica (forthcoming) notes that liberalization of services trade has been either in terms of cross-border supply or commercial presence. Executive Order 29 issued in 2011 opened up secondary gateways to international flights. In banking, RA 10641 was signed in 2014, which allowed the full entry of foreign banks in the country.

Liberalization in the services trade is to be undertaken under commitments to the GATS and AFAS. It is noted that there are other agreements where the Philippines committed to liberalize trade in services i.e., Philippines–Japan Economic Partnership Agreement, and various ASEAN agreements on services with dialogue partners such as China, Korea, Japan, India, Australia and New Zealand. The Interagency Committee on Trade in Services chaired by the NEDA coordinates the formulation of the country's position on services in bilateral, regional and multilateral trade agreements. Government agencies such as the Department of Trade and Industry and the Board of Investments make offers under the AFAS packages. The Philippines has already completed the ninth package of commitments and signed the Protocol to Implement the said package under the AFAS. The ninth package includes an offer to increase the foreign equity participation on repair of vessels to 70 per cent (threshold set for mode 3). The Protocol is now undergoing the ratification process.

The Philippines' transport and logistics commitments under AFAS are shown in Table 4.7. The offers under the GATS constitute the baseline of what the Department of Transportation and NEDA offered in AFAS 9, which covers 106 sectors and subsectors.

The maritime cargo freight services by foreign registered shipping companies, repair of vessels, vessel and salvage re-floating services provided in oceans and seas, domestic freight forwarding and international freight forwarding, routine cleaning and maintenance services limited to vehicle laundry and car-wash services, parking services, and others such as packaging, crating, are fully liberalized, which means that 100 per cent foreign equity participation in these subsectors is allowed. In contrast, those sectors or subsectors that are considered to be public utilities are limited by the Philippine Constitution to a maximum foreign equity participation of 40 per cent. The Philippine Constitution provides that "no franchise, certificate, or any form of authorization for the operation of a public utility shall be granted except to citizens of the Philippines or to corporations or associations organized under the laws of the Philippines, at least sixty per cent of whose capital is owned by such citizens" (Article XII, Section11, 1987 Philippine Constitution). Dee (2011) noted that in the maritime transport services, the foreign equity limit of 40 per cent and the monopolistic structure of public ports deter FDI inflows. There are current moves by the Congress and the Senate of the Philippines to amend the economic provisions of the Constitution that deter FDI inflows to certain sectors such as public utilities.[8]

A liberalized environment for FDI should be enhanced by reforms aimed at improving regulatory quality as discussed above in Project

TABLE 4.7
Philippine International Commitments on
Transportation and Logistics Services

Sector/Subsector	CPC Code	Current Regime	AFAS 9 Limitation on Market Access	AFAS 9 Limitation on National Treatment
A. Maritime Transport Services				
International transport (passenger and freight), except cabotage transport and government-owned cargoes		Max. 40 per cent FE allowed	M1: None M2: None M3: None	M1: None M2: None M3: None
Maritime cargo freight services by foreign registered shipping companies	7212**	100 per cent FE allowed	M1: None M2: None M3: None, except that up to 70% FE participation is allowed.	M1: None M2: None M3: None
Leasing/rental of vessels without crew	83103	Max. 40 per cent FE allowed	M1: None M2: None M3: Bareboat charter or lease contract subject to approval by the Maritime Industry Authority (MARINA)	M1: None M2: None M3: None
Maintenance of vessels		Max. 40 per cent FE allowed	M1: Unbound due to lack of technical feasibility. M2: Any repairs, conversion or dry docking of Philippine-owned or registered vessels are required to be done at domestic ship repair yards registered with the MARINA. M3: None	M1: Unbound due to lack of technical feasibility. M2: None M3: None

TABLE 4.7 (*continued*)

Sector/Subsector	CPC Code	Current Regime	AFAS 9 Limitation on Market Access	AFAS 9 Limitation on National Treatment
Repair of vessels		100 per cent FE allowed	M1: Unbound due to lack to technical feasibility. M2: Any repairs, conversion or dry docking of Philippine-owned or registered vessels are required to be done at domestic repair yards registered with the MARINA. M3: None except that up to 70 per cent FE participation is allowed.	M1: Unbound due to lack of technical feasibility. M2: None M3: None
Pushing and towing services	72140	Max. 40 per cent FE allowed	M1: Unbound due to lack of technical feasibility. M2: None M3: Up to 40 per cent FE participation is allowed	M1: Unbound due to lack of technical feasibility. M2: None M3: None
Supporting services for maritime transport Container yard and depot services	745**	Max. 40 per cent FE allowed	M1: Unbound due to lack of technical feasibility. M2: None M3: None	M1: Unbound due to lack of technical feasibility. M2: None M3: None
Port and waterway operation services	74510	Max. 40 per cent FE allowed	M1: Unbound due to lack of technical feasibility. M2: None M3: Up to 40 per cent FE participation is allowed.	M1: Unbound due to lack of technical feasibility. M2: None M3: None

TABLE 4.7 (*continued*)

Sector/Subsector	CPC Code	Current Regime	AFAS 9 Limitation on Market Access	AFAS 9 Limitation on National Treatment
Other supporting services for water transport	74590	Max. 40 per cent FE allowed	M1: Unbound due to lack of technical feasibility. M2: None M3: Up to 40 per cent FE participation is allowed.	M1: Unbound due to lack of technical feasibility. M2: None M3: None
Classification societies		Max. 40 per cent FE allowed	M1: None M2: None M3: Unbound, except up to 40 per cent FE allowed	M1: None M2: None M3: Unbound
Vessel and salvage re-floating services provided in oceans and seas	745**	100 per cent FE allowed	M1: None M2: None M3: Unbound, except up to 40 per cent FE is allowed	M1: None M2: None M3: Subject to issuance of permits and supervision by the Philippine Coast Guard for the salvage of vessels and marine salvage operation, respectively, within the maritime jurisdiction of the Philippines
Maritime agency services	7454	Max. 40 per cent FE allowed	M1: None M2: None M3: None	M1: None M2: None M3: None
B. Rail Transport Services				
Passenger transportation	7111	Max. 40 per cent FE allowed	M1: Unbound due to lack of technical feasibility. M2: None M3: Up to 40 per cent FE participation is allowed.	M1:Unbound due to lack of technical feasibility. M2: None M3: None

Sector/Subsector	CPC Code	Current Regime	AFAS 9 Limitation on Market Access	AFAS 9 Limitation on National Treatment
Freight transportation	7112	Max. 40 per cent FE allowed	M1: Unbound due to lack of technical feasibility. M2: None M3: Up to 40 per cent FE participation is allowed.	M1: Unbound due to lack of technical feasibility. M2: None M3: None
Maintenance and repair of rail transport equipment	8868**	Max. 40 per cent FE allowed	M1: Unbound due to lack of technical feasibility. M2: None M3: None	M1: Unbound due to lack of technical feasibility. M2: None M3: None
Supporting services for rail transport services	743	Max. 40 per cent FE allowed	M1: Unbound due to lack of technical feasibility. M2: None M3: Up to 40 per cent FE participation is allowed.	M1: Unbound due to lack of technical feasibility. M2: None M3: None
C. Road Transport Services				
Passenger transportation (CPC 7121 + CPC 7122) Freight transportation (CPC 7123) Rental of commercial vehicles with operator (CPC 7124)	7124	Max. 40 per cent FE allowed	M1: Unbound due to lack of technical feasibility. M2: None M3: Up to 40 per cent FE is allowed.	M1: Unbound due to lack of technical feasibility. M2: None M3: None

TABLE 4.7 (*continued*)

Sector/Subsector	CPC Code	Current Regime	AFAS 9 Limitation on Market Access	AFAS 9 Limitation on National Treatment
Maintenance and repair of road transport equipment	8867	Max. 40 per cent FE allowed	M1: Unbound due to lack of technical feasibility. M2: None M3: None	M1: Unbound due to lack of technical feasibility. M2: None M3: None
Routine cleaning and maintenance services limited to vehicle laundry and car-wash services	6112**	100 per cent FE allowed	M1: Unbound due to lack of technical feasibility. M2: None M3: Up to 70 per cent FE participation is allowed.	M1:Unbound due to lack of technical feasibility. M2: None M3: None
Supporting services for road transport services Parking services	7443	100 per cent FE for parking service is allowed	M1: Unbound due to lack of technical feasibility. M2: None M3: Up to 70 per cent FE participation is allowed.	M1: Unbound due to lack of technical feasibility. M2: None M3: None
Pipeline transport	713	Max. 40 per cent FE allowed	M1: Unbound due to lack of technical feasibility. M2: None M3: Up to 40 per cent FE participation is allowed.	M1: Unbound due to lack of technical feasibility. M2: None M3: None

Sector/Subsector	CPC Code	Current Regime	AFAS 9 Limitation on Market Access	AFAS 9 Limitation on National Treatment
D. Services Auxiliary to All Modes of Transport				
Cargo-handling services	741	100 per cent FE is allowed if located in a free port like Subic Free Port; those outside are limited to 40 per cent under existing regime	M1: Unbound due to lack of technical feasibility. M2: None M3: None	M1: Unbound due to lack of technical feasibility. M2: None M3: None
Cargo handling services at the Subic Bay Freeport Zone	741**	100 per cent FE is allowed if located in a free port like Subic Free Port; those outside are limited to 40 per cent FE	M1: Unbound due to lack of technical feasibility. M2: None M3: None, except up to 70 per cent FE participation is allowed.	M1: Unbound due to lack of technical feasibility. M2: None M3: None
Storage and warehouse services	742	Max. 40 per cent FE allowed	M1: Unbound due to lack of technical feasibility. M2: None M3: None	M1: Unbound due to lack of technical feasibility. M2: None M3: None
Storage and warehouse services at the Subic Bay Freeport Zone	742**	100 per cent FE is allowed if located in a free port like Subic Free Port; those outside are limited to 40 per cent	M1: Unbound due to lack of technical feasibility. M2: None M3: None, except up to 70 per cent FE participation is allowed.	M1: Unbound due to lack of technical feasibility. M2: None M3: None

TABLE 4.7 (*continued*)

Sector/Subsector	CPC Code	Current Regime	AFAS 9 Limitation on Market Access	AFAS 9 Limitation on National Treatment
Freight forwarding services		Max. 40 per cent FE allowed; air sector has pending case with the Supreme Court allowing 100 per cent FE to a certain company.	M1: None M2: None M3: None	M1: None M2: None M3: None
Freight transport agency services International freight forwarding by sea	74800**	100 per cent FE is allowed subject to certain conditions	M1: None M2: None M3: Up to 100 per cent FE is allowed, provided that paid-in equity capital is not less than $200,000. Otherwise, maximum FE participation is 40 per cent.	M1: None M2: None M3: None
Domestic freight forwarding by sea		Max. 40 per cent FE is allowed	M1: None M2: None M3: Up to 40 per cent FE participation is allowed.	M1: None M2: None M3: None
Others; Packaging and crating and unpackaging and de-crating services	749**	100 per cent FE is allowed	M1: None M2: None M3: Up to 70 per cent FE equity participation is allowed.	M1: None M2: None M3: None

Notes:
1. Modes: M1 – Cross-border supply; M2 – Consumption abroad; M3 – Commercial presence; M4 – Presence of natural persons; M4 is no longer covered in the most recent AFAS; it is already under the ASEAN Movement of Natural Persons Agreement.
2. Definitions: Market Access – In terms of access to the market of a country, services and services suppliers of any other countries must be accorded the same treatment specified in its schedule of commitments; National Treatment – Services and services suppliers of a country must be permitted access to the market of another country on the same terms as those accorded to domestic services or services provider.
3. This rule applies to all transport services subsectors included in the schedule under Mode 3: no franchise, certificate, or any other form of authorization for the operation of a public utility shall be granted except to citizens of the Philippines or to corporations or associations organized under the Laws of the Philippines at least 60 per cent of whose capital is owned by such citizens. Limitations listed in the horizontal section shall also apply.[9]
4. FE = allowed foreign equity participation
5. Double asterisks on the CPC indicates that the corresponding service subsector in this schedule only covers a part or parts of the service subsector classified under the given CPC code number.

Source: International Cooperation Desk (ICD) under the DOTC, as of 21 June 2016. Validated by Trade, Services and Industry Staff under the National Economic and Development Authority (NEDA).

Repeal. Domestic regulations leaning toward protection of certain sectors or investors can thwart efforts to attract FDI inflows. There is a case for reviewing domestic regulations in order to harmonize them with market openness brought about by liberalization measures. For example, under mode 3 supply of services, to lease or rent vessels without crew, the bareboat charter or lease contract is subject to approval by the Maritime Industry Authority; for passenger transportation, provisional authority or a certificate of public conveyance must be secured from the Land Transportation Franchising and Regulatory Board, and new entrants are subject to economic needs test to protect investments of transport operators in so-called "unserved areas".

FDI inflows into the logistics services depend on a number of factors and a competitive environment certainly provides a good incentive for both domestic and foreign investors. Producing a competitive environment for the logistics sector will certainly involve the following: (i) the quality of investments in the sector, e.g., hard infrastructure already present or yet to be actually constructed, (ii) market-enhancing domestic policies and regulations, and (iii) elimination of entry barriers and foreign equity restrictions.

FDI AND LOGISTICS SERVICES

Like in other countries as reported in this volume, the available evidence and data on the impact of liberalization of services on FDI inflows are rather thin. Most of the approved FDI reported in the Board of Investments are in the manufacturing sector and are mostly confined to the economic zones. There are a few FDI in transportation and logistics, which may be partly explained by the constitutional barrier to such investments as explained above.

A joint venture with a domestic company, the formation of subsidiaries, branches or representative offices, and equity investments are the usual channels used to penetrate the domestic logistics market. Table 4.8 shows investments made in the transport and logistics sector in 2015. Air transport services, tollway operation and maintenance, water transport, expressways, airport, seaport and container yard are the preferred areas for investments. Four of eighteen projects reported in Table 4.8 are FDI, namely: Metro Manila Skyway Stage 3 Project, PPP Project for Mactan Cebu International Airport Phase 1, Manila International Container Terminal Project Berth 7, and Petron's Pandacan Terminal Relocation Project. The rest are investments by 100 per cent Filipino-owned companies.

TABLE 4.8
Private Investments in the Transport and Logistics Sector, 2015

Type of Product	Amount of Investment (US$ million)
New Operator of Cold Storage Facilities	7.28
New Domestic Shipping Operator/Oil Tanker (MT Jamie Faith)	6.0
New Domestic Shipping Operation (Fast Cat M11) and Operator Water Transport (Fast Cat M9)	16.5
New Domestic Shipping Operator (Fast Cat M10)	8.25
New Domestic Shipping Operator Water Transport	16.5
New Operators of various Air Transport Services	268.07
New Operator of Cold Storage and Blast Freezing Facilities	6.59
New Operator of Cold Storage Facilities	0.55
New Operator of Cold Storage and Blast Freezing Facilities	7.35
New Domestic/Inter-Island Shipping Operator (One Container Cargo Vessel)	3.28
Expanding Provider of Logistic Services to Exporters (Bulk Handling and Cold Storage Facilities)	1.84
New Domestic Shipping Operator Water Transport (One Oil Tanker –MT Chelsea Denise II)	9.89
New Domestic Shipping Operator/Inter Island Shipping Activity	8.89
PPP Project under the Preferred Activities – Infrastructure Project (NAIA EXPRESSWAY Phase 2 Project pursuant to the Build-Transfer-Operate Arrangement under the Concession Agreement with DPWH)	515.0
New Operator of Tollways (Metro Manila Skyway Stage 3 Project) *75% Filipino; 25% FDI*	648.42
PPP Project for Mactan Cebu International Airport Project (Phase I Manitenance and Renovation of Terminal 1) *60% FDI; 40% Filipino*	139.02
Expanding Operator of Seaport and Container Yard (Manila International Container Terminal Project Berth 7) *62% Filipino; 32% FDI; remaining 6% mixed*	116.56
Relocation of Oil Terminal under Infrastructure – Logistics (Petron's Pandacan Terminal Relocation Project) *97% Filipino; 3% FDI*	86
Total	**1,865.99**

Note: Foreign exchange rate used PHP45.503/USD (2015 average FOREX).
Source: Department of Trade and Industry – Board of Investments.

OUTSTANDING CHALLENGES AND
POLICY SUGGESTIONS

Outstanding Challenges

Logistics services perform a critical role and function in regional and global value chains and the Philippines stand to gain if it can successfully attract FDI that will bring in capital, technology, innovations, and management expertise to improve the logistics sector. Liberalization and deregulation efforts undertaken by the country since the end of martial rule in the late 1980s have been contributing factors in sustaining the economy's growth momentum. Domestic policy and regulatory reforms have likewise been instrumental in improving economic performance.

The main outstanding challenge to policymakers is to intensify and make more comprehensive the reform effort in the logistics sector. There is a need to pursue full liberalization of the sector and going by the previous experiences with liberalization in other sectors, piece-meal liberalization would not be enough to attract FDI. Half-hearted liberalization will work against the better interest of the country. This will consist of implementing the commitments in GATS and AFAS to ensure a competitive environment and non-discriminatory treatment of any investor. For the Philippines, this has three dimensions: (i) removing constitutional and legal restrictions to FDI inflows; (ii) complementing liberalization with the establishment of market-enhancing domestic policies and regulations and resisting attempts to introduce or maintain protectionist domestic policies; and (iii) making significant investments in hard infrastructure, with emphasis on transport and logistics.

Policy Recommendations

Removing Constitutional and Legal Restrictions to FDI

A major barrier to entry of FDI in the logistics sector is the Constitutional provision limiting foreign equity participation to 40 per cent in sectors that are considered public utilities. A positive signal is coming from the present Congress and Senate about amending the 1987 Constitution to remove the provisions that restrict foreign investments.

A companion effort is the proposed amendment of the Public Service Act (Commonwealth Act no. 146). This is a good strategic move by Philippine lawmakers because amending the 1987 Constitution will be a tedious process. The proposed amendments to the Public Service Act want to clarify the ambiguity between the understanding of "public service" and "public utility". It will have to define clearly what public utilities are and remove some industries from the list of public utilities. A precedent to this legislative move is the removal of power generation from the public utilities definition through the enactment of the Electric Power Industry Reform Act of 2001. If passed into law, the amendments to the Public Service Act will remove certain industries performing a public service, e.g., transportation and logistics, from the list of public utilities, which in effect will address the constitutional restriction on foreign equity participation. Transportation and logistics will be classified as a regulated public service that will be open both to domestic and foreign investors. This legislative initiative has to be supported by stakeholders of the sector.

Aligning Domestic Policies with Liberalization Commitments

Liberalization of services trade has to be complemented by reforms in domestic ("behind-the-border") policies and regulations, and investments in hard logistics infrastructure in order to have a wholistic competitive environment for investors, domestic and foreign alike. The recent enactment of the Philippine Competition Act (Republic Act 10667), which recognizes the efficiency of market competition for allocating goods and services, and the Foreign Ships Co-Loading Act of 2015 (Republic Act 10668), which seeks to improve shipping services are steps in the right direction. There is a need to sustain congressional efforts such as this.

A low hanging fruit that can yield immediate results in terms of improving the investment climate and reducing the cost of doing business in the country is Project Repeal, an initiative of the NCC and the Department of Trade and Industry to identify, amend or repeal regulations in order to reduce the cost of doing business in the country. The NCC has recently announced the initial repeal of 1,900 issuances in eight government agencies. The NCC has formed a technical working group to review and identify regulations for repeal or amendment (Pillas 2016). The government should adopt RIA as a whole-of-government policy together with the requirement to government agencies, including local government units, to conduct a RIA as a default whenever new regulations are being proposed.

The NLMP will provide a practical platform for developing the logistics sector. The government also calls it an "action document" because it will identify the specific logistics investments that government should undertake and the key strategies and specific policies required of government to attain the Plan's goal of a seamless, efficient transport and logistics system for the country. A critical issue here is the funding required for the government's ambitious spending plan for the logistics sector. The government should give it an adequate, multi-year budgetary appropriation. It should also work with the private sector in monitoring and conducting an independent review of NLMP implementation to ensure compliance with government commitments to improve the transport and logistics sector.

The government should also designate the Department of Transportation as the national competent body for multimodal transport, which will take care of policy coordination of various transport agencies, among others, to implement its commitment to the ASEAN Framework Agreement on Multimodal Transport. It is noted that a draft Executive Order in this respect is currently under review by the Department of Transportation's legal unit. Following this, the Department of Transportation should establish the proposed Bureau of Multimodal Transport and Logistics, which will take responsibility for the registration and accreditation procedures currently undertaken by the Department of Trade and Industry for sea freight, the Civil Aeronautics Board for air freight, and by the Land Transportation and Franchising Regulatory Board for trucks.

Complementary Investment in Infrastructure

There is a critical need for increased investments in modern airports, seaports and the RORO maritime transport system, which connect the different islands of the archipelago and likewise, the southern part of the country (Mindanao) to Indonesia, Brunei and Malaysia (Sabah). The Philippines currently enjoys ample fiscal space for additional spending in infrastructure, social protection and other public goods but this has to be shored up, given the big ticket items in the spending envelope.

The government announced plans to increase infrastructure spending, which includes investments in transport and logistics infrastructure, to 5 to 7 per cent of GDP under the present administration. It should exploit the fiscal space to improve the logistics infrastructure but at the same time, the government has to increase its tax effort through reforms in tax administration and tax policy. It has submitted to Congress a tax reform package to create additional substantial fiscal space. There is a need for government to work on public and congressional support for its tax reform proposal.

Aside from tax-financed provision of infrastructure, the country should continue to tap PPP arrangements that have successfully attracted private investments in power and water for investments in transport and logistics.

CONCLUSION

Logistics services is a key growth driver of the Philippine economy and occupies a prominent place in the country's development agenda. Recent economic performance shows the efficacy of pursuing domestic policy and regulatory reforms and liberalization. They have been instrumental in the creation of an environment that is conducive to investments, growth and employment. The private sector has responded positively to reforms and liberalization in logistics services and policymakers have to continue with efforts to remove barriers to entry of FDI, which can bring much needed capital, management and technical expertise and wider market reach.

A major barrier to entry that has deterred foreign investors from making significant investments is the constitutional provision limiting foreign equity participation to 40 per cent in subsectors of the logistics sector that are classified as public utility. It is noted that there are current moves to amend the 1987 Constitution. This is the ideal solution but it may face an uphill battle given the complexity attending any constitutional amendment. The situation is not irremediable. Lawmakers have filed legislative bills seeking to amend the Public Service Act that governs the operation of public utilities. Stakeholders and the general public should support passage of the proposed bills amending the Public Service Act. At the same time such efforts as domestic policy reforms, reducing the cost of doing business, tapping PPPs, and providing multi-year funding support to critical infrastructure to remove other legal barriers to FDI should be continued.

At the regional level, the importance of an efficient maritime connectivity in the ASEAN's economic development cannot be ignored. In October 2010, ASEAN leaders adopted the Master Plan on ASEAN Connectivity that included RORO as a flagship project. Development of a RORO maritime transport system should be given more serious attention by the ASEAN leaders and private sector. The different ASEAN member states

(AMSs) have different maritime policies. Trace, Frielink and Hew (2009, p. 21) pointed to Indonesia's regulation PP17 (1988), which

> reserves coastal trades for Indonesian flag vessels, provides operating subsidies for vessels used on selected inter-island routes, and requires that crews be Indonesian citizens. Malaysia's Cabotage Act (1980) requires all vessels employed in coastal trades, including vessels trading between Peninsular Malaysia and East Malaysia, to be licensed by the Domestic Shipping Licensing Board.

As noted above, the Philippines has amended its decades-old cabotage law through the Foreign Ships Co-Loading Act of 2015 (RA 10668). A review of the AMSs coastal shipping policies for seamless operation across the region is in order. The harmonization of those policies will lead to better marine connectivity and more significant trade in goods and services among the AMSs.

Another important area for regional action is the establishment of the ASEAN Single Window (ASW). The respective national single windows are in varying states of development and preparedness to link to the planned ASW. AMS should take the establishment of the ASW much more seriously than in the past by modernizing their bureaus or entities in charge of customs, harmonizing customs and trade procedures, and facilitating the exchange of cross-border information.

APPENDIX 4.1
List of Public–Private Partnership (PPP) Projects, National

	Current Status	Project Cost (US$ billion)	Agency
East–West Rail Project	Upcoming project	TBD	**Project Name**
Integrated Transport System–North Terminal Project	Projects with on-going studies	0.09	DOTr
Road Transport Information Technology (IT) Infrastructure Project	Projects under Procurement	0.01	DOTr & LTFRB
LRT Line 6 Project	Projects under Procurement	1.38	DOTr
Davao Sasa Port Modernization Project	Projects under Procurement	0.40	DOTr
Bacolod Airport Operations, Maintenance & Development Project	Projects under Procurement	0.43	DOTr & CAAP
Operation and Maintenance of LRT Line 2	Projects under Procurement	No CAPEX	DOTr & LRTA
Davao Airport Operations, Maintenance & Development Project	Projects under Procurement	0.86	DOTr & CAAP
New Bohol (Panglao) Airport Operations, Maintenance & Development Project	Projects under Procurement	0.10	DOTr & CAAP
Iloilo Airport Operations, Maintenance & Development Project	Projects under Procurement	0.65	DOTr & CAAP
Laguindingan Airport Operations, Maintenance & Development Project	Projects under Procurement	0.31	DOTr & CAAP
Manila Bay Integrated Flood Control, Coastal Defense and Expressway Project	Projects under Evaluation	106.88	DPWH
Central Spine Roll-on/Roll-off (RoRo)	Projects under Conceptualization/ Development	TBD	DOTr
R-1 R-10 Link Mass Transport System Development Project	Projects under Conceptualization/ Development	TBD	DOTr
Motor Vehicle Inspection System	Projects under Conceptualization/ Development	TBD	DOTr
LRT Line 4 Project	Projects under Conceptualization/ Development	TBD	DOTr

APPENDIX 4.1 (*continued*)

	Current Status	Project Cost (US$ billion)	Agency
Manila–East Rail Transport System Project	Projects under Conceptualization/ Development	TBD	DOTr
North–South Railway Project (South Line)	For Approval of Relevant Government Bodies; For NEDA Board Approval	4.54	DOTr
LRT Line 1 Cavite Extension and Operation & Maintenance	Awarded Projects under Pre-Construction	1.38	DOTr
South Integrated Transport System Project	Awarded Projects under Pre-Construction	0.11	DOTr
MRT Line 7	Awarded Projects under Pre-Construction	1.47	DOTr
Mactan–Cebu International Airport Passenger Terminal Building	Awarded Projects under Construction	0.37	DOTr
Southwest Integrated Transport System (ITS) Project	Awarded Projects under Construction	0.05	DOTr
Automatic Fare Collection System	Awarded, Completed and Operational Projects	0.04	DOTr
NAIA PPP Project	Approved Projects for Procurement	1.58	DOTr & MIAA

Notes: CAAP – Civil Aviation Authority of the Philippines
DOTr – Department of Transportation
DPWH – Department of Public Works and Highways
LRTA – Light Rail Transit Authority
LTFRB – Land Transportation Franchising and Regulatory Board
MIAA   – Manila International Airport Authority
PNR – Philippine National Railways
CAPEX – capital expenditure
TBD – to be determined
Foreign Exchange used: PHP47.1/USD

Source: Public-Private Partnership Center, Projects Database, available at <http://ppp.gov.ph/?page_id=26068> (accessed 9 November 2016).

Notes

1. The author thanks Ma. Kristina Ortiz and Christine Ma. Grace Salinas for research assistance, and Tham Siew Yean, Sanchita Basu Das, Amelia Menardo, and Ramonette Serafica for helpful comments.
2. The Domestic Logistics Performance Index is part of larger survey (i.e. Logistics Performance Index) which is conducted by the World Bank starting 2012. The LPI also comprises the International LPI. It is a benchmarking tool that is used to assess the performance of the logistics supply chain in different countries. This online survey was conducted in two phases (i.e. October–December 2015 and in March–April 2016) using the Uniform Sampling Randomized approach. Respondents are represented by operators from various logistics firms and are asked about the qualitative and quantitative aspects of the logistics environment of each country in which they operate.
3. The government is currently preparing the successor plan for the period 2017–21.
4. Drafting the Philippine Multimodal Transportation and Logistics Industry Roadmap, which is yet to be finalized, is an initiative led by the private sector, including the Philippine International Seafreight Forwarders Association (PISFA). The Department of Transportation and Communication (DOTC) was reorganized into the Department of Transportation.
5. The PPPC reports in its website various local and international awards that it has received since the launching of the PPP Program in 2010. Available at <http://ppp.gov.ph/?page_id=29286>.
6. <http://www.gov.ph/2016/02/29/dti-transportation-logistics-services/>.
7. <http://www.gov.ph/2012/07/30/dot-dole-and-dof-to-strengthen-government-efficiency/>. Malaysia has a formal regulatory management system, a mechanism to filter unnecessary regulations proposed or implemented by government bodies. Llanto (2016b) describes the Philippines regulatory management system. See Gill and Ponciano Intal (2016).
8. There are current discussions on calling for a constitutional convention to amend the Constitution.
9. The horizontal section stipulates that limitations shall apply to all of the sectors included in the schedule; often referring to a particular mode, notably commercial presence and presence of natural persons.

References

Aldaba, Rafaelita. "Philippine New Industrial Policy". Presentation, Philippine House of Representatives, 16 October 2013.

Dee, Philippa. "Services Liberalization Towards an ASEAN Economic Community". In *Toward a Competitive ASEAN Single Market: Sectoral Analysis*, edited by

Shujiro Urata and Misa Okabe. Jakarta: Economic Research Institute for ASEAN and East Asia, 2011, pp. 17–136.

Department of Trade and Industry. National Logistics Master Plan (Draft). Makati City: Department of Trade and Industry, Philippines, 2016.

Economic and Social Commission for Asia and the Pacific (ESCAP). *Asia-Pacific Trade and Investment Report 2015: Supporting Participation in Value Chains*. Bangkok: ESCAP, 2015.

Gill, Derek and Ponciano Intal, Jr., eds. *The Development of Regulatory Management Systems in East Asia: Country Study*. Jakarta: Economic Research Institute for ASEAN and East Asia, 2016.

Gonzalez, Anabel. "Preface". In *Valuing Services in Trade: A Toolkit for Competitiveness Diagnostics*, by Claire H. Hollweg, Erik Leendert Van Der Marel, Juan Sebastian Saez, Daria Taglioni, and Veronika Zavacka. Washington, D.C.: World Bank, 2014.

Grossman, Gene M. and Esteban Rossi-Hansberg. "Trading Tasks: A Simple Theory of Offshoring". *American Economic Review* 98, no. 5 (2008): 1978–97.

Hollweg, Claire H., Erik Leendert Van Der Marel, Juan Sebastian Saez, Daria Taglioni, and Veronika Zavacka. *Valuing Services in Trade: A Toolkit for Competitiveness Diagnostics*. Washington, D.C.: World Bank, 2014.

Llanto, Gilberto M. "Reduce Regulatory Burden, Improve Regulatory Quality". In *PIDS 2014 Economic Policy Monitor: Effective Regulations for Sustainable Growth*. Quezon City: Philippine Institute for Development Studies, 2015, pp. 44–70.

———. "Philippine Infrastructure and Connectivity: Challenges and Reforms". *Asian Economic Policy Review* 11, no. 2 (2016a): 243–61.

———. "Regulatory Coherence: The Case of the Philippines". In *The Development of Regulatory Management Systems in East Asia: Country Study*, edited by Derek Gill and Ponciano Intal, Jr. Jakarta: Economic Research Institute for ASEAN and East Asia (ERIA), 2016b, pp. 231–93.

Llanto, Gilberto M. and Adoracion M. Navarro. "The Impact of Trade Liberalization and Economic Integration on the Logistics Industry: Maritime Transport and Freight Forwarders". *Philippine Journal of Development* 36, nos. 1–2 (2012): 95–117.

Local Government Academy–Department of the Interior and Local Government (LGA–DILG). *Primer on RA 9485: The Anti-Red Tape*. Manila: LGA–DILG, 2008.

McKinsey Global Institute. "Manufacturing the Future: The Next Era of Global Growth and Innovation". Seoul: McKinsey and Company, 2012.

North, Douglas C., John Joseph Wallis and Barry R. Weingast. *Violence and Social Orders: A Conceptual Framework for Interpreting Recorded Human History*. New York: Cambridge University Press, 2009.

Nye, John. "Taking Institutions Seriously: Rethinking the Political Economy of Development in the Philippines". *Asian Development Review* 28, no. 1 (2011): 1–21.

Philippine Statistics Authority. "Census of Philippine Business Industries". Quezon City: Philippine Statistics Authority, 2012.

Pillas, Catherine. "NCC Rolls Out 'Project Repeal' to Cut Red Tape in Several Government Agencies", 13 June 2016. Available at <http://www.investphilippines.info/arangkada/ncc-rolls-out-project-repeal-to-cut-red-tape-in-several-government-agencies/> (accessed 28 February 2016).

Serafica, Ramonette B. "Sustaining the Competitiveness of Philippine Services". *Philippine Journal of Development.* (Forthcoming).

Trace, Keith, Barend Frielink and Denis Hew. "Maritime Connectivity in Archipelagic Southeast Asia: An Overview". Southeast Asia Working Paper Series no. 1. Manila: Asian Development Bank, 2009.

Transport Intelligence. "Philippines Transport & Logistics 2015". The United Kingdom: Transport Intelligence, 2015.

United Nations Industrial Development Organization (UNIDO). "Emerging Trends in Global Manufacturing Industries". Vienna: UNIDO, 2013.

5

SERVICES SECTOR LIBERALIZATION IN SINGAPORE: CASE OF THE LOGISTICS SECTOR

Sanchita Basu Das and Evelyn Peiqi Ooi Widjaja

INTRODUCTION

Singapore's economy has been growing at a tepid pace since 2012 due to a modest performance of the US economy, uncertainties surrounding the European Union (EU), weak growth in the East Asian region, particularly with China's structural economic slowdown and, a general slowdown in global trade. During 2011–16, Singapore's real Gross Domestic Product (GDP) grew at an average rate of 3.8 per cent per annum, compared to an average of 7.3 per cent during 2002–7 (Singapore Department of Statistics 2017*a*). The lackluster output is matched by an unemployment rate of around 2 per cent during 2011–16 (Singapore Department of Statistics 2017*b*). It has been estimated that the economy will grow at a rate of 1–3 per cent in 2016 (Ministry of Trade and Industry Singapore 2017).

It is during this time of restrained economic outlook that Singapore is also undergoing a structural adjustment. In 2010, the city-state embarked on a ten-year programme to boost its productivity growth to 2 to 3 per cent per annum, from around 1 per cent during the 2000s

(Economic Strategies Committee 2010). The target was to be achieved by curbing the growth of low-skilled foreign labour supply, encouraging capital deepening and increasing automation. Programmes were put in place to help the local workforce to develop new skills according to new growth areas. While the manufacturing sector had undergone restructuring several times in past decades, it was the first time the entire economy was subject to such a process. Since then, this strive for transformation has been a challenge for domestic-oriented businesses, particularly those in the services sector, which are trying hard to lower their dependence on foreign labour and re-position themselves by investing in technology and talent (Menon 2015).

A further policy boost came in February 2017, when Singapore released the Committee on the Future Economy (CFE) Report that laid down seven strategies to secure the city-state's economic success over the longer term. These seven strategies are: (a) deepen and diversify international connection through trade and investment cooperation; (b) acquire and utilize deep skills; (c) strengthen enterprise capabilities to innovate and scale up; (d) build strong digital capabilities; (e) develop a vibrant and connected city of opportunity; (f) develop and implement industry transformation maps; and (g) partner each other to enable growth and innovation.

Singapore made a strategic shift to the services sector in the mid-1980s. The city-state decided to move beyond manufacturing activities by shifting to the services sector, especially in businesses and financial services, as it felt constrained by the lack of natural resources and the small land size and population (Ministry of Trade and Industry Singapore 1986*a*). By the early 2000s, Singapore had recognized services as its twin engine of growth, along with the manufacturing sector (Ministry of Trade and Industry Singapore 2003). It aimed to promote services activities, especially exportable ones, given the growing middle class population in China and India. The Economic Review Committee Report of 2003 categorically mentioned that "We are well-placed to [....] be a regional services hub. We must continue to upgrade, liberalize and develop established industries like trading and logistics, information, communication and technology (ICT), financial services and tourism. We should also promote promising new areas such as healthcare, education and creative industries" (p. 13). However, policymakers in Singapore realize that services, as an industry, is more varied and complex than the manufacturing industry. The sector is regulated by multiple bodies because of its implications on many social policies. In addition, with rising importance of the services sector in many Asian economies, Singapore faces tough competition in attracting foreign investment.

Singapore has always viewed external demand, i.e. exports of goods and services, and Foreign Direct Investment (FDI) as propellers for growth (Abeysinghe 2007). The role of exports is well reflected in the export-to-GDP ratio. In 2015, the merchandise trade-to-GDP ratio stood at around 120 per cent, and the domestic merchandise exports (excluding re-exports) stood at around 60 per cent. The major value-adding export good is non-oil domestic (merchandise) export (NODX), which accounted for 35 to 40 per cent of total exports during 2014–15. For FDI, the inward flows have gone up from US$5.6 billion in 1990 to US$16.5 billion in 2000 and further to US$67.5 billion in 2014. There were a few periods of sharp decline — 2002–3 and again in 2008 — but inflows rose thereafter, surpassing the level in 2007. The percentage ratio of inward FDI to GDP was 15.4 per cent in 1990 and 21.9 per cent in 2014, while the ratio of inward FDI to gross domestic capital formation stood at 31.7 per cent and 25.4 per cent over the same time period.

Given this background on Singapore's economy and its interest in the services sector and trade and investment, this chapter seeks to take a closer look at two aspects. First, Section 2 discusses the importance of the services sector and examines to what extent the sector is liberalized both at the regional level of ASEAN and multilateral level of the World Trade Organization (WTO). How far are liberalization measures matched by a domestic enabling environment to attract FDI? Second, in Section 3, we zero down to a case study of logistics services with the purpose of observing how far liberalization and facilitation efforts have helped in attracting FDI. What are the challenges in the logistics sector for attracting future FDIs? The chapter concludes in Section 4 and provides policy recommendations.

The methodology adopted throughout the chapter is research from secondary sources (government position papers and academic and newspaper articles) and data from domestic and international sources. The authors have also conducted informal discussions from June to October 2016 with Singapore government agencies and the private sector to develop better understanding about the logistics sector in the economy.

SINGAPORE SERVICES SECTOR — DEVELOPMENT TRENDS AND INVESTMENT LIBERALIZATION

Trends in Services Sector

Services have always played a predominant role in Singapore's economy since the 1970s. Out of the country's total GDP, the sector accounted for 65.1 per cent in 2000 and grew to 75.0 per cent in 2014. Its share of employment has also risen, accounting for 70.9 of total employment in 2014 (see Table 5.1). The services sector is a relatively stable source of growth compared to the manufacturing industry. While the latter is subject to volatility in global demand, the former appears to be more resilient because of its nature that it cannot be stored and is less sensitive to variations in credit and trade finance conditions (World Bank 2017). This can also be observed in Figure 5.1, as the growth rate of the services sector has been within a narrower band (between –2.6 per cent and 12.8 per cent) compared to the manufacturing sector (between –11.6 per cent and 26.7 per cent). Nevertheless, the services sector has also encountered slowdowns due to the financial market turmoil during 1997–98 and 2008–9 and the dotcom bust in early 2000 (see Figure 5.1).

TABLE 5.1
Share of Services in Total GDP and Employment

Year	Share in Total GDP		Share in Total Employment	
	Manufacturing	Services	Manufacturing	Services
2000	27.75	65.07	20.76	65.54
2005	27.78	67.58	20.51	68.70
2010	21.36	72.33	16.70	70.30
2014	18.40	75.02	14.80	70.90

Source: World Bank, World Development Indicators (various years); Ministry of Manpower Singapore, *Singapore Yearbook of Manpower Statistics* (various issues).

FIGURE 5.1
Growth Rate of Manufacturing and Services, 1990–2015

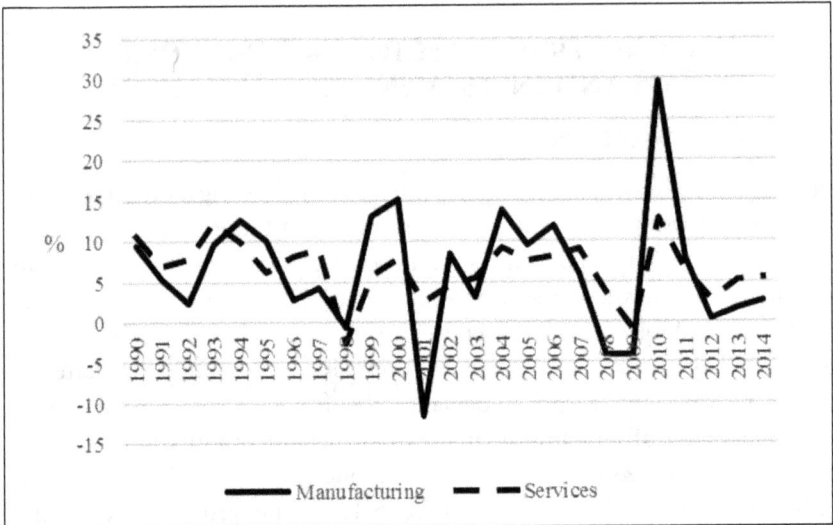

Source: World Bank, World Development Indicators (various years).

The rising importance of the services industry is also reflected in Singapore's trade statistics. In gross value terms, although trade in goods account for a major share in total exports, the share of services in total exports has gone up from 16 per cent in 2003 to 23 per cent in 2013. With regard to the composition of services export, in 2013, the share of transport related exports account for around 34 per cent, followed by other business services at 18 per cent, travel services at 15 per cent and financial services at 14 per cent. The relatively high share of transport related service export reflects Singapore's significance in entrepôt trade. These kinds of exports are related to the movement of goods, charter of vessels, port services, commissions and income from goods traded (Ministry of Trade and Industry Singapore 2014).

The services sector accounts for a majority share of FDI in Singapore economy: approximately 83.7 per cent of FDI stock in 2014 (see Table 5.2). In the last five years, inward FDI stock has grown in the financial and insurance services. In terms of geographic distribution, the US, Netherlands, Japan, and the UK are the top source countries, while some Southeast Asian countries like Malaysia and Indonesia are countries with increasing investment in value terms (see Table 5.3).

TABLE 5.2
Sectoral Distribution of FDI Stock, 1990–2014 (% of total)

Industries	1990	1995	2000	2005	2010	2014
Manufacturing	39.65	36.34	36.08	32.01	21.35	14.40
Construction						
Services	58.99	62.47	62.74	67.57	76.89	83.71
Wholesale & Retail Trade*	13.08	13.88	14.34	16.85	17.37	17.23
Transport & Storage*	2.47	3.15	4.41	5.45	5.88	3.66
Financial & Insurance Services*	43.21	45.38	35.75	37.57	43.17	50.32
Total FDI Stock (S$ billion)	49.83	84.26	191.45	323.82	625.78	1,024.59

Note: * Figures pertain to percentage share of total services sector FDI.
Source: Singapore Department of Statistics, *Yearbook of Statistics Singapore* (various issues).

TABLE 5.3
Geographic Distribution of Singapore FDI Stock (S$ million)

Country	2009	2010	2011	2012	2013
United States	58,968.80	67,082.00	74,648.50	104,636.00	114,191.30
Netherlands	61,511.70	60,546.50	69,372.90	75,371.30	84,350.90
Japan	50,515.40	53,577.40	53,722.10	58,701.70	71,992.00
United Kingdom	49,499.40	48,947.30	55,654.00	48,865.30	58,545.70
India	18,145.80	19,066.10	23,468.10	29,053.20	34,602.60
Malaysia	15,864.90	14,437.60	19,867.90	27,684.50	27,302.00
Indonesia	21,954.80	24,515.80	23,204.50	23,487.60	24,415.40
China	9,725.70	14,028.70	13,612.10	14,669.70	16,491.70
Australia	6,004.30	7,145.50	9,197.50	9,922.40	10,028.20
Taiwan	6,169.40	5,772.10	7,195.40	7,265.70	8,218.20
Total	574,703.60	625,780.40	677,772.50	755,974.30	853,339.50

Source: Singapore Department of Statistics, *Yearbook of Statistics Singapore* (2015).

Services Sector Liberalization under ASEAN and WTO

Singapore accounted for half of total FDI flows in the Association of Southeast Asian Nations (ASEAN) as at the end of 2015. In fact, Singapore's share of FDI inflows into ASEAN has increased from 41 per cent in 1995 to 51 per cent in 2013 (see Table 5.4). This can be attributed in part to the city-state's efforts through unilateral actions and liberalization efforts under regional initiatives like ASEAN integration and the WTO multilateral framework of General Agreement on Trade in Services (GATS). The services sector is regarded as more open to inward FDI, when compared to the manufacturing sector or to the other economies in the region. This is shown in the FDI Restrictiveness Index estimated by Thangavelu (2015) (see Table 5.5).[1]

TABLE 5.4
FDI Inflows into ASEAN Countries (US$ million)

	Singapore	Indonesia	Malaysia	Thailand	Philippines	Others	ASEAN
1995	11,943	4,419	5,815	2,070	1,459	2,927	28,632
2000	15,515	-4,550	3,788	3,410	2,240	2,112	22,515
2005	18,090	8,336	4,065	8,004	1,854	2,763	43,112
2010	55,076	13,771	9,060	14,568	1,298	16,771	1,10,544
2013	66,067	18,817	12,115	16,652	2,430	12,559	1,28,639

Source: ASEAN Secretariat, ASEAN FDI Database.

TABLE 5.5
FDI Restrictiveness Index for Manufacturing and Services Sector in ASEAN, 2015

	Manufacturing	Services
Brunei	0.569	0.680
Cambodia	0.686	0.644
Indonesia	0.536	0.558
Laos	0.597	0.617
Malaysia	0.618	0.573
Myanmar	0.563	0.650
Philippines	0.640	0.626
Singapore	0.669	0.846
Thailand	0.637	0.459
Vietnam	0.588	0.6276

Source: Thangavelu (2015).

According to the ASEAN Secretariat and the World Bank (2015), which has estimated the Services Trade Restrictiveness Index (STRI)[2] for ASEAN countries, Singapore's applied policies are more liberal than its ASEAN Framework Agreement on Services (AFAS) commitments. Singapore is also ahead of its Blueprint goals for 2015, and the gap between applied policy and Blueprint commitments is around eight STRI points. In multilateral commitments, Singapore's commitments during the WTO Doha negotiations and Uruguay Round are more restrictive than the AFAS ones: the gap is at thirty STRI points. Hence, as in the case of AFAS, applied policies are significantly liberal than the WTO commitments (see Table 5.6). For example, in the case of the fixed-line telecommunication sector, although Singapore limits foreign investment to 73.99 per cent under its multilateral and regional AFAS commitments, and allows for foreign (ASEAN) equity partnership of not less than 70 per cent under AEC Blueprint 2015, in practice, there is no restriction on foreign ownership in the sector (except that at least one member of the board of directors shall be a resident in Singapore).

TABLE 5.6
Comparing Restrictiveness of Singapore's ASEAN and WTO Commitments and Applied Policies

	Singapore	ASEAN Average
Restrictiveness of GATS Commitments	60.4	70.1
Restrictiveness of Doha Offers	59.8	68.2
Restrictiveness of AFAS Commitments	30.5	46.6
Restrictiveness of Applied Policy	10.8	34.5
Restrictiveness of Blueprint Goals	19.1	19.1

Source: Adapted from ASEAN Secretariat and the World Bank (2015).

Enabling Environment for Drawing FDI

In addition to liberalizing the services sector, Singapore has an enabling environment to attract foreign investments in the sector. The country aims to position itself as a global services hub in certain industries such as finance and logistics. The enabling environment could be divided in three major categories: Institution, Infrastructure and Human Capital.

a) *Institutions*

Motivated by growing competition in international commerce, Singapore provides a good institutional environment to start a foreign business. Almost all manufacturing sectors and a large number of services are fully open to foreign equity ownership. The regulatory framework provides a level-playing field for foreign investors. The sectors that have restricted foreign ownership are port and airport operation companies, television broadcasting channels and print media.

In Singapore, the Economic Development Board (EDB) plays the primary role of an Investment Promotion Authority (IPA) and has been successful in targeting specific multinationals and broad sectors to invest in the country. Other government agencies like International Enterprise (IE) Singapore and SPRING Singapore are also important for enhancing FDI inflows. The city-state has modernized and simplified its regulations related to FDI flows in its economy. According to the World Bank (2016), it takes only three procedures and 2.5 days to set up a company in Singapore. Other than that, it takes an additional procedure to register with Singapore customs to obtain a certificate of origin of a foreign company that wants to trade across border. Investment approval is not required unless and until a company needs financial assistance from the EDB. Application with business registration can be done and monitored online. Foreign companies can also open and operate a bank account in foreign currency.

In terms of accessing industrial land, although the city-state does not allow for private ownership of land, it offers considerable leasing rights that allows investors to use land as collateral and to sublease or subdivide it. Information on land is mostly available publicly except for land valuation and documents on environmental impact assessment. Singapore Land Authority is accountable for all land related issues and information in the country. The legal, institutional and administrative regimes are also conducive for foreign investments. Singapore offers several arbitral institutions, reflecting a thriving arbitration practice. On average, it takes around eight weeks to enforce an arbitration award rendered in Singapore, from filing an application to a writ of execution attaching assets and seven weeks for a foreign award.

Besides streamlining regulations, with its strong fiscal position, Singapore uses a combination of low tax rates and aggressive fiscal strategies to attract FDI. Indeed, the city-state has the lowest corporate tax rate of 17 per cent in the ASEAN region. It does not have tax on capital gains and dividend income. Over the years, it has added a wide range of incentives to promote FDI inflows. It provides subsidies to investors that go beyond traditional tax measures and involves training, expenditure, pricing of land and utilities.[3] Moreover, Singapore has signed a network of double taxation agreements (DTAs) with more than seventy countries, which lowers taxes for businesses. The main benefits of DTAs are avoidance of double taxes, lower withholding taxes and provision of preferential taxes.

Singapore also boasts of other non-fiscal advantages for foreign investors, including: political and social stability; good governance and a network of bilateral and regional Free Trade Agreements (FTAs) that covers comprehensive and well-coordinated foreign investment policies. The city-state provides a robust intellectual property (IP) rights regime, supported by a strong legal system and IP infrastructure. The IP policy is in line with the government's aim to encourage innovation, creativity and growth of industry and commerce in the country. The Global Information Technology Report 2012 of the World Economic Forum has ranked Singapore as having the best IP protection regime among the Asian countries.

b) *Infrastructure*

Singapore has a unique location as it is at the crossroads of the main global trade and shipping routes of the world, including the major sea route between India and China. It is located within seven-hour flight radius to half of the world's population in the Asia-Pacific region. Taking advantage of its location, the city-state aspires to be a transportation hub in the region. Both its airport and seaport have been awarded the best in the world. The city-state's Changi Airport is one of the largest cargo airports in Asia and serves over 6,500 weekly flights connecting 280 cities across sixty countries. It handles two million tonnes of cargo annually. Singapore's seaport handles 30.9 million TEUs of containers in 2015, second after Shanghai, China (World Shipping Council n.d.). The country's port is connected by 200 shipping lines to 600 ports across 123 countries. Both the airport and the seaport are easily accessible through road and rail networks domestically, ensuring smooth operating procedures from Singapore to the rest of the world (Singapore Economic Development Board n.d.).

Singapore's physical connectivity is further supported by robust institutional connectivity and advance technological capability. For example, the Singapore Customs provides TradeNet facility in collaboration with EDB and the Infocomm Development Authority of Singapore (IDA)[4] to facilitate exchange of information for international trade and logistics services. TradeNet also offers a single electronic window facility that simplifies documentation processes, saving time and cost. It permits traders and freight forwards to apply for and receive trade permits from thirty-five government agencies for trade and trans-shipment of goods. All these together improves efficiency and strengthens Singapore's competitiveness in global trade, which benefits the logistics services industry (Singapore Information Services n.d.). The World Economic Forum has ranked Singapore's telecommunication infrastructure as one of the best that can leverage on information and communication technologies to boost its competitiveness. It is the only Asian country in the top ten in the Report's rankings of 142 countries worldwide (Dutta and Bilbao-Osorio 2012). In Singapore's CFE report, the government reiterated its commitment to invest in external connectivity such as through the upcoming seaport in Tuas and Changi Airport Terminal 5 (Committee on the Future Economy 2017).

c) *Human Capital and Migration*

Singapore has a strong focus in education in order to develop an educated workforce and to meet manpower capability requirements for industries. In the mid-1980s, the Singapore government identified tertiary education as one of its eighteen services industries to be nurtured and promoted (Ministry of Trade and Industry Singapore 1986*b*). Education is valued not just as its contribution to net worth to economy but also through its revenue growth stream and export earning potential (Ministry of Trade and Industry Singapore n.d.). This mindset has developed a productive and motivated workforce in the country, which is again conducive for foreign investors.

However, Singapore has a small workforce. To overcome the issue, the country, while welcoming foreign workers, has also developed different mechanisms to manage the inflow. As of mid-December 2015, Singapore's total labour force was 3.6 million, of which resident workforce, covering Singapore citizens and permanent residents, was 2.2 million. This implies that the rest of the 1.4 million of workforce, or approximately 39 per cent of the total labour force, are foreigners (Singapore Department of Statistics 2016a). The services sector uses most of the foreign labour force (Teng n.d.). While the vast majority of foreign labour force are Work Permit holders (low-skilled workers), there are also S-Pass (semi-skilled workers) and Employment Pass (professionals and highly qualified workers) holders.

Singapore adopts a twin strategy with respect to foreign workers, one for the low-skilled and the other for skilled professionals and entrepreneurs/investors. The latter category of foreigners has a bigger share in terms of their economic contribution to the city-state. Low-skilled foreign workers are viewed as short-term labourers, who are to be repatriated after their jobs are completed or when their contracts end. In recent years, it has been acknowledged that a growing share of foreign population is not sustainable in the country. Hence, the Economic Strategies Committee in 2010 recommended that the share of the foreign labour force be maintained at about one third of the total labour force and this share should not grow significantly overtime (Economic Strategic Committee 2010). Following this, while Singapore signed trade agreements to facilitate movement of skilled workers to support its growing industries,[5] it also imposed levies on companies for their use of foreign labour. The government raised levy rates between S$30 and S$100 and reduced dependency ratios for Work Permit holders on 1 July 2016 compared to the previous year (see Table 5.7). Putting the change in levy rates into perspective, the levy rate for the basic tier has increased from S$170 for skilled workers in February 2011 to S$300 in July 2016 — close to doubling the levy rates in five years. This raises operation cost and makes it difficult for businesses to find workers across all industries.

Despite certain challenges, the three enablers, along with the government's emphasis on policy reform to bolster services sector integration regionally and multilaterally, are constantly trying to position Singapore as a leader in several services sectors. One such targeted sector is logistics. Singapore serves as the global logistics centre for DHL. In logistics services, the Port of Singapore plays a focal point to offload cargo for the region and pick up cargo through feeder services for their destination markets in Asia, the US and the EU. This reflects Singapore's role in ASEAN's regional connectivity, as described in the Master Plan on ASEAN Connectivity (MPAC) (ASEAN Secretariat 2011). MPAC recognizes the role of logistics services in meeting ASEAN's overall goal of facilitating movement of goods, services, investment and people.

TABLE 5.7
Changes in the Work Permit Levy Rate for the Services Sector, 2011–16

Tier	R1/R2	DR	Feb-11 $	DR	Jul-11 $	DR	Jan-12 $	DR	Jul-12 $	DR	Jan-13 $	DR	Jul-13 $	DR	Jul-15 $	DR	Jul-16 $
Basic Tier	R1	≤25%	170	≤20%	180	≤20%	210	≤15%	240	≤15%	270	≤10%	300	≤10%	300	≤10%	300
	R2		270		280		310		340		370		400		420		450
Tier 2	R1	>25–40%	300	>20–35%	300	>20–30%	330	>15–25%	360	>15–25%	380	>10–25%	400	>10–25%	400	>10–25%	400
	R2		400		400		430		460		480		500		550		600
Tier 3	R1	>40–50%	450	>35–50%	450	>30–50%	470	>25–50%	500	>25–50%	550	>25–50%	600	>25–40%	600	>25–40%	600
	R2														700		800

Notes:

- DR is dependency ratio, referring to the percentage of foreign workers to total workers in a business.
- R1 and R2 refer to higher skilled and basic skilled respectively. Accepted qualifications for higher skills category include Sijil Pelajaran Malaysia for Malaysians; diploma certification for Chinese citizens; Workforce Skills Qualification (WSQ) administered by the Workforce Development Agency (WDA) of Singapore.
- The tiers represent the difference in foreign worker dependency ratio in a business.

Source: Ministry of Manpower Singapore (2011); Ministry of Finance Singapore (2015).

CASE OF LOGISTICS SERVICES

The World Bank ranked Singapore as the No. 1 Logistics Hub in Asia in the 2016 Logistics Performance Index. This is contributed by the country's strategic location in Southeast Asia. Its connectivity to major shipping lanes has helped it become a logistics hub and conduit for world trade, in addition to its comparative advantage in infrastructure, institution, and human capital as explained in the earlier section.

About the Logistics Industry

Broadly, the logistics industry is defined as transporting, freight forwarding, warehousing, and some supporting activities. Specifically, the industry includes activities as described under the SSIC 2015 industry classification (Singapore Department of Statistics 2016*b*) (see Table 5.8). The industry contributes around 8 per cent to Singapore's total GDP and employs 227,000 workers. It is a key enabler for manufacturing, trading and services industries (Lee 2014).

TABLE 5.8
Singapore Logistics Industry

Land Transport and Transport via Pipelines	Water Transport	Air Transport	Warehousing and Support Activities for Transportation	Information and Communications
Transport via railways; Passenger and freight rail transport; Other land transport; Passenger land transport; Aerial cableways; Freight land transport; Transport via pipelines	Passenger water transport; Freight water transport	Airlines (passenger, freight, foreign airlines and others)	Warehousing and storage; Storage activities for transportation; Supporting services to land transport; Supporting services to water transport; Supporting services to air transport; Cargo handling; Marine surveying services; Other support activities (value-added logistics providers, freight forwarding, packing and crating); National post activities; Courier activities other than national post activities	Development of e-commerce applications hardware consultancy; Computer facilities management activities; Computer systems integration facilities

Note: All categories except for Information and Communication are as per SPRING Singapore's definition. The sub-categories in Information and Communication are selected by the authors based on its relevance to the logistics sector.
Source: Singapore Department of Statistics and Ministry of Trade and Industry Singapore (2015).

In 2013, the logistics industry had an operating profit of S$166 billion. It grew from S$124 billion in 2009 and contributed 5.2 per cent to the city-state's national income, which has remained steady in the last few years. During 2009–13, the number of establishments has increased from 7,169 to 7,606 and top twenty of the twenty-five global logistics players have set up operation here (such as DHL, Toll, UPS, Yusen logistics, Sankyu). In order to meet the growing and changing demands of the supply chain industry, logistics companies in Singapore not only provide freight, warehousing and transportation services but also offer specialized logistics.

Government's Domestic Policies for the Logistics Industry

Logistics is a strategic industry for Singapore's economy due to the city-state's role in entrepôt trade, leading to business opportunities in warehousing, cargo handling, insurance and freight forwarding and distribution. There are two global trends that can affect the future of logistics industry in Singapore and the broader region. First, the shift of economic weight from the West to the East is likely to change the flows of trade and investment across borders. For example, multinationals in search of economies of scale, will explore consolidation of businesses and increase their cross-border activities in Asia. Second, is the emergence of "frugal engineering", that is "a product design approach that emphasises using the bare minimum of resources to create basic, no-frills products" (Singapore Economic Development Board n.d.).

Singapore is positioning its logistics industry to compete based on these two trends. It is encouraging firms to innovate and to develop greater capability in higher value-added services. As advanced infrastructure is a pre-requisite to the growth of logistics sector, the city-state is providing the infrastructure that can support niche specialized logistics services, such as the Airport Logistics Park of Singapore, the Changi International LogisPark and the Banyan LogisPark on Jurong Island. While some of these facilitate regional distribution, some are catering to the specific demands of chemicals and oil companies.

In 2012, the EDB and SPRING Singapore drew a five-year productivity roadmap to increase the long-term productivity of Singapore's logistics and transportation industry (Singapore Economic Development Board and SPRING Singapore 2012). The industry has also been promised S$42 million as government funding. It is strongly believed that a competitive logistics services industry has spillover effects and is expected to raise productivity of manufacturing and services industries in the country.

The five-year roadmap emphasizes two key areas for development of logistics in the city-state: developing supply chain management expertise and enhancing innovation and efficiency. While the former is needed to help logistics providers to navigate Asia's trade landscape and lock-in its growth opportunities, the latter is aimed at assisting the industry to align itself continually with changing demands of new customers. The EDB is working with several logistics companies in the country (such as DHL and YCH) to provide on-the-job training for their supply chain managers. The programme, which was launched in March 2012, has benefitted 180 logistics enterprises. To address new challenges, the Republic Polytechnic has started a Centre of Innovation for Supply Chain Management. In addition, SPRING's customized Logistics Productivity Toolkit is likely to benefit firms to identify opportunities for upgrading and enhancement within their organizations (Singapore Economic Development Board 2012).

The logistics industry is also one of the sixteen priority sectors to benefit from the National Productivity and Continuing Education Council (NPCEC) initiative. Set up in April 2010, the NPCEC aims to achieve national productivity growth of 2 to 3 per cent per annum by 2030 through its focus on developing:

- national productivity initiatives at the sectoral, enterprise and worker levels;
- a comprehensive, first-class national Continuous Education and Training (CET) system; and
- a culture of productivity and continuous learning and upgrading.

Other recent initiatives that have been undertaken in light of the government's encouragement to increase productivity includes the "Mobileye" and "Software-as-a-System (SaaS) Total Logistics Information System". These initiatives are supported by SPRING Singapore. The former initiative is an effort by the Singapore Transport Association to incorporate the use of assistive driver technology for safety.[6] It can help to increase the productivity of trucking companies by about 20 per cent by reducing the number of accidents. Since its launch in 2014, fifteen trucking companies have signed up for the programme. The "SaaS Total Logistics Information System"[7] is a low-cost cloud computing technology solution tailor-made to support logistics management. Since May 2014, six pioneering companies have signed up for the system, which provides shared services and enable better management of resources. This will increase productivity by up to 50 per cent (Lee 2014).

As a continuation of the government's support of the logistics industry, the government included an Industry Transformation Map (ITM) in the Committee on the Future Economy Report, released in February 2017. It will develop a Logistics Skills Framework with information on career pathways. More significantly, the government intends to revamp the system for goods delivery. Instead of having point-to-point distribution, the report suggests creating an "urban logistics system", where goods are consolidated in offsite consolidation centres, before being re-distributed to the malls. In recognizing the trend in e-commerce, it intends for the goods from malls to be distributed to federated lockers and collection points in neighbourhood areas, reducing the need for consumers to stay at home to wait for the delivery of goods. Essentially, the government would like to see the adoption and integration of technology among logistics players, to optimize resources and to re-skill executives to take on less labourious jobs in the future.

As more businesses adopt the Internet of Things in their operations, such technology is likely to become standard tools for logistics operations. Logistics companies that succeed in implementing real-time management of their operations will be able to improve service offerings and reduce costs. Capabilities such as fleet optimization, dynamic supply-chain tracking and tracing, big data management and analytics, and real-time security will play an integral role in the sector.

State of Liberalization

Being part of ASEAN and WTO, Singapore has offered liberalization commitments under AFAS and GATS. In 2007, the ASEAN countries have signed the Sectoral Integration Protocol for the Logistics Services Sector that covers eight subsectors[8] and planned to increase the foreign equity cap (mode 3 — services trade through commercial presence) to 49 per cent by 2008 to 51 per cent by 2010, and to 70 per cent by 2013. The city-state has also committed to GATS liberalization efforts, as described below.

Table 5.8 shows Singapore's commitments in nine logistics subsectors at the WTO and ASEAN level. Under the WTO's Uruguay Round, Singapore committed to have no restrictions under modes 1, 2 and 3 for international freight shipping and for shipping agencies and brokerage services, which are categorized under the auxiliary services category. Market access commitments for modes 1 and 3 for courier services are unbound, while for mode 2, there is no restriction. There are no commitments made for all nine subsectors under WTO GATS in the unconcluded Doha Round.

At the ASEAN level, Singapore has no investment restrictions in most subsectors. It has no restrictions in the following sectors for modes 1, 2 and 3: packaging services; courier services; rail freight transport and other auxiliary services. Road freight transport has similar treatment as well except for mode 1 under market access, where restrictions are "unbound". Two subsectors — maritime cargo handling and maritime freight — have no limitations specified, whereas the extent of access for storage and warehousing is to be negotiated in bilateral agreements.

This confirms the earlier prognosis that Singapore has more liberal commitments under AFAS than in WTO. Singapore's GATS commitments in logistics services are limited to only three subsectors. But its commitments under AFAS cover around seven out of nine subsectors, as shown in Table 5.9.

FDI in Singapore Logistics Industry

It will be wrong to say that services sector liberalization or Singapore's efforts to place priority on its logistics sector are the sole reasons of FDI flows into the sector. There could be other factors that influence the investment decision for an investor, including the favourable FDI enabling environment as explained earlier in the chapter. Given this understanding and limited FDI data availability on public domain, Table 5.10 gives some broad indications about FDI flows in Singapore's logistics sector.

FDI stocks in Singapore's transport and storage sector has gone up from S$17.6 billion to S$37.4 billion during 2005–14, reflecting an average annual growth rate of around 8 per cent per annum (*vis-à-vis* a 12 per cent growth rate of total FDI stock in the country and 16 per cent of FDI growth in the services sector). Of the components, while FDI stock in water transport and supporting services grew by 7 per cent per annum, the same grew by 14 per cent for warehousing, post and courier services, reflecting the growing importance of the sector in the post-Global Financial Crisis (GFC).

TABLE 5.9

Singapore's Commitments in Logistics Subsectors under GATS and AFAS 9

Subsector	CPC	GATS: UR		GATS (Doha Round Offers) (2006)		AFAS 9	
		Market Access (MA)	National Treatment (NT)	MA	NT	MA	NT
Packaging services	876	M1: NA M2: NA M3: NA	M1: NA M2: NA M3: NA	M1: NA M2: NA M3: NA	M1: NA M2: NA M3: NA	M1: N M2: N M3: N	M1: N M2: N M3: N
Courier services	7512	M1: unbound M2: N M3: unbound	M1: NA M2: NA M3: NA	M1: NA M2: NA M3: NA	M1: NA M2: NA M3: NA	M1: N M2: N M3: N	M1: N M2: N M3: N
Maritime freight transportation, excluding cabotage	7212	M1: N M2: N M3: N	M1: N M2: N M3: N	M1: NA M2: NA M3: NA	M1: NA M2: NA M3: NA	M1: N M2: N M3: N, except on the registration of Singapore flag ships as specified in the Merchant Shipping Act	M1: N M2: N M3: N, except on the registration of Singapore flag ships as specified in the Merchant Shipping Act
Rail freight transportation	7112	M1: NA M2: NA M3: NA	M1: NA M2: NA M3: NA	M1: NA M2: NA M3: NA	M1: NA M2: NA M3: NA	M1: N M2: N M3: N	M1: N M2: N M3: N

Road freight transportation	7123	M1: NA M2: NA M3: N	M1: NA M2: NA M3: NA	M1: NA M2: NA M3: NA	M1: NA M2: NA M3: NA	M1: unbound M2: N M3: N	M1: N M2: N M3: N
Maritime cargo handling services	741	M1: NA M2: NA M3: NA	M1: NA M2: NA M3: NA	M1: NA M2: NA M3: NA	M1: NA M2: NA M3: NA	M1: NA M2: NA M3: NA	M1: NA M2: NA M3: NA
Storage and warehouse services: covering private bonded warehousing services only	742	M1: NA M2: NA M3: N	M1: NA M2: NA M3: NA	M1: NA M2: NA M3: NA	M1: NA M2: NA M3: NA	M1: Y# M2: Y# M3: Y#	M1: Y# M2: Y# M3: Y#
Maritime freight	748	M1: NA M2: NA M3: NA	M1: NA M2: NA M3: NA	M1: NA M2: NA M3: NA	M1: NA M2: NA M3: NA	M1: NA M2: NA M3: NA	M1: NA M2: NA M3: NA
Other auxiliary services	749	M1: N M2: N M3: N	M1: N M2: N M3: N	M1: NA M2: NA M3: NA	M1: NA M2: NA M3: NA	M1: N M2: N M3: N	M1: N M2: N M3: N

Note: M1: mode 1, M2: mode 2, M3: mode 3, N: none, NA: not-applicable (i.e. no commitments), Y#: The undertaking of the commitments to bind the current level of market access and treatment to services and services supplier, will be through the conclusion of bilateral shipping agreements.

Source: WTO n.d.; Ministry of Trade and Industry Malaysia (2013).

TABLE 5.10
FDI Stocks (end-year) in Singapore Logistics Industry (S$ million)

	Transport & Storage	Water Transport & Supporting Services	Freight Water Transport	Other Water Transport	Land & Air Transport & Supporting Services	Warehousing, Post & Courier Services	Total FDI Stock in Services	Total FDI Stock in the Country
2005	17,652	15,894	–	–	-88.7	1,846	218,809	323,821
2006	23,225	20,670	–	–	-93.8	2,649	260,999	370,495
2007	30,525	27,575	–	–	-206.4	3,157	346,355	466,567
2008	36,329	32,879	–	–	-312.5	3,763	398,187	510,585
2009	36,661	33,954	28,474	5,481	-180.9	2,888	439,351	574,704
2010	36,794	33,152	26,808	6,343	-321.6	3,964	481,179	625,780
2011	34,005	29,916	23,372	6,544	-309	4,399	521,098	677,392
2012	38,425	32,222	24,488	7,735	-209.4	6,412	619,426	761,637
2013	33,176	27,048	23,684	3,365	-164.4	6,292	700,996	868,149
2014	37,449	30,959	27,195	3,765	-172.1	6,662	857,663	1,024,586

Note: Total services cover wholesale and retail trade, transportation and storage, accommodation and food services, information and communications, financial and insurance services, professional services and real estate activities. The category of transport and storage includes water transport, land and air transport and warehousing, post and courier services.

Source: Singapore Department of Statistics, *Yearbook of Statistics Singapore* (various issues).

In 2014, the share of FDI in transport and storage amounted to 4 per cent of total FDI stock and 4.4 per cent of total FDI stock in the services sector. Water transport and supporting services attracted most of the FDI amount in transport and storage services (82 per cent in 2014). Share of warehousing, post and courier services went up from 10.5 per cent in 2005 to 17.8 per cent of the total FDI stock in transport and storage in 2014. A negative value of FDI stock in land and air transport services depicts a decrease in foreign assets in the sector. This could be due to excess capacity in this subsector. Electronic components — high-value goods typically transported by air — come in reduced sizes in recent years, hence air logistics and cargo companies have smaller, lighter amounts to transport than expected. This excess capacity may have caused some foreign investors to pull out some of their initial investments.

Besides attracting FDI in the country, Singapore is also a leading source of outward FDI (OFDI). Its stock of OFDI has gone up from S$245,998 million in 2006 to S$619,997 million in 2014. Of this, transport and storage account for 3.2 per cent in 2006 (S$7,878 million), which has fallen to 2.7 per cent in 2014 (S$17,131 million). However, it should be noted that Singapore has a notable share of OFDI of 7 per cent in 2014 in real estate activities and this may include premises for logistics services.

Challenges in the Logistics Industry

The development of the logistics services industry in Singapore is not without challenges. The industry faces headwinds due to rising business operating costs and labour shortages in the country and growing competition from the neighbouring countries. As Singapore is an open and entrepôt economy, it is also negatively affected by slowdowns in global economy and international trade.

a) *Rising Cost for Businesses*

A key concern of those operating logistics businesses in Singapore is the growing manpower and rental costs in the economy, which in turn is affecting the operating cost and hence the profit margin (Singapore Business Federation 2016). The Ministry of Trade and Industry (MTI) has recently estimated that freight and transportation costs make up 33.6 per cent of business costs for large companies in the transportation and storage sector and this proportion goes up to 50.2 per cent for small firms (Soon 2016). With an expanding e-commerce sector in Singapore, last-mile delivery companies such as Singapore Post, Ninja Van and Yamato Asia compete with one another, with the side benefit of lowering costs to other upstream logistics suppliers. Raising efficiency is important as Singapore is also restructuring its own economy towards more innovation capabilities and higher productivity.

b) *Labour Shortages*

One of Singapore's perennial challenges for companies operating in the country is its labour force.[9] Employers in the logistics industry find it difficult to hire skilled and low-skilled workers due to the following reasons: a mismatch in expectation between employers and new recruits; the small size of Singapore's talent pool and tougher rules in hiring foreigners (Singh 2014). Employers in the logistics sector have to fight for the same pool of graduates who are drawn to more lucrative careers in consultancy, law and banking. Furthermore, employers expect fresh graduates to have some sort of experience in supply chain and logistics, while new graduates, in general, expect to hold jobs that are comfortable without much physical labour. The EDB has proposed initiatives, like web-based supply chain simulation game among local polytechnics and universities, to align the expectations of employers and graduates before they join the industry (Ho 2016).

Besides the demands of physical labour in the low-skilled worker category, it is difficult for logistic companies to attract Singaporeans due to its relatively low pay. The industry is not popular among graduates, who would rather seek jobs in banking and finance, where they can earn a more lucrative pay. It is common to have foreigners work in this category, but even then, the industry finds it difficult to hire migrant workers due to the Ministry of Manpower's local-to-foreigner quota and the extra costs (such as work permit application costs and levy) that have to be paid with the hiring of each foreigner. The challenges that the sector face with its manpower makes Singapore less cost-competitive compared to neighbouring countries like Malaysia.[10]

c) *Competition from Neighbouring Countries*

Singapore's port faces strong competition from neighbouring countries, particularly from Malaysia. The busy port of Singapore handles one of the largest cargo trans-shipment volumes in the world. However, due to Singapore's lack of land, it is unable to expand fast enough to accommodate high shipment volume. At times, there are insufficient cargo containers to meet the demands of customers. As such, the port has lost business opportunities to Port Tanjung Pelepas (PTP) in Johor, Malaysia and Port Klang in Selangor, Malaysia, which have lower costs and spare capacity.[11] In June 2016, the PTP has announced a US$2bn investment plan to increase its capacity over the next fifteen years.

In addition, Indonesia is also developing its container-port capacity. There are plans to expand the Port of Tanjung Priok — the country's busiest port, located in north Jakarta — while the Patimban Port in Subang, West Java province, is under construction. Indonesian government has put in a lot of focus on its maritime connectivity that will include building seaports, industrial areas and upgrading vessels. All these together are expected to give stiff competition to Singapore's port in due course.

Apart from the ASEAN region, Colombo International Container Terminal in Sri Lanka, a deep seaport that came in operation in 2014, is adding to the growing level of competition as well. The country is adjacent to a big market of India, which lacks a deep seaport and has a double taxation avoidance treaty with Sri Lanka.

d) Uneven Liberalization and Facilitation Efforts in ASEAN

As Singapore is a small-sized economy, most often foreign investors view ASEAN as the city-state's immediate hinterland that offers scale economy. They treat Singapore as a headquarter economy, while operating their business in the rest of the region. However, of late, companies in the e-commerce industry, such as Rakuten, Lazada and Zalora, are losing money and are deliberating whether to stay or leave the ASEAN region.[12] A key challenge for these companies in the region is inadequate infrastructure and an inefficient logistics network. Most of them have cited inconsistent duties, inefficient customs procedures and illegal fees as crucial impediments to service an enlarged ASEAN market.

Many of these issues arise from the reluctance of ASEAN countries to implement their respective liberalization or facilitation commitments for sectoral integration. This could be due to the countries' desire to protect its domestic logistics industry, based on standard infant industry argument. It is possible that some of the ASEAN members do not have the capacity in terms of financial and human resources in their logistics industry and may lack institutional and regulatory framework to implement their respective commitments. Differences in efficiency in customs clearance across ASEAN countries also act as a hindrance to integrate the region's logistics services. In addition, disparities in human resource capability, leading to a shortage of skilled professionals in many ASEAN countries, is another major obstacle to develop a competitive and integrated logistics industry in the region.

e) *Uncertain Global Trade Environment*

Singapore's trade-sensitive logistics and transport sector is also affected by falling global demand, as lacklustre trade growth and uncertain global economic outlook reduces the trans-shipment of goods through Singapore. Growth slowdown in China is a concern for Singapore's maritime and the related logistics sectors, as trans-shipment from China is likely to fall. These concerns are reflected in container throughput. According to the Maritime and Port Authority of Singapore, container throughput in the Port of Singapore has declined from 33.9 million TEUs in 2014 to 30.9 million TEUs in 2016. It was the lowest container throughput volume since 2011, when 29.9 million TEUs passed through Singapore's port. The Singapore Logistics Association (SLA) stated that the slowdown in trade and the manufacturing sector is being "keenly felt, especially amongst small and medium-sized (logistics) enterprises" (Koh 2016).

CONCLUSION AND POLICY RECOMMENDATIONS

Singapore's success in the services industry is not achieved by default. It is by deliberate and careful design of domestic policies as well as tapping on regional and to a lesser extent, multilateral liberalization initiatives. Since a large number of services sector are fully open to foreign equity participation, its applied policies are more liberal than its liberalization commitments under ASEAN and WTO. In particular, Singapore's commitments under GATS Uruguay Round are more restrictive than the commitments in ASEAN. In this case, it is the domestic policies, as enablers, that play a much bigger role in differentiating the city-state as an attractive investment destination in the region. Strong institutions, political stability, good regulatory practices and availability of infrastructure are important determinants to attract FDI in the city-state's services industry. However, it is the manpower constraint that is stalling a rapid expansion of the services economy. While Singapore is undergoing a structural adjustment to boost its economy's productivity growth by curbing the supply of low-skilled foreign labour, encouraging capital deepening and increasing automation, much needs to be seen on how services firms manage this period of transition.

Similar characteristics and issues are observed in the case of the logistics services industry in Singapore. The government views logistics as a strategic sector to promote trade and investment, which in turn is expected to deepen regional integration among Southeast Asian countries and beyond. It views changes in global economy and technology as two key variables that may affect the future of the industry. Accordingly, domestic policymaking is focused on developing supply chain management expertise and enhancing innovation and efficiency. These together are expected to push for the overall economy-wide objective of improving productivity. For sectoral liberalization, it is more liberal under AFAS compared to the WTO GATS arrangement.

That said, FDI stock in the transport and storage activities, taken as a proxy for logistics services, has gone up in the last decade. Within the industry, it is the warehousing, post and courier services that has attracted more FDI, showcasing its growing importance in the economy. However, there are many challenges — rising business operating cost, labour shortages, growing competition from the neighbouring countries, slow liberalization and facilitation efforts in ASEAN as well as slowdown in international trade — that need to be overcome during the period of structural adjustment in the broader domestic economy. Given this, below are few policy recommendations that are provided for Singapore's logistics industry and the services sector, in general.

Policy Recommendations

a) *Assisting Local Enterprises to Access Government Grants*

As Singapore faces labour shortage challenges, it is continuously encouraging companies to automate their business. This is more so in the logistics industry (e-commerce business) where it is necessary to reduce cost in the last-mile of service delivery. The government offers various grants — the Productivity and Innovation Credit (PIC), the Capability Development Grant (CDG), Automation Support Package and others — and urges local enterprises to use them to upgrade and automate their business processes. However, it has been found that while businesses are aware of the grants, they have not used them extensively (PwC 2015).

This could be due to lack of awareness of the schemes available or not knowing how to apply for the grants. The government has since created a one-stop portal in late 2016 — Business Grants Portal — for small and medium enterprises (SMEs) to view and apply for business grants. The government can further build on this initiative by having a dedicated person be a point of contact for different industries. The appointed person has to have sufficient knowledge of the challenges say the logistics sector to be able to make a sensible judgement call on the legitimacy of grant applications. Currently, government officers are savvy with administrative processes, but lack the industry knowledge to grasp the technological improvements and challenges that has been happening in the logistics sector.

b) *Attract Leading Operators*

The logistics industry in Singapore is highly fragmented. The majority of the businesses are SMEs: 72 per cent of the companies has turnover of less than S$1 million. While those with turnover of more than S$10 million account for around 7 per cent of the total number of establishments, they contribute more than 85 per cent of the industry's value add.[13] This implies that Singapore still needs to continue to attract leading logistics players to base their operations in Singapore and encourage increased collaboration within the industry. For this to happen, Singapore needs to review some of its policies, such as the ones related to manpower, that is currently challenging logistics operation in the city-state. The government, for instance, can offer flexibility in employing foreign workers so that the firms can have a higher foreign worker quota than manufacturing.

c) *Develop Domestic Infrastructure*

For a sustainable logistics and transport service delivery in a land-scarce country, Singapore needs to look for new kinds of domestic infrastructure. It has been reported that about 4,000 trucks are making more than 20,000 delivery trips daily and are occupying a quarter of the available road network (Ng 2015). The government has recognized the truck congestion on roads as a problem to address in the CFE report. One way to manage the issue is to explore underground goods movement system. Singapore has an existing Mass Rapid Transit System, which is fast expanding to span the entire city, for people's movement. A system, in similar lines, can be contemplated for goods movement too. It can facilitate by connecting with the future port of Singapore in Tuas[14] to different industrial estates in the city-state, as well as within the city to support other business operations, such as e-commerce. The entire system can be developed as energy-efficient and can be fully automated, thus reducing congestion on road, manpower requirement and fuel cost. The idea has already surfaced among the policymakers in Singapore. JTC Corporation is working on a feasibility study for an underground goods movement system in Singapore.

d) *Capacity Building in ASEAN Countries*

As Singapore suffers from uneven implementation of liberalization and facilitation initiatives in the ASEAN region, it should work with less developed members, especially in the area of capacity development, for better logistics service delivery in their domestic economies. Most of the countries in the region suffer from a shortage of skilled and qualified logistics professionals. They also do not have resources for on-the-job training opportunities, especially for workers in the SMEs. Singapore can take a lead in developing a common understanding of the region's logistics industry. It can, in partnership with other ASEAN government agencies, establish teaching or training institutions offering logistics as an area of specialized education. It can promote a common curriculum for logistics education so that a mutually recognized standard can facilitate cross-border movement of logistics professionals in the region.

e) *Collaboration between Government Agencies, Think-Tanks/Academic Institutes and Private Sector*

The government and the educational institutes should collaborate on research to reconfigure logistics business models for the future. Some are already underway. For example, earlier in 2016, Procter and Gamble (P&G) and the Logistics Institute–Asia Pacific of National University of Singapore (NUS) embarked on a three-year collaboration to engage in supply chain and logistics research. A search is undertaken across countries for good PhD candidates in NUS, who will engage in more research for supply chain operations, among other sectors. However, much more needs to be done. With Singapore's ambition to be a regional logistics hub, it needs to understand how other developed countries are dealing with the issue of goods transportation and distribution. Singapore can work with researchers and the private sector to see if similar models used in developed countries can be replicated for the city-state and the region. It can work with other ASEAN governments and their stakeholders too to explore new and sustainable ways for a seamless movement of goods in the region based on tripartite research arrangements.

Notes

1. The index covers parameters like foreign ownership, i.e. market access, national treatment, screening and approval procedure, board of directors and management composition, movement of investors and performance requirements. The higher the scores, the more open are the FDI rule (Thangavelu 2015).
2. STRI – This helps to identify which policy measures restrict trade.
3. Local Industrial Upgrading Programme by EDB.
4. Since 1 October 2016, the Infocomm Development Authority and Media Development Authority merged to become one government agency, known as Infocomm Media Development Authority (IMDA).
5. One such agreement is the ASEAN Economic Community which promotes the movement of skilled workers, through Mutual Recognition Agreements (MRAs) for eight professions – doctors; dentists; nurses; engineers; accountants; architects; surveyors; and tour guides.
6. The Mobile initiative is launched by Singapore Transport Association and supported by SPRING Singapore.
7. The Software as a System (SaaS) Total Logistics Information System is a cloud computing solution specially customized for the logistics industry. The SaaS model is built upon a purely subscription-based shared platform model. SPRING Singapore is supporting the logistics companies that subscribe to the system.
8. The logistics liberalization scheme of ASEAN covers the following subsectors: railway transport, road transport, maritime transport, cargo handling, storage and warehousing, transport agency, postal and courier and packaging.
9. This came out as a key factor both throughout interviews conducted during July–October 2016 and in newspaper articles.
10. This came out during our discussion with policymakers and industry players during July–October 2016.
11. Ibid.
12. *ASEAN Today*, 31 December 2016.
13. Source: <https://www.spring.gov.sg/Developing-Industries/LOG/Pages/Statistics-Logistics.aspx>.

14. Singapore is currently investing in a new port infrastructure to match the needs of the maritime industry. The government has planned to relocate the existing port from Tanjung Pagar to Tuas (west of Singapore) with automated built-in port equipment, which is expected to handle 65 million TEUs of cargo when completed in 2027.

References

Abeysinghe, Tilak. "Singapore: Economy". Singapore: National University of Singapore, August 2007. Available at <https://courses.nus.edu.sg/course/ecstabey/singapore%20economy-tilak.pdf>.

ASEAN Secretariat. "Master Plan on ASEAN Connectivity". Jakarta: ASEAN Secretariat, January 2011. Available at <http://www.asean.org/storage/images/ASEAN_RTK_2014/4_Master_Plan_on_ASEAN_Connectivity.pdf>.

―――. ASEAN FDI Database [online]. Jakarta: ASEAN Secretariat.

ASEAN Secretariat and the World Bank. "ASEAN Services Integration Report". Jakarta: ASEAN Secretariat; Washington, D.C.: World Bank, 2015. Available at <http://documents.worldbank.org/curated/en/759841468178459585/pdf/100637-Revised-WP-PUBLIC-Box393257B-ASEAN-Report-web.pdf>.

ASEAN Today. "Battle of the E-Commerce Giants: Amazon comes to ASEAN", 31 December 2016. Available at <https://www.aseantoday.com/2016/12/battle-of-the-e-commerce-giants-amazon-comes-to-asean/> (accessed 16 February 2017).

Committee on the Future Economy. "Report on the Committee on the Future Economy". Singapore: Committee on the Future Economy, February 2017. Available at <https://www.gov.sg/~/media/cfe/downloads/mtis_full%20report.pdf>.

Dutta, Soumitra and Beñat Bilbao-Osorio. "The Global Information Technology Report 2012". Geneva: World Economic Forum and INSEAD, 2012.

Economic Strategies Committee. "Report of the Economic Strategies Committee – High Skilled People, Innovative Economy, Distinctive Global City". Singapore: Economic Strategies Committee, February 2010. Available at <http://www.mof.gov.sg/Portals/0/MOF%20For/Businesses/ESC%20Recommendations/ESC%20Full%20Report.pdf>.

Ho, Olivia. "Supply Chain and Logistics Sector Look to Train More Young Professionals". Straits Times, 19 May 2016. Available at <http://www.straitstimes.com/singapore/manpower/supply-chain-and-logistics-sector-look-to-train-more-young-professionals> (accessed 11 November 2016).

Koh, Jeremy. "Tough Year for Logistics, Pockets of Growth in Trade". Straits Times, 8 March 2016. Available at <http://www.stjobs.sg/career-resources/workplace-success/tough-year-for-logistics-pockets-of-growth-in-trade/a/242304> (accessed 9 November 2016).

Lee, Yi Shyan. "Speech by Mr Lee Yi Shyan at the Opening Ceremony of the Logistics and Transportation Conference, 26 August 2014". 2014. Speech. Available at <http://www.spring.gov.sg/NewsEvents/PS/Pages/Speech-by-Mr-Lee-Yi-Shyan-at-the-Opening-Ceremony-of-the-Logistics-and-Transportation-Conference-20140826.aspx> (accessed 7 June 2016).

Menon, Ravi. "An Economic History of Singapore: 1965–2065". Keynote Address by Mr Ravi Menon, Managing Director, Monetary Authority of Singapore, at the Singapore Economic Review Conference 2015, 5 August 2015. Available at <http://www.mas.gov.sg/News-and-Publications/Speeches-and-Monetary-Policy-Statements/Speeches/2015/An-Economic-History-of-Singapore.aspx>.

Ministry of Finance Singapore. "Annex A-5: Changes to Foreign Worker Levies". Singapore: Ministry of Finance Singapore, 2015. Available at <http://www.singaporebudget.gov.sg/data/budget_2015/download/annexa5.pdf> (accessed 26 December 2016).

Ministry of Manpower Singapore. "Annex A – Schedule of Foreign Worker Levy Changes until July 2013". Singapore: Ministry of Manpower Singapore, 2011. Available at <http://www.mom.gov.sg/~/media/mom/documents/press-releases/2011/annex%20a%20schedule%20-%20foreign%20worker%20levy%20changes%20(210211).pdf> (accessed 26 December 2016).

———. *Singapore Yearbook of Manpower Statistics*. Singapore: Ministry of Manpower Singapore, various issues.

Ministry of Trade and Industry Malaysia. "Singapore – Schedule of Specific Commitments for the 9th Package of Commitments under ASEAN Framework Agreement on Services". Kuala Lumpur: Ministry of Trade and Industry Malaysia, 2013. Available at <http://www.miti.gov.my/miti/resources/AFAS_9_Consolidated_Schedule_-_SG_SOC_(20130509).pdf>.

Ministry of Trade and Industry Singapore. "Report of the Economic Committee, The Singapore Economy: New Directions". Singapore: Ministry of Trade and Industry Singapore, 1986a, pp. 12–13.

———. "Report of the Economic Committee, The Singapore Economy: New Directions – Executive Summary". Singapore: Ministry of Trade and Industry Singapore, 1986b. Available at <https://www.mti.gov.sg/ResearchRoom/Documents/app.mti.gov.sg/data/pages/885/doc/econ.pdf>.

———. "Report of the Economic Review Committee, New Challenges, Fresh Goals – Towards a Dynamic Global City". Singapore: Ministry of Trade and Industry Singapore, February 2003. Available at <https://www.mti.gov.sg/ResearchRoom/Documents/app.mti.gov.sg/data/pages/507/doc/1%20ERC_Main_Committee.pdf>.

———. "Economic Survey of Singapore Second Quarter 2014". Singapore: Ministry of Trade and Industry, 2014. Available at <https://www.mti.gov.sg/ResearchRoom/SiteAssets/Pages/Economic-Survey-of-Singapore-Second-Quarter-2014/BA2_2Q14.pdf>.

————. "MTI Maintains 2017 GDP Growth Forecast at '1.0 to 3.0 Per Cent'". *Press Release*, 17 February 2017. Available at <http://www.singstat.gov.sg/docs/default-source/default-document-library/news/press_releases/gdp4q2016.pdf> (accessed 26 February 2017).

————. "Developing Singapore's Education Industry". Singapore: Ministry of Trade and Industry Singapore, n.d.

Ng, Kelly. "Singapore Logistics Sector Must Evolve to Stay Competitive". *Today*, 23 October 2015. Available at <http://www.todayonline.com/business/singapore-logistics-sector-must-evolve-stay-competitive> (accessed 16 April 2017).

PricewatershouseCoopers (PwC). "Tax Outlook: An Outlook on Recent Tax Changes", September 2015. Available at <https://www.pwc.com/sg/en/tax-lookout/assets/taxlookout_201509.pdf> (accessed 16 February 2017).

Singapore Business Federation. "SBF National Business Survey 2015/2016 Executive Summary". Singapore: Singapore Business Federation, 2016. Available at <http://www.sbf.org.sg/images/pdf/NBS/SBF_NBS_Summary_2015-16.pdf>.

Singapore Department of Statistics. *Yearbook of Statistics Singapore 2015*. Singapore: Singapore Department of Statistics, 2015.

————. *Yearbook of Statistics Singapore 2016*. Singapore: Singapore Department of Statistics, 2016a. Available at <http://www.singstat.gov.sg/docs/default-source/default-document-library/publications/publications_and_papers/reference/yearbook_2016/yos2016.pdf>.

————. "Informal Discussions with Singapore Department of Statistics, June to August 2016". 2016b. Informal Discussions.

————. *Yearbook of Statistics Singapore*. Singapore: Singapore Department of Statistics, various issues.

————. "Real Economic Growth". Singapore: Singapore Department of Statistics, 2017a. Available at <http://www.singstat.gov.sg/statistics/visualising-data/charts/real-economic-growth>.

————. "Summary Table: Unemployment". Singapore: Singapore Department of Statistics, 2017b. Available at <http://stats.mom.gov.sg/Pages/Unemployment-Summary-Table.aspx>.

Singapore Department of Statistics and Ministry of Trade and Industry Singapore. "Singapore Standard Industrial Classification 2015". Singapore: Singapore Department of Statistics, 2015.

Singapore Economic Development Board. "Singapore Business News – Adaptability and Advantage". Singapore: Singapore Economic Development Board, 2012. Available at <https://www.edb.gov.sg/content/dam/edb/en/resources/pdfs/publications/SingaporeBusinessNews/Singapore-Business-News-July-2012.pdf> (accessed 7 June 2016).

————. "Logistics and Supply Chain Management". Singapore: Singapore Economic Development Board, n.d. Available at <https://www.edb.gov.sg/content/edb/en/industries/industries/logistics-and-supply-chain-management.html> (accessed 7 June 2016).

Singapore Economic Development Board and SPRING Singapore. "$42 Million Committed to Improving Productivity of Singapore's Logistics and Transportation Industry". Singapore: Singapore Economic Development Board and SPRING Singapore, 2012. Available at <http://www.rp.edu.sg/uploadedFiles/Contents/RP/MEDIA/Press_Release/2012/Media_Release-EDB-SPRING_Launch_Log_Productivity_Roadmap_02Mar2012.pdf> (accessed 6 November 2016).

Singapore Information Services. "The Logistics Industry in Singapore – The Past, Present and Future". Singapore: Singapore Information Services, n.d. Available at <http://www.insis.com/articles/se/the-logistics-industry-in-singapore-the-past-present-and-future> (accessed 7 June 2016).

Singh, Malminderjit. "S'pore's Growing Logistics Sector Tackles Hiring Challenges". *Business Times*, 17 October 2014. Available at <http://www.businesstimes.com.sg/transport/spores-growing-logistics-sector-tackles-hiring-challenges> (accessed 11 November 2016).

Soon, Weilun. "Logistics Players Ponder the Industry's Future as Deliveries Grow". *Business Times*, 20 June 2016. Available at <http://www.businesstimes.com.sg/transport/logistics-players-ponder-the-industrys-future-as-deliveries-grow> (accessed 9 November 2016).

Teng, Mui Yap. "Chapter 10: Singapore's System for Managing Foreign Manpower". Singapore: Lee Kuan Yew School of Public Policy, n.d. Available at <http://lkyspp.nus.edu.sg/ips/wp-content/uploads/sites/2/2013/04/pa_MT_Managing-International-Migration-for-Development-in-East-Asia-Research-Papers_240215.pdf> (accessed 9 November 2016).

Thangavelu, Shandre Mugan. "FDI Restrictiveness Index for ASEAN: Implementation of AEC Blueprint Measures". ERIA Discussion Paper Series 2015-43. Jakarta: Economic Research Institute for ASEAN and East Asia, 2015. Available at <http://www.eria.org/ERIA-DP-2015-43.pdf>.

World Bank. "Doing Business 2016". Washington, D.C.: World Bank, 2016. Available at <http://www.doingbusiness.org/~/media/WBG/DoingBusiness/Documents/Annual-Reports/English/DB16-Full-Report.pdf>.

———. "Global Economic Prospects: Weak Investment in Uncertain Times". Washington, D.C.: World Bank, 2017.

———. World Development Indicators Database [online]. Washington, D.C.: World Bank. Available at <http://wdi.worldbank.org/tables>.

World Shipping Council. "Top 50 World Container Ports", n.d. Available at <http://www.worldshipping.org/about-the-industry/global-trade/top-50-world-container-ports> (accessed 26 February 2017).

World Trade Organization (WTO). "Singapore and the WTO". Geneva: WTO, n.d. Available at <https://www.wto.org/english/thewto_e/countries_e/singapore_e.htm> (accessed 7 November 2016).

6

LOGISTICS SERVICES LIBERALIZATION IN THAILAND

Ruth Banomyong

INTRODUCTION

Trade in services plays an important role in the economic development of a country. The Asian Development Bank (ADB) in 2012 reported that the services sector of ASEAN member countries contributed around 28.1 per cent to 70.1 per cent to their Gross Domestic Product (GDP) from 2000 to 2007 respectively (Park and Shin 2012, p. 35). Among ASEAN countries, Singapore's services sector accounts for around 70.1 per cent of its GDP — highest in the region, followed by the Philippines (50.3 per cent), Malaysia (50 per cent), Thailand (47.7 per cent), and Vietnam (43.3 per cent). Wholesale and retail business has taken up the highest proportion in terms of value added in the services sector in ASEAN, followed by finance and insurance. Singapore has the highest employment share in the services sector, followed by Malaysia, the Philippines, Indonesia, and Thailand.

According to the ASEAN Economic Community (AEC) Blueprint 2025, ASEAN member states (AMS) are required to cooperate under the ASEAN Framework Agreement on Services (AFAS). AMS need to be compliant with the agreed upon liberalization programmes, procedures, and timeframe. One of the objectives of the AFAS is to decrease and eliminate restrictions to trade in services based on the twelve types of services, as classified in the General Agreement on Trade in Services (GATS). These are business services, communication services, construction services, distribution services, education services, environmental services, financial services, health and social services, transport and tourism services, leisure, cultural and sports services, transportation services, and other services that are not included in the above eleven fields, such as spa and beauty services.

According to the established protocols, if any AMS has any reservations or limitations with regard to any measures, these should be specified in the horizontal commitment table. These commitments are legally binding between members. Logistics and other related services fall mostly within the domain of the transport sector and that complicates matters as logistics is much more than just transport related services. Logistics in ASEAN has been identified as a priority integration sector with its own liberalization roadmap by 1 January 2013 (Tongzon 2011).

The purpose of this chapter is to identify key challenges to the liberalization and promotion of foreign direct investment (FDI) in the logistics sector in Thailand as per the ASEAN priority integration sector logistics roadmap of 2007 (Banomyong et al. 2008). Policy guidelines will be then derived based on the identified challenges to enable full logistics service liberalization.

SERVICES LIBERALIZATION IN THAILAND

The Importance of Services to the Thai Economy

Thailand is a classic example of how to achieve rapid economic growth in less than a generation. A low-income country in the 1980s, Thailand was upgraded to an "upper-middle income economy" by the World Bank (Gil and Burgard 2011, p. 96). The transition of this Southeast Asian economy did not only take place within a short span of time, but it also occurred against a backdrop of domestic political turmoil, which is still ongoing. The Thai economy, referred to as a "tiger" economy, grew at a fast pace of 8–9 per cent during the latter part of the 1980s and the early 1990s before it got caught up in the Asian Financial Crisis (AFC) of 1997–98. The "tiger" has now become a "kitten" that is struggling with structural issues in terms of the needed economic transformation for sustaining growth.

The economy, nonetheless, recovered from the AFC in the subsequent years with moderate and occasional spurts of growth before the global financial crisis (GFC) of 2008–9. Since then, economic growth has again slowed down due to economic and political events, along with a few natural disasters. In 2011, one of the worst floods to hit the country in five decades resulted in an economic loss of approximately US$45.7 billion. Political uncertainties and tensions arose in 2010 and yet again in 2013–14. To make things worse, the nation faced a drought in 2015 and floods in the south of the country in 2017. The military dictatorship in charge of the country has not been able to stimulate higher growth level. According to the ADB,[1] Thailand's GDP growth in 2014 and 2015 was 0.8 per cent and 2.8 per cent and it was forecasted to reach 3.2 per cent and 3.5 per cent in 2016 and 2017 respectively. The future still remains unclear as the military junta is struggling with its agenda for the country and numerous mega-projects designed to kick-start the economy has been delayed. Nonetheless, the ADB has also stated that tourism played an important role in driving the moderate growth in the first half of 2016. In fact, growth in tourism combined with weak imports is generating a larger current account surplus than projected.

According to the World Bank's statistics, Thailand's GDP in 2013 and 2015 was US$419.9 billion and US$395.2 billion respectively.[2] In 2014, the primary sector accounted for about 12 per cent of the GDP while industry and tertiary industry accounted for 42 per cent and 46 per cent respectively.

a) *Agriculture*

Agricultural development has played a major role in the transformation of Thailand's economy. The primary sector in the country has undergone two main phases in its development. The first was characterized by agricultural growth that is primarily driven by the utilization of unemployed labour and vacant land. This phase lasted from the early 1960s to the early 1980s, during which time the economy was heavily dependent on agriculture as the main economic driver for growth. Agriculture employed around 70 per cent of Thailand's active working population during the first phase.

During the second phase, rural labour had shifted to urban areas and no new land was utilized. Nevertheless, agricultural sector continued to grow, albeit at a slower rate, led by productivity improvements through mechanization and availability of formal credit, unlike the first phase of agricultural development. Figure 6.1 depicts the value-added to GDP of agriculture in Thailand.

FIGURE 6.1
Value of Agriculture
(% of GDP)

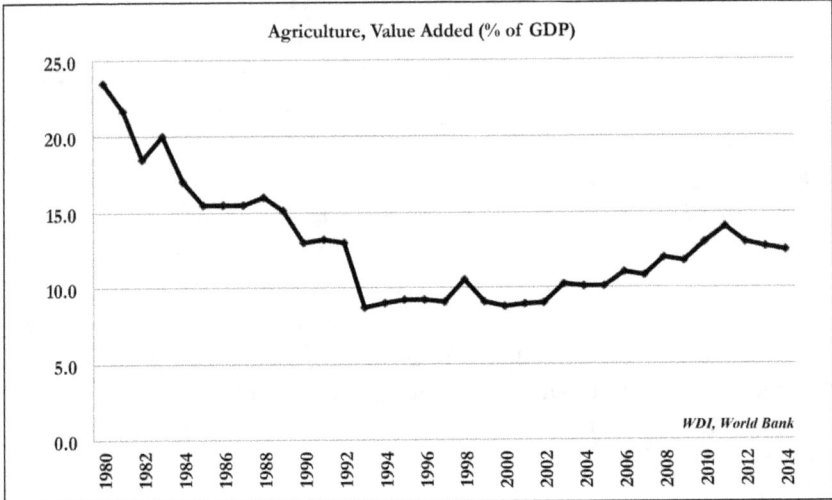

Source: World Development Indicators, World Bank, available at <http://data.worldbank.org/
data-catalog/world-development-indicators> (accessed 1 December 2016).

With growth in the other sectors of the economy, the dependence of Thailand's economic base on agriculture has gradually declined over the years. Nevertheless, this sector still accounts for about 12 per cent of GDP and employs 32 per cent of the population in 2014. This figure is relatively high compared to the United States, the United Kingdom and Japan, where only around 1 to 2 per cent of GDP comes from the primary sector, while it is comparable to China and Malaysia where agricultural contribution to GDP touches around 10 per cent. Thailand's main agricultural output is rice, rubber, corn, sugarcane, coconuts, palm oil, pineapple, cassava (manioc, tapioca) and fish products.

b) *Industry*

The industrial sector comprising mainly of manufacturing but including mining, construction, electricity, water and gas, contributes more than 40 per cent to Thailand's GDP. This share has gradually increased as the share of agriculture progressively declined. The growth in Thailand's manufacturing occurred over two periods, with two different strategies: the first, from 1960–85, was led by import substitution policies; the second era, from 1986 to the present, focuses on export promotion. However, continuous shrinkages in Thailand's export volumes and value in recent years,[3] indicate that the use of the same export promotion policies may have become less effective as it occurred with the weakening of global growth and external demand from the European Union (EU), the United States and China.

In the initial years, manufacturing in Thailand was highly intertwined with agriculture, especially as the country's manufacturing started with the food processing industry. Over time, with changes in the industrial policies, industries like petrochemicals, electronics, automobile and automobile parts, computer equipment, iron and steel, minerals and integrated circuits have emerged, as they received policy support and investment incentives. Figure 6.2 shows the industrial value-added percentage to the Thai GDP.

FIGURE 6.2
Value Added of Industry to GDP

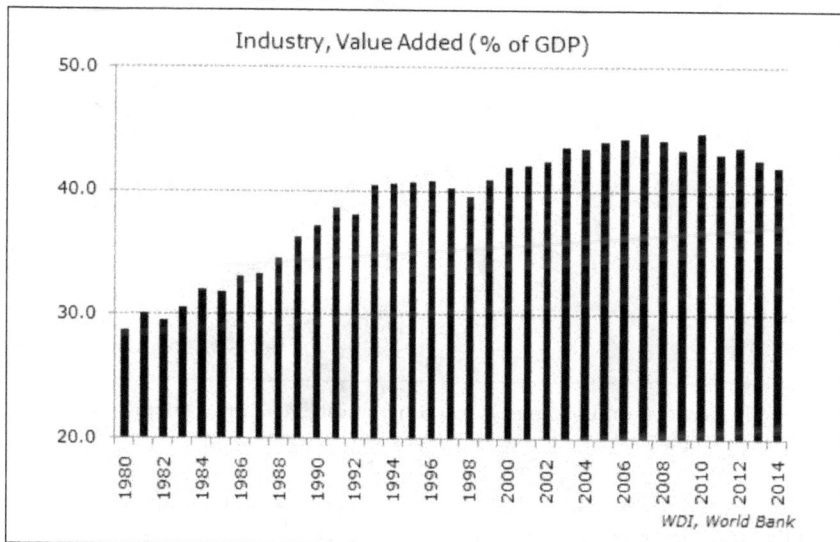

Source: World Development Indicators, World Bank, available at <http://data.worldbank.org/data-catalog/world-development-indicators> (accessed 1 December 2016).

c) *Services*

The services sector accounts for more than 45 per cent of Thailand's GDP in 2014 while providing employment to around 38 per cent of total employment in 2013. It is interesting to note that the share of the service sector has gone down from over 50 per cent to 2000 to just over 45 per cent in 2014. This indicates that the major structural shift in the Thai economy occurred between agriculture and industry. Within services, transportation, wholesale and retail trade (which includes repair of motor vehicles and motorcycles as well as personal and household goods), and tourism and travel-related activities have been the prominent contributors to the GDP and employment generators. The value-added of the service sector to the Thai GDP is shown in Figure 6.3.

FIGURE 6.3
Value Added of Service to GDP

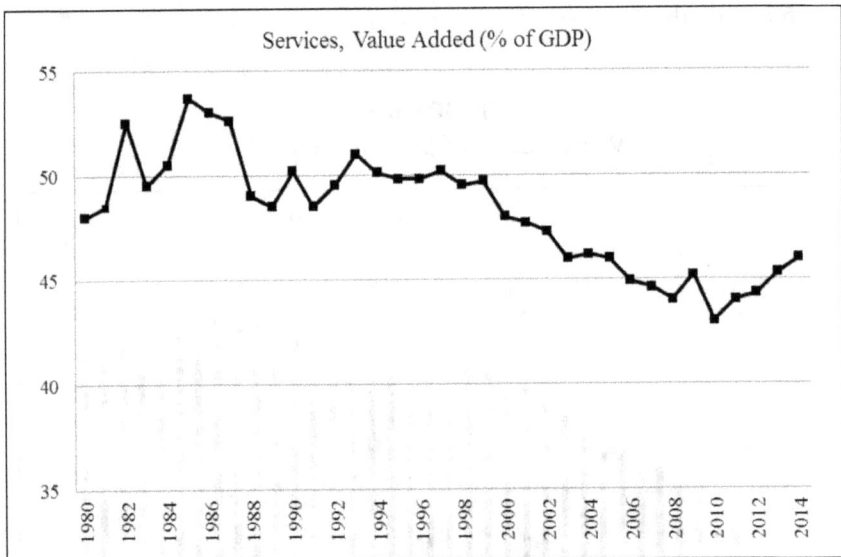

Source: World Development Indicators, World Bank, available at <http://data.worldbank.org/data-catalog/world-development-indicators> (accessed 1 December 2016).

Thailand has several definitions for the service sector, and agencies collect data for different purposes, which can create complexities in understanding the scope and categories of services in the country. As illustrated in Table 6.1, the National Economic and Social Development Board (NESDB) has a different definition of services when compared to GATS. Thailand's services sector is based on the ISIC revision 3, as used by the NESDB, while GATS as well as the AFAS uses the Central Product Classification (CPC) codes for liberalization commitments. This may cause difficulties when trying to compare service sector definitions in Thailand against international definitions used for liberalization commitments.

TABLE 6.1

Definitions of the Services Sector

Services Sector: NESDB Concept	Scope of Services: GATS concept
1. Electricity, gas and water supply	1. Business services
2. Construction	2. Communication services
3. Wholesale and retail trade; repair of motor vehicles, motorcycles, and personal and household goods	3. Construction and related engineering services
4. Hotels and restaurants	4. Distribution services
5. Transport, storage and communications	5. Educational services
6. Financial intermediation	6. Environmental services
7. Real estate, renting, and business activities	7. Financial services
8. Public administration and defence; compulsory social security	8. Health-related and social services
9. Education	9. Tourism and travel-related services
10. Healthcare and social work	10. Recreational, cultural, and sporting services
11. Other community, social, and personal service activities	11. Transport services
12. Private households with employed persons	12. Other services not included elsewhere

Source: Koonnathamdee (2013).

According to Koonnathamdee (2013), Thailand needs to start revising its system of data collection as quickly as possible and in as much detail as possible. The proposed revised system should include regional and provincial data. Informal service activities such as street vending, driving taxis, and offsite tutoring should be collected and included in estimates as these activities are important and contributes to the Thai economy.

Services Liberalization under GATS and AFAS

Thailand has not made much progress in its ninth package of commitments under the AFAS. The unofficial policy since 2015 is not to move forward as the country is facing much internal uncertainties in terms of future directions. The country is therefore adopting a wait-and-see attitude towards numerous regional and international cooperation agreements and commitments, unlike its previous leadership, which took a proactive role in developing a regional agenda and direction. This does not bode well as the country seems to be getting more inward-looking with limited interest in opening up.

Thailand's sector-specific commitments in mode 3 or commercial presence in both the World Trade Organization (WTO) and ASEAN agreements, defer to the respective horizontal commitments in these agreements. In the case of GATS, the horizontal commitments for market access is the same as that stated in 3.3*a* and 3.3*b* of the horizontal commitments in AFAS 9 (see Table 6.2) while it is unbound for national treatment (WTO undated). AFAS 9 allows for a higher percentage of foreign equity ownership, as seen in 3.1 and 3.2 of Table 6.2. Therefore, although it is possible for foreign service providers, including logistics to establish physical presence in the country, 70 per cent of foreign equity ownership is the highest percentage allowed.

However, to obtain the right to have 70 per cent of foreign ownership in Thailand, the foreign service provider must apply for a certificate of business operation pursuant to a treaty or obligation under section XI of the Foreign Business Act (FBA); Ministerial Regulation Prescribing Rules and Procedures Pertaining to the Application for a Foreign Business certificate B.E. 2546 (2003). The same requirement is also needed when the foreign logistics service provider would like to have more than 51 per cent of equity in the juristic person in Thailand. But, even if the established firm has more than 51 per cent of foreign capital, it will not be able to buy land in the country as acquisition and usage of land is unbound under national treatment as shown in Table 6.2.

This is why the main business model for investing in Thailand for foreign logistics service providers is for the foreign partner to have 49 per cent of the capital and to work with Thai partners even though in theory it is possible to have more than 51 per cent. Obtaining the certificate of business operation is almost impossible as it will require the signature of the Minister of Commerce.

Most-Favoured-Nation (MFN) exemptions related to service activities, including logistics in Thailand can only be obtained under a reciprocal basis (see Table 6.3). This means that if a country is willing to give the

TABLE 6.2

Schedule of Horizontal Commitments: Thailand for the Ninth Package of Commitments under AFAS

Mode of Supply	1) Cross-border supply	2) Consumption abroad	3) Commercial presence
Sector or Subsector	Limitation on Market Access	Limitation on National Treatment	Additional Commitments
HORIZONTAL COMMITMENTS			
ALL SECTORS INCLUDED IN THIS SCHEDULE	3) Commercial presence in sectors or subsectors in this schedule is permitted only through limited liability company which is registered in Thailand or the other type of legal entity as specified in the sector-specific commitments of which the company is incorporated and registered, pursuant to Thai laws and regulations and will have to meet one of the following condition as indicated in the sector-specific commitments: 3.1 Foreign equity participation must not exceed 70 per cent of the registered capital and shall only operate through joint venture with a juridical person of Thai national; or 3.2 Foreign equity participation must not exceed 51 per cent of the registered capital and shall only operate through joint venture with a juridical person of Thai national; or 3.3*a*. Foreign equity participation must not exceed 49 per cent of the registered capital; and	3) For 3.3, legal entity which is owned or controlled by foreigner(s) must meet the requirements as stipulated by laws and regulations regarding foreign investment. For 3.1 and 3.2, prior to obtaining a license or certificate, legal entity which is owned or controlled by foreigner(s) must meet the criteria required by the relevant authorities. In establishing its commercial presence, a legal entity which is owned or controlled by foreigner(s) must apply for a certificate of business operation pursuant to a treaty or obligation under section XI of the FBA; Ministerial Regulation Prescribing Rules and Procedures Pertaining to the Application for a Foreign Business certificate B.E. 2546 (2003). According to article XIV and XIV of GATS, service supplier is required to comply with section V of the FBA.	

TABLE 6.2 (continued)

Mode of Supply	1) Cross-border supply	2) Consumption abroad	3) Commercial presence
Sector or Subsector	Limitation on Market Access	Limitation on National Treatment	Additional Commitments
	3.3b. The number of foreign shareholders must be less than half of the total number of shareholders of the company concerned.	For legal entity incorporated pursuant to Thai laws and regulations with foreign equity participation not exceeding 49 per cent of the registered capital: None Unbound for the measures pertaining to subsidies or privileges, minimum capital requirements, acquisition and usage of land, taxation measures, and nationality requirement.	
	3) Acquisition and usage of land: according to the Land Code of Thailand, foreign nationals or domestic companies which are deemed foreigners are not allowed to purchase or own land in Thailand. However, they may lease land and own buildings. For 3.1 and 3.2, a natural person or juridical person of another member that acquires or gains ownership of land, shall be deemed ineligible to exercise rights and privileges under this agreement	3) The board of directors, including administrative and executive position or alike in the legal entity must be of Thai national and have permanent domicile in Thailand. The person or the representative of the juridical person who apply for a license must be of Thai nationality. For 3.1 and 3.2, a natural person or a juridical person who receives other special privileges or incentives from Thai authorities other than those provided under this agreement may not claim benefits under this agreement	

Source: Thai Ministry of Commerce.

TABLE 6.3

Thailand's List of MFN Exemptions for the Ninth Package of Commitments under AFAS

Sector or Subsector	Description of Measure Indicating its Inconsistency with Article II	Countries to which the Measure Applies	Intended Duration	Conditions Creating the Need for the Exemption
Business services – Auditing services – Publishing newspapers	Bilateral agreement based on reciprocity treatment Thailand will grant permission to a natural person of the countries which have treaties with Thailand.	Countries which allow Thai nationals to practise auditing in their territories. Countries which have treaties with the Thai Government.	Indefinite Indefinite	Reciprocal basis Reciprocal basis
Computer reservation system services	Only airlines/CRS partners which are in Amadeus system can bring in and install their own systems in Thailand.	Countries whose CRS operators are in Amadeus system and intend to bring in and install the systems to any travel agencies in Thailand.	Indefinite	To ensure that local operators are able to have complete access to the Amadeus system within a certain period of time.
Transport services – Selling and marketing of maritime transport services – Selling and marketing of air transport services	The value-added tax in use comprises three rates, namely 10 per cent, zero per cent and exempted. VAT collection is based on a reciprocal basis.	– Countries which have the same zero rate VAT system as Thailand; – Countries which exempt Thai persons from VAT or other taxes of similar nature by virtue of the treaties concluded or to be concluded with Thailand; – Countries which exempt juristic persons constituted in accordance with Thai law from VAT or other taxes of similar nature on the basis of reciprocity; – Countries which do not levy VAT or other taxes of similar nature on juristic persons constituted in accordance with Thai law on the basis of reciprocity.	Indefinite	Reciprocal basis

TABLE 6.3 *(continued)*

Sector or Subsector	Description of Measure Indicating its Inconsistency with Article II	Countries to which the Measure Applies	Intended Duration	Conditions Creating the Need for the Exemption
International maritime transport of cargoes	1) Rights to carry all products: – Treaty of Amity and Economic Relations between the Kingdom of Thailand and the United States of America	The United States of America	10 years	Bilateral agreement
	2) Cargo sharing: – Commercial Maritime Navigation Agreement between the Government of the Kingdom of Thailand and the Government of the Socialist Republic of Vietnam	The Socialist Republic of Vietnam	10 years	Bilateral agreement
	– Agreement of Maritime Transport between the Government of the Kingdom of Thailand and the Government of the People's Republic of China	The People's Republic of China	10 years	Bilateral agreement
International road tranport services – Passenger transportation – Freight transportation – Rental of non-commercial vehicles with/without driver	Reciprocity treatment	Countries that have the agreement on international road transport with Thailand	Indefinite	Reciprocal basis

		Indefinite	Reciprocal basis
Aircraft repair and maintenance services	Thailand will grant permission to airlines of those countries which treat Thai carriers on reciprocal basis.	– Countries whose airline is accepted as a designated airline by Thailand under bilateral air services agreements; – Countries whose regulations do not prevent Thai carriers from performing similar activities in that country.	
Service sectors stipulated in the relevant articles of the Treaty of Amity and Economic Relations especially Articles 4 and 10	Only American citizens and entities are granted national treatment with respect to operating business and providing services in Thailand.	The United States of America	10 years	Bilateral agreement

Source: Thai Ministry of Commerce, available at <http://myservices.miti.gov.my/documents/10180/19d4fc7a-c2d5-442b-a17d-9c03a470a53c>.

same treatment to a Thai person, then the foreign person will receive the same treatment in Thailand such as in the case of value-added tax exemption for the selling and marketing of transport services.

Bilateral agreements are another way to allow for MFN exemption. For example, the Treaty of Amity and Economic Relations between the Kingdom of Thailand and the United States of America allows American citizens and juristic persons to be granted Thai national treatment, thereby allowing Americans to conduct their business, without any restrictions. Nonetheless, they would need to invoke Articles 4 and 10 of the Treaty before they can obtain their certificate of business operations. In ASEAN, the only country that has a bilateral agreement with Thailand is Vietnam, for cargo sharing.

It can therefore be observed from Tables 6.2 and 6.3 that Thailand is not willing to open much of its service sector under AFAS, except under a reciprocal basis.

The Thailand FBA

Under the FBA, a foreigner is classified as an alien and the definition of an alien is as follows:

a. A natural person who is not of Thai nationality;
b. A juristic entity which is not registered in Thailand;
c. A juristic entity incorporated in Thailand with foreign shareholding accounting;
d. A partnership or ordinary partnership whose managing partner is a foreigner.

Business laws in Thailand reserve certain rights only for Thai nationals. Therefore, foreign investors face certain restrictions when doing business in Thailand. The law separates foreigners in terms of juristic persons into two different kinds:

a. Juristic person not registered in Thailand;
b. Juristic person registered in Thailand having the characteristics as follows:
    • Limited company or public limited company whereby over 50 per cent of its capital shares are owned by foreigner(s);
    • Limited partnership or registered ordinary partnership whereby over 50 per cent of its capital is invested by foreigner(s); or
    • Limited partnership or registered ordinary partnership having a foreigner as the managing partner or manager.

Moreover, according to Thailand FBA B.E. 2542, there are three types of business activities (see Table 6.4):

TABLE 6.4

Categories of Businesses as Listed in the FBA in Thailand

List 1: Businesses Not Permitted for Foreigners to Operate due to Special Reasons	List 2: Businesses Related to the National Safety or Security or Affecting Arts and Culture, Tradition, Folk Handicraft or Natural Resource and Environment	List 3: Businesses which Thai Nationals Are Not Yet Ready to Compete with Foreigners
(1) Newspaper business, radio broadcasting or television station businesses	*Group 1: Businesses related to the national safety or security*	(1) Rice milling and flour production from rice and farm produce
(2) Rice farming, farming or gardening	(1) Production, selling, repairing and maintenance of: (a) Firearms, ammunition, gun powder, explosives; (b) Accessories of firearms, ammunition and explosives; (c) Armaments, ships, aircrafts or military vehicles; (d) Equipment of components, all categories of war materials.	(2) Fishery, specifically marine animal culture
(3) Animal farming	(2) Domestic land, waterway or air transportation, including domestic airline business.	(3) Forestry from forestation
(4) Forestry and wood fabrication from natural forest	*Group 2: Businesses affecting arts and culture, traditional and folk handicraft*	(4) Production of plywood, veneer board, chipboard or hardboard
(5) Fishery for marine animals in Thai waters and within Thailand specific economic zones	(1) Trading antiques or art objects being Thai arts and handicraft	(5) Production of lime
(6) Extraction of Thai herbs	(2) Production of carved wood	(6) Accounting service business
(7) Trading and auctioning Thai antiques or national historical objects	(3) Silkworm farming, production of Thai silk yarn, weaving Thai silk or Thai silk pattern printing	(7) Legal service business

196 Ruth Banomyong

TABLE 6.4 (continued)

List 1: Businesses Not Permitted for Foreigners to Operate due to Special Reasons	List 2: Businesses Related to the National Safety or Security or Affecting Arts and Culture, Tradition, Folk Handicraft or Natural Resource and Environment	List 3: Businesses which Thai Nationals Are Not Yet Ready to Compete with Foreigners
(8) Making or casting Buddha images and monk alms bowls	(4) Production of Thai musical instruments	(8) Architecture service business
(9) Land trading (estate agent)	(5) Production of goldware, silverware, nielloware, bronzeware or lacquerware	(9) Engineering service business
	(6) Production of crockery of Thai arts and culture	(10) Construction, except for: (a) Construction rendering basic services to the public in public utilities; (b) Other categories of construction as prescribed by the ministerial regulations.
	Group 3: Businesses affecting natural resources or environment	(11) Broker or agent business, except: (a) Being broker or agent for underwriting securities or services connected with future trading; (b) Being broker or agent for trading or procuring goods or services necessary for production; (c) Being broker or agent for trading, purchasing or distributing or seeking both domestic and foreign markets.

(1) Manufacturing sugar from sugarcane	(12) Auction, except: (a) Auction in the manner of international bidding not being the auction of antiques; (b) Other categories of auction as prescribed by the ministerial regulations.
(2) Salt farming, including underground salt	(13) Internal trade connected with native agricultural products or produce not yet prohibited
(3) Rock salt mining	(14) Retailing all of goods having the total minimum capital less than 100 million baht
(4) Mining, including rock blasting or crushing	(15) Wholesaling all categories of goods having minimum capital of each shop
(5) Wood fabrication for furniture and utensil production	(16) Advertising business
	(17) Hotel business, except for hotel management service
	(18) Guided tour
	(19) Selling food or beverages
	(20) Plant cultivation and propagation business
	(21) Other categories of service business except that prescribed

Source: Adapted from Narakorn (1999), p. 21.

- List 1: Business Not Permitted to Foreigners;
- List 2: Business Permitted to Foreigners under Conditions;
- List 3: Business Not Yet Permitted to Foreigners, unless permission is granted by the Director-General of the Commercial Registration Department.

Based on the above definitions, if majority of the shares of a limited company are held by Thais, it is regarded as a Thai company and thus not subject to the FBA. This means that aliens are generally allowed to participate up to 49 per cent in a company that is engaged in restricted businesses. Beyond that, the approval requirement must be complied with. Strictly speaking, any company with majority of foreign shareholders is required to apply for the Foreign Business License (FBL), if it engages in a restricted business. The minimum capital requirement for foreigners is two million baht or around US$64,000 in general, and three million baht or around US$96,000 for those under List 2 or List 3.

There are some exemptions, which allow the foreigner to set up business in Thailand where majority of the owners are foreigners. The Thailand–United States Treaty of Amity is one of such exemption. Under this treaty, the majority of share and the director have to be U.S. citizens to enjoy the exemption from FBL.

Similar to the Thailand–United States Treaty of Amity, the Thailand Board of Investment (BOI) is another exemption which might allow foreigners to operate their businesses in Thailand by holding majority of share capital or even 100 per cent ownership depending on the investment and BOI regulation. The amount of equity capital that can be held by foreign investors is determined by BOI considerations. Such BOI-promoted company will not be restricted by the requirements of the FBA.

However, in the case of logistics, the BOI is still very much confused on how to promote as BOI can only promote investment in warehousing or distribution centres but not on trucking related services. The reason for this confusion is that there is no national definition of what constitutes the logistics industry in Thailand. Depending on the government agency, the understanding of logistics will be different as it is based on their respective mandate. The mandate of the BOI is to promote FDI but because the scope of logistics service is vague, there is a need for the BOI to fall back on incentive schemes that they are familiar with. Real estate investment, in the case of logistics, is related to the establishment of a warehouse or a distribution centre and therefore it is easier for the

BOI to provide incentives in contrast to the establishment of a trucking fleet. This means that the BOI can only support non-movable asset based logistics investment.

Foreigners wishing to engage in businesses indicated in List 2 or List 3 of FBA in Thailand will need to obtain a FBL from the relevant authorities before starting their business operations. An application needs to be filed with the Commercial Registration Department, which will be reviewed by the Cabinet or Foreign Business Committee, as the case may be. Various criteria are used to consider the impact of the proposed business operation, such as the advantages and disadvantages to the nation's safety and security, economic and social development, size of enterprise, local employment, etc. Approval of a business license application is more likely when the authorities view the business as providing significantly more economic benefits, and/or protecting and promoting Thai interests. These criteria are in principle transparent but in reality the decision is made based on a qualitative assessment and it is often ad-hoc in nature.

The application process for a FBL can be at times very time consuming, complicated, with unpredictable outcomes. Therefore, in general, most of foreign investors will rarely go through this process even if they think they have a serious chance to get it. On the other hand, they will not hesitate to go through the BOI application process even when there is only a slim chance of getting it as the process is more transparent and streamlined to provide rapid response to the foreign investor. Moreover, BOI allows for 100 per cent foreign equity with the opportunity to buy land in designated industrial zones. The latter is particularly important for large scale investments, especially in logistics investments in warehouses.

Logistics services fall under List 2 where FBL is needed if foreigners would like to have majority shareholding. As discussed above, the process is long and tedious with an uncertain outcome. It is much easier to find nominee Thai shareholders than to actually comply with the FBA.

Although the FBA may seem restrictive, in reality it has never stopped foreign investors in establishing businesses with the help of willing Thai nominees. This is why it is not surprising at all to see that the major foreign logistics service providers are well established in Thailand without having obtained the FBL. The Thai partner can also play an important lobbying role when necessary, so the selection of the nominee is often based on network of contacts more than actual expertise.

Reform of the FBA has been in discussion for many years. The various foreign chambers of commerce have repeatedly asked the Thai Ministry of Commerce (MoC) to amend and make the FBA more foreign investment friendly with a relaxation of the 49 per cent rule. However, because of the political turmoil in the country, the revised draft of the FBA has become in fact even more stringent with a focus on identifying and instituting penalties against firms that have Thai nominees. The revised draft has not been presented to the legislative assembly and therefore the existing FBA is still in place.

LOGISTICS SERVICES IN THAILAND

Definition and Scope of Logistics Services in Thailand

The NESDB is responsible for the logistics development of the country. The NESDB, based on its mandate to develop and implement the national logistics development plan views logistics from a macro-level perspective that includes infrastructure development and also policy support to Thai logistics service providers. The plan's policy objective focuses on non-asset based providers as the majority of Thai logistics providers are small and medium-enterprises (SMEs) with limited capital. This is why the definition of logistics offered by the NESDB also focuses on non-asset based operators such as freight forwarders and customs brokers with no reference to warehouse or ICT consulting firms

On the other hand, the Department of Business Development at the MoC is responsible for company registration and for assigning business codification of juristic persons in line with the International Standard Industrial Classification (ISIC) (Thailand) developed in 2001. This department has a broader classification of logistics services as shown below:

- **Category 1:** Freight Transport and Forwarding — this group includes logistics services related to domestic and international freight transport and forwarding such as roads, rail, sea, and air transportation. Under the Thai classification, the following codes are used to refer to these juristic persons: 49120, 49331, 49332, 49333, 49334, 49339, 49400, 50121, 50122, 50221, 50222, 51201, and 51202.
- **Category 2:** Warehousing/Inventory Management and Packing — including Distribution. Under the Thai classification, the following codes are used to refer to these juristic persons: 52101, 52102, 52109, 52291, and 52293.

- **Category 3:** Non-Asset Based Logistics Services — this group includes customs clearance, documentary services related to import or export. Under the Thai classification, the following code is used to refer to these juristic persons: 52292.
- **Category 4:** Information and Communication Technology and Consulting — under the Thai classification, the following codes are used to refer to these juristic persons: 52211, 52213, 52214, 52219, 52221, 52229, 52231, 52239, 52241, 52241, and 52299.
- **Category 5:** Courier and Postal Services — concerns both domestic and international delivery services. Under the Thai classification, the following codes are used to refer to these juristic persons: 53100 and 53200.

The scope of logistics services is therefore different between the NESDB and the MoC. The issue here is that there is a clear lack of harmonization of what constitutes logistics services within the country itself. Additionally, policy goals also differ: NESDB focuses on promoting local logistics service providers becoming more international while the scope of the MoC covers a broader range of services for logistics, focusing more on FDI.

Commercial Registration of Logistics Services Related Firms

The majority of logistics businesses established in Thailand are primarily in Category 1 with more than 6,000 registered logistics firms, or around 54 per cent of the total number of logistics related firms. The total number of logistics service firms was 11,377 in 2013. The average growth rate is 0.07 per cent year-on-year. In terms of revenue or sales, Category 1 of services logistics has the highest revenue or sales. Total revenue of Category 1 in 2013 was estimated at 135,886 million baht or around US$3,800 million.

Table 6.5 compares the numbers of registered logistics juristic persons and each category's sales revenue between 2012 and 2013. It can be seen that the largest increase in sales revenue from 2012 to 2013 is in Category 5. The sales figure increased due to the expansion of e-commerce activities in the country but the number of juristic persons fell slightly. It is possible that this reduction is derived from the fact that such services require nationwide capability, which not all providers in Category 5 are able to provide due to their limited size.

TABLE 6.5
Logistics Services Firms' Registration in Thailand

	2013		2012		Per Cent Change, 2012–13	
	No. of juristic persons	Sales (mil. baht)	No. of juristic persons	Sales (mil. baht)	No. of juristic persons	Sales
Category 1	6,142	135,886	6,138	128,927	0.07%	5.40%
Category 2	1,754	60,563	1,705	69,133	2.87%	–12.40%
Category 3	2,420	49,455	2,455	55,532	–1.43%	–10.94%
Category 4	766	109,895	766	113,928	0.00%	–3.54%
Category 5	295	35,903	305	23,344	–3.28%	53.80%
Total	11,377	391,703	11,369	390,865	0.07%	0.21%

Source: Department of Business Development, Thai Ministry of Commerce.

Table 6.6 shows the number of registered juristic persons by regions in 2013. In terms of geographical distribution, logistics firms registered in Bangkok are the largest in numbers, representing around 49 per cent of all logistics services firms registered in the country.

TABLE 6.6
Geographical Distribution of Registered Logistics Services Firms in Thailand, 2013

(unit: firm)

	Bangkok	North	Northeast	Central	West	East	South	Total
Category 1	2,156	407	442	1,541	209	864	523	6,142
Category 2	973	118	34	384	21	161	63	1,754
Category 3	1,747	62	31	350	4	103	123	2,420
Category 4	450	31	34	119	11	57	64	766
Category 5	200	6	4	55	3	10	17	295
Total	5,526	624	545	2,449	248	1,195	790	11,377

Source: Department of Business Development, Thai Ministry of Commerce.

Estimated Value of the Logistics Market in Thailand

Although the global economy continues to be weak with increased debts in the Euro zone combined with a deceleration of manufacturing and growth in China, the domestic logistics market seems to be still robust up to a certain extent. Some research institutes such as the Kasikorn Research Center in 2012 considered that the establishment of the AEC in 2015 and potential new regional groupings such as the Regional Comprehensive Economic Partnership (RCEP) will continue to support logistics market growth, with the development of linkages with ASEAN and its Plus-6 partners. Cross-border trade remains a key driver that will sustain growth in the logistics service sectors. Kasikorn Research Center (2014) estimated an average annual growth rate for the logistics market between 6.3 per cent and 8 per cent, as shown in Figure 6.4. The value of the Thai logistics market was estimated from 2008 to 2013 to be US$123 million, US$127 million, US$130 million, US$128.5 million, US$147 million and US$154 million, respectively.

FIGURE 6.4
Estimated Annual Growth Rate of the Thai Logistics Market

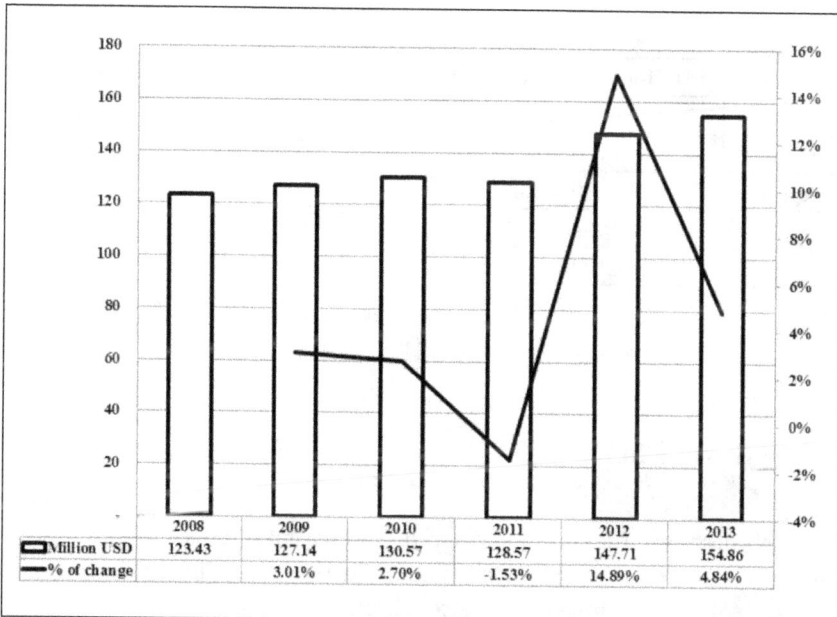

	2008	2009	2010	2011	2012	2013
Million USD	123.43	127.14	130.57	128.57	147.71	154.86
% of change		3.01%	2.70%	-1.53%	14.89%	4.84%

Source: Adapted from Kasikorn Research Center, *Economic Insight* no. 2451 (2014).

According to the Department of Business Development, it was estimated that assets owned by the Thai logistics sector reached 742,924.85 million baht or US$21,226 million in 2013. The category with the highest assets is Category 4 that covers the communication sector (see Table 6.7). Service providers in this category have to invest continuously in telecommunication technology in order to provide their services as the value of their assets tend to diminish over time because of technological obsolescence.

Service providers in Category 1 have more overall assets than those in Category 2. This is due mainly to the sheer number of providers as the majority of Category 1 service providers pursue a light asset strategy (see Table 6.6). It is possible that there are some vessels operators in this category but most of the Thai ship owners prefer to fly foreign flags and therefore do not have these assets in their Thai ledger. Category 2 service providers, which are substantially fewer in number than those in Category 1, need to have the land to build their warehouse and distribution centres thus forcing them to have more assets per firm, compared to firms in Category 1.

TABLE 6.7
Assets Owned by Logistics Firms in Thailand

	2013	2012
	Total assets (Mil. US$)	Total assets (Mil. US$)
Category 1	220,594.01	217,739.56
Category 2	114,800.81	123,262.83
Category 3	39,836.48	39,663.84
Category 4	345,552.07	351,127.03
Category 5	22,141.48	38,164.62
TOTAL	742,924.85	769,957.88

Source: Department of Business Development, Thai Ministry of Commerce.

LOGISTICS SERVICES LIBERALIZATION CHALLENGES IN THAILAND

Table 6.8 describes the challenges faced by Thai logistics service providers based on a survey that was conducted during the annual meeting of the national freight forwarders association in 2014. Not all members were present but around eighty respondents provided answers from a membership roster of 300 members. This meant that the survey had a 27 per cent response rate and thereby providing the perspectives of the service providers alone. Based on the survey results, the main challenges can be summarized as a lack of competitiveness of local service providers, weak policy support and legal barriers.

Lack of Competitiveness of Local Logistics Service Providers (LSPs)

The biggest problem for the logistics service sector in Thailand is not from the lack of liberalization but more related to the local providers themselves. Ninety per cent of the local logistics service providers in Thailand are SMEs and do suffer from inherent weaknesses in their operations. Local Thai LSPs often provide their services as subcontractors to large multinational logistics providers which have limited access to the end clients. They also suffer from a lack of scale in the provision of integrated logistics services where the service providers need to be in control of all logistics activities from door to door. Most local LSPs have expertise in only one or two specific logistics activities such as customs brokerage or sea freight forwarding.

Inadequate Policy Support

The Thai logistics service industry sees itself as un-competitive when compared with their foreign counterparts and hence they would like to have government support. According to the NESDB, in their lessons learned from the first national logistics plan, Thai LSPs have business disadvantages in terms of integrated services, international standard administrative management, IT innovation sufficiency as well as difficulties in accessing finance.

The most often request for support relates to access to finance but this is a difficult issue from a policy perspective. Access to finance for SMEs has always been an issue in the country and the establishment of an SME development bank did not help the local LSPs much. Even though there is a specific fund in this SME bank earmarked for local logistics providers but there is not enough collateral to guarantee the loan due to limited assets. The logistics service industry is different from manufacturing where production equipment can be used to guarantee loans. In the case of small and medium LSPs, the only asset may be their truck fleet, which may already be under a leasing contract. Contracts with clients are not long term enough or of a sufficient value to be used collaterals. Moreover, if financial aid is to be provided to this specific sector, then other sectors will also ask for similar support.

The country has had two national logistics development plan and it is currently undergoing consultations for the development of a new plan for the period 2018 to 2022. The national logistics development plan (2011–16) focused on enhancing the competitiveness of Thai logistics service providers with specific policies to support Thai providers to achieve international quality standards and develop regional logistics networks in ASEAN and beyond. But, the success of the two plans is quite limited due to a lack of implementation capability. There is also no unified understanding on the actual of scope of logistics, with many agencies competing in the same development area. The most common example is the overlap between the Thai Ministry of Commerce and the Thai Ministry of Transport when trying to implement support policies for Thai LSPs that are SMEs. The SMEs that are benefitting are the same and the support activities are similar too.

Another reason for the limited success in the two earlier plans is the lack of clear measures on how to achieve these goals. The performance indicators that are used to measure if targeted goals have been achieved do not reflect or explain how or what the line agencies such as the MoC should do in order to achieve them. This has led the MoC, in the case of internationalizing local LSPs, to organize events or exhibitions in neighbouring countries with local LSPs, having their respective booths offered by the MoC. Such an approach enables the MoC to achieve the quantitative criteria of having local providers going abroad but not in terms of actually establishing a presence or offering logistics services in a foreign country.

The current tangible support policy that is being implemented, not by the MoC, but by the Thai Ministry of Transport focuses on assisting Thai trucking providers expand their operations to neighbouring countries. This is because of the opening up of land borders and the establishment of bilateral agreements with Cambodia for the exchange of traffic rights as well as the implementation of the Greater Mekong Subregion Cross Border Transport Agreement (GMS-CBTA) that have opened up opportunities for cross border transport with Thailand's neighbouring countries. The help provided is to take Thai trucking firms to neighbouring countries and organize business-matching activities. There are no financial or even legal and advisory services support if Thai operators should decide to enter the foreign market.

This approach is not sustainable as there is no real support after the Thai logistics provider enters the foreign market. For a Thai provider to be successful it will need to go with a Thai manufacturing or trading firm into that market and provide logistics services for the Thai owner of the goods. It is impossible for a Thai provider to come and just provide logistics services in the domestic market in the foreign country as local cargo owners in that country would prefer to use their own local providers.

Legal Barriers

Services liberalization in Thailand is a sensitive subject (Banomyong 2014). The services sector represents almost half of the country's GDP and would benefit from higher levels of liberalization. Thailand is well aware of its international and regional commitments but the country is still struggling in terms of implementation. Within the context of ASEAN, logistics services liberalization should have been a reality since 2013 in Thailand with ASEAN nationals, both natural and juristic persons, being able to have as much as 70 per cent of capital in a logistics service firm. This is not the case as foreign investment is subject to the FBA of 1999 that restricts activities as well as shareholding of foreigners. The other explanation is that most transport logistics related services are classified under List 2 (see Table 6.4) and these services would need to have not only the approval of the Minister of Commerce but also the Cabinet.

In the case of logistics, the sector itself is not closed but it is still subject to the 49 per cent rule for foreign investors. From an operational perspective this is not a real issue. In terms of promotion for the logistics sector, the BOI in Thailand can provide exemptions to the FBA as well as other incentives. However, logistics services need to have land related investment such as the buying of land to build a warehouse or a distribution centre in order to qualify for BOI status. In the case of transport logistics services, the BOI cannot provide incentive or special status as these assets are not considered as secure.

However, the existing legal restrictions have not really limited access of foreign providers to the Thai market. Foreign logistics service providers have been operating in the country for a long time and the trend will continue. Hence, there needs to be a clear distinction between legal requirements and operational services being provided.

TABLE 6.8
Challenges Faced by Thai Logistics Service Providers

Activities	Challenges
Freight Transportation and Forwarding	
Trailers and Semi-trailers Transport Services	Idle transportation vehicles and inefficient use of trailers Severe price competition Does not feel competitive enough to compete with other countries
Truck Transport	Limited business operating standards Difficult access to new customers Lack of updated technology Lack of skilled human resources
Barge Transport	Thai legislative environment challenging for efficient operations Limited international connectivity
Rail Transport	Laws and regulations are obsolete Outdated technology Lack of professional management system Weak infrastructure
Air Freight Transport	Congestion at main airport Limited use of provincial airports
Warehousing and Distribution	Cannot compete against foreign providers Commercial warehouses in Thailand need to have more professional management systems. Distribution centres are dominated by foreign-owned interests.
Courier and Postal Services	Thai local firms are just subcontractors. Local users do not have access to good services.
Packing	Lack of skilled employees Lack of expertise in using new technologies
Customs Clearance	Competitive pricing Access to funds to advance duty payment for customers
Transport Agents	Most Thai service providers are only subcontractors of foreign service providers. Limited Thai service providers can offer integrated logistics service providers. Unable to access their target markets Lack of investment promotion factors Limited access to updated information technology Are not aware of modern management techniques

Source: Banomyong (2014).

CONCLUSION

In order for Thailand to meet its commitment under AFAS and in the priority integration sector logistics roadmap of 2007, it is necessary for the country to amend its FBA on 1999. However, it may take a very long time to change the law as there is a general lack of political will to change its content. Operationally, this does not pose a problem to foreign logistics provider to establish a commercial presence in the country as it is possible to find Thai nominee partners who will help fill in the necessary legal requirements with respect to the allowed foreign shareholding ceiling.

The best case situation would be to amend the FBA to enable full liberalization but if this cannot be done, apart from the operational flexibility offered in the country, foreign logistics providers may choose to ask for their investment projects to be approved by the BOI for equity ownership purposes as well as to have access to buying land in the country. This option is more suited for large foreign providers that plan to establish warehouses, distribution centres or logistics parks in the country. Smaller scale foreign investment in moveable assets would not qualify for BOI and therefore these investments will fall under the jurisdiction of the FBA.

The competitiveness of local LSPs is considered important by the Thai government in their national logistics development plan. However, the implementation of the plan has mostly focused on achieving the quantitative targets such as the number of Thai LSPs going abroad (even if it is just for an event) than on the establishment of a successful commercial presence in a foreign country. If this policy is to be taken seriously, there is a need to establish a support agency for all Thai businesses that are planning to invest in commercial presence abroad. Such an agency can be similar to the Japan External Trade Organisation (JETRO) model. JETRO has primarily three major roles: (1) provision of market information; (2) organization of Trade Tie-Up Promotion Programmes (TTPP); and (3) establishment of Business Support Centres (IBSC). JETRO also provides free office space and professional advisors for consulting services. Such an organization would be beneficial for Thai LSPs that plan to expand to other countries.

Thai LSPs are by nature opposed to liberalization as they consider themselves at a disadvantage. However, if the perspective of the cargo owners and users of logistics services is taken into account, liberalization will further enhance competition in the logistics services market and enable users to have access to efficient and effective logistics services. It is a question of perspective and since there are more users of logistics services than LSPs in the country, the benefit of liberalizing logistics would be more beneficial to the users of logistics services than to the LSPs themselves. The Thai government should therefore choose between supporting local LSPs or local traders, manufacturers, or importers and exporters. The benefit of supporting local LSPs is minimal on the country.

The PIS roadmap for logistics is a typical example of an ASEAN plan, where liberalization and facilitation for logistics integration is encouraged though the implementation aspect is kept flexible. In other words, this implies while liberalization is a good starting point for ASEAN countries, the final decision to open up the logistics sector resides with each AMS and at a pace that is decided internally. But, it is also important for ASEAN to consider the perspective of the users of logistics services rather than from the perspective of the providers alone. The latter may have a vested interest in maintaining the current status quo. Therefore, liberalization efforts have to bear in mind that it should foster lowering costs to the users of logistics services and the pace of liberalization should not cater to the demands of logistics providers alone.

Notes

1. <https://www.adb.org/countries/thailand/economy> (accessed 14 February 2017).
2. World Development Indicators, World Bank, available at <http://data.worldbank.org/data-catalog/world-development-indicators> (accessed 14 February 2017).
3. <http://tnsc.com/news/news/view/20> (in Thai language) (accessed 13 December 2016).

References

ASEAN. *The ASEAN Economic Community Blueprint 2025*. Jakarta: ASEAN Secretariat, 2015.
Banomyong, Ruth. *The Impact of the ASEAN Framework Agreement on Services: The Case of the Logistics and Retail Industry*. Bangkok: Institute for Trade and Development, 2014. (in Thai language)

Banomyong, Ruth, Peter Cook and Paul Kent. "Formulating Regional Logistics Development Policy: The Case of ASEAN". *International Journal of Logistics Research and Applications* 11, no. 5 (2008): 359–79.

Gil, Sander F. and Anthony Burgard. "Thailand Economic Monitor: April 2011". *Thailand Economic Monitor*. Washington, D.C: World Bank, 2011.

Kasikorn Research Center. "Thai Logistics, 2H12: Supported by Regional Networks Ahead of AEC". Business Brief no. 3314 Full Ed. Bangkok: Kasikorn Research Center, July 2012.

———. "Land Transport, 2014: Thai Entrepreneurs Bracing for AEC". Current Issue no. 2451 Full Ed. Bangkok: Kasikorn Research Center, January 2014.

Koonnathamdee, Pracha. "A Turning Point for the Service Sector in Thailand". ADB Economics Working Paper no. 353. Manila: Asian Development Bank, June 2013.

Nanakorn, Pinai. "Official Translation of the Foreign Business Act (1999)". Bangkok: Department of Business Development, Thai Ministry of Commerce, 1999. Available at <http://www.dbd.go.th/dbdweb_en/ewt_dl_link.php?nid=4047> (accessed 1 June 2016).

Park, Donghyun and Kwanho Shin. "The Service Sector in Asia: Is it an Engine of Growth?". ADB Economics Working Paper Series no. 322. Manila: Asian Development Bank, December 2012.

Tongzon, Jose. "Liberalisation of Logistics Services: The Case of ASEAN". *International Journal of Logistics Research and Applications* 14, no. 1 (2011): 11–34.

World Trade Organization (WTO). "Services: Commitments". Geneva: WTO, n.d. Available at <https://www.wto.org/english/tratop_e/serv_e/serv_commitments_e.htm> (accessed 18 February 2017).

7

SERVICES LIBERALIZATION IN VIETNAM: THE CASE OF FDI IN LOGISTICS SECTOR

Nguyen Anh Thu, Vu Thanh Huong and Nguyen Thi Minh Phuong

INTRODUCTION

Since the *Doi Moi* in 1986, Vietnam has been progressively opening up its services sector. In recent years, it has made significant efforts to liberalize the sector by participating in various trade agreements, including bilateral, and multilateral agreements related to trade in service, namely GATS (General Agreement on Trade in Services), AFAS (ASEAN Framework Agreement on Services), different ASEAN+1 FTAs and recently the EU–Vietnam FTA (EVFTA) and Trans-Pacific Partnership (TPP) agreement. In line with its commitments, Vietnam has reviewed, revised and issued numerous legislative regulations and policies towards a freer flow of services. Consequently, the regulatory framework related to the services sector in Vietnam has become more transparent and open to foreign suppliers, enabling them to have better access to its domestic services market.

However, the ease of doing business in Vietnam remains at a relatively low ranking — the 90th among 189 countries (World Bank 2016), partly because the services-related policies are still relatively restrictive towards foreign direct investment (FDI). Therefore, there is a need for Vietnam to evaluate its challenges in services liberalization, especially in the aspect of commercial presence (i.e. mode 3), by examining the impediments to FDI inflows in services so as to enable Vietnam to benefit from ASEAN's initiatives to liberalize services.

This chapter analyses the development and contribution of the services sector to Vietnam's economy. It also discusses services trade liberalization under AFAS and GATS along with the domestic FDI policies in the services sector. The logistic sector was selected as a case study for a deeper analysis of Vietnam's services liberalization. Based on these economy-wide and sector-specific discussions, the chapter will identify key challenges facing Vietnam in attracting FDI into the services sector. The chapter concludes with policy recommendations for Vietnam as well as for ASEAN.

SERVICES SECTOR IN VIETNAM

Overview of Services Sector

The services sector plays an increasingly important role in Vietnam's economy. In 2014, the sector accounted for 39.0 per cent of Vietnam's GDP,[1] 6.8 per cent of total exports and 8.9 per cent of total imports. The employment in services accounts for 32.3 per cent of total employment in Vietnam (GSO 2015). Subsequently in 2015, the sector contributed 39.7 per cent to Vietnam's GDP.[2] Its contribution to trade and employment also increased to 6.9 per cent of total exports, 10.0 per cent of total imports and 33.2 per cent of total employment (GSO 2016).

According to Vietnam's overall strategy for services development towards 2020, priorities are given for developing the services that have comparative advantages and potentials, especially in the field of science and technology. It includes Information and Communication Technology (ICT), education, logistics, finance, business services, tourism, transport, distribution, and healthcare services. These sectors are identified based mainly on an assessment of Vietnam's services productivity, efficiency and demand, and the trend in the development of the world's services (Lakatos et al. 2009).

Economic liberalization, in general, and investment liberalization, in particular, seem to have a positive impact on Vietnam's FDI inflows. After opening up the economy during 1991–97, Vietnam received the first wave of FDI with total registered capital of nearly US$34 billion (see Figure 7.1). The period 2007–9 saw a boom in the FDI inflows

FIGURE 7.1
Vietnam's FDI Inflows, 1991–2015
(US$ million)

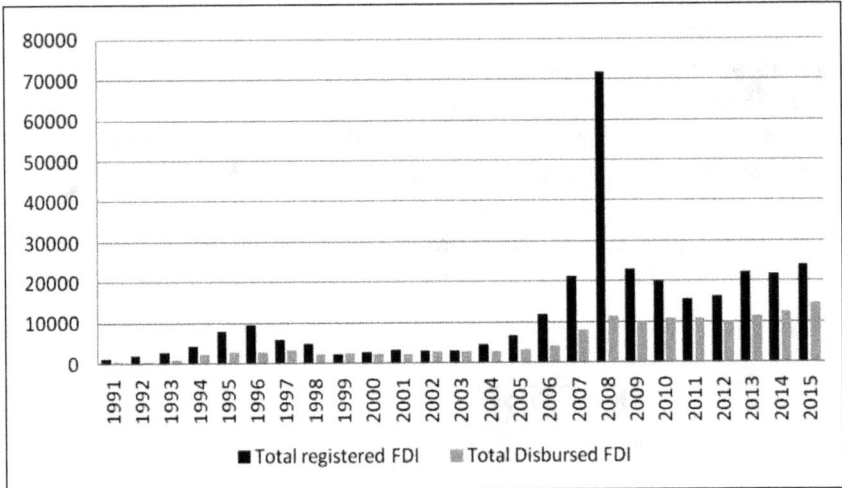

Source: General Statistics Office; Foreign Investment Agency of Vietnam, available at <http://fia.mpi.gov.vn/>.

to Vietnam, thanks to the country's accession to the World Trade Organization (WTO). In 2007, the registered FDI capital soared to US$21.3 billion and the total disbursed FDI was more than US$8 billion, twice as much as that of the year 2006. Even in the subdued global economic environment in 2008, Vietnam's total registered or approved FDI capital reached a record level of more than US$72 billion and the implemented or actual capital of US$11.5 billion. For the period 2009–14, Vietnam maintained relatively stable FDI inflows, attracting from US$10 billion to US$12.5 billion of realized or actual FDI capital each year. The year 2015 marked a turning point in the international economic integration process of Vietnam with the establishment of the ASEAN Economic Community (AEC) and the completion of negotiations of key FTAs, including the EVFTA and the TPP. Vietnam's FDI inflows again saw an increase in 2015, which likely remains as a trend in the coming years.

The manufacturing and services sectors have received the most FDI inflows. As of 31 December 2015, cumulative FDI in manufacturing and services respectively accounted for 58 per cent and 35 per cent of the total registered FDI capital (see Figure 7.2). Although the services sector attracted a high share of registered FDI soon after Vietnam's accession to the WTO,[3] its share fell from a high of 83.2 per cent in 2009 to as low as 13.4 per cent in 2013, before recovering moderately to 19.1 per cent in 2015. The impact of investment liberalization on manufacturing seems to be greater when compared to that of services, suggesting that there are other factors affecting FDI in services besides investment liberalization (see Figure 7.3).

Among the subsectors in services, business services[4] attracted more than half of the total registered FDI in services. Real estate business is the largest FDI recipient within the business services. Tourism and travel related services and construction services attracted 12 per cent and 11 per cent of the total registered services FDI, respectively. Each of the sectors, including distribution services; recreational, cultural and sporting services; transport services and health related and social services, received 4–5 per cent of the total registered FDI in services. FDI in other subsectors are insignificant at around 1–2 per cent for each (see Figure 7.4).

FIGURE 7.2
Vietnam's Registered FDI Inflows by Group,
Accumulated as of 31 December 2015
(%)

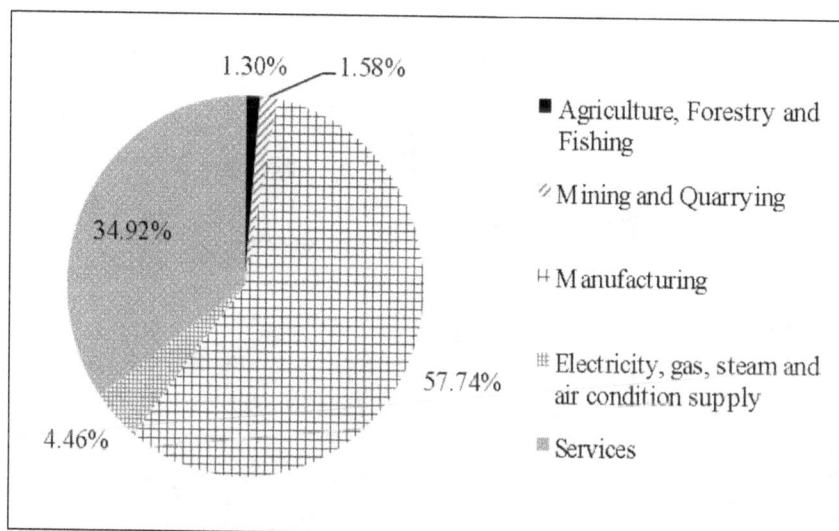

- Agriculture, Forestry and Fishing
- Mining and Quarrying
- Manufacturing
- Electricity, gas, steam and air condition supply
- Services

1.30% 1.58%
34.92%
4.46%
57.74%

Source: Foreign Investment Agency of Vietnam, available at <http://fia.mpi.gov.vn/>.

FIGURE 7.3
Vietnam's Registered FDI Inflows by Group, 2008–15
(%)

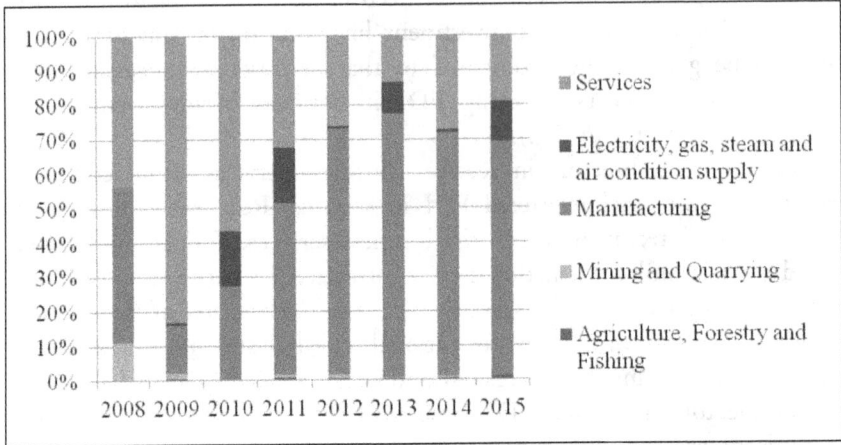

Source: Authors' calculations from General Statistics Office and Foreign Investment Agency of Vietnam, 2009–16.

FIGURE 7.4
Vietnam's Registered Cumulative FDI in Services by Sector,
as of 31 December 2015
(%)

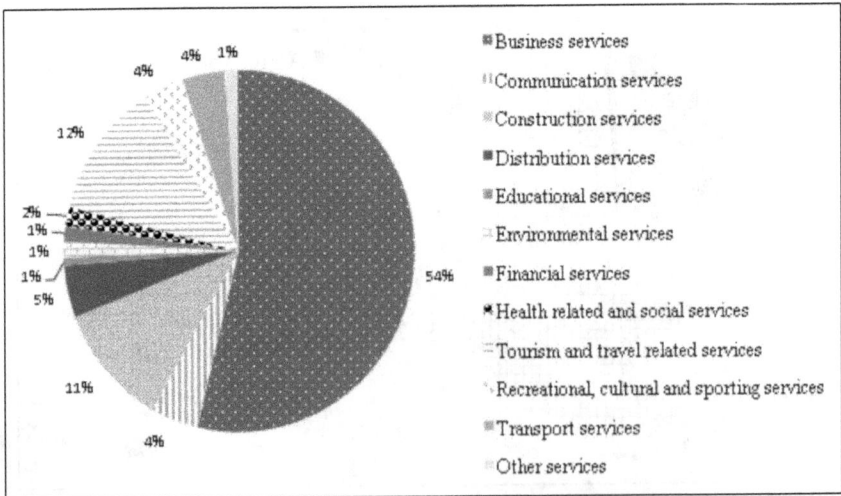

Source: General Statistics Office; Foreign Investment Agency of Vietnam, available at <http://fia.mpi.gov.vn/>.

Services Liberalization in Vietnam
FDI Policies in Vietnam

Seen as the milestone towards a freer and fairer investment regime in Vietnam, the Law on Investment in 2005 was promulgated to create a more liberal and transparent investment regime. Vietnam for the first time legislated a common Law on Investment that is applied to both domestic and foreign investors (replacing the Law on Foreign Investment in 1987, which was revised in 1990, 1992, 1996, 2000 and the Law on Promotion of Domestic Investment in 1998). More recently, the Law on Investment in 2014 was enacted to replace the Law on Investment in 2005 with some important amendments towards more liberal and transparent investment policies, including investment assurance and procedures.

The provisions of the Law on Investment in 2005 and in 2014 have extended autonomy to provincial governments and provided better conditions for investors in business activities. It has also removed barriers inconsistent with market-economy rules and Vietnam's liberalization commitments at the multilateral, regional and bilateral levels. Along with the Law on Enterprise in 2014 and in 2006, Vietnam has built a legal framework towards non-discrimination between domestic and foreign investors.

The trend of decentralization in FDI management that arose since the issuance of the Law on Investment in 2005 allows for the autonomy of provincial governments in investment promotion activities and has helped to reduce burdensome and investment costs for investors, thereby improving the investment environment. However, this policy also led to a number of shortcomings in recent years, such as "a race to the bottom" or excessive competition for FDI among provinces, disruption of industrial and regional planning and attracting low quality FDI. Consequently, in the Law on Investment in 2014, the authority of National Assembly, the Prime Minister and the People's Committees of provinces are more clearly defined in order to avoid such problems.

Besides, Vietnam has revised and issued laws and policies to implement its commitments in specific sectors, especially in the distribution service sector, banking, insurance, securities, and telecommunications. For the priority services sectors including health care, tourism, logistics, e-ASEAN, and aviation, Vietnam has strictly complied with its commitment and it has been actively implementing ASEAN agreements.

The country has given priorities to projects in the five areas. They are: (i) projects related to some selected production activities (e.g. production of high tech products, green energy, IT products, key electronics, mechanical products, cars, car parts, etc., and productions in labour-intensive sectors) (Article 16 of the Law on Investment 2014); (ii) projects in services such as collection, treatment and recycling of waste; public passenger transportation; preschool, compulsory and vocational education; medical examination and treatment; protection and development of cultural heritage; people's credit funds and microfinance institutions are also among prioritized sectors (Article 16 of the Law on Investment 2014); (iii) projects with capital of at least VND 6,000 billion (about US$263.5 million) and disbursement within three years; (iv) projects in rural areas employing at least 500 workers; and (v) high tech enterprises (Article 15 of the Law on Investment 2014).

Other incentives have also been taken to further attract FDI, including (i) preferential corporate tax policy, e.g. exemption of corporate income tax in the first two to four years; reduction of 50 per cent of the corporate income tax for another four to nine years; preferential rate for corporate income tax of 10–20 per cent for fifteen years compared to the standard rate of 22 per cent; (ii) exemption of the import tax for necessary goods serving for the FDI project; (iii) allowing losses to be carried forward within five years; (iv) exemption and fee reduction for rental of land or water surface.

Vietnam's Services Liberalization Commitments under GATS and AFAS

Vietnam has participated in different bilateral and multilateral agreements with services liberalization such as the US–Vietnam Bilateral Trade Agreement, AFAS, Trade in Services agreements in the ASEAN–China FTA, ASEAN–Korea FTA, ASEAN–Japan FTA, and ASEAN–Australia–New Zealand FTA. Recently concluded agreements namely the EVFTA also require Vietnam to open up its services sector. However, so far, the two most important agreements for services liberalization are GATS under the WTO framework and AFAS under the ASEAN framework. While the former should be regarded as the benchmark in making services commitments with other partners in the world, the latter shows the willingness and determination of Vietnam to improve its services liberalization post-GATS.

Under the latest package of AFAS 9, *in terms of services coverage*, Vietnam has committed to liberalize all twelve services sectors, with a total of 117 services subsectors out of 155 (see Table 7.1). In AFAS 9, Vietnam has committed to liberalize six more subsectors compared to

TABLE 7.1
Vietnam's Services Commitments under GATS and AFAS 7, 8 and 9

No.	Sector	Number of Subsectors as Defined in GATS[5]	Number of Committed Subsectors in GATS	Number of Committed Subsectors in AFAS 7	Number of Committed Subsectors in AFAS 8	Number of Committed Subsectors in AFAS 9
1	Business	46	26	21	25	30
2	Communication	24	19	20	20	20
3	Construction	5	5	5	5	5
4	Distribution	5	4	4	4	4
5	Education	5	4	4	4	5
6	Environment	4	3	3	4	4
7	Finance	17	16	16	16	16
8	Health care	4	2	3	4	4
9	Tourism	4	2	3	3	3
10	Recreation, culture and sport	5	2	2	2	2
11	Transport	36	17	14	24	24
12	Other services	–	0	0	0	3**
	Total*	155	100	95	111	117

Notes: * Excluding other services
        ** Laundry collection services; Dry cleaning services; and Pressing services
Source: Vu Thanh Huong and Tran Viet Dung (2015); authors' calculations from
        Vietnam's services schedule in AFAS 8 and the seventh package of commitments on
        air transport services.

AFAS 8, and twenty-two more subsectors compared to AFAS 7, showing its determination and willingness to further opening up of the services sector with the region. However, the increase of only six more subsectors has not yet resulted in significant additional liberalization under the AFAS 9 commitments, compared with AFAS 8.

Comparing GATS and AFAS, the coverage of Vietnam's commitments in terms of the number of subsectors committed to be liberalized in ASEAN before AFAS 7 was relatively fewer compared to GATS (see Table 7.1). From AFAS 8 to AFAS 9, Vietnam has gradually enhanced its liberalization commitments within ASEAN by increasing more main sectors and subsectors in AFAS. As a result, up to AFAS 9, Vietnam has opened more subsectors in AFAS than in GATS, such as business services, communications services, education, health care, tourism, transport, and environment. This is expected because health care, tourism, air transport and logistics are prioritized sectors in ASEAN. In addition, the signing of the ASEAN Movement of Natural Persons (MNP) in 2012 and eight Mutual Recognition Agreements (MRAs) have contributed to improving professional services (in business sector) liberalization in Vietnam.

In terms of degree of openness by subsectors, based on the Hoekman index, environmental services has the highest degree of liberalization, followed by financial services and health care. The degree of openness was lowest for culture, recreation and sport services, and educational services (Vu Thanh Huong 2013). Under AFAS 9, Vietnam has kept the same level of commitments for nine out of eleven services sectors, as in AFAS 8. The degree of openness has increased by two additional sectors, such as education and business services mainly because Vietnam added more sectors in its commitments in AFAS 9. However, in total, the degree of openness of Vietnam has only increased marginally under AFAS 9 when compared to its previous commitments in AFAS 8.

In terms of degree of openness by modes, under AFAS 8, Vietnam had the highest level of liberalization in mode 2. Vietnam was relatively reluctant in liberalizing modes 1 and 3, and it is mostly unbound in mode 4 (Vu Thanh Huong 2013). The committed level of other modes including mode 3 increases in AFAS 9, but only marginally, as Vietnam was very reluctant to improve on its commitments in AFAS 8.

More specifically to mode 3, which is in nature related to FDI in services, the Hoekman index for Vietnam in AFAS 8 is 0.49 (Vu Thanh Huong 2013), implying that the "Unbound" commitments is slightly higher than "Partially" and "None" commitments. The most restricted sectors in mode 3 are education and recreation, followed by tourism. Even though the level of commitments made are higher than those of modes 1 and 4, nevertheless it shows that Vietnam continues to have some barriers to entry in terms of policies and regulations towards ASEAN services providers that aim to enter the Vietnamese services market.

In short, Vietnam has made gradual improvements in services liberalization in terms of the number of subsectors and depth of commitments, and its commitment level in AFAS surpasses those made under GATS. Vietnam has also progressively reduced entry barriers in mode 3 for ASEAN service providers, especially in terms of obtaining permission for branch establishments and a reduction of the cap on foreign equity ownership. All of these efforts have created more opportunities and better advantages for ASEAN compared to non-ASEAN services providers.

OVERVIEW OF THE LOGISTICS SECTOR IN VIETNAM

Concept of Logistics in Vietnam

In Vietnam, under the Decree No. 140/2007/ND-CP dated 5 September 2007, logistics services is defined as a commercial activity that is broadly classified into three main subsectors: (i) principal logistics services; (ii) transport-related logistics services; and (iii) other related logistics services, as shown in Table 7.2.

TABLE 7.2
Vietnam's Classification of Logistics Services

Principal Logistics	Transport-related Logistics	Other Related Logistics
• Cargo handling services, including container handling services • Storage and warehouse services, including container station and material treatment warehouse • Transportation agency services, including custom clearance and cargo unloading plan services • Other auxiliary services including cargo receipt and warehouse, and information services on transportation and storage of goods throughout the entire logistic process	• Maritime transport services Inland waterway transport services • Air transport services • Railway transport services • Road transport services • Pipe transport services	• Technical check and analysis services • Postal and courier services • Wholesales services • Retail services • Other supporting transport services

Source: Vietnam's Decree No. 140/2007/ND-CP.

Logistics Performance in Vietnam

Logistics sector's value added contribution to GDP in Vietnam is quite low. Although the value added of transportation and storage (main statistics for logistics sector) has been increasing in 2012–15, its share in GDP is declining from 2013 (see Figure 7.5).

In 2016, Vietnam's Logistics Performance Index (LPI) is 2.98, ranking at 64th among the investigated countries. This indicates that the development of logistics sector in Vietnam needs further improvement as there are still numerous challenges confronting this sector.

In terms of *transport-related logistics services*, Vietnam has a geographical advantage to develop many kinds of transportation services, including

FIGURE 7.5
Value and Share of Transportation and Storage in GDP

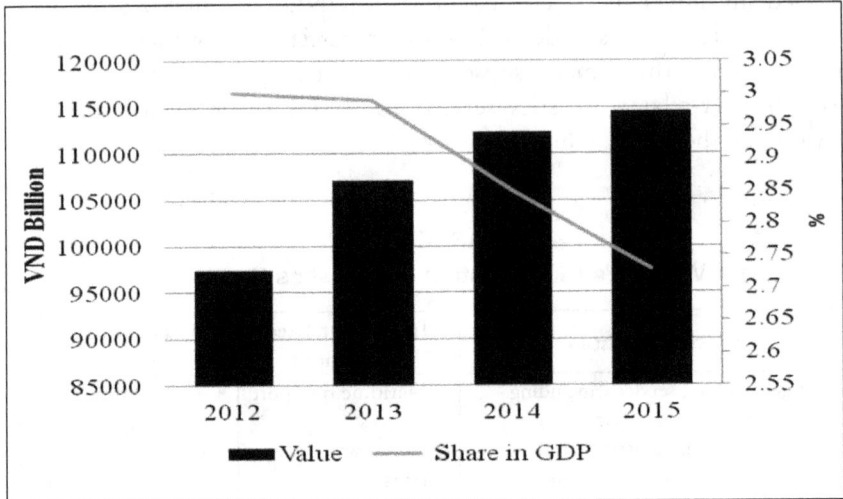

Source: GSO (2016).

maritime, inland waterway, road, railway transport services. With a long coastline of 3,200 kilometres, maritime transport is the most important mode of transport for facilitating trade in Vietnam. The national seaport system is comprised of six main groups along the coast, of which the sea cargo throughput is concentrated at the ports of Ho Chi Minh City and Hai Phong. Together, they account for more than 70 per cent of the country's total cargo throughput (Ministry of Industry and Trade 2016). The road network in Vietnam is connected with the neighbouring countries of ASEAN, Asia and Greater Mekong Subregion. It is also connected to the seaports in Vietnam. This partly explains why road transport accounts for more than 70 per cent in terms of domestic cargo transport volume in Vietnam. Although marine and road transport are the two main modes of transport services in Vietnam, there are shortcomings related to quality of infrastructure, poor connection between infrastructure and production centres.

In terms of *principal logistics services*, Vietnam's logistics companies provide mainly transport agency services, cargo handling and storage and warehouse services. Only a few companies have developed the distribution centre services with the use of technology to meet the demands of supply chain management from the producer to the consumer (Ministry of Industry and Trade 2016).

In terms of *logistics service providers*, according to Vietnam Logistics Association (VLA), there are about 2,253 logistics firms in the country, as at the end of 2015. Logistics services is mainly concentrated in international freight forwarding, maritime transport agencies and road transport. Table 7.3 shows that 36 per cent of these providers are located in Ho Chi Minh (HCM) city.

TABLE 7.3
Number of Logistics Companies in Vietnam, 2015

No.	Subsector	Total	Location				
			Ha Noi	HCM city	Da Nang	Hai Phong	Others
	Total number of transport agencies*	2,253	273	821	246	89	824
a	International freight forwarding	1,885	257	1,139	36	48	405
b	Maritime transport agencies	963	103	486	36	65	273
c	Road transport	633	51	164	11	17	390
d	Air freight services	417	47	220	11	14	125
e	Customs clearance services	367	43	183	5	19	117
f	Other logistics services	287	28	144	4	18	93
g	Postal and courier services	286	52	108	6	1	119
h	Container transport	283	20	124	7	21	111
i	Warehousing	127	10	60	1	2	54
j	Loading, unloading	125	4	56	5	20	40
k	Rail freight transport	97	4	56	3	2	32
	Percentage of each location in total	100%	12%	36%	11%	4%	37%

Note: All are registered as transport agencies.
Source: VLA (2015).

Although domestic companies represent 80 per cent of the total number of logistics firms, they only account for about 25 per cent of the total market share. Most of them are small-and-medium-sized private companies with very limited owners' equity. State-owned companies with up to thirty-year-experience, large capital, well-equipped facilities, large warehouses and abundant staff still do not have sufficient capability to provide value-added logistics and multimodal transport services since they lack active and effective management as well as well-trained human resources. In general, domestic logistics companies have only limited services and they are not internationally competitive. It can be said that Vietnamese logistics companies are mainly second party logistics (2PL) providers.[6] Only 15 per cent of the companies take part in third party logistics (3PL)[7] segment (Ministry of Industry and Trade 2016).

Preferential investment policies, the emergence of 100 per cent foreign invested enterprises, and a lack of technology transfer make it difficult for domestic companies to seize market opportunities and secure resources. Given this situation, it is difficult for Vietnam's domestic logistics service providers to provide competitive logistics services even within the domestic market.

LOGISTICS ENABLING ENVIRONMENT IN VIETNAM

Policies and Regulations in Logistic Services

Regulations

Before 2005, Vietnam did not have any legal documents containing provisions on logistics services. The Commercial Law in 2005 was the first one that provided a concept of logistics services (Articles 233–240). In the Commercial Law, logistics services are defined as commercial activities whereby a trader organizes the performance of one of many jobs including reception, transportation, warehousing, yard storage of cargoes, completion of customs procedures and other formalities and paperwork, provision of consultancy to customers, services of packaging, marking, delivery of goods, or other services related to goods according to agreements with customers in order to enjoy service charges. In 2007, the Government issued Decree No. 140/2007/ND-CP providing detailed regulations on Commercial Law regarding conditions for engaging in the business of logistic services, and limitations on the liability of logistic service business entities.

In Decree No. 140/2007/ND-CP, conditions for engaging in logistic services for foreign businesses are made stricter than their domestic counterparts. Foreign business entities are only permitted to engage in logistic services business based on Vietnam's commitments in the WTO, e.g. limitations on modes and percentage of capital contributed (see Table 7.4). But almost all these limitations have been eliminated since 2014. This implies that currently, foreign investors do not face many obstacles when entering and operating in Vietnam's logistics market. This increases the challenges faced by domestic investors and service providers in the domestic market.

TABLE 7.4
Limitations on Mode and Capital Contribution Ratio of Foreign Investors Engaging in Logistics Services

Logistic Services Business	Limitations on Mode and Contribution Ratio
Cargo handling services	Joint venture; not exceeding 50 per cent
Storage and warehouse services	Joint venture; not exceeding 51 per cent; no limitations since 2014
Transportation agency services	Joint venture; not exceeding 51 per cent; no limitation since 2014
Other auxiliary services	Joint venture; not exceeding 49 per cent; not exceeding 51 per cent since 2010; no limitation since 2014
Maritime transport services	• Fleet operation: Joint venture; not exceeding 49 per cent since 2009 • International maritime transport services: not exceeding 51 per cent; no limitation since 2012
Inland waterway transport services	Joint venture; not exceeding 49 per cent
Air transport services	Law on Civil Aviation in 2006, Decree No. 76/2007/ND-CP Investment by foreign investors must be approved by the Government Joint venture; not exceeding 49 per cent
Railway transport services	Joint venture; not exceeding 49 per cent
Road transport services	Joint venture; not exceeding 49 per cent; not exceeding 51 per cent since 2010
Pipe transport services	No permitted; except other regulation in Vietnam's international treaties

TABLE 7.4 *(continued)*

Logistics Services Business	Limitations on Mode and Contribution Ratio
Technical check and analysis services	Restricted in geographical locations reasons due to security and defense • Services to be provided to implement the authority of the Government: Joint venture after three years or other mode after five years from the time the private companies are accepted to supply these services. • Services of testing and issuance of certificates for transportation facilities: not permitted
Postal services	Postal Law in 2010; Decree No. 47/2011/ND-CP Projects with foreign investment must be examined; scale of VND 15 billion or more must be proposed to the Prime Minister for acceptance.
Wholesale and retail services	• Scope of activities: Commission Agent (CPC 621, 61111, 6113, 6121); Wholesales (CPC 622, 61111, 6113, 6121); Retail (CPC 631 + 632, 61112, 6113, 6121); Franchising (CPC 8929) • Not allowed to distribute some goods (e.g. tobacco and cigars, recorded items, books, magazines and newspapers, pharmaceuticals, oil, rice, sugar cane, precious metals and gems, etc.) • Establishment of retail store based on economic needs test (ENT)
Other supporting transport services	Not permitted; except other regulations in Vietnam's international treaties

Source: Decree No. 140/2007/ND-CP, Law on Civil Aviation in 2006, Decree No. 76/2007/ND-CP, Postal Law and Decree No. 47/2011/ND-CP.

Foreign investors may have to satisfy the conditions in the specialized legal documents, e.g. those engaging in maritime transport services have to follow the regulations in the Maritime Code, Decree No. 49/2006/ND-CP on the procedure for ship registration; Decree No. 115/2007/ND-CP on condition for maritime transport business, etc. Although Vietnam's logistics legal framework has gradually improved in line with deeper international and regional commitments, the legal system still reveals several shortcomings: (i) the logistics-related provisions are scattered in many different legal documents; (ii) lack of synchronization and consistency among legal documents, e.g. conditions for operating business in logistics sector regulated in Decree No. 140/2007/ND-CP, Decree No. 87/2009/

ND-CP and Decree No. 89/2011/ND-CP on multimodal transportation; (iii) frequent amendments of legal documents as the provisions were inconsistent with reality; and (iv) the legislation has not clearly defined the responsibilities of state agencies in the management of logistics activities.

Institutions

Logistics cover a large range of subsectors therefore logistics-related institutions include many state management agencies. In Vietnam, the Ministry of Industry and Trade is the lead agency responsible for managing and developing the logistics sector. The Ministry of Transport also plays an important role because of the large proportion of the transport subsector in the logistics services sector. This Ministry is also responsible for the implementation of logistics cooperation projects in ASEAN. To further promote cooperation in logistics sector in ASEAN, at the end of 2016 Vietnam established the National Steering Committee for the ASEAN Single Window, national single window and trade facilitation.

Institutions related to FDI activities in the logistics services are basically similar to those in FDI activities in general. However, as many subsectors are classified as conditional business lines,[8] FDI activities in these subsectors are also under the management and inspection of relevant ministries and state agencies, such as Ministry of Transport, Ministry of Industry and Trade, Ministry of Information and Communication, General Department of Customs, etc.

The VLA was established in 1993, with the aim of: (i) connecting logistics enterprises with each other; (ii) linking logistics business sector with the State management agencies on policy issues in order to solve difficulties and to foster favourable conditions for the development of the logistics industry; as well as, (iii) building relationships with regional and international logistics organizations. Over the twenty-three years of its development, the VLA has increased its membership from 7 in 1993 to 292 as of May 2016. This covers 50 per cent of the total capital and human resources in Vietnam's logistic industry. Since 1999, Vietnam has become a member of the ASEAN Freight Forwarders Association (AFFA), which helps to stimulate Vietnam's integration into the regional logistics industry. However, VLA is still operationally limited due to a shortage of funds, professional personnel as well as the still relatively low rate of participation of logistics enterprises.

In short, Vietnam is relatively open in the logistics market, so that foreign investors currently face few restrictions on capital contribution ratio and forms of investment. However, obstacles remain mostly due to beyond the border measures such as cumbersome procedures and a complicated legal and institutional system. Activities in the logistics services sector are under the management of many ministries and regulated by many legal documents. The complexity and overlapping management of different ministries and regulations are a significant hindrance to foreign investors in joining and operating in this sector.

Development Plans and Priorities

Vietnam's logistics industry has rapidly developed and contributed to the country's economic development. Recognizing the growing importance of logistics, Vietnam has developed an Action Plan to improve the competitiveness and development of logistics services in Vietnam. A draft of the Action Plan had been completed and is pending for government's approval. This is the first document that specifies the development orientation for the logistics sector as a whole. Prior to this, there was only an overall development plan of services sectors and development schemes and plans for some selected logistics subsectors, e.g. transport services and port system. According to the draft Action Plan, logistics services sector is identified as an important service sector that contributes to the improvement of the whole economy's competitiveness. The government plans to develop logistics services into a key, high value-added service sector that meets the domestic demand and that can gradually expand to regional and international markets. Several specific targets are given, including: (i) an annual growth rate of 15–20 per cent; (ii) an increase in the sectoral contribution to GDP from 2–3 per cent to 5 per cent; (iii) to achieve a rate of outsourcing logistics of 40 per cent; (iv) to decrease logistics cost from 25 per cent to 18 per cent of GDP; and (v) to be ranked 55th in the world in the LPI, by the year of 2020.

The Action Plan provides short- and medium-term solutions to improve Vietnam's logistics sector. Specifically, the Action Plan focuses on six areas: (i) improvement of the legal system and supporting policies for logistics sector; (ii) development of infrastructure, from bridges, ports, terminals, bonded warehouses to logistics centres; (iii) capacity building for enterprises and improving services quality; (iv) market development;

(v) training and raising awareness of the importance of logistics and improving the quality of human resource in logistics sector; and (vi) other solutions, e.g. establishing the National Steering Committee for logistics; maintaining Vietnam's logistics forum; building statistical and assessment indicators of the logistics sector, etc.

However, until now Vietnam has not yet developed a comprehensive strategy for the long-term development of this sector. The country has not identified the prioritized subsectors in logistics industry. As Vietnam plans to increase its integration to international and regional economies, along with its expectation to increase the growth of its logistics services, it is essential for the country to build a comprehensive development strategy as well as to clarify the priorities in the logistics sector.

Logistics Services Commitments under AFAS 9

As a prioritized sector under the AFAS framework, Vietnam has made commitments to liberalize eight subsectors in logistics services. This section will focus on examining Vietnam's commitments in mode 3 as this mode is directly related to FDI. It is noted that logistics is a provisional business sector by which both domestic and foreign enterprises must satisfy certain conditions as stipulated in Vietnam's Commercial Law 2005 to be eligible to operate in this sector.

In *Maritime Transport Services*, ASEAN service providers establishing commercial presence in Vietnam are allowed to invest at maximum of 70 per cent in a joint venture. In all other subsectors, except for maintenance and repair of vessels, 100 per cent foreign invested enterprises are allowed to be established in Vietnam. ASEAN enterprises that desire to invest in supporting services for maritime transport in Vietnam can be established without any limitation in commercial presence.

Four of five subsectors in *Railway Transport Services* have the same foreign equity limitation in a joint venture of 51 per cent, which is lower than that in maritime services. ASEAN enterprises can establish commercial presence in Vietnam with no equity limitation only in freight transportation. Vietnam is more cautious in opening up its market for passenger transportation and maintenance and repair of rail transport equipment services as it only allows joint ventures to be established.

With *Road Transport Services*, besides the limitation of foreign equity ranging from 49 to 71 per cent in a joint venture, 100 per cent foreign-invested enterprises are prohibited in Vietnam. There are also conditions related to "the needs of the market" and nationality of drivers. It seems that Vietnam is more reluctant to have ASEAN investment in railway transport services compared with the three other above-mentioned transport services.

ASEAN services providers in cargo handling services can establish joint ventures in Vietnamese providers. Equity limits for maritime cargo handling services is 49 per cent, while it is 50 per cent for container handling services, and 70 per cent for rail handling services. It is not allowed for ASEAN enterprises to set up 100 per cent foreign-invested company in Vietnam in maritime cargo handling services and container handling services (except services provided at airports).

ASEAN enterprises can invest in *Storage and Warehouse Services*, and *Postal and Courier Services* without any equity limitation.

Concerning *Transport Agency Services*, ASEAN companies investing in freight transport agency services can be established in Vietnam without any equity limitations while those in maritime agency services can only establish joint venture with a maximum of 49 per cent in foreign equity share. However, Vietnam does not commit maritime agency services in mode 3 for national treatment.

With *Packaging Services*, Vietnam limits foreign equity to 70 per cent.

In nine of the twenty-two committed subsectors in logistics services, ASEAN enterprises cannot establish branches and representative offices.

In summary, besides the conditions stipulated in Vietnam's Commercial Law 2015, Vietnam is relatively open to the ASEAN enterprises for its logistics services. In all committed subsectors of the logistics services, Vietnam allows ASEAN service suppliers to establish joint ventures with Vietnamese companies. In almost all committed subsectors (namely sixteen out of twenty-two), 100 per cent of foreign invested companies are allowed to be established. The main barriers for the ASEAN logistics enterprises are foreign equity limitations and the right to establish representative offices and branches in Vietnam.

The implementation of logistics commitments of Vietnam is incorporated with the overall implementation of its services commitments. As stated above, the commitments of Vietnam on FDI are implemented based on Vietnam's Law on Investment and Decree No. 07/2016/ND-CP. These two important documents stipulate that the ratio of ownership of foreign investors, and the establishment of representative offices and branches in Vietnam are subject to other relevant laws and international treaties of which Vietnam is a member. This stipulation creates a strong ground for Vietnam to fulfill its logistics commitments not only in AFAS but also in other FTAs of Vietnam.

TABLE 7.5
Vietnam's Commitments in Logistics Services under AFAS 9

Sector or Subsector	Limitation on Market Access	Limitation on National Treatment
1. Maritime Transport Services		
Passenger transportation less cabotage	(1) None (2) None (3) Establish joint ventures with foreign capital contribution not exceeding 70 per cent of total legal capital; under the national flag of Vietnam (or registered in Vietnam); foreign seafarers not exceeding one-third of total employees of the ships; the Master or First Chief Executive must be Vietnamese citizen. Other forms of commercial presence: 100 per cent foreign invested enterprises are allowed.	(1) None (2) None (3) None
Freight transportation less cabotage	(1) None (2) None (3) Establish joint ventures with foreign capital contribution not exceeding 70 per cent of total legal capital; under the national flag of Vietnam (or registered in Vietnam); foreign seafarers not exceeding one-third of total employees of the ships; the Master or First Chief Executive must be Vietnamese citizen. Other forms of commercial presence: 100 per cent foreign invested enterprises are allowed.	(1) None (2) None (3) None
Rental of vessels with crew	(1) None (2) None (3) None, except joint venture with the foreign capital contribution not exceeding 70 per cent shall be permitted.	(1) None (2) None (3) None, except as indicated in the market access column
Maintenance and repair of vessels	(1) None (2) None (3) Commercial presence may be in the form of joint venture. Maximum share of foreign equity in the joint venture company allowable up to 70 per cent.	(1) None (2) None (3) None

TABLE 7.5 (*continued*)

Sector or Subsector	Limitation on Market Access	Limitation on National Treatment
Supporting services for maritime transport: custom clearance	(1) Unbound (2) None (3) None	(1) Unbound (2) None (3) None
Supporting services for maritime transport: container station and depot services	(1) None (2) None (3) None	(1) None (2) None (3) None
2. Railway Transport Services		
Passenger transportation	(1) None (2) None (3) Unbound except: foreign suppliers are permitted to provide freight transport services through the establishment of joint ventures with Vietnamese partners in which the capital contribution of foreign side not exceeding 51 per cent of the total legal capital.	(1) None (2) None (3) None
Freight transportation	(1) None (2) None (3) None	(1) None (2) None (3) None
Pushing and towing services	(1) None (2) None (3) None, except that joint ventures with foreign capital contribution not exceeding 51 per cent can be established.	(1) None (2) None (3) None, except as indicated in the market access column
Maintenance and repair of rail transport equipment	(1) None (2) None (3) Foreign service suppliers are permitted to provide services only through the establishment of joint ventures with Vietnamese partners in which the capital contribution of foreign side not exceeding 51 per cent of total legal capital.	(1) None (2) None (3) None

Sector or Subsector	Limitation on Market Access	Limitation on National Treatment
Supporting services for rail transport services	(1) None (2) None (3) None, except that joint ventures with foreign capital contribution not exceeding 51 per cent can be established.	(1) None (2) None (3) None, except as indicated in the market access column
3. Road Transport Services		
Passenger transportation	(1) Unbound (2) None (3) Since 11 January 2007, foreign service suppliers are permitted to provide passenger and freight transport services through business cooperation contracts or joint ventures with the capital contribution of foreign side not exceeding 49 per cent. Since 11 January 2014, subject to the needs of the market, joint ventures with foreign capital contribution not exceeding 70 per cent may be established to provide freight transport services. Hundred per cent of joint venture's drivers shall be Vietnamese citizen.	(1) Unbound (2) None (3) None
Freight transportation	(1) Unbound (2) None (3) Since 11 January 2007, foreign service suppliers are permitted to provide passenger and freight transport services through business cooperation contracts or joint ventures with the capital contribution of foreign side not exceeding 49 per cent. Since 11 January 2014, subject to the needs of the market, joint ventures with foreign capital contribution not exceeding 70 per cent may be established to provide freight transport services. Hundred per cent of joint venture's drivers shall be Vietnamese citizen.	(1) Unbound (2) None (3) None
Maintenance and repair of road transport equipment	(1) None (2) None (3) None, except that joint ventures with foreign capital contribution not exceeding 51 per cent can be established.	(1) None (2) None (3) None, except as indicated in the market access column

TABLE 7.5 (*continued*)

Sector or Subsector	Limitation on Market Access	Limitation on National Treatment
4. Cargo Handling Services		
Maritime cargo handling services	(1) None (2) None (3) Commercial presence may be in the form of joint venture. Maximum share of foreign equity in the joint venture company allowable up to 49 per cent.	(1) None (2) None (3) Unbound
Container handling services, except services provided at airports	(1) None (2) None (3) Foreign service suppliers are only permitted to provide services through the establishment of joint ventures with Vietnamese partners with the capital contribution of foreign side not exceeding 50 per cent.	(1) None (2) None (3) None
Container handling services	(1) Unbound (due to the lack of technical feasibility) (2) None (3) None, except that joint ventures with foreign capital contribution not exceeding 50 per cent can be established.	(1) None (2) None (3) None, except as indicated in the market access column
Rail handling services	(1) None (2) None (3) None, except that joint ventures with foreign capital contribution not exceeding 70 per cent can be established.	(1) None (2) None (3) None
5. Storage and Warehouse Services		
	(1) None (2) None (3) None	(1) None (2) None (3) None
6. Transport Agency		
Freight transport agency (excluding road transport)	(1) None (2) None (3) None	(1) None (2) None (3) None

Sector or Subsector	Limitation on Market Access	Limitation on National Treatment
Maritime agency services	(1) None (2) None (3) Commercial presence may be in the form of joint venture. Maximum share of foreign equity in the joint venture company allowable up to 49 per cent.	(1) None (2) None (3) Unbound
7. Postal and Courier		
	(1) None (2) None (3) None	(1) None (2) None (3) None
8. Packaging Services		
	(1) None (2) None (3) None, except joint venture with the foreign capital contribution not exceeding 70 per cent shall be permitted.	(1) None (2) None (3) None, except as indicated in the market access column

Source: Vietnam's Services Schedules under AFAS 9.

In addition, as the coordinator for the logistics sector, Vietnam has actively participated in a great deal of integration activity in ASEAN in this sector. Vietnam held successfully a business forum on logistics services during the 42nd ASEAN Economic Ministers Meeting and the 4th ASEAN Economic Community Meeting in 2010. Vietnam also signed the Protocol on ASEAN Roadmap for the integration of logistics services and it is committed to liberalize almost all of the subsectors of logistics services. Vietnam has also assessed the opportunities arising out of the ASEAN logistic connectivity programme (Cao Ngoc Thanh 2014).

FDI in Logistics Sector

Foreign companies dominate Vietnam's logistics market, particularly in the international transportation segment. There are about forty foreign shipping firms in Vietnam, handling more than 80 per cent of the country's imports and exports, primarily with respect to trade with the European and American markets. It is expected that many more foreign logistics services suppliers will expand their activities in Vietnam with improved access to the domestic logistics market.

Foreign Logistics Providers Focus on 3PL

In Vietnam, 2PL service is very popular with domestic enterprises. Foreign logistics companies pioneered and developed the 3PL service market in Vietnam. FDI enterprises in Vietnam often focus on integrated logistics services (3PL), which includes not merely transporting goods, but also other value-added services (customs procedures, warehousing, packaging and distribution of products). According to a Report of the Ministry of Industry and Trade (2016), Vietnam has 287 3PL logistics providers, of which 200 are foreign logistics enterprises or 70 per cent of the total number of these providers in the country. Some major 3PL service providers in Vietnam are foreign companies such as DHL Logistics, Damco, APL Logistics (Lam Tran Tan Sy and Phan Nguyen Trung Hung 2015).

Foreign Logistics Services Providers Expand Logistics Infrastructure

Many foreign logistics services providers are strengthening their presence in Vietnam through expanding warehousing and improving productivity. Japan's Yusen Logistics, for example, has set up a new logistics complex in Haiphong in 2014, comprising a warehouse of 12,000 square metre (sqm) and a 23,800 sqm container depot with 3,000 TEUs storage capacity (VLA 2015). In 2013, DHL Supply Chain invested US$3 million to expand the invested project. The company is expected to build 141,000 sqm of warehouse capacity (Lam Tran Tan Sy and Phan Nguyen Trung Hung 2015).

Merger and Acquisition of Foreign Logistics Enterprises Increases

In 2014–15, as Vietnam officially opened to FDI enterprises to invest in logistics, foreign service providers began to look for opportunities to buy up Vietnamese local logistics companies. The development of new markets outside the traditional markets offered additional opportunities for transport and logistics industry. The number of FDI logistics enterprises has increased rapidly and has expanded under the process of merger and acquisition and new investments.

In general, the trend of more FDI companies setting up their business in Vietnam can be illustrated by Table 7.6. This is the statistics of FDI in transportation and warehousing in Vietnam from 2012 to 2015. It can be seen that the number of projects is increasing over

TABLE 7.6
FDI in Transportation and Storage, 2012–15

Year	Number of New Projects	New Registered Capital (US$ million)	Number of Capital Extended Project	Additional Registered Capital of Existing Projects (US$ million)	New and Additional Registered Capital of Existing Projects (US$ million)	Number of Projects	Accumulated Registered Capital (US$ million)
2015	55	72.6	25	72.4	145	505	3,829
2014	53	125.17	7	28.05	153.22	435	3,730
2013	29	34.66	9	33.44	68.09	382	3,563
2012	28	209.48	7	5.61	215.09	346	3,476

Source: Foreign Investment Agency, Vietnam, available at <http://fia.mpi.gov.vn/>.

time, especially in 2014 and 2015. Registered capital reached a high level of US$3,827 million in 2015. Both new and additional registered capital projects have increased dramatically in 2015, showing that foreign investors are finding increased investment opportunities in Vietnam. This can be attributed to liberalization efforts and revisions of the country's investment laws, which provides more opportunities for foreign enterprises to operate in Vietnam.

CONCLUSION AND POLICY RECOMMENDATIONS

Over the last three decades, Vietnam has gradually opened up its services sector. This liberalization process has led to a deeper integration of the country with the world and especially with the region. Investment liberalization can be seen in the revisions of investment laws and this constitutes the most important policy change in Vietnam. The main motivation is to create a more liberal, transparent and non-discriminatory investment environment for all investors. More importantly, the liberalization commitments in WTO and AFAS are embedded in the new investment laws. However, the main constraint lies in the cumbersome bureaucratic measures for establishing foreign presence.

Vietnam's logistics services sector in particular has taken off with the country's active participation in multilateral and bilateral agreements. However, Vietnam's logistics services sector is still relatively under-developed. The major drawback in the development of this sector is the transport infrastructure and related issues such as road safety, road and bridge quality. It is difficult to develop multimodal transportation because of the poor connection between infrastructure and production centres. Another issue is the lack of qualified human resource in the logistics sector. Only the professional level is evaluated above average according to logistics providers. Soft skills, foreign language skills and information technology qualifications remain inadequate (Ministry of Industry and Trade 2016). Additionally, the regulations and procedures relating to the entry and operation in the logistics sector are still quite complicated. The institutions involve many ministries and state agencies. As a result, both domestic and foreign investors in the logistics sector bear high cost and low competitiveness. The legal framework on logistics operation also lacks transparency and consistency. Thus, the legal framework relating to logistics needs to be reviewed and updated to ensure transparency, consistency and compliance with new commitments.

Regarding the services liberalization in ASEAN, even though Vietnam has made progress in liberalizing services trade within ASEAN, Vietnam's commitments in AFAS 9 have not produced significant additional liberalization because the level of openness is only marginally higher than that of AFAS 8 and does not go far enough beyond the current applied regime. Therefore, it requires Vietnam to consider improving its services commitments in AFAS 10. The task for this future package is to consider what sectors/subsectors should be put in the negotiation agenda and what sectors/subsectors should be more open.

For ASEAN as a whole, the way to enhance services liberalization in the future is to go beyond the current liberalization measures by working towards regulatory coherence in the priority sectors. In addition to FDI liberalization, other initiatives should also be considered to enhance the development of the regional services sector, for example: (i) promoting the implementation of ASEAN Single Window; (ii) extending logistics infrastructure connections among ASEAN, Northeast Asia and other regions; (iii) strengthening the linkages among logistics associations and enterprises in ASEAN regions; (iv) building a common vocational training framework of logistics in ASEAN; and (v) building an ASEAN statistical databank with assessment indicators of logistics performance in each country.

Finally, Vietnam lacks a comprehensive strategy to develop the logistics sector in the long term. The country has not identified prioritized logistics subsectors. Without a clear national strategy, Vietnam's logistics industry in general and logistics companies in particular will not have long-term orientation and adequate support. The government, therefore, needs to quickly approve and effectively implement the short- and medium-term solutions suggested in the Action Plan to improve the competitiveness of logistics services sector in Vietnam; and concurrently build a comprehensive and long-term development strategy as well as supportive policies for the domestic enterprises in this sector to grow. Policies and solutions must be synchronized with the entire national logistics system, creating a corridor of multimodal connectivity. In this regard, Vietnam should take advantage of the opportunities from economic integration to develop the domestic logistics industry by encouraging domestic enterprises to become more competitive and to expand to the ASEAN region. In addition, Vietnam should also improve its logistics infrastructure as well as human resources in the logistics sector. In order to develop the infrastructure, the state can mobilize resources through public–private partnerships (PPP). Meanwhile, professional and practical education and training programmes on logistics can help increase the quantity and the quality of workers in the logistic services industry.

Notes

1. Excluding construction services
2. Excluding construction services
3. 2008: 43.8 per cent; 2009: 83.2 per cent; 2010: 56.7 per cent of the total registered FDI inflows
4. Comprising real estate business and professional services as classified by Foreign Investment Agency.
5. Services sectoral classification list can be seen in Document MTN.GNS/W/120 dated 10 July 1991.
6. A second-party logistics provider is an asset-based carrier, which actually owns the means of transportation.
7. A third-party logistics provider provides outsourced or "third party" logistics services to companies for part or sometimes all of their supply chain management functions.
8. An industry in which the conduct of business investment activities must satisfy conditions for the reason of national defense or security, social order or safety, social ethics or the health of the community.

References

Cao, Ngoc Thanh. "The Logsitics Services in Front of the WTO Commitments". *VINAFREIGHT International*, 18 February 2014. Available at <http://vinafreight.com/tin-tuc-su-kien/canh-cua-logistics-truoc-cam-ket-wto.html> (accessed 12 April 2016).

General Statistics Office of Vietnam (GSO). *Statistical Handbook of Vietnam – 2008*. Hanoi: Vietnam Statistical Publishing House, 2009.

——. *Statistical Handbook of Vietnam – 2009*. Hanoi: Vietnam Statistical Publishing House, 2010.

——. *Statistical Hankbook of Vietnam – 2010*. Hanoi: Vietnam Statistical Publishing House, 2011.

——. *Statistical Hankbook of Vietnam – 2011*. Hanoi: Vietnam Statistical Publishing House, 2012.

——. *Statistical Hankbook of Vietnam – 2012*, Hanoi: Vietnam Statistical Publishing House, 2013.

——. *Statistical Hankbook of Vietnam – 2013*, Hanoi: Vietnam Statistical Publishing House, 2014.

——. *Statistical Hankbook of Vietnam – 2014*. Hanoi: Vietnam Statistical Publishing House, 2015.

―――. *Statistical Hankbook of Vietnam – 2015*. Hanoi: Vietnam Statistical Publishing House, 2016.

Government of Vietnam. "Decree No. 47/2001/ND-CP on the Function, Tasks, Power and Organization of the Tourist Inspectorate". Hanoi: Government of Vietnam, 2001.

―――. "Decree No. 49/2006/ND-CP on Ship Registration, Purchases and Sale". Hanoi: Government of Vietnam, 2006.

―――. "Decree No. 140/2007/ND-CP on Providing Detailed Regulations on the Commercial Law Regarding Conditions for Engaging in Logistic Services Business, and Limitations on Liability of Logistic Services Business Entitites". Hanoi: Government of Vietnam, 2007*a*.

―――. "Decree No. 76/2007/ND-CP on Air Transportation Business and General Aviation". Hanoi: Government of Vietnam, 2007*b*.

―――. "Decree No. 115/2007/ND-CP on Conditions for Sea Shipment Services Business". Hanoi: Government of Vietnam, 2007*c*.

Lakatos, Andras, Michel Kostecki, Andrea Spears, Daniel Linotte, and Nguyen Hong Son. "Comprehensive Strategy for Service Sector Development to the Year 2020 (CSSSD) with a Vision up to 2025". Hanoi: MUTRAP (EU-Vietnam MUTRAP III), 2009.

Lam, Tran Tan Sy and Phan Nguyen Trung Hung. "Report on Logistics Sector 2015: Facing Competition and Growth". Vietnam: FPT Securities, 2015. Available at <www.fpts.com.vn/FileStore2/File/2015/08/05/Logistics%20Report.pdf> (accessed 12 April 2016).

Ministry of Industry and Trade (MOIT). "Action Plan on Improving Competitiveness and Development of Logistics Services". Hanoi: MOIT, 2016.

National Assembly. "Law on Investment". Hanoi: National Assembly of Vietnam, 2005.

―――. "Law on Enterprises". Hanoi: National Assembly of Vietnam, 2006*a*.

―――. "Law on Civil Aviation". Hanoi: National Assembly of Vietnam, 2006*b*.

―――. "Law on Post". Hanoi: National Assebly of Vietnam, 2010.

―――. "Law on Investment". Hanoi: National Assembly of Vietnam, 2014*a*.

―――. "Law on Enterprises". Hanoi: National Assembly of Vietnam, 2014*b*.

Vietnam Logistics Business Association (VLA). "Current Situation of Vietnam's Logistics Sector". Hanoi: Vietnam Logistics Institute, 2015.

Vu, Thanh Huong. "Assessing the Committed Integration of Vietnam's Distribution Services in AEC 2015". *Journal of Science, Economics and Business* 29, no. 5E (2013): 43–55.

Vu, Thanh Huong and Tran Viet Dung. "Vietnam with Service Trade Liberalization towards ASEAN Economic Community". *Journal of Science and Development* 13, no. 3 (2015): 474–83.

World Bank. "Doing Business 2016: Measuring Regulatory Quality and Efficiency". Washington, D.C: World Bank, 2016.

8

SERVICES LIBERALIZATION: CASE OF LOGISTICS IN BRUNEI

Tham Siew Yean

INTRODUCTION

Brunei's economy is in the middle of a critical transition from an oil-rich and oil-dependent state to a diversified economy that is dynamic and sustainable. The rich natural endowment of oil resources has enabled Brunei to become one of the richest state in ASEAN and the world. According to IMF (2016a), based on Gross Domestic Product (GDP) (in PPP terms) per capita, Brunei is the fifth wealthiest state in the world and the second wealthiest in ASEAN in 2016, after Singapore which is ranked at number four in the world. The oil wealth, in turn, has enabled the country to depend primarily on oil for its revenue since there is no income nor sales tax for locals. Free education through university and subsidized housing is additionally provided for its citizens. It has also led to a dominant role of the state in terms of its control over the economy as well as employment, as an estimated 70–80 per cent of the Bruneians work for the government or government-linked institutions (Prusak 2016).

Economic diversification, although viewed in terms of a more balanced contribution of manufacturing and services, may in reality entail far more than that. It may necessitate, for example, a reconsideration of the country's fiscal budgeting and its ensuing implications on the extent of public goods provided by the state. The sharp drop in global price of oil in 2014 and after, had a detrimental impact on the state revenue, leading to a fiscal deficit of 16 per cent of its GDP for the fiscal year

2015/16 (Prusak 2016). Economic growth was also affected, with the country's annual growth falling into negative rates from 2013 to 2016. Current forecasts of future oil prices do not seem to indicate that there will be a price recovery to its peak value in 2010 (Knoema n.d.). Hence sustainability will require considering diversifying sources of fiscal revenue, tightening government expenditure and a restructuring of the privileges enjoyed by the citizens. Injecting dynamism into the economy will also require rebalancing the role of the state and the private sector in generating economic growth.

In a world dominated by global value chains (GVCs), participation in value chain activities has become an important development strategy (UNIDO 2015). Therefore, it is important for Brunei's diversification into manufacturing and services to engage in GVC activities in these sectors, through liberalization and regulatory reforms. Foreign direct investment (FDI) has an important role to play in this transition due to its prevalence in GVCs. In particular, economic diversification into services will necessitate improving the overall FDI enabling environment, including FDI liberalization in services. This chapter seeks to examine the FDI environment in Brunei's services sector, focusing on its regulations and liberalization. A case study of the logistics sector is included in view of its importance in moving goods and services within an economy and to the external world as well as connecting an economy with GVCs. The chapter concludes with some policy suggestions for improving the FDI enabling environment in the services sector, including logistics. The chapter is organized as follows: an overview of the services sector is provided following the introduction. This is followed by an analysis of the FDI regulations, reforms and liberalization efforts in the country. A case study of the logistics sector is presented after that while the conclusion summarizes the main findings of this chapter.

OVERVIEW OF SERVICES SECTOR IN BRUNEI

Brunei's economy is heavily dependent on oil and gas. In 2010, it is more than one and a half times the non-oil and gas sector. Even after the fall in oil prices, it is still 1.3 times the non-oil sector in 2015 (see Table 8.1). Therefore, the industrial sector, which includes mining, the largest sector in its GDP, followed by services (see Figure 8.1). It also means that this sector's share in the country's GDP is particularly vulnerable to oil and gas prices, as shown by its relatively large contribution in the 1970s when oil prices were relatively high (see Figure 8.1).

TABLE 8.1
Nominal GDP by Economic Activity, 2010–15
(Brunei million dollars)

	2010	2011	2012	2013	2014	2015
Gross domestic product (GDP)						
Oil and gas sector	12,200	16,433	16,437	14,957	13,930	10,120
Oil and gas mining	9,575	12,757	12,656	11,424	10,635	7,737
Manufacture of liquefied natural gas & methanol	2,625	3,676	3,781	3,534	3,295	2,383
Non-oil and gas sector	6,843	7,243	7,744	8,124	8,100	7,994
Government	1,993	2,111	2,136	2,175	2,273	2,136
Private sector	4,850	5,132	5,608	5,948	5,827	5,858
Vegetables, fruits, and other agriculture	19	19	26	21	24	26
Livestock and poultry	52	57	62	62	64	63
Forestry	17	15	14	15	38	33
Fishery	50	43	54	57	60	74
Manufacture of wearing apparel and textile	30	28	33	35	36	36
Manufacture of food and beverage products	24	28	32	31	29	29
Other manufacturing	107	97	110	136	134	135
Electricity and water	132	131	134	138	144	148
Construction	339	450	547	556	425	441
Services (non-government)	*6,073*	*6,375*	*6,732*	*7,073*	*7,146*	*7,009*
Wholesale and retail trade	755	812	891	952	916	900
Land transport	20	12	14	14	14	13

Water transport	128	113	150	192	170	163
Air transport	70	68	56	54	50	51
Other transport services	74	79	108	128	137	111
Communication	254	276	284	286	280	258
Finance	760	794	864	912	936	923
Real estate and ownership of dwellings	620	634	649	664	668	738
Hotels	23	24	22	29	23	21
Restaurants	126	135	142	155	161	163
Health services	212	223	233	252	269	267
Education services	519	536	547	555	572	637
Business services	353	389	463	529	490	443
Domestic services	69	70	72	73	75	76
Other private services	100	99	101	103	111	108
Government services/Public administration	1,993	2,111	2,136	2,175	2,273	2,136
Taxes less subsidies on products	-353	-373	-379	-442	-335	-337
Memorandum items						
Population ('000)	387	393	400	406	412	417
GDP per capita (in Brunei dollars)	48,319	59,238	59,536	55,733	52,670	42,610

Source: IMF (2016b).

FIGURE 8.1
Brunei Darussalam Value Added, 1974–2015
(% of GDP)

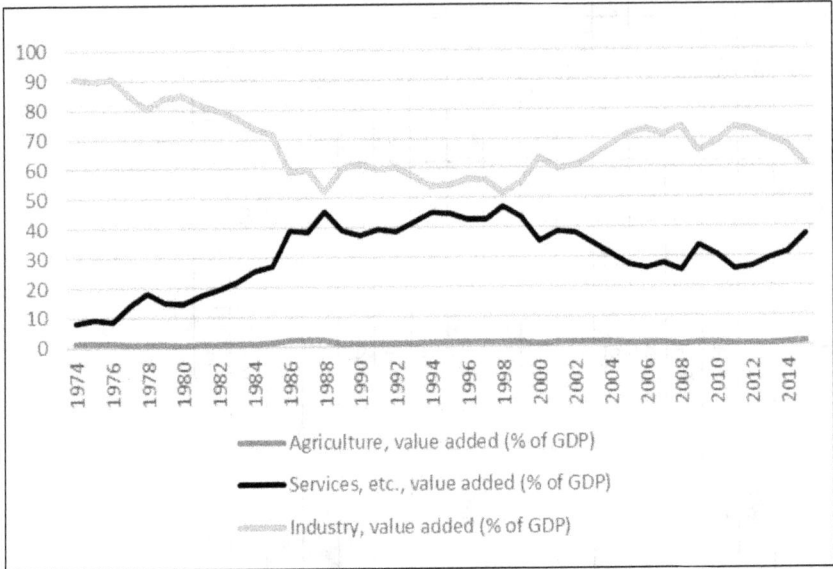

Agriculture, value added (% of GDP)

Services, etc., value added (% of GDP)

Industry, value added (% of GDP)

Source: World Bank, *World Development Indicators*, available at <http://wdi.worldbank.org/tables> (accessed 20 March 2017).

When Brunei's economy was hit simultaneously by falling oil prices and regional currency depreciation stemming from the region's economic crisis in 1998, the share of the industrial sector in the country's GDP fell to a low of 52 per cent. Likewise, the fall in oil prices from 2011 onwards has also caused the industrial sector's share in GDP to contract. Agriculture's contribution is marginal throughout the period as shown in Figure 8.1.

The services sector expanded progressively with the decline of the industrial sector's share in GDP to a peak of 47 per cent of the GDP in 1999, before its share contracted until 2011.[1] Services share in the GDP has increased as the share of the industrial sector shrank progressively after 2011.

In the non-oil and gas sector, aggregated services is far more important than agriculture and manufacturing combined as its share in non-oil and gas is 89 per cent and 93 per cent respectively in 2010 and 2015 (see Table 8.1). Within services, government services/public administration dominates (see Table 8.1), which is not surprising given the larger government sector in the economy due to its control over the oil resources. Wholesale and retail trade, finance, real estate, education and business services are other services subsectors that are important in terms of their size in the GDP. Total transport services (i.e., the sum of land, water, air and other transport services) is the sixth largest in 2015.

Plans to diversify the economy from its heavy dependence on oil and gas have been attempted since 2001 when the Brunei Economic Development Board (BEDB) was established for this purpose (Department of Foreign Affairs and Trade, Australian Government n.d.). Attracting FDI into the country became part of the diversification strategy. Despite this early attempt, Brunei's economy continued to be dependent on income derived from sales of oil and gas. The main reason for the failure to diversify was attributed to a poor enabling environment, such as a lack of clarity of purpose on diversification objectives and strategies, bureaucratic hindrances, a weak private sector, lack of scale due to size of economy, weak human capital, a high cost structure, lack of FDI outside of the oil and gas sector and unexploited potential growth areas (Bhaskaran 2007).

Efforts to diversify were reinvigorated in 2008 when the government revealed its Wawasan 2035 (Vision 2035) plan, which laid out the development strategies of the country. This vision has the ultimate aim of delivering economic diversification by 2035. Sectors prioritized for development as stated in the Tenth Year Development Plan (2012–17), include several services activities such as logistics, financial services, tourism, ICT logistics, financial services, tourism, and information, technology and communication (ICT) (BEDB n.d.*a*). Again, attracting FDI is an important component of this strategy for joining GVCs, technology and knowledge transfer.

FDI REGULATIONS, REFORMS AND LIBERALIZATION
Domestic Regulations and Reforms

In general, it has been reported that there are no restrictions on total foreign ownership of companies incorporated in Brunei (US Department of State 2016). It has also been highlighted that the country allows for 100 per cent foreign ownership at promotional talks from the BEDB, which acts as a "one-stop" agency to facilitate and support foreign investments (*Borneo Bulletin*, 13 May 2015). Nevertheless, the website of BEBD (<http://www.bedb.com.bn/invest-bd>) does not provide any information to that effect. WTO (2015)'s review of the country's trade policy, however, indicates some caveats. Prohibited sectors for domestic and foreign investment are the manufacture of liquor and armaments. Restricted sectors include the use of natural resources related to food security, and certain locations where 30 per cent minimum local equity participation is required. Sectors where public provision prevail such as telecom and energy require approval from the relevant authorities, while market concentration and nationality requirements may also restrict both domestic and foreign investors. In the case of retail trade, investment approvals are based on a case-by-case basis. The Companies Act, which requires registration of all businesses in the country, stipulates that at least one of two directors of a locally incorporated company to be a resident of the country, unless an exemption is granted by relevant authorities (Oxford Business Group n.d.). There is, however, no available and clearly stated negative list or conditions for foreign ownership to guide investors along the lines of these caveats.

Previous studies have indicated that bureaucratic red tapes as one of the factors have deterred foreign investment from entering the country (OECD 2013a; Jones 2014). There were efforts made to improve its business environment, especially in terms of more efficient company registration procedures, using electronics for speeding up processes such as name searches, customs, shorter waiting times for excavation permits, and reducing corporate tax rates from 30 per cent from 2007 to 18.5 per cent in 2015 (OECD 2013a; US Department of State 2016). Nevertheless, WTO's trade policy review of the country (2015, p. 15) concludes that "there remains considerable scope for Brunei to improve its business climate. Moreover, Brunei's FDI policies could be more transparent, particularly with respect to limits on foreign equity participation, partnership requirements, and the identification of sectors in which FDI is restricted."

The drop in oil prices in 2011 and again after 2014 and its negative impact on the economy prompted the government to step up its efforts to attract FDI. A new delivery unit was established at the Prime Minister's Office in 2014, called PENGGERAK.[2] Although this is similar to Malaysia's delivery unit, PEMANDU, its composition of committee members differs in one significant aspect, namely the role of the private sector. PENGGERAK's task force comprises ministers, civil servants, researchers, consultants, school leaders or doctors as well as skilled professional staff, indicating the subdued role of the private sector in Brunei's economy. The main goal of the delivery unit is to improve the ease of doing business in order to attract more FDI. Some laws were amended to facilitate this. For example, the Business License Act was amended to exempt several businesses from the need to obtain a business licence and the Miscellaneous Licence Act was also amended to reduce the time needed for new business registrants to start operations (US Department of State 2016). These efforts contributed to a jump in the country's ranking in World Bank Ease of Doing Business 2016 report from 105th place in 2015 to 84th place in 2016 (Oxford Business Group n.d.).

Institutional support was improved with the restructuring of the BEDB to enhance its focus on attracting FDI. New agencies were also established to facilitate investors such as the FDI Action and Support Centre (FAST). FAST works with the BEDB to hasten the approval process, especially for high-value investment by coordinating and obtaining high level approvals (BEDB n.d.*b*).

Investment incentives are also provided as shown in Table 8.2. These incentives are granted to both domestic and foreign investors based on the Investment Incentives Order 2001 (WTO 2015). To promote services development, pioneer status is provided for services that are innovative and that can contribute to the economic development of the country. In addition, expansion of service companies and export of services are encouraged through incentives.

TABLE 8.2
Investment Incentives

	Incentives	Tax Relief Period (not exceeding)
Pioneer industries	Exemption from income tax; Carry forward of losses and allowances; Exemption from customs and import duties	5–8 years (11 years), depending on the amount of fixed capital expenditure; 11 years (20 years) for industries established in high tech park
Pioneer service companies	Exemption from income tax; Carry forward of losses and allowances; Exemption from customs and import duties	8 years (11 years); 5 years (10 years) for financial services
Post-pioneer companies	Exemption from income tax; Deduction of losses; Adjustment of capital allowances and losses	6 years (11 years)

TABLE 8.2   (*continued*)

	Incentives	Tax Relief Period (not exceeding)
Expansion of established enterprises	Exemption from income tax	3–5 years (15 years), depending on the amount of new capital expenditure
Expanding service companies	Exemption from income tax	11 years (20 years)
Production for export	Exemption from income tax	6 years (11 years) for pioneer enterprises, depending on sales volume; 8 years for the remaining enterprises, depending on sales volume; 15 years, depending on the amount of fixed capital expenditure
Export of services	Exemption from income tax; Deduction of allowances and losses	11 years (20 years)
International trade incentives	Exemption from income tax	8 years
Foreign loans for productive equipment	Exemption from withholding tax on interests paid to non-resident lenders	Depends on the financial agreement with the foreign lender
Investment allowances	Exemption from income tax	5 years; 11 years for tourism
Warehousing and servicing incentives	Exemption from income tax	11 years (20 years)
Investment in new technology companies	Deduction of losses	
Overseas investment and venture capital incentives	Deduction of losses	

Source: Investment Incentives Order 2001, as amended by S 15/10 and S 5/11 in WTO (2015).

The US Department of State in its 2016 statement on the investment climate of Brunei Darussalam concludes that further improvements in the transparency of Brunei's FDI policies are still needed. This is especially pertinent with respect to limits on foreign equity participation, partnership requirements, and a list of sectors that are restricted to FDI.

Moreover, the immigration of foreign labour is strictly regulated to prevent social disruptions in Brunei's tiny society. Work permits are issued only for short periods and need to be continually renewed. In 2014, it is estimated that about half of the population of 411,900 is in the labour force, with an unemployment rate of 6.9 per cent, while the number of migrant workers are estimated at 120,000 (Department of Economic Planning and Development n.d.*a*; US Department of State 2016). The government appears to be the largest employer (Prusak 2016; US Department of State 2016). Economic expansion towards the aspired high value-added segments of manufacturing and services will need to focus on capital and knowledge-intensive activities and may still require the import of knowledge workers that are not available domestically.

In view of the extent of the economy that is controlled by the state, the enactment of a competition law is critical for attracting more private investment. The enactment of the Brunei Competition Order in January 2015, which was subsequently gazetted in March of the same year, represents an important step forward in terms of regulatory changes (Department of Economic Planning and Development, n.d.*b*). Apart from establishing a legal framework for prohibiting anti-competitive activities, the Order also provides for the establishment of Brunei Competition Commission (BCC) and Competition Tribunal. It is expected to take effect in four phases: establishment of the BCC and the enforcement infrastructure, then the provisions on anti-competitive agreements, followed by unilateral conduct prohibitions and finally merger control. Since implementation is still a work-in-progress, the effectiveness of the Competition Order has yet to be tested.

In the case of intellectual property rights, Brunei has adequate provisions in the laws of the country while enforcement is reportedly improving. It was removed from the United States Special 301[3] report in 2013 and has stayed off the list from 2014 to 2016.

Although Brunei has not adopted any Regulatory Impact Assessment (RIA) processes, it does have a Law Review Committee. The Committee's main responsibilities include reviewing and updating laws that are administered by all ministries and departments as well as facilitating the formulation and/or amendment of laws. Its monitory role is assisted by the Attorney General's Chambers.

Inflows of FDI

Figure 8.2 indicates inflows of FDI increasing steeply from 2008 to 2012 before falling sharply after that due to the fall in world oil prices and its ensuing negative impact on Brunei's economy. According to WTO (2015), average FDI inflows over the 2008–13 period amounted to US$600 million a year, almost double the average of US$328 million for the period 2005–7.

Brunei has not succeeded in attracting much FDI outside the energy sector. The oil and gas sector remains the largest recipient of FDI, followed by manufacturing and services (see Table 8.3). The drop in world oil prices has affected foreign investment in this sector and total inflows after 2013. Disinvestment occurred within manufacturing and services in 2014 and 2015 due to the contraction of the economy during these two years. Within services, wholesale and retail trade is the highest recipient. Logistics services, which is lumped under other services, is a relatively less important recipient of FDI. The major investors come from the European Union (EU), especially from the United Kingdom, and the Netherlands, with increasing investment from Hong Kong (see Table 8.3).

FIGURE 8.2
Brunei Darussalam FDI, 2001–15
(current US$)

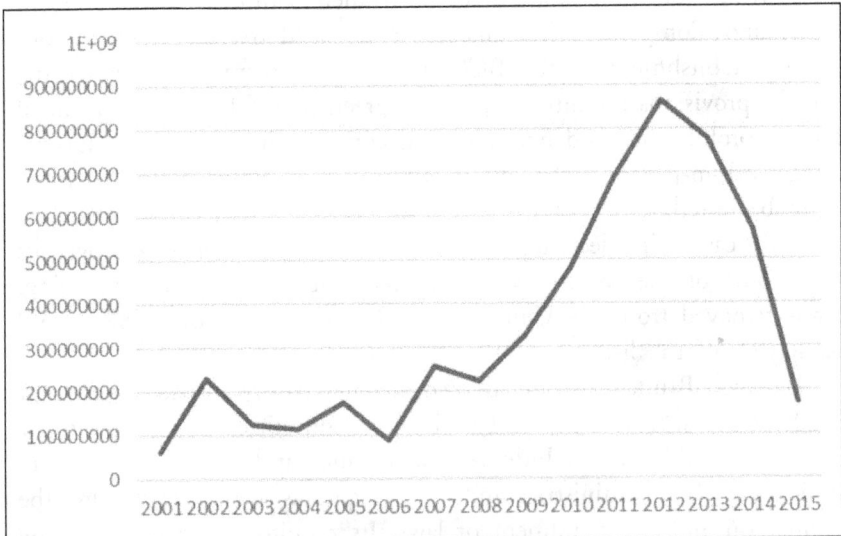

Source: World Bank Development Indicators, World Bank.

TABLE 8.3
FDI Inflows by Sector and Country, 2008–15

	2008	2009	2010	2011	2012	2013	2014*	2015*
Total inflows of FDI (B$ million)	457	538	655	869	1,081	971	720*	238*
Total inflows of FDI (US$ million)	323	370	481	691	865	775	566**	173**
Total inflows of FDI (% of GDP)**	1.5	3.0	3.5	3.7	4.5	4.3	3.3	1.3
(B$ million)								
Mining and quarrying	231	385	185	557	709	698	537	244
Manufacturing	80	–28	63	97	97	142	77	–67
Construction	0	0	4	0	48	–53	29	12
Wholesale and retail trade	0	1	13	1	51	48	75	–34
Financial activities	66	114	338	55	151	92	–25	5
Others	80	66	53	158	25	43	27	–77
(B$ million)								
ASEAN	1.3	4.5	122.1	84.9	39.3	–10.5	178.8	122.1
Malaysia	0.7	3.4	61.2	42.4	6.5	4.3	116.8	52.8
Singapore	0.6	0.6	59.5	41.9	32.8	–14.8	62.0	69.2
EU	300.3	415.5	189.8	569.7	747.7	704.2	462.7	115.4
Germany	0	0	3.0	0	–20.1	19.2	10.3	7.6
Netherlands	66.2	134.5	30.8	0.9	265.7	143.1	68.1	34.8
United Kingdom	231.2	277.6	152	565.8	498.7	539.0	380.6	59.1
Others	2.9	3.5	4.1	3.0	3.4	2.9	3.7	13.9
Hong Kong, China	n.a.	n.a.	n.a.	17.2	108.8	116.4	122.1	1.3
Japan	36.8	–7.1	30.0	69.7	69.4	19.8	33.7	–50.2
United States	5.5	2	20.7	23.2	40.1	–6.7	–49.2	–9.7
Others	84.2	88.3	274.5	182.7	75.4	147.3	131.3	59.3

Note: – indicates divestment
Sources: 2008–13 data are extracted from WTO (2015); 2014–15* data are extracted from *Brunei Statistical Yearbook 2015*; 2014–15** data are extracted from World Development Indicators, World Bank.

FDI Liberalization in Trade Agreements

Apart from being a founding member of the WTO, Brunei has eight regional trade agreements (RTAs) encompassing sixteen partners. These include ASEAN partners and also the extra ASEAN partners, namely Australia and New Zealand; India; Japan; and the Republic of Korea. There is one bilateral agreement with Japan, and a plurilateral agreement under the Trans-Pacific Partnership.

Under the General Agreement on Trade in Services (GATS), Brunei's commitments are limited to four out of twelve services: business services, communication services, financial services, and transport services (WTO 2001). The number of services subsectors committed is only twenty-two and this has improved to ninety-two subsectors in AFAS 9 (WTO n.d.*a*; CARI 2016). Thangavelu (2015)'s assessment of the extent of FDI restrictiveness[4] in Brunei's commitments in AFAS 8, indicated that Brunei is relatively open in terms of horizontal commitments (see Table 8.4). It is completely closed for distribution services and also relatively closed for transportation services. Health-related and social services is the most open sector for FDI in the list.

TABLE 8.4
Brunei's Scores for AFAS 8 in FDI Restrictiveness

Commitments	Scores
Horizontal commitments	0.900
Specific Commitments	
(Average)	0.680
Business services	0.697
Communication services	0.426
Engineering services	0.820
Distribution services	0.000
Education services	0.740
Environmental services	0.820
Financial services	0.825
Health-related and social services	0.900
Tourism and travel-related services	0.820
Recreational, cultural and sporting services	0.820
Transport services	0.617

Source: Thangavelu (2015).

CASE OF LOGISTICS

Given that there is no definition of logistics available, transportation and storage is used as a proxy for the sector. Based on the most recent published data available, this sector is the fourth largest sector in services, according to the number of establishments, employees as well as value added (see Table 8.5). The number of employees in this sector is 60 per

TABLE 8.5
Key Statistics of Private Enterprises by Sector, 2010

Sectors	Number of Enterprises	Total Employees	Gross Value of Output (B$ million)	Gross Value Added (B$ million)
Agriculture, Forestry and Fishery	289	1,754	79.4	19.2
Mining and Quarrying	40	5,277	12,479	9,568
Manufacturing	695	8,187	6,467	2,792
Electricity, Gas, Water Supply and Other Industrial Activities	20	283	86	12
Construction	691	22,719	1,949	382
Wholesale and Retail Trade	1,907	22,750	1,418	794
Accommodation and Food Service Activities	536	9,563	278	135
Transportation and Storage	166	4,972	1,309	307
Information & Communication	98	2,345	554	286
Financial & Insurance Activities	102	3,368	961	686
Real Estate Activities	67	675	39	15
Professional, Technical, Administrative & Support Services	437	11,234	716	361
Education	128	3,126	119	99
Human Health & Social Work Activities	41	664	69	30
Other Service Activities	349	2,690	74	50
Total	5,566	99,607	2,637	15,536

Source: Department of Economic Planning and Development, Prime Minister's Office, *Brunei Darussalam Statistical Yearbook 2015*, available at <http://www.depd.gov.bn/SitePages/Statistical%20Publications.aspx> (accessed 3 March 2017).

cent and 94 per cent, respectively, of that employed in manufacturing and mining and quarrying, indicating its relative importance in terms of employment generation. However, in terms of gross value of output, it is the second largest service subsector. Most of the establishments are micro, small and medium enterprises (SMEs).

Four main issues characterize the logistics market in Brunei, namely imbalanced trade, public provision of transportation with weak private sector involvement, and a fragmented and uncompetitive logistics industry.

Given the predominant role played by the oil and gas sector, exports of this product constitutes almost 90 per cent of Brunei's exports in 2016, with machinery and transport equipment and chemicals contributing respectively another 5 per cent of exports each (Trading Economics n.d.). In the case of imports, 33 per cent of it comes from machinery and transport equipment while manufactured goods comprise another 20 per cent. Food constitutes another 16 per cent, followed by fuels and lubricants (9 per cent); chemical products (9 per cent); miscellaneous manufactured articles (9 per cent); and beverages and tobacco (2 per cent) (Trading Economics n.d.). The relatively smaller exports of manufacturing goods in total exports indicates that Brunei is not linked to GVCs in manufacturing activities, which is also confirmed by the relatively smaller amount of FDI in manufacturing. This implies that the non-oil transport and logistics market is dependent mainly on the domestic market. In turn, this has important implications on the cost structure of logistics as there is a severe imbalance between import and export freight volumes, leading to about 92 per cent of the containers leaving the country empty in 2010 (Teo n.d.). Certainly this is not peculiar to Brunei alone as imbalanced trade typically characterizes less developed regions such as Sabah and Sarawak in East Malaysia.

Second, the present transport infrastructure consists of a main maritime port, namely Muara Port, Brunei International Airport, and a road network connecting the country to Sabah and Sarawak in East Malaysia (Teo n.d.). The infrastructure is owned, managed and operated mainly by public authorities such as the civil service, wholly owned government companies and statutory bodies (Jones 2014). For example, the Ports Department in the Ministry of Communications, manages Muara Port, including its berthing operations and terminal services and facilities such as cranes, warehouses, trans-shipments, and logistics schedule. The private sector is only involved in capital projects with respect to upgrading and expansion of infrastructure, which follows the public procurement process. It has little to do with the management and operations of any of public transport infrastructure. Not surprisingly, there is very little public–private partnerships (PPP) in infrastructure management. Jones (2014) postulates that the availability of finance, prior to the fall in oil prices in 2014, has reduced the need to raise private finance, while the state is reluctant to forego its overall control of the economy, including key infrastructure such as ports and airports. Lack of capable private firms imply that private management will have to rely on foreign companies that may have the expertise but may not be attracted to the Brunei market because of its size and its implications on scale and returns.

The domestic logistics market is generally fragmented due to the smallness of the market relative to the number of establishments. Teo (n.d.) reported that industry sources seem to indicate that there are over 500 freight forwarding companies, although not all operate regularly and most are rather small. The membership roll of the Brunei Freight Forwarders Association (BRUFA) suggests that the number of active players are around twenty-six and these are likely to be the larger ones. As shown in Table 8.3, FDI in logistics which is included in other services, is not significant. Multinationals in this market are limited to express couriers and are relatively less significant as most of them outsource their activities to local agents. This leads to inefficiencies in the market, as each firm needs to operate its own set of assets, leading to lower levels of utilization of assets and higher operating costs and charges. These inefficiencies, in turn, are reflected in the higher charges quoted by Brunei's freight forwarders as compared to their counterparts in Sabah and Sarawak in East Malaysia.

Customs clearance is still considered to be relatively slow in Brunei, as compared with its ASEAN neighbours. Intal Jr. (2015)'s analysis of the relative performance of Brunei using the World Bank Trading Across Borders methodology found that customs clearance and technical control for exports took twice the number of days for Brunei in 2014, compared to Indonesia and Malaysia, despite the larger volume of exports in the two latter countries. The ease of doing business ranking may be high even though there are weaknesses in the customs system compared to best practice because the volume of non-oil gas trade is very small compared to other member countries in ASEAN. The country is working towards improving this with the launch of the Brunei Darussalam National Single Window (or BDNSW) in 2013, which will facilitate and expedite customs declaration processes and other services under the Royal Customs and Excise Department. This online system allows involved government agencies to provide faster feedback. It is being implemented progressively in stages with increasing functions added over time as well as the number of government agencies that are integrated with the system.

The Logistics Performance Index 2016 of the World Bank (2016) shows that Brunei is underperforming as it is below its potential for its given level of income, as well as compared with its ASEAN neighbours. It is ranked at 70, compared to Singapore, which is ranked number 5 in the world. In terms of ranking, Brunei is closer to Cambodia (ranked at 73) and the Philippines (ranked at 71) despite its higher level of income and better infrastructure. Its performance is closer to that of resource rich economies such as Equatorial Guinea and Gabon.

Logistics Liberalization in GATS and AFAS

Since the horizontal commitments are unbound except where indicated in the specific commitments, the analysis in this section will refer only to the sector specific commitments that pertain to logistics. There are no commitments for any of the logistics subsectors identified for liberalization in the Roadmap for Logistics Integration in ASEAN, in Brunei's commitments for GATS. Hence, there is improvement in terms of the number of subsectors committed for liberalization in Brunei's AFAS 9 package. But based on Table 8.6, it can be seen that Brunei has not liberalized up to 70 per cent for all subsectors and there are still two sectors that have no commitment as yet.

TABLE 8.6

Brunei's Commitments in ASEAN for Logistics Sector, as of 2016

Sector	CPC	AFAS 9	
		MA	NT
Packaging services	876	M1: N M2: N M3: Foreign equity participation should not exceed 70 per cent.	M1: N M2: N M3: N
Courier services	7512	M1: N M2: N M3: Joint venture corporation with Bruneian individuals or Bruneian-controlled corporations or both the aggregate foreign shareholding in the joint venture corporation shall not exceed 70 per cent foreign equity.	M1: N M2: N M3: N
Maritime freight transportation, excluding cabotage	7212	M1: N M2: N M3: a) The supply of international maritime transport, excluding vessels for the carriage and transportation of energy goods, foreign equity participation shall not exceed 51 per cent. b) The supply of international maritime transport of energy goods: unbound.	M1: N M2: N M3: None, except as indicated in the horizontal section.
Rail freight transportation	7112	M1: N M2: N M3: Foreign equity participation should not exceed 51 per cent.	M1: N M2: N M3: N
Road freight transportation	7123	No commitments	No commitments
Maritime cargo handling services	741	M1: N M2: N M3: Foreign equity participation should not exceed 51 per cent.	M1: N M2: N M3: N
Storage and warehouse services: covering private bonded warehousing services only	742	M1: N M2: N M3: Foreign equity participation should not exceed 51 per cent.	M1: N M2: N M3: N

TABLE 8.6 *(continued)*

Sector	CPC	AFAS 9	
		MA	NT
Maritime freight forwarding services only	748	M1: N M2: N M3: Foreign equity participation should not exceed 51 per cent.	M1: N M2: N M3: N
Other auxiliary services	749	No commitment	No commitment

Note: M1: mode 1; M2: mode 2; M3: mode 3; N: None
Source: ASEAN Secretariat, "Member Countries' Horizontal Commitments, Schedules of Specific Commitments and the List of Most-Favoured Nation Exemptions", available at <http://asean.org/?static_post=member-countries-horizontal-commitments-schedules-of-specific-commitments-and-the-list-of-most-favoured-nation-exemptions> (accessed 2 March 2017).

POLICY SUGGESTIONS

Since the issue of imbalanced trade affecting logistics cost is related to both the level and scale of economic activities in a country, continuing and accelerating the diversification plans of Brunei is essential for creating a demand for logistics services. A critical step in diversification is joining GVCs. The dominant business model in the world is production fragmentation as a means of increasing productivity and competitiveness. Consequently, GVCs have proliferated, intensifying the interconnectedness in production activities within manufacturing and between manufacturing and services as well as interdependencies between markets. As activities constituting a value chain are generally inter-firm in nature, and on a global scale, MNC-coordinated GVCs account for 80 per cent of global trade in terms of gross exports (Serafica 2014). Currently, Brunei's participation in GVCs is mainly confined to the mining sector, with insignificant GVC activities in the non-oil and gas sector (WTO n.d.*b*). Although the OECD Trade in Value Added (TiVA) data show that transport and storage in Brunei has a small domestic value-added component in its exports, the use of this sector is also tied to the oil and gas sector. In other words, transportation and storage also serves primarily the needs of the oil and gas sector since oil and gas is the country's primary export good. The country therefore needs to join GVCs in non-oil and gas activities, be it manufacturing or services.

To secure entry to GVCs, attracting FDI is an important first step (Taglioni and Winkler 2016). UNESCAP (2015, Chapter 10), suggests three crucial policies, namely infrastructure development, reducing trade costs and reforms in domestic regulations. Infrastructure in Brunei is adequate currently, with excess capacity in its Muara port and airport (Teo n.d.).[5] Reducing trade costs include liberalization of trade in goods and services and the removal or reduction of direct and indirect barriers. Given Brunei's late-comer disadvantage at FDI liberalization compared with most of its ASEAN neighbours, it is important for Brunei to accelerate its FDI liberalization measures which is still relatively closed for transportation and logistics based on the analysis in the earlier sections. It will also entail improving the country's trade facilitation measures since this is an important aspect of trade costs reduction. A review of the country's trade facilitation measures and their effectiveness will enable it to focus on new areas of improvements for smoothening and facilitating the flow of trade.[6] In this regard, accelerating the complete integration of the National Single Window will complement diversification strategies as an expansion of the non-oil sector will benefit from improved customs processing. It will also need to consider including the implementation of good regulatory practices to ensure that regulatory barriers do not hinder trade and investment in the country. An important component of regulatory reform is transparency and making investment rules and regulations readily available, especially on websites. In this regard, the current website of BEDB (<http://www.bedb.com. bn/>) has little information to offer investors and compares poorly with its some of its ASEAN neighbours.[7]

Producers can overcome size constraints in the domestic economy by internationalizing their operations to overseas market. Since SMEs made up 97.5 per cent of the total number of active enterprises in 2010, helping SMEs to export is critical for scaling up these enterprises. Although there are incentives offered for exporting,[8] it is unclear whether these incentives have contributed to exports and whether firms have problems accessing these incentives. Reviewing the effectiveness of these incentives will enable the government to know which incentives are meaningful to keep. However, studies on the internationalization of SMEs indicate that the main export problems encountered by these enterprises are their limited capacity to analyse, penetrate and access foreign markets. There are also technical limitations to act as suppliers to foreign buyers and investors. SMEs need market information such as "market intelligence, marketing research, brand promotion, bid intervention, trade fairs and exhibitions, channels and distributions, buyer-seller matching, logistics systems, publicity literature, creditworthiness of importers and marketing outlet and consortia formation" (Abe et al. 2012, p. 178). In particular, meeting the standards of foreign markets and standard certification is important to penetrate export markets. Establishing a dedicated institution for facilitating exports of SMEs like MATRADE in Malaysia can assist in providing the marketing support needed. A common finding on the utilization of trade agreements, including ASEAN, is a general lack of awareness of these agreements and how to utilize these agreements for market expansion. More dissemination efforts of market opening measures under the ASEAN Economic Community (AEC) can help to create better awareness and stimulate SMEs to strive to export to the ASEAN region.

Another important finding on helping SMEs to export points to the use of modern ICT as the most important factor in increasing the probability of SMEs participation in both direct exports and international production networks (Duval and Chorthip 2014). Brunei can assist SMEs in the adoption of ICT for their business development and internationalization strategies by reducing cost, increasing speed and broadband penetration in the country.

Enhancing connectivity will also help to expand the horizons of enterprises. Teo (n.d.) points to the need to leverage on better connectivity with its neighbours and the region. She suggests an incremental approach by first improving links with cities from Bintulu to Kota Kinabalu so that Brunei can become the core hub for a North Borneo Economic Region. Subsequent to that, the links can be further expanded to Sabah and Sarawak through the Brunei Darussalam–Indonesia–Malaysia–Philippines East ASEAN Growth Area (BIMP-EAGA), and then towards the ASEAN market. Creating links and better connectivity is another way to overcome the scale issue in Brunei. She therefore recommends improving road links with key economic nodes in Sabah and Sarawak as an important first step towards better connectivity. Although this is consistent with internal plans, it will require bilateral cooperation between Brunei and Malaysia and collaborations to improve these road connections.

CONCLUSION

Brunei is strategically located in Southeast Asia as it is situated on the South China Sea, which is one of the busiest shipping lanes in the world.

It is in the midst of diversifying its economy from its dependence on oil as well as improving the role of the private sector. Attracting FDI is an important part of its diversification strategy as evidenced by the on-going efforts to improve the ease of doing business, FDI promotion and regulatory changes such as the enactment of the Competition Order in 2015.

Nonetheless, the country is a late-comer in FDI liberalization and reforms as there are many competitors within the region that have also moved aggressively in the same direction and for the same reasons. Despite the regulatory changes, inflows in FDI fell sharply after 2012 and it is still concentrated in the mining sector. Liberalization in terms of commitments have been improving but it is still far short of the bold liberalization efforts in some of its neighbouring countries. While to a certain extent the limited success in attracting more FDI can be attributed to the issue of scale due to the relatively small domestic economy, further liberalization and regulatory reforms should be considered, especially in terms of improving transparency.

The broader issue of scale can be addressed by using FDI to join GVCs, especially in non-oil and gas activities in line with its diversification strategies. The other issue of improving private sector's role will require appropriate policies for assisting SMEs to attain scale through internationalization strategies. Finally improving connectivity with its immediate neighbours and the region is another way of addressing the scale problem.

Notes

1. Services in the World Bank indicators correspond to ISIC divisions 50–99 and include wholesale and retail trade (including hotels and restaurants), transport, and government, financial, professional, and personal services such as education, health care, and real estate services.
2. Or "Piloting Exclusive National Goals, Gearing Excellent Results and KPIs". See <http://www.pmo.gov.bn/SitePages/PENGGERAK.aspx#anchor-1> (accessed 3 March 2017).
3. The Special 301 Report (Report) is the result of an annual review of the state of intellectual property rights (IPR) protection and enforcement in U.S. trading partners around the world, which the Office of the United States Trade Representative (USTR) conducts pursuant to Section 182 of the Trade Act of 1974, as amended by the Omnibus Trade and Competitiveness Act of 1988, the Uruguay Round Agreements Act, and the Trade Facilitation and Trade Enforcement Act of 2015.

4. The index gave an overall score between 0 and 1, with higher scores indicating greater openness. It is constructed based on a weighted average of six areas relevant for services liberalization, namely foreign ownership or market access, national treatment, screening and approval procedure, board of directors and management composition, movement of investors, and performance requirements.

5. It is estimated that based on forecast of its growth rate, Muara Port is expected to have sufficient container handling capacity up to 2035 while Brunei Airport has capacity to handle twice the current cargo throughput (Teo n.d.).

6. OECD (2013*b*)'s assessment of trade facilitation in Brunei highlighted the need for improvements in the areas of information availability and streamlining of procedures; involvement of trade community; advance rulings; simplification and harmonization of documents and automation. There has been no published review since then.

7. Compare, for example, with Myanmar's website information for foreign investors at <http://www.dica.gov.mm/en/invest-myanmar> (accessed 6 March 2017).

8. See Table 8.2 and also a list of other financial incentives at APEC (n.d.).

References

Abe, Masato, Michael Troilo, J.S. Juneja and Sailendra Narain. "Market Access" (Chapter VIII). In *Policy Guidebook for SME Development in Asia and the Pacific*. Bangkok: UNESCAP, 2012. Available at <http://www.unescap.org/resources/policy-guidebook-sme-development-asia-and-pacific> (accessed 6 March 2017).

Asia-Pacific Economic Cooperation (APEC). "Brunei Economic Development Board", n.d. Available at <http://www.we-apec.com/directory/brunei-economic-development-board> (accessed 6 March 2017).

Brunei Economic Development Board (BEDB). "Tenth National Development Plan (2012–2017) — Brunei Darussalam", n.d.*a*. Available at <http://www.depd.gov.bn/DEPD%20Documents%20Library/NDP/RKN%20English%20as%20of%2011.12.12.pdf> (accessed 7 March 2017).

———. "FDI Action and Support Centre (FAST)", n.d.*b*. Available at <http://business.gov.bn/SitePages/Your%20Partners.aspx> (accessed 5 March 2017).

Bhaskaran, Manu. "Economic Diversification in Negara Brunei Darussalam". A report submitted for the Centre for Strategic and Policy Studies, Brunei Darussalam, 2007. Available at <http://www.csps.org.bn/publications/CSPS_Report_3_-_Economic_Diversification_in_Brunei_-_Manu_Bhaskaran_-_Aug2007.pdf> (accessed 2 March 2017).

Borneo Bulletin. "BEBD as a 'One-Stop' Agency to Support, Facilitate Foreign Investment". 13 May 2015. Available at <http://borneobulletin.com.

bn/bebd-as-a-one-stop-agency-to-facilitate-support-foreign-investments/> (accessed 2 March 2017).

CIMB ASEAN Research Institute (CARI). "Liberalization of the Trade in Services". *AEC Blueprint 2025 Analysis*, vol. 1, paper 3 (3 March 2016).

Department of Economic Planning and Development, Prime Minister's Office. *Brunei Darussalam Statistical Yearbook 2015*, n.d.*a*. Available at <http://www.depd.gov.bn/SitePages/Statistical%20Publications.aspx> (accessed 3 March 2017).

––––––. "Competition Order", n.d.*b*. Available at <http://www.depd.gov.bn/SitePages/Competition%20Order.aspx> (accessed 3 March 2017).

Department of Foreign Affairs and Trade, Australian Government. "Brunei Darussalam Country Brief", n.d. Available at <http://dfat.gov.au/geo/brunei-darussalam/Pages/brunei-darussalam-country-brief.aspx> (accessed 2 March 2017).

Duval, Yann and Chorthip Utoktham. "Enabling Participation of SMEs in International Trade and Production Networks: Trade Facilitation, Trade Finance and Communication Technology". Trade and Investment Working Paper Series no. 3. Bangkok: United Nations Economic and Social Commission for Asia and the Pacific, June 2014.

Intal, Jr., Ponciano. "AEC Blueprint Implementation Performance and Challenges: Trade Facilitation". ERIA Discussion Paper Series, ERIA-DP-2015-41. Jakarta: Economic Research Institute for ASEAN and East Asia, 2015. Available at <http://www.eria.org/ERIA-DP-2015-41.pdf> (accessed 7 March 2017).

International Monetary Fund (IMF). "List of Countries by Projected GDP Per Capita", 2016*a*. Available at <http://statisticstimes.com/economy/countries-by-projected-gdp-capita.php> (accessed 3 March 2017).

––––––. "Brunei Darussalam: Statistical Appendix". IMF Staff Country Report no. 16/310, 2016*b*. Available at <http://www.imf.org/external/pubs/cat/longres.aspx?sk=44303.0> (accessed 3 March 2017).

Jones, David S. "Brunei Country Report". In *Financing ASEAN Connectivity*, edited by Fauziah Zen and Michael Regan. ERIA Research Project Report FY2013, no. 15. Jakarta: Economic Research Institute for ASEAN and East Asia, 2014, pp. 39–62.

Knoema. "Crude Oil Price Forecast: 2017 to 2030", n.d. Available at <https://knoema.com/yxptpab/crude-oil-price-forecast-long-term-2017-to-2030-data-and-charts> (accessed 3 March 2017).

Organisation for Economic Co-operation and Development (OECD). "Structural Policy Country Notes: Brunei Darussalam". In *Economic Outlook for Southeast Asia, China and India 2014: Beyond the Middle-Income Trap*. Paris: OECD, 2013*a*. Available at <https://www.oecd.org/site/seao/Brunei%20Darussalam.pdf> (accessed 3 March 2017).

———. "OECD Trade Facilitation Indicators – Brunei Darussalam", 2013*b*.
    Available at <http://www.oecd.org/trade/facilitation/indicators.htm> (accessed
    6 March 2017).
Oxford Business Group. "Brunei Darussalam Reforms Regulations to Attract
    Foreign Investment in Key Industries", n.d. Available at <https://www.
    oxfordbusinessgroup.com/overview/targeted-approach-regulator-reforms-are-
    under-way-attract-foreign-investment-key-industries-while> (accessed 2 March
    2017).
PENGGERAK (Delivery Unit at the Prime Minister's Office, Brunei Darrusalam).
    Available at <http://www.pmo.gov.bn/SitePages/PENGGERAK.aspx#anchor-1>,
    n.d. (accessed 3 March 2017).
Prusak, Matthew. "Brunei's Economy Running on Empty". *The Diplomat*,
    17 February 2016. Available at <http://thediplomat.com/2016/02/bruneis-
    economy-running-on-empty/> (accessed 3 March 2017).
Serafica, Ramonette B. "Why Global Value Chains and Services Matter:
    Implications for APEC 2015". Philippine Institute for Development
    Studies (PIDS) Policy Notes no. 2014–22. Manila: PIDS, December 2014.
    Available at <http://dirp3.pids.gov.ph/webportal/CDN/PUBLICATIONS/
    pidspn1422.pdf> (accessed 6 March 2017).
Taglioni, Daria and Deborah Winkler. *Making Global Value Chains Work for
    Development*. Washington, D.C.: World Bank, 2016.
Teo Siew Yean. "A Study on the Transportation and Logistics System of Brunei
    Darussalam", n.d. Unpublished manuscript.
Thangavelu, Shandre M. "FDI Restrictiveness Index for ASEAN: Implications of
    AEC Blueprint Measures". ERIA Discussion Paper Series, ERIA-DP-2015-43.
    Jakarta: Economic Research Institute for ASEAN and East Asia, 2015.
Trading Economics. "Brunei Exports and Imports", n.d. Available at <http://www.
    tradingeconomics.com/brunei/exports> (accessed 3 March 2017).
US Department of State. "2016 Investment Climate Statement – Brunei". Bureau
    of Economic and Business Affairs, July 2016. Available at <https://www.
    state.gov/e/eb/rls/othr/ics/2016/eap/254265.htm> (accessed 2 March 2017).
World Bank. *Connecting to Compete 2016: Trade Logistics in the Global Economy*.
    Washington, D.C.: World Bank, 2016.
    <https://wb-lpi-media.s3.amazonaws.com/LPI_Report_2016.pdf> (accessed
    3 March 2017).
World Trade Organisation (WTO). "Schedule of Commitments and Lists of
    Article II Exemptions", n.d.*a*. Available at <https://www.wto.org/english/
    tratop_e/serv_e/serv_commitments_e.htm> (accessed 2 March 2017).
———. "Trade in Value-Added and Global Value Chains: Statistical Profiles",
    n.d.*b*. Available at   <https://www.wto.org/english/res_e/statis_e/miwi_e/
    countryprofiles_e.htm> (accessed 6 March 2017).

————. "Trade Policy Review: Brunei Darussalam", May 2001. Available at <https://www.wto.org/english/tratop_e/tpr_e/tp164_e.htm> (accessed 22 March 2017).

————. "Trade Policy Review: Brunei Darussalam". Report by the WTO Secretariat. Geneva: WTO, 2015. Available at <https://www.wto.org/english/tratop_e/tpr_e/tp409_e.htm> (accessed 2 March 2017).

United Nations Economic and Social Commission for Asia and the Pacific (UNESCAP). "GVCs and Supporting Policies" (Chapter 10). In *Asia-Pacific Trade and Investment Report 2015: Supporting Participation in Value Chains*. Bangkok: UNESCAP, 2015. Available at <http://www.unescap.org/resources/asia-pacific-trade-and-investment-report-2015-supporting-participation-value-chains> (accessed 3 March 2017).

United Nations Industrial Development Organization (UNIDO). *Global Value Chains and Development: UNIDOs Support Towards Inclusive and Sustainable Development*. Vienna: UNIDO, 2015. Available at <https://www.unido.org/fileadmin/user_media/Research_and_Statistics/GVC_REPORT_FINAL.PDF> (accessed 7 March 2017).

US Department of State. "Brunei", 5 July 2016. Available at <https://www.state.gov/e/eb/rls/othr/ics/2016/eap/254265.htm> (accessed 6 September 2017).

9

FDI, SERVICES LIBERALIZATION AND LOGISTICS DEVELOPMENT IN CAMBODIA

Vannarith Chheang

INTRODUCTION

Over the last two decades, inflows of foreign direct investment (FDI) to Cambodia has increased significantly, due to its relatively liberal investment law and pace of services liberalization, including the logistics sector. Liberalization of the services sector started soon after the country's accession to the World Trade Organization (WTO) in 2004 through the General Agreement on Trade in Services (GATS) and later in 2007 through the ASEAN Framework Agreement on Services (AFAS). The services sector, accounting for 42.3 per cent of Gross Domestic Product (GDP) in 2015, plays a critical role in socio-economic development through job creation and productivity improvement. Within it, logistics is regarded as a strategic sector for national and regional connectivity, socio-economic development, and poverty reduction.

This chapter reviews Cambodia's economic development and FDI climate, along with its efforts in services liberalization. The chapter also looks at the liberalization initiatives in logistics services and the current state of logistics development and connectivity in Cambodia. Investment in logistics, especially in infrastructure, and enhancing regional connectivity is one of the key areas of national development as it can help to improve the country's economic performance and competitiveness by reducing transactions cost, improving broad investment climate, and promoting international trade.

Investment Climate

As a small economy, Cambodia has been performing well in the last two decades in terms of sustaining high economic performance and reducing poverty significantly. It has achieved a high average growth rate of 7.9 per cent from 2000 to 2015, thus making it one of the fastest growing economies in ASEAN. The poverty rate has reduced from more than 53.2 per cent in 2004 to 13.5 per cent in 2014. Per capita income has increased from US$417 in 2004 to US$1,215 in 2015, making Cambodia a lower middle-income country, according to the classification by the World Bank Group. Cambodia aims to become an upper middle-income country by 2030 and a high-income country by 2050, if it can sustain an annual growth rate of around 7 per cent.

The GDP growth rate in 2016 was 7.2 per cent and it is forecasted to be around 7 per cent for 2017 (ADB 2016). Attracting FDI has been the main development strategy for the country. The annual average net FDI inflows to Cambodia from 2000 to 2015 is 7.7 per cent of GDP[1] (see Table 9.1). In terms of trade openness, total export volume reached US$9,231 million (46.3 per cent of GDP) and total import volume hit US$12,404 million (64.2 per cent of GDP) in 2016. Garments and footwears are the main export products. The United States, Europe, ASEAN, and Japan are the main export destinations of Cambodia.

TABLE 9.1
GDP and FDI Inflows, 2000–15

Year	2000	2007	2008	2009	2010	2011	2012	2013	2014	2015
GDP Growth Rate	8.8	10.2	6.7	0.1	6.0	7.1	7.3	7.5	7.1	7.0
GDP (US$ billion)	3.65	8.63	10.35	10.40	11.24	12.82	14.03	15.44	16.77	18.04
FDI (% of GDP)	3.01	9.97	7.83	4.90	6.49	6.16	10.26	8.68	10.32	9.42
FDI (US$ billion)	0.11	0.86	0.81	0.51	0.73	0.79	1.44	1.34	1.73	1.70

Source: World Development Indicators, World Bank.

The laws and regulations governing foreign investment in Cambodia have been developed with the objective of encouraging inward FDI. FDIs are treated in a non-discriminatory manner, except for land ownership. Foreign investors are allowed to invest, without discrimination, in many areas with the provision of investment incentives such as exemptions, in whole or in part, of custom duties and taxes.[2] In return, investors are expected to provide adequate training to Cambodian nationals.

Under the Investment Law of Cambodia in 2003, the investors, who are given Final Registration Certificates[3] are entitled to various incentives. The incentives include profit tax exemption or use of special depreciation and duty free import of production equipment, construction materials, raw materials, intermediate goods and accessories for the export-oriented investment projects. The tax exemption period is composed of a Trigger Period,[4] plus additional three years and Priority Period[5] (as determined by the Financial Management Law).

The investment projects that are not qualified to get tax incentives are: (a) all kinds of commercial activity, import, export, wholesale, and retails, including duty free shops, (b) any transportation services by waterway, by road, by air except investment in the railway sector, (c) restaurants, karaoke parlors, bars, nightclubs, massage parlor, fitness, (d) tourism services, (e) casino and gambling business, (f) currency and financial business and services such as banks, financial institutions, and insurance companies, (g) business activities related to newspaper and media, including radio, television, press, magazine, etc. (h) professional services, (i) production and processing of wood products using wood from natural forest with a legal domestic supply source for raw materials, (j) complex resort, including hotel, theme park, sport facilities, zoo with less than 50 hectares, (k) hotel below 3-star grade, and (l) real estate development, warehouses facilities.

Besides the investment incentives provided in the Investment Law, investment facilitation services have gradually improved over time. For example, the government has established the Cambodian Special Economic Zone Board (CSEZB) in 2005 under the Council of Development of Cambodia to promote special economic zones (SEZs) in the country. The SEZs are expected to provide one-stop service to investors, i.e. from registration of investment projects to routine export-import approvals. It is observed that the firms located in SEZs are relatively more integrated with the global markets or value chains compared to the local production networks. The main logistics issue facing the SEZ firms is the high cost of getting containers from their factory to and from the port (Warr and Menon 2015).

There are no sectors in Cambodia that are closed to foreign investment. There are only two restrictions on foreigners: land ownership and work permit requirement. For any approved project, ownership of land is only permitted for Cambodian citizens. The use of land is permitted to foreign investors, including concessions and long-term or short-term leases. Also, a foreign investment project is entitled to obtain visas and work permits for foreign employees as managers, technicians and skilled workers, if the qualifications needed and expertise are not available in Cambodia.

China, Japan, South Korea and ASEAN are the main sources of FDI to Cambodia. In 2015, China accounted for 32 per cent (48 per cent of total manufacturing FDI) and ASEAN accounted for 25 per cent of the total FDI (30 per cent of investment in finance). The accumulated FDI to Cambodia from 1994 to 2015 reached US$23.8 billion. In 2015, the approved investment capital hit a record high of US$4,644 million. FDI in finance and insurance activities increased from US$325 million to US$515 million in 2015, contributing significantly to the services sector (*ASEAN Investment Report 2016*). Service liberalization, including logistics is one of the factors attracting foreign investors.

The main challenges and constraints in attracting FDI are relatively high uncertainties and costs associated with business operations. Weak governance and the rule of law, legislative gaps, high corruption, and unstable democratic institutions are the main challenges to Cambodia's development (ADB 2012*a*). Similar constraints are observed in two important production clusters in the economy: firms in SEZs and firms in the informal sector (World Bank 2016*c*).

SERVICES SECTOR LIBERALIZATION

Cambodia's Services Sector

The services sector (including tourism, financial services, information and communication technology, postal services, transport and logistics) is the biggest contributor to GDP, accounting for 42.3 per cent of the GDP in 2015. Agriculture and manufacturing sectors respectively, account for 28.2 per cent and 29.4 per cent of GDP. The average annual growth rate of the services sector is 8.3 per cent over the last fifteen years (see Table 9.2). To sustain the dynamism of economic growth, Cambodia has gradually diversified its sources of growth from labour-intensive industry to a skills-based economy. Enhanced productivity and innovation are the core elements of the development vision. Services sector is regarded as the

TABLE 9.2
Structure of Output
(% of GDP at current basic prices)

Sectors	2000	2005	2010	2015	Average Change Rate (%)
Agriculture	37.9	32.4	36.1	28.2	3.8
Industry	23.0	26.4	23.2	29.4	12.0
Services	39.1	41.2	40.8	42.3	8.3

Source: Asian Development Bank, Key Indicators for Asia and the Pacific 2016.

main driving force of future growth. Therefore, further liberalization of services sector is needed for achieving the economic development vision of becoming an upper middle-income country by 2030.

However, the development of the services sector is a long and challenging process. Improving the competitiveness and productivity of the services sector require institutional and legal reforms. Investing in logistics infrastructure is vital for a strong services sector (Noland et al. 2012). The study by the Asian Development Bank (ADB) shows that the future of the sector will also be defined by a dynamic and open competitive environment. It further argues that "more competition will raise service sector productivity which can, in turn, lift productivity in other sectors" (ADB 2013, p. 390).

After three decades of civil war and two decades of centrally planned economy, Cambodia embarked on a market economy in the early 1990s with a remarkable speed of liberalization and privatization. After becoming a full member of the WTO in 2004, Cambodia is required to reform and liberalize many of its services sector to other members of the WTO. WTO accession is a "positive externality to stimulate and make irreversible substantial trade liberalization and more broadly based reforms" (Sok 2005, p. x).

Cambodia's WTO Commitment and Status

In compliance with WTO requirements, Cambodia conducted its first review of trade policies and practices in November 2011. In response to the trade policy review recommendations, many reforms were undertaken. Some of these are: elimination of the Certificate of Origin requirement for exports to countries where a certificate is no longer required; enactment of the Law on Telecommunications in December 2015; and enactment of the Law on Animal Health and Production in February 2016.[6]

Moreover, in addition to the above, ongoing or planned reforms include the following: Amendment to the Law on Standards; Enacting a Competition Law; Enacting a Law on Special Economic Zones; Enacting a Law on Food Safety; and Enacting a Law on E-Commerce. In January 2016, the Ministry of Commerce launched an online business registration portal that allows all existing and new businesses to register their companies. To summarize, in a few years after joining WTO, economic liberalization in Cambodia has gained momentum in order to attract FDI but nonetheless many FDI barriers are still encountered, such as corruption and a weak legal framework (Chea et al. n.d.).

The WTO defines trade in services in four modes — mode 1 on cross-border supply; mode 2 on consumption abroad; mode 3 on commercial presence; and mode 4 on presence of natural persons. Cambodia has largely committed to all modes of liberalization, with the exception of mode 4 (presence of natural persons). It is fully in compliance with WTO's rules on the conditions of ownership, management, operation, judicial form and scope of activities as set out in a license or other forms of approval for establishing or authorizing the operation or supply of services by the foreign service suppliers. Notably, for its GATS commitments, modes 1–3 have mainly no restrictions in market access while mode 4 remains largely unbound across subsectors. Maritime international transport (freight and passengers) is unbound in all four modes.

Cambodia's AFAS Commitments

In addition to the WTO, the conclusion of the AFAS in 2007 further accelerated the speed of liberalization of trade in services in Cambodia. The main subsectors that are liberalized are computer and related services, courier, telecommunication, commission agents, wholesale trade, retailing, franchising, higher education, adult education and other education services, sewage, refuse disposal, sanitation and similar services, environmental services, travel agencies and tour operation, tour guides, and road transport (Hikari 2011). Under the AFAS 8, Cambodia's overall score is 0.45, which is higher than Laos (0.39) and Vietnam (0.43). Service liberalization under mode 4 is restricted in Cambodia (see Table 9.3).

TABLE 9.3

Service Liberalization AFAS 8, Simple Average of 154 Subsectors

	Market Access				National Treatment				Average
	M1	M2	M3	M4	M1	M2	M3	M4	
Cambodia	0.56	0.64	0.59	0.00	0.59	0.64	0.61	0.00	0.45
Laos	0.53	0.55	0.37	0.07	0.53	0.55	0.43	0.07	0.39
Vietnam	0.47	0.68	0.52	0.03	0.48	0.68	0.56	0.00	0.43

Note: M1: mode 1: M2: mode 2; M3: mode 3; M4: mode 4.
Source: Isono and Ishido (2016).

Issues and Challenges in Services Liberalization

Although Cambodia has liberalized its services sector in terms of foreign ownership on a non-discriminatory basis in a wide range of sectors as explained in the section above, good governance and implementing capacity are the core issues. Regulatory frameworks on land use are weak and opaque, causing difficulties for foreign investors. Ambiguities of land entitlements, improper land transactions and registration, and corruption lead to land disputes or conflicts, which are the main challenges for investors (Sekiguchi and Hatsukano 2013). Regarding land use, Article 44 of the Constitution provides that only Cambodian citizens and legal entities have the right to own land.

Cambodia needs to address several bottlenecks that hinder the services sector. Based on the reports by the ADB in 2013 and the World Bank in 2014, the services sector in Cambodia is mired by inadequate transport and infrastructure in the rural areas, high costs of electricity, transportation and logistics, weak governance and institutional capacity, lack of information relating to regulatory requirements, inconsistent application and interpretation of regulations across agencies, frequent changes in administrative practices, and a general lack of skilled workforce (ADB 2013; World Bank 2014c).

Institutional capacity and logistics are regarded as the main constraints in smoothly operationalizing trade in services. According to the Transparency International's annual corruption perception index, Cambodia is ranked 105th in 2015, scoring only 21 points out of 100 (Transparency International 2015). The enterprise survey conducted by the World Bank in 2016 shows that the corruption rate in Cambodia is much higher than the average rate in East Asia and Pacific (see Table 9.4).

TABLE 9.4
Enterprise Survey 2016

Indicator	Cambodia	East Asia and Pacific
Bribery incidence (per cent of firms experiencing at least one bribe payment request)	64.7	30.4
Bribery depth (per cent of public transactions where a gift or informal payment was required)	59.4	23.9
Per cent of firms expected to give gifts in meetings with tax officials	58.7	21.6
Per cent of firms expected to give gifts to secure government contracts	87.5	47.3

Source: World Bank, Enterprise Survey 2016, available at <http://www.enterprisesurveys.org/data/exploreeconomies/2016/cambodia>.

The rule of law is another concern for foreign investors (Sperfeldt 2016). The courts are perceived as unreliable and susceptible to external political influence or bribery. In the annual Rule of Law Index in 2015, Cambodia is ranked 112 out of 113 countries surveyed globally by the World Justice Project.

To strengthen the competitiveness of the services market, the government needs to remove a wide range of internal and external policy distortions sector (Noland et al. 2012, p. v). To effectively implement services liberalization, Cambodia needs to develop and strengthen logistics governance, promote dialogue and coordination among regulators, trade officials and other stakeholders to have effective services liberalization (Hoekman and Mattoo 2013). Good governance, institutional coordination, regulatory capacity, infrastructure development, and human capital are critical to services sector development.

LOGISTICS DEVELOPMENT

Cambodia does not have an official definition of logistics. Logistics, regarded as a strategic subsector of the services sector, is generally understood as a combination of four main subsectors, namely transportation infrastructure (land, rail, maritime, air), logistics service providers (such as trucking, warehousing, freight forwarding, shipping, materials handling, inventory, packaging, courier and postal services), institutional framework relating to logistics (such as custom clearances and border reforms), and logistics users (such as traders and manufacturers).

Current State of Logistics

The logistics sector in Cambodia is less developed compared with neighbouring countries due to the lack of a reliable network of transportation, telecommunications, warehousing, trucking services, and related infrastructure. High logistics "service-link" costs have an adverse impact on attracting FDI, besides slowing down industrial development and the process of economic integration with the world and the region (Banomyong 2010). Based on the assessment by the World Bank in its annual Logistics Performance Index (LPI),[7] Cambodia ranked the 73rd with the score of 2.8 (5 is the perfect score). Infrastructure, logistics competence and customs have the lowest performance (see Figure 9.1).

FIGURE 9.1
Logistics Performance of Cambodia

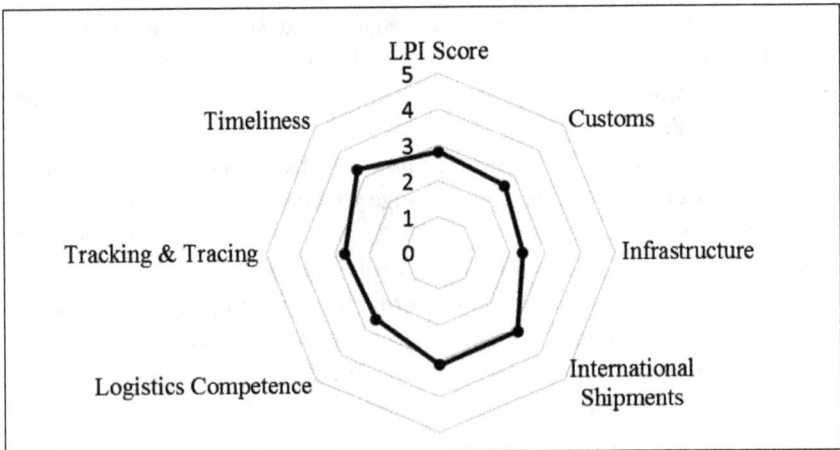

Source: World Bank (2016*a*).

The logistics cost in Cambodia is high, relatively to other ASEAN member countries. Cambodia's export costs are about 33 per cent higher than that of Thailand and 30 per cent higher than that of Vietnam (World Bank 2014*a*). Cambodia's farmers and manufacturers encounter difficulties in moving goods to internal and external markets. Logistics is the main challenge faced by exporters in supplying goods to overseas customers and in integrating producers into regional production networks (World Bank 2014*a*).

For instance, the study by the World Bank on Rice Monitoring in 2014 shows that transport costs of rice in Cambodia is higher than that in neighbouring Thailand and Vietnam. The transport cost of one ton of rice from a farmer to a rice miller is US$247 in Cambodia compared with US$126 in Thailand and US$122 in Vietnam. The transport cost of one ton of rice from the miller to the port is US$43 in Cambodia compared with US$25 in Thailand and US$23 in Vietnam (World Bank 2014b).

The transportation cost for a twenty-foot container from Phnom Penh to Sihanoukville port is around US$400 (including trucking, documentation fee, export clearance fee, loading charge, Certificate of Origin, toll fee, agency fee, VAT, and miscellaneous charges). The charge at the port is around US$350 and it takes around eight hours by road from Phnom Penh to Sihanoukville port (CDC 2016a). The export cost from Phnom Penh to Ho Chi Minh City in Vietnam is about US$880 for a forty-foot container and US$820 for a twenty-foot container. These include the customs clearance fee in Cambodia, but exclude the charges at Vietnam's port. It takes around fifteen hours by road. Using the waterway, the export cost is slightly lower. It costs around US$800 for a twenty-foot container from Phnom Penh Port to Cai Mep, including customs fee in Cambodia and Vietnam, though it takes around thirty-six hours by the Mekong River (CDC 2016a).

Institutional Framework

Since logistics is one of the development priority areas in Cambodia, there are several plans that include the development of this sector such as the Rectangular Strategy Phase III (2013–18); National Strategic Development Plan 2014–18; Cambodia Trade Integration Strategy 2014–18; and the Industrial Development Policy 2015–25. In order to create more coherence within the sector, in his key address at the 2016 Cambodia Outlook Conference, Prime Minister Hun Sen stressed on the need to improve coordination between key agencies as well as the regulatory framework and support system (Hun Sen 2016).

Institutional and legal reforms have been underway to develop the logistics sector. Various laws have been adopted to facilitate the investment in logistics sector such as the Law on Concessions[8] adopted in 2007, which aims to promote and facilitate the implementation of private financing through contractual concessions,[9] for infrastructure development. Progressively other laws related to the logistics sector are being put in place such as the law on electricity in 2001 to govern and to prepare a framework for the electric power supply and services throughout the country and the Sub-Degree on the Establishment and Management of Special Economic Zone in 2005. More recently, additional laws such as the Law on Civil Aviation in 2008, Law on Road in 2014, Law on Water Resources Management in 2007, Law on Telecommunications in 2015, are added to the regulatory structure.

With the support from the World Bank, trade facilitation reforms have undergone quite well, which led to the improvement of logistics performance. Procedures for issuing and applying Certificate of Origin have been abolished where unnecessary, and when needed, simplified through an automated system. An automated customs system has been rolled out in twenty-one border checkpoints. The duration of customs clearance fell from 5.9 days (2010) to 1.4 days (2014) and the duration of physical inspection fell from 29 per cent (2010) to 17 per cent (2014) (World Bank 2014a). In 2016, Cambodia's LPI ranked 73 with the LPI score of 2.80, Customs score of 2.62, Infrastructure score of 2.36, International Shipment score of 3.11, Logistics Competence of 2.60, Tracking and Tracing score of 2.70, and Timeliness score of 3.30 (5 being the perfect score) (World Bank 2016a).

The National Single Window (NSW) is developed in line with the ASEAN Single Window (ASW)[10] project to promote ASEAN Connectivity through trade and investment. The objective of NSW is to strengthen coordination and relationship between government agencies, between enterprises, and between the government and private sector (General Department of Customs and Excise of Cambodia 2016a). The NSW Blueprint has been developed with the financial support of the World Bank, incorporating technical and functional specifications for the system, governance and operational model, procurement strategy and a project implementation plan. But, it is not fully operational yet due to a lack of institutional and technical capacity. Cambodia has yet to implement ASEAN Trade in Goods Agreement (ATIGA) Form D using the ASW enabling system. The credibility of the automation of the customs clearance system and the electronic exchange of customs data with other ASEAN members are the main technical issues that need to be addressed. Cambodia is learning from the experiences of other advanced ASEAN members in implementing NSW. It is committed to joining the testing on the electronic exchange of ATIGA (or e-ATIGA) Form D by mid of 2017 and the full implementation is expected to start by the end of 2017 (ASEAN Single Window n.d.)

In addition, with the financial and technical support from development partners, especially the World Bank under the Trade Facilitation and Competitiveness Project (TFCP) and Trade Development Support Program (TDSP), the ASYCUDA WORLD system, which is a system to expedite custom clearance through electronic system, has been implemented at fifty-four major customs branches and offices, which covered almost 99 per cent of Single Administrative Declaration (SAD) and approximately 87 per cent of trade volume (General Department of Customs and Excise of Cambodia 2016*b*).

The Customs–Private Sector Partnership Mechanism (CPPM), launched in January 2010, aims to further enhance fair business and investment climate. The CPPM is responsible for coordinating cooperation and mutual understandings between Customs Administration and Private Sector, as well as resolving all customs related matters before problems and issues are moved to other dispute settlement bodies, or to the Government–Private Sector Forum. This is also an important factor to ensure the effectiveness of the implementation of the government's trade facilitation policy (General Department of Customs and Excise of Cambodia 2016*c*).

Transport Infrastructure

The transport infrastructure mainly includes road network, railway, waterway, and air transport. Transport infrastructure development projects have been mainly funded by ADB, China, Japan, and the World Bank. The movement of goods within the country is heavily based on road network. There are three main cross-border transport networks under the regional connectivity projects of the Greater Mekong Subregion Southern Corridor and ASEAN Highway System, linking Cambodia with neighbouring countries. Cambodia is developing a master plan to develop expressway. Based on the study by China's expert group, Cambodia needs to develop 2,230 km of national expressway network by 2040 with the investment amount of approximately US$26 billion (Agence Kampuchea Press, 28 May 2014). The first expressway connecting Sihanoukville and Phnom Penh will be built by China under the Belt and Road initiative (*The Khmer Times*, 12 August 2016).

Two single-track railways, the Northern Line and the Southern Line, serve the country. The container train service restarted its operation in 2014 between Phnom Penh and Sihanoukville (three times a week) with a total volume of container of 17,836 TEUs in 2014. The railway was privatized in 2009 with a thirty-year concession. The Railway Master Plan is being developed in cooperation with the Korea International Cooperation Agency.

Besides this, there are seven seaports in Cambodia: Sihanoukville port, Koh Kong port, Sre Ambel port, Oknha Mong port, Stunghav port and Oil terminal, Kampot port, and Kaeb port. Sihanoukville Port is the largest international deep seaport. There is a plan to build a multipurpose terminal to accommodate larger vessels with a loading capacity from 30,000 to 40,000 DWT, new container terminal, and tourism terminal. It is estimated that the container volume will increase up to 450,000 TEUs by 2018. The development project costs approximately US$71.7 million, which is to be completed by May 2017 (Sihanoukville Autonomous Port, Development Plan).

There are also seven dry ports[11] in Cambodia, located in three main areas: Bavet (Cambodia–Vietnam border), Poi Pet (Cambodia–Thailand border), and around the capital city Phnom Penh. The dry ports are invested by the private sector under the investment scheme of Build–Own–Operate (BOO) in partnership with the Ministry of Economy and Finance. Dry ports are developed to process goods from the point of entrance. For instance, containers arriving at Sihanoukville could be transported by road to the dry ports near Phnom Penh for customs clearance to save time and reduce inconvenience for customers based in Phnom Penh.

Inland waterway has improved remarkably in the last five years while railway and airports are slowly rehabilitated and expanded. Cambodia's navigable inland waterway has a total length of 1,750 km in which the Mekong mainstream accounts for 30 per cent of the total, the Tonle Sap River 15 per cent, the Bassac River 5 per cent, and other tributaries 50 per cent. There are six major river ports out of which Phnom Penh river port is the international gateway to Vietnam and beyond. The Agreement on Waterway Transportation between Cambodia and Vietnam in 2009 establishes a legal framework for the effective implementation of freedom of navigation in the Mekong river system (Sar 2010).

The overall condition of the transport infrastructure and the infrastructure connectivity between the urban and rural areas are not good. A strategy on multimodal mode of transport connecting these transport infrastructures has not yet been developed. The study by the ADB argues that "the strategic challenges facing the transport sector are lack of connectivity to services and markets, resulting in lost economic opportunity; high operating, maintenance, and logistics costs; lack of competitiveness; and unsafe and unsustainable infrastructure" (ADB 2011, p. 6).

Logistics Service Providers (LSP)

Logistics service providers (LSP) are private agencies or professionals that "serve clients like manufacturers, raw materials suppliers, distributors, retailers, and shippers within the supply chain" (Chow et al. 2005, p. 272). LSPs are involved in almost all sectors with a wide variety of services such as transport, storage, packaging and many others that add more values to products and services (Kovacs et al. 2016). The logistics process is to "merge and organize all activities involved in acquiring, converting and distributing goods from raw materials to finished goods to the customers to achieve customer service objectives in an efficient cost effective manner" (Sheik and Rana 2014, p. 1).

Cambodia's national logistics providers mainly offer domestic services, with a limited service range and low service quality. Local companies are dominant in Dry Port operations and trucking. The Kampuchea Shipping Agency and Brokers (KAMSAB) is the largest domestic freight forwarding company that offers a wide range of logistics services including transport, brokerage, and warehousing. Therefore, it is challenging for Cambodian logistics service providers to provide competitive logistics services even within the domestic market, let alone in international or global markets. Knowledge and technology transfer, capital injection will be required to improve the quality and competitiveness of the logistics service providers in Cambodia.

The logistics sector is heavily run by several multi-national companies, most of whom are also customs brokers and airfreight GSA (General Sales Agent). Global logistics operators in Cambodia significantly contribute to trade facilitation and they also help strengthen the capacity of the local operators either through partnerships or joint ventures. However, these global operators face the problem of a lack of adequately trained manpower that would be required to ensure efficient operations.

Logistics Service Users

Traders and manufacturers are the main users of logistics services. The Cambodian traders and manufacturers are generally not aware of the importance of managing logistics and the supply chain as well as the potential associated benefits. Thus, logistics is often equated with transport. Another issue is the outsourcing of logistics services excluding transportation to foreign logistics service providers because there is a lack of confidence in the quality of the services provided by domestic logistics providers.

Liberalization in Logistics

In line with its WTO commitments, Cambodia has also placed no
limitations in market access and national treatment for the logistics
services subsectors, as identified in the Roadmap for the Integration of
Logistics Services (see Table 9.5). This makes the country relatively open
to FDI in services compared to the other member countries in ASEAN.

TABLE 9.5
Cambodia's Commitments in ASEAN for Logistics Sector, as of 2016

Sector	CPC	AFAS 9	
		MA	NT
Packaging services	876	M1: N M2: N M3: N	M1: N M2: N M3: N
Courier services	7512	M1: N M2: N M3: N	M1: N M2: N M3: N
Maritime freight transportation, excluding cabotage	7212	M1: N M2: N M3: N	M1: N M2: N M3: N
Rail freight transportation	7112	M1: N M2: N M3: N	M1: N M2: N M3: N
Road freight transportation	7123	M1: N M2: N M3: N	M1: N M2: N M3: N
Maritime cargo handling services	741	M1: N M2: N M3: N	M1: N M2: N M3: N
Storage and warehouse services: covering private bonded warehousing services only	742	M1: N M2: N M3: N	M1: N M2: N M3: N
Maritime freight forwarding services only	748	M1: N M2: N M3: N	M1: N M2: N M3: N
Other auxiliary services	749	M1: N M2: N M3: N	

Source: ASEAN Secretariat, available at <http://asean.org/?static_post=member-countries-horizontal-commitments-schedules-of-specific-commitments-and-the-list-of-most-favoured-nation-exemptions> (accessed 2 March 2017).

Investment in Logistics Infrastructure

Investment in logistics sector is in high demand (currently there is no statistics on FDI in logistics in Cambodia). Cambodia would need about US$15 billion in infrastructure development from 2013 to 2020 to keep up with its economic growth rate of around 7 per cent (ADB 2012*b*). The infrastructure investment projects need to focus on the development of multimodal and cross-border transport systems, improvement and expansion of inland waterway transport systems, thereby linking SEZs with strategic industrial areas, electricity supply, postal and courier services, and telecommunications.

A study by the Cambodia Resource Development Institute indicates, "One per cent increase in the stock of infrastructure directly contributes to a 0.8 per cent increase in GDP" (CDRI 2016, pp. 1–2). The quantity of committed investment capital to Cambodia hit US$4.5 billion in 2015, with investment in infrastructure at US$3.1 billion (see Table 9.6). Cumulatively, investment projects from 2011 to 2015 concentrate mainly on infrastructure (41 per cent), followed by industries (35 per cent), agriculture (14 per cent), and tourism (10 per cent) (see Table 9.7). Local investments account for two thirds of the total investment capital. The largest foreign investor is China, accounting for almost 90 per cent of total foreign investment capital (Council for the Development of Cambodia 2016*b*).

TABLE 9.6
Investments by Sector, 2011–15

	2011	2012	2013	2014	2015
Agriculture	794.5	556.6	1,128.8	264.7	482.6
Industries	1,340.8	1,489.7	1,106.7	2,835.6	919.3
Infrastructure	2,782.3	227.8	2,620.8	353.5	3,129.8
Tourism	845.6	691.5	106.0	479.6	111.9

Source: Council for the Development of Cambodia (2016*b*).

TABLE 9.7
Investment Capital, 2011–15
(total of US$22.3 billion)

Infrastructure	Industries	Agriculture	Tourism
41%	35%	14%	10%

Source: Council for the Development of Cambodia (2016*b*).

Public–Private–Partnership (PPP) investment in logistics remains limited. The sources of infrastructure financing mainly come from the government, multilateral development agencies (especially ADB and the World Bank), and bilateral donors (especially China, Japan, Korea, Australia). There are several potential infrastructure development projects that are open and attractive to domestic and foreign investors. For example, dry ports are the main transport subsectors that mostly attract private investment. In fact, the seven dry ports are invested by the private sector under the investment scheme of BOO. Another potential infrastructure that is attractive to investors is riverports development and waterway transport service. Transport by the inland waterway from Phnom Penh port to Cai Mep (Vietnam) is more efficient and costs less than overland transport (Kingdom of Cambodia 2014, p. 85).

Likewise, airport infrastructure is another potential investment area. Cambodia has concluded fourteen air service agreements, seven of which are with ASEAN member states. Based on the ASEAN Open Sky Agreement in 2008, Vietnamese carriers are granted 5th freedom rights for route Ho Chi Minh–Phnom Penh–Vientiane. There are already three international airports (Phnom Penh, Siem Reap, and Sihanouk) that are managed by the French company (SCA) under the Build–Operate–Transfer (BOT) investment scheme.

ISSUES AND CHALLENGES IN LOGISTICS DEVELOPMENT

The main issues and challenges in developing seamless logistics in Cambodia, as pointed out by Prime Minister Hun Sen, are low public and private investment in transport infrastructure, limited number of domestic logistics service providers, poorly integrated multimodal transport system, lack of healthy competition in trucking, part and freight services, poor rural roads connections, little investment in inland waterways, weak links of rail network, port inefficiency, limited electricity supply with high unit costs ($0.177/Kwh) (Hun Sen 2016).

Moreover, an earlier draft action plan on logistics development prepared by the Ministry of Commerce in 2010 identified several issues and challenges facing the logistics sector, including complex and overlapping institutional arrangement, lack of coordination among related government agencies, lack of single state agency responsible for logistics, lack of government officials with expertise on logistics, lack of logistics statistical indicators, lack of operational standards for logistics service, weak professional associations or organizations, limited information and communication technology (ICT) usage, low quality level of logistics service, lack of skilled manpower, and limited international coverage (Ministry of Commerce 2010). The plan was not implemented due to lack of leadership, which is critical for dealing with the multiple subsectors, agencies, and stakeholders in logistics.

According to the former coordinator of the Cambodia Freight Forwarders Association (CAMFFA),[12] the main issues in logistics development are lack of quality and safety of transport infrastructures and connectivity (although it is improving), lack of understanding among key stakeholders on the importance of logistics sector, lack of transparency, high cost of red tape and unofficial fee of custom clearances, the credibility of the automation system of the NSW, and the lack of qualified or adequately trained manpower in logistics. Currently there are no container repairing-service education for truck drivers, and proper inspection of vehicles.[13]

The transport sector is facing four main issues namely a lack of laws and institutions, lack of transport infrastructure and efficiency in roads and railways, lack of sustainability through low maintenance capability, and low participation of the private sector. Further regulation and transparency are required to attract private investment in transport infrastructure (ADB 2011, pp. 8–13). In addition, the issues faced by the urban transport are lack of consultation and consensus among the related government ministries and agencies on the responsibilities and measures to tackle urban transport issues, policies to manage urban traffic are not implemented effectively, and there is insufficient dialogue between transport regulators, operators, and enterprises (UNESCAP 2016).

The findings from the field interview with the management staff at the Phnom Penh Autonomous Port (PPAP),[14] the largest river port operator and the second largest international container terminal port after Sihanoukville port, illustrate that container congestion due to the delay in custom clearance and unofficial fees paid to custom officers are the main issues. Specific problems of border crossing faced by the company are no official tariff fee and exact time frame as documents can be delayed by customs officers who are waiting for more unofficial fees. The main constraints for the logistics providers are weak governance (corruption or unofficial fee, lack of transparency, poor coordination among government agencies), low quality and connectivity of transport infrastructure, and qualified manpower. Hun Sakhalay, manager of sales/marketing office at the PPAP, said "good governance, quality infrastructure development, institutional coordination, and regional economic integration are vital to logistics development and economic competitiveness".[15]

The report on Cambodia Trade Integration Strategy 2014–18 highlights corruption and informal fees as the main challenges in developing logistics. It observes that

> A fundamental problem underlying the logistics market in Cambodia is the opacity of the cost elements that determine the final price for shipments. This is one of the reasons manufacturing firms do not invest in in-house logistics capability — because they wish to avoid having to deal with some of the informal practices that are encountered along the trade corridors. (Kingdom of Cambodia 2015, p. 85)

The report continues:

> Informal payments are reported to take place at weighbridges, en-route checkpoints, and customs [...] The informal fees are also levied at border crossing and during customs clearance. Most operators are reluctant to even discuss informal fees [...] There are also high levels of informal payments to clear cargo. Typically, agents pay $180 to $210 to clear each twenty-foot container. The payments are shared between the clearing agent and border officials. Stakeholders view the border processes as the main contributor to high trade costs in the country [...] The informal costs are passed on to shippers, but without supporting receipts, leading to opacity about the real rate of informal payments that are truly required for clearance of each shipment and exacerbating the distrust between agents and shippers. (Kingdom of Cambodia 2015, p. 86)

Specific problems of border crossing encountered by traders and freight forwarders are those relating to border agencies, more particularly Customs and CamControl. The following issues relating to the General Department of Customs and Excise (GDCE) are: (a) No official fee tariff, all fees paid to Customs are considered as "non-official handling fees", and it varies according to weight, volume of cargo and nature of commodity; (b) No official time frame, documents can be delayed by Customs waiting for more fees, and no back up for persons in charge at Customs; (c) No clear process mapping for Customs formalities. Documents and process are all depending and vary as per commodities; (d) Lack of information flows from Customs to traders, Customs often applies new regulations without considering whether information reach traders. No grace/free time left before apply new regulations; and (e) Risk management targets physical inspection at 20 per cent, but in practice there is for no exception an inspection "un-official" handling fee for all Customs cleared shipment even though there is no requirement for physical inspection of cargo (Ministry of Commerce 2010).

Similarly, procedures established and followed by CamControl still cause some problems, despite considerable operational improvements. These include: (a) CamControl permit is required for nearly all export commodities and some import commodities. CamControl officers are present at all checkpoints and clearance places. Inspection fees and service fees are charged for nearly all operations; (b) Service provided is relatively time consuming (Ministry of Commerce 2010).

Logistics is a "strategic subject" and a "political fight" among government ministries (Ministry of Public Works and Transport, Ministry of Economy and Finance, Ministry of Commerce, Ministry of Land Management, and the Council for the Development of Cambodia). The government ministries are competing for a higher stake and more dominant role in regulating the logistics sector — an emerging industry with high financial returns. There is currently no clear division of responsibilities among the government ministries and agencies regarding logistics development. Therefore, to avoid the power competition among the agencies, it is necessary to establish a national logistics council to coordinate the logistics industry.

With regards to private investment in logistics infrastructure, the private sector is reluctant to invest in hard infrastructure such as roads and rails given the high risks and low returns. Land issue and resettlement of local people are politically sensitive issues, which lead to high investment risk.[16]

For the logistics sector to be more competitive, Cambodia needs to get access to the transport networks in neighbouring countries, particularly for the border provinces located in proximate to Thai and Vietnamese seaports. For instance, Cambodia uses its Mekong waterway to ship its export products via the ports in Vietnam. And in July 2016, the Cambodian government approached the Thai counterpart to discuss the possibility of allowing Cambodia to use Laem Chabang port to export its agriculture products to a third country in order to reduce transportation cost. However, the differences in traffic rules and transport regulations between the two countries are the main challenges in promoting cross-border land transport. Both countries agreed to increase the quota of vehicles from 150 per day in 2016 to 500 per day in 2018 as part of implementing the ASEAN Framework Agreement on Facilitation of Inter-

State Transport and the Greater Mekong Subregion Cooperation Framework (400 for trucks and 100 for buses) (*Phnom Penh Post*, 25 May 2015).

Cambodia acceded to the Greater Mekong Subregion Cross-Border Transport Facilitation Agreement (CBTA) in 2001 to improve its regional logistics connectivity. The CBTA aims to: (a) facilitate the cross-border transport of goods and people between and among the contracting parties; (b) to simplify and harmonize legislation, regulations, procedures, and requirements relating the cross-border transport of goods and people; and (c) to promote multimodal transport.

The private sector plays a critical role in delivering logistics services. Logistics services are provided by numerous brokers, each contributing one activity to the final clearance of the goods. However, the multiplicity of actors makes it more difficult for traders to track payments (Ministry of Commerce, *Cambodia Trade Integration Strategy 2014–18*, p. 85). Another challenge is a lack of management capacity and professionalism of the logistics services providers. Rithy Sear, chairman of the WorldBridge International Group, said:

> Logistics is the way of the future, and in Cambodia many companies don't understand the market or the value of managing the whole supply chain... In terms of the supply chain, it is very important to operate the whole thing. However, most logistics companies in Cambodia lack that [ability] of professionalism. Only a few companies have been able to operate well" (*Phnom Penh Post*, 8 April 2016).

Another issue in logistics development is the price of electricity, which is much higher than the neighbouring countries. The electricity price is around US$0.8 per kWh in Phnom Penh[17] higher than Ho Chi Minh City which is US$0.11 per kWh and Bangkok which is US$0.15 per kWh (World Bank 2016*b*). Cambodia is importing electricity from its neighbours to supply its domestic needs. In 2013, it imported 1,691 megawatts from Vietnam, 579 megawatts from Thailand, and 10.73 megawatts from Laos (*Phnom Penh Post*, 12 May 2015).

CONCLUSION

FDI plays a critical role in socio-economic development. Services sector liberalization under the framework of WTO and AFAS are the main strategies used to attract FDI to Cambodia. FDI in services sector has grown remarkably in Cambodia due to conducive investment environment such as liberal and open services sector, favourable investment law and other related laws and regulations, and various investment incentives. However, weak governance (includes the principles of accountability, transparency and rule of law), corruption, the cost of electricity and logistics are the core constraints in attracting FDI.

As part of the strategy to further attract FDI and facilitate trade (export-led growth), the Cambodian government has started, at a preliminary stage, to promote logistics development in its industrial development strategy and trade promotion policies. However, logistics performance is still weak and investments in logistics remain relatively low. The government does not have a clear and comprehensive policy on logistics. Corruption has hindered logistics development. Attracting foreign investment in logistics sector is critical to strengthening national logistics performance and competitiveness.

Liberalization is not sufficient in logistics sector development since the country is already open. Soft infrastructure (i.e. good governance, transparency, rule of law, regulatory capacity, human capital, ICT, international institutional framework) and hard infrastructure (i.e. roads, rails, seaports, airports, dry ports, river ports, warehousing), and robust participation from the private sector are required to develop a competitive and seamless logistics sector.

The main bottlenecks in logistics in Cambodia are corruption, lack of quality and reliability of transport systems, lack of integrated multimodal transport networks, poor coordination between government agencies and institutions, informal payments occurring especially at the border checkpoints and customs clearance, lack of integrated logistics service providers, and domestic logistics users, who are less seasoned in the knowledge and use of comprehensive logistics services.

Policy Recommendations

Cambodia needs to develop a comprehensive master plan on logistics and establish a national council on logistics to strategically connect logistics to national development strategy and trade facilitation policy, coordinate line ministries and agencies to reduce corruption and informal fees, develop multimodal logistics approach, and work towards administrative and regulatory reform. Such a council can help to overcome the political fight among government ministries to exert regulatory control over the sector. It can also serve to monitor and oversee implementation of the goals and targets in the master plan.

Domestic infrastructure connectivity, especially linking urban and rural transport and logistics, is necessary to reduce development gaps between the rural and urban areas as well as to realize an inclusive growth. Integrating multimodal transport systems, such as connecting land (rails, roads) and waterway (inland, maritime) transport networks, is needed to enhance domestic connectivity and cross-border transport.

Since PPP is needed to finance infrastructure development, to promote PPP investments in logistics sector, Cambodia needs to develop a regulatory framework to promote and facilitate PPP investment projects on logistics sector (Sotharith 2014). Transparency, investment protection, market opportunities, and risks mitigation measures are required to attract private investment in logistics. The government should also consider establishing a PPP unit that is tasked to manage the government's PPP policy and strategy, identify and coordinate projects, provide advices and coordination services, oversight and approve projects, and build the capacity of government employees in line with ASEAN–Public Private Partnership Guidelines (Zen and Regan 2014, p. 12).

Customs reform is critical to reducing the cost of logistics. In this regard, it needs to further reduce customs formalities. Although some progress has been made, it should prioritize the implementation of the NSW in compliance with the ASW by improving the credibility of the automation system and accelerating electronic exchange of customs data with the ASEAN Member States (e-ATIGA). Capacity building for both the public and private sectors are needed. Knowledge sharing between the ASEAN members regarding the implementation of NSW is essential. For instance, in 2013, Malaysia hosted and shared Malaysian experiences in implementing NSW with the Cambodian customs officers.

Cambodia needs to negotiate with Thailand and Vietnam to reach agreements on an integrated road transport and cross-border shipments to facilitate cross-border trade and to maximize the utilization of its dry ports. Given that human resource development and capacity building in logistics are critical for effective policy implementation, ASEAN should promote regional cooperation on capacity building, especially in human resource development. The more developed ASEAN members can assist the less developed members in narrowing the logistics performance gap through human resource development and institutional improvements. ASEAN member states also need to assist each other in logistics performance for the effective implementation of the ASEAN Master Plan on Connectivity.

Notes

1. There are no data for 2001–6.
2. See the details of investment incentives at <http://www.cambodiainvestment. gov.kh/investment-scheme/investment-incentives.html>.
3. These are the investment projects that are qualified and approved by the Council for the Development of Cambodia, which is a one-stop service organization responsible for the rehabilitation, development and the oversight of investment activities.
4. Maximum Trigger Period is the first year of profit or three years after the qualified investment project starts earning its revenue, whichever is sooner.
5. Priority Period is determined by the Financial Management Law, within the period of three years, according to the type of project and investment capital (for light industries: zero year in case of investment capital of below US$5 million, one year in case of investment capital between US$5 million and US$20 million, two years in case of investment capital over US$20 million).
6. Other institutional reforms include the implementation of online business registration; adoption of a competitive hiring process for Ministry of Commerce staff; implementation of risk assessment measures for the Cambodia Import–Export Inspection and Fraud Repression Directorate General (CamControl) and creation of a CamControl risk management unit; enactment of the Law on Public Procurement; enactment of three judicial system laws (the Law on Court Structures, the Law on the Duties and Discipline of Judges and Prosecutors, and the Law on the Organization and Functioning of the Supreme Council of Magistracy); creation of the Commercial Court as a specialized Court of First Instance; the creation of a credit bureau; establishment of a Telecom Regulator of Cambodia (TRC) (in 2012, the Ministry of Posts and Telecommunication transferred the regulatory role to the TRC).
7. The logistics performance index (LPI) is the weighted average of the country scores on six key dimensions:
    - Efficiency of the clearance process (i.e., speed, simplicity and predictability of formalities) by border control agencies, including customs;
    - Quality of trade and transport related infrastructure (e.g., ports, railroads, roads, information technology);
    - Ease of arranging competitively priced shipments;
    - Competence and quality of logistics services (e.g., transport operators, customs brokers);
    - Ability to track and trace consignments;
    - Timeliness of shipments in reaching destination within the scheduled or expected delivery time.
8. The "concession" means any attribute to the state whereby a competent institution entrusts to a private third party the total or partial implementation

of an infrastructure project for which that institution would normally be responsible and for which the third party assumes a major part of the construction and/or operating risks or receives a benefit by way of compensation from government revenue or from fees and charges collected from users or customers.

9. A concession contract is granted through the following means: (a) Build, Operate and Transfer, (b) Build, Lease and Transfer, (c) Build, Transfer and Operate, (d) Build, Own and Operate, (e) Build, Own, Operate and Transfer, (f) Build, Cooperate and Transfer, (g) Expand, Operate and Transfer, (h) Modernize, Operate and Transfer, (i) Modernize, Own and Operate, and (j) Lease and Operate or management arrangements, including joint public–private implementation of infrastructure facilities.

10. The ASEAN Single Window aims to serve as a one-stop service, which allows parties involved in trade and transport to lodge standardized information and documents with a single-entry point to fulfill all import, export, and transit-related regulatory requirements.

11. A dry port is an inland intermodal terminal directly connected by road or rail to a seaport and operates as a centre for the trans-shipment of sea cargo to inland destinations.

12. Currently CAMFFA has sixty-seven members.

13. Based on the interview with a former coordinator of the Freight Forwarders Association in Cambodia on 27 July 2016.

14. Based on the field interview on 23 August 2016 at the office of the PPAP.

15. Ibid.

16. Based on the interview with Freight Forwarding Association in Cambodia on 27 July 2016.

17. This is the electricity price in Phnom Penh, the capital city. The price is higher in the provinces and rural areas.

References

Agence Kampuchea Press. "China Presents the Report of Expressway Development Master Plan to Cambodia", 28 May 2014. Available at <http://www.akp.gov.kh/?p=45843> (accessed 3 January 2017).

ASEAN Secretariat. "Cambodia – Schedule of Specific Commitments". Protocol to Implement the Fifth Package of Commitments on Financial Services under the ASEAN Framework Agreement on Services. Available at <http://investasean.asean.org/files/upload/01%20KH%20AFAS%205%20FS%20HC.pdf> (accessed 5 December 2016).

ASEAN Secretariat and the United Nations Conference on Trade and Development (UNCTAD). *ASEAN Investment Report 2016: Foreign Direct Investment and MSME Linkages*. Jakarta: ASEAN Secretariat, September 2016. Available at <http://asean.org/storage/2016/09/ASEAN-Investment-Report-2016.pdf> (accessed 5 January 2017).

ASEAN Single Window. "Cambodia General Information", n.d. Available at <http://asw.asean.org/nsw/cambodia/cambodia-general-information> (accessed 4 March 2017).

Asian Development Bank (ADB). *Cambodia, Transport Sector Assessment, Strategy, and Road Map.* Manila: ADB, September 2011. Available at <https://www.adb.org/sites/default/files/institutional-document/33102/files/cam-transport-assessment.pdf> (accessed 8 January 2017).

————. *Cambodia, Country Governance Risk Assessment and Risk Management Plan.* Manila: ADB, 2012a. Available at <https://www.adb.org/sites/default/files/institutional-document/33292/files/cgra-cam.pdf> (accessed 8 January 2017).

————. *Assessment of Public-Private Partnerships in Cambodia: Constraints and Opportunities.* Manila: ADB, 2012b. Available at <https://www.adb.org/sites/default/files/publication/29921/assessment-ppp-cambodia.pdf> (accessed 8 January 2017).

————. *Bright Spots for Cambodia's Service Sector, But Hard Reforms Needed.* ADB Country Office in Phnom Penh, 12 November 2013. Available at <http://www.adb.org/news/bright-spots-cambodias-service-sector-hard-reforms-needed> (accessed 8 January 2017).

————. "Cambodia: Economy". *Asian Development Outlook 2016 Update.* Manila: ADB, 2016. Available at <http://www.adb.org/countries/cambodia/economy> (accessed 5 January 2017).

Banomyong, Ruth. "Logistics Challenges in Cambodia, Lao PDR, Myanmar, and Vietnam". In *A Study on Upgrading Industrial Structure of CLMV Countries*, ERIA Research Project Report 2009-7-3, edited by Ruth Banomyong and Masami Ishida. Jakarta: Economic Research Institute for ASEAN and East Asia, 2010, pp. 392–420.

Cambodia Development Resource Institute (CDRI). *Cambodia Outlook Brief.* Phnom Penh: CDRI, 2016. Available at <http://cdri.org.kh/webdata/policybrief/ob16/ob16e.pdf> (accessed 5 January 2017).

Chea Samnang, Denora Sarin and Hach Sok. "Trade in Services in Cambodia". ASEAN Economic Forum, World Bank, n.d. Available at <http://siteresources.worldbank.org/INTRANETTRADE/Resources/Topics/Services/Cambodia-Asean_services.pdf> (accessed 7 January 2017).

Chow, Harry K.H., K.L. Choy, W.B. Lee and Felix T.S. Chan. "Design of a Knowledge-Based Logistics Strategy System". *Expert Systems with Applications* 29, no. 2 (2005): 272–90.

Council for the Development of Cambodia (CDC). "Logistics Cost", CDC 2016a. Available at <http://www.cambodiainvestment.gov.kh/investment-enviroment/cost-of-doing-business/logistics-cost.html> (accessed 2 November 2016).

————. "Investment Trend", CDC 2016*b*. Available at <http://www.cambodiainvestment.gov.kh/investment-enviroment/investment-trend.html> (accessed 2 November 2016).

General Department of Customs and Excise of Cambodia. "National Single Window", 2016*a*. Available at <http://www.customs.gov.kh/trade-facilitation/national-single-window/> (accessed 2 November 2016).

————. "ASYCUDA Project", 2016*b*. Available at <http://www.customs.gov.kh/trade-facilitation/customs-automation/> (accessed 2 November 2016).

————. "Customs-Private Partnership", 2016*c*. Available at <http://www.customs.gov.kh/trade-facilitation/customs-private-sector-partnership-mechanism-cppm/> (accessed 2 November 2016).

Hikari, Ishido. "Liberalization of Trade in Services under ASEAN+n: A Mapping Exercise". ERIA Discussion Paper. Jakarta: Economic Research Institute for ASEAN and East Asia, May 2011.

Hoekman, Bernard and Aoditya Mattoo. "Liberalizing Trade in Services: Lessons from Regional and WTO Negotiations". *International Negotiation* 18, no. 1 (2013).

Hun Sen. "Keynote Address at the 2016 Cambodia Outlook Conference". Phnom Penh: Cambodia Development Resource Institute, 2016. Available at <http://www.cdri.org.kh/oc2016/Samdaech%20Prime%20Minister's%20Speech-English.pdf> (accessed 5 January 2017).

Isono, Ikumo and Hikari Ishido. "Service Liberalization in Laos PDR". IDE Discussion Paper no. 559. Institute of Developing Economies-Japan External Trade Organization (IDE-JETRO), 2016.

Kovacs, Zoltan, Laszlo Szabo and Beata G. Pato. "Characteristics of Logistics Service Providers and Their Services". *Studia Universitatis Babes-Bolyai* 61, no. 1 (2016).

Kingdom of Cambodia. *Cambodia Trade Integration Strategy 2014–2018*. Phnom Penh: Kingdom of Cambodia, 2014. Available at <http://www.kh.undp.org/content/dam/cambodia/docs/PovRed/Cambodia%20Trade%20Integration%20Strategy%202014-2018.pdf> (accessed 5 January 2017).

Ministry of Commerce. "Logistics Development Cambodia". Draft Action Plan prepared by the Ministry of Commerce with support from the Asian Development Bank (Project RETA 6450), February 2010 (unpublished document).

Noland, Marcus, Park Donghyun, and Gemma B. Estrada. "Developing the Services Sector as Engine of Growth for Asia: An Overview". Working Paper Series. Manila: Asian Development Bank, October 2012. Available at <https://www.ciaonet.org/attachments/22045/uploads> (accessed 5 January 2017).

Phnom Penh Post. "PM Rebuts Cuts to Electricity Tariffs", 12 May 2015. Available at <http://www.phnompenhpost.com/business/pm-rebuts-cuts-to-electricity-tariffs> (accessed 5 January 2017).

———. "Cambodia, Thailand to Discuss Raising Border-Crossing Quota", 25 May 2015. Available at <http://www.phnompenhpost.com/business/cambodia-thailand-discuss-raising-border-crossing-quota> (accessed 5 January 2017).

———. "Logistics Firm Takes Shape", 8 April 2016. Available at <http://www.phnompenhpost.com/business/logistics-firm-takes-shape> (accessed 5 January 2017).

Sar, Vutha. "Current Conditions of Waterway Systems and Transport-Related Infrastructure in Cambodia". Presentation at Seminar on the Promotion of the Mekong River Cruise Tourism, Hotel Pacific Tokyo, 10 September 2010. Available at <http://www.jterc.or.jp/koku/koku_semina/pdf/100910_seminer_Vutha.pdf> (accessed 19 April 2017).

Sekiguchi, Manami and Naomi Hatsukano. "Land Conflicts and Land Registration in Cambodia". In *Land and Post-Conflict Peacebuilding*, edited by Jon Unruch and Rhodri Willams. London: Routledge, 2013.

Sheikh, Zaryab and Shafaq Rana. "The Role of Logistics Service Providers in Supply Chain Management: A Comprehensive Literature Review". *International Journal of Academic Research in Business and Social Sciences* 4, no. 5 (2014).

Sihanoukville Autonomous Port, Development Plan [online]. Available at <http://www.pas.gov.kh/en/page/development-plan> (accessed 5 January 2017).

Sok, Siphana. "Lessons from Cambodia's Entry into the World Trade Organization". ADBI Policy Papers no. 7. Tokyo: Asian Development Bank Institute, 2005.

Sotharith, Chap. "Cambodia Country Report". In *Financing ASEAN Connectivity*, edited by Fauziah Zen and Michael Regan. ERIA Research Project Report no. 15. Jakarta: Economic Research Institute for ASEAN and East Asia, 2014.

Sperfeldt, Christoph. "Cambodia's Unruly Rule of Law". *East Asia Forum*, 19 May 2016. Available at <http://www.eastasiaforum.org/2016/05/19/cambodias-unruly-rule-of-law/> (accessed 4 March 2017).

The Khmer Times. "Cambodia–China Talk Expressway", 12 August 2016. Available at <http://www.khmertimeskh.com/news/28412/cambodia-china-talk-expressway/> (accessed 5 January 2017).

Transparency International. *Corruption Perceptions Index 2015*. Berlin: Transparency International, 2015. Available at <https://www.transparency.org/cpi2015/> (accessed 5 January 2017).

United Nations Economic and Social Commission for Asia and the Pacific (UNESCAP). "Country Report on Sustainable Urban Transport Cambodia". Expert Group Meeting on Planning and Assessment of Urban Transportation Systems, Kathmandu, Nepal, 22–23 September 2016.

Warr, Peter and Jayant Menon. "Cambodia's Special Economic Zones". ADB Economics Working Paper Series no. 459. Manila: Asian Development Bank, October 2015.

World Bank. "Improving Trade and Logistics in Cambodia", 2014*a*. Available at <http://www.worldbank.org/en/results/2014/04/11/cambodia-trade-development-support-program> (accessed 20 December 2016).

————. "Rice Monitor Note". Phnom Penh: World Bank Country Office in Cambodia, 2014*b*.

————. *Cambodia Service Trade: Performance, Regulatory Framework Assessment.* Washington, D.C.: World Bank, 2014*c*.

————. *Logistics Performance Index 2016.* Washington, D.C.: World Bank, 2016*a*. Available at <http://lpi.worldbank.org/international/scorecard/radar/200/C/KHM/2016> (accessed 5 January 2017).

————. *Doing Business Report 2016.* Washington, D.C.: World Bank, 2016*b*. Available at <http://www.doingbusiness.org/~/media/WBG/DoingBusiness/Documents/Annual-Reports/English/DB16-Full-Report.pdf> (accessed 28 December 2017).

————. *Enterprise Surveys – Cambodia 2016 Country Profile.* Washington, D.C.: World Bank, 2016*c*. Available at <http://www.enterprisesurveys.org/~/media/GIAWB/EnterpriseSurveys/Documents/Profiles/English/cambodia-2016.pdf> (accessed 2 February 2017).

Zen, Fauziah and Michael Regan, eds. *ASEAN Public–Private Partnership Guidelines.* Jakarta: Economic Research Institute for ASEAN and East Asia, 2014. Available at <http://asean.org/storage/2016/09/Public-Private-Partnership-in-South-East-Asia.pdf> (accessed 2 February 2017).

10

SERVICES LIBERALIZATION IN LAO PDR: FDI IN LOGISTICS SECTOR OF A LAND-LINKED COUNTRY

Phanhpakit Onphanhdala and
Vanvisa Philavong

INTRODUCTION

Lao PDR is known as one of the poorest countries in ASEAN. In recent years, the economy has performed well. In 2015, its Gross Domestic Product (GDP) has increased by about 6.7 per cent, implying that Lao PDR is one of the top ten world's fastest growing economy (ADB 2016). This growth is a result of exports in energy, mostly in mining and electricity, which is due to an increase in Foreign Direct Investment (FDI) in these sectors, given its high return. FDI inflows to Laos rose remarkably, with more than 80 per cent in 2012–15 compared with 2009–11 (UNESCAP 2015). It is worth noting that FDI is a major source of investment that supports the growth of the economy.

It is a well-accepted fact that FDI has both positive and negative impact on an economy. For an open economy, higher FDI flows may contribute positively to GDP growth. Alternatively, at the sectoral level, higher investment, particularly in the mining sector, may lead to declining economic growth when both energy and mining sectors have reached a saturation level. It is difficult to keep up economic growth by only depending on these sectors. This implies that countries that focus on natural resources only may face an economic slump eventually. However, in Lao PDR, services sector value added as percentage of GDP is growing faster than the industrial and agricultural sectors' growth rates since 2013 (ADB 2016). Thus, the services sector is likely to be an alternative source of growth for the economy.

Lao PDR is a latecomer in services sector liberalization in ASEAN. The country opened up to FDI in 1988, but significant investment inflows only occurred after the early 2000s. In recent years, Lao PDR has achieved steady economic growth, mainly fuelled by large FDI inflows and exports of natural resources. Of the total accumulated FDI stock during 1989–2015, services sector was ranked fourth, after electricity, mining and agricultural sectors (IPD 2016*a*). Vietnam, Thailand and China are the three key investors in Lao PDR.

As a landlocked country that is surrounded by four ASEAN member states (AMS), the development of the logistics sector assumes great importance in Lao PDR's economy. The sector is not only seen as a facilitator for the country's growth and development but it is also expected to help the country to deepen its economic integration in ASEAN. However, the logistics sector in its current form faces many challenges. This chapter will first examine trends in FDI flows in the country, especially in the context of historical changes in policies, before proceeding to discuss Laos' domestic policies, including FDI liberalization in its logistics sector under the ASEAN Framework Agreement on Services (AFAS). It will also discuss the policy incentives, institutional and regulatory reforms that Laos PDR offers for promotion of FDI into the country. The main source of data for our analysis is obtained from Key Informant Interviews (KIIs), which was undertaken during May to November 2016. Finally, the chapter will identify the main challenges in FDI liberalization and other related policies for the development of the logistics sector. It also provides some policy suggestions for addressing these challenges.

Data Collection

This study aims to assess the impact of FDI liberalization on inflows of foreign investment in the logistics sector of Lao PDR. The AFAS is used as a guideline for FDI liberalization assessment and it is analysed in conjunction with other related foreign investment policies, laws and regulations in this sector. During May and August 2016, secondary data was collected from different government sources, including the Ministry of Planning and Investment (MPI), Ministry of Public Works and Transport (MoPWT) and Ministry of Industry and Commerce (MoIC).

A quantitative survey was conducted in Vientiane Capital where the largest number of freight forwarding joint venture firms are found. The chosen sample is taken from Lao International Freight Forwarder Association (LIFFA). LIFFA was established in 2003 under the MoPWT with ten members at the beginning. At present, there are forty members from all over the country, and includes various modes of transportation such as air, maritime, inland waterway and land transportation. Two air and maritime freight forwarding firms, six specific freight forwarding firms that transport fuel and construction materials, eight shipping and supportive services and one freight association are omitted from the study. Out of the twenty-three land freight transportation, only fourteen were available for the survey, which are joint venture freight transport firms (see Table 10.1). Domestic freight transport firms are too small and provide only specific services in their local area. The main respondents are high ranking officials, either chairman or owners of these firms.

TABLE 10.1
Survey Respondents

Total	Omitted	Availability	Response
40 LIFFA members	1 Air freight 1 Maritime freight 6 Specific freight 8 Shipping 1 Association	23 land freight transportation	14 land freight transportation

Source: Onphanhdala, Sirisack, and Khantiyavong (2017).

In addition, a qualitative KII was conducted through face-to-face interviews with representatives from the MoPWT, MoIC and LIFFA. The main respondents are the chairman and senior advisors of LIFFA, technical staff of Department of Transport (MoPWT), Department of Planning and Cooperation (MoIC) and Savan-Seno Special Economic Zone Authority (SEZA) and owners of domestics and joint venture freight forwarding firms as shown in Table 10.2.

TABLE 10.2
List of Key Informants

No.	Player	Location	Person
1.	Chairman of LIFFA	Vientiane C.	1
2.	Senior Advisor of LIFFA	Vientiane C.	1
3.	Technical Staff of Department of Transport (MoPWT)	Vientiane C.	1
4.	Technical Staff of Department of Planning and Cooperation (MoIC)	Vientiane C.	1
5.	Owner of a transport company (Domestics)	Bolikhamxay	1
6.	Former General Manager of a transport company (Joint Venture)	Savannakhet	1
7.	Technical Staffs of Savan-Seno Special Economic Zone Authority (SEZA)	Savannakhet	1
	Total		7

Source: Onphanhdala, Sirisack, and Khantiyavong (2017).

Data Analysis

For the qualitative analysis, law on investment promotion and transport regulations are used along with FDI liberalization assessment, especially to assess Lao PDR's commitments on the logistics sector under the ninth package of the ASEAN Framework Agreement on Services (or AFAS 9). In addition, the results from KII matched with the quantitative analysis from the survey, will provide tools for an appraisal of the logistics sector. For the KII, questionnaires were prepared for obtaining information from chairman and owners of land freight forwarding firms. The data from the interviews are used to provide the status and main challenges that Lao freight forwarders face in their sector.

The next section discusses changes in FDI flows from 1988 to 2015, policies related to investment promotion and logistics business in Lao PDR.

CHANGES IN FDI, 1988–2015

FDI in Laos is a recent phenomenon that emerged only after the late 1980s. Prior to that it was insignificant and was mostly found in the mining sector. It was in 1988 that the first law on FDI was formulated. According to the statistics of Investment Promotion Department (IPD)[1] under MPI,[2] FDI inflows to Lao PDR in 1988 was very small, less than

US$3 million, and mainly from Thailand, United States and France. Investment inflows to Lao PDR started to rise to US$800 million in the early 1990s due to large investments in the energy sector and the global economic boom. The Asian Financial Crisis (AFC) in the late 1990s temporarily affected FDI inflows to the ASEAN countries, including Lao PDR. However, in 2015, Lao PDR received a significant amount of total FDI of US$1.26 billion, with US$1.17 billion invested in hydropower, plantation agriculture and mining.

FDI by Countries and Sectors

Before examining the FDI data for Lao PDR, it is worth noting that all data need to be treated with some caution given the potential for inaccuracies.[3] This is particularly true for data before the year 2000.[4] Therefore, the FDI data provided here should be regarded as an approximate indicator. The discussion below focuses only on trends and patterns of FDI in Lao PDR since 2000.[5]

As suggested by Menon (1999) and Freeman (2001),[6] there have been some big fluctuations in FDI flows during 1988–99 and especially since 1991, as the hydroelectric power sector was licensed only in 1993. FDI inflows tend to be much smaller in Lao PDR for the years when there were no approved power projects due to the difference in scale of investment needed between power and non-power projects. According to Menon (1999), the power sector received more than 70 per cent of the total FDI inflows from 1988 to 1996. The other sectors that were significant during that period included banking, telecommunications and transport, and tin mining. However, the actual implemented investments based on data reported by Foreign Investment Management Committee (FIMC),[7] was found to be only about one-fourth of the registered investment after five years from the date of approval. Freeman (2001) reported that Lao PDR had approved around 844 foreign investment projects worth roughly US$5.8 billion over 1988–99. Of these, half were wholly foreign-owned and two-thirds were small-scale projects of less than US$1 million.

Not surprisingly, the largest investor in Lao PDR was its immediate neighbour, Thailand, followed by the United States, South Korea, France and Malaysia.[8] Even after the AFC, Thailand continued to be the main investor in Lao PDR, albeit at a much lower level than in the early 1990s. Moreover, the largest proportion of FDI was located predominantly in and around Vientiane. A smaller amount of FDI was received in other major cities including Luang Prabang, Savannakhet and Champasack provinces. There was not much FDI in the agricultural sector due in part to the inadequacy of rural transportation.

The implemented investment values and number of projects in each sector for the period 2005 to 2015, still shows considerable fluctuations due to the prevalence of large-scale investments in the mining and hydropower sectors (see Figure 10.1). During 2008 and 2009, Lao PDR approved 102 foreign investment projects, worth US$4.3 billion. This records the highest value in the history of FDI inflows in Lao PDR. Figure 10.1 also shows that services sector is ranked the fourth recipient of FDI after energy, mining and agricultural sectors during 2005–15.

FIGURE 10.1
FDI Approvals by Sector, 2005–15
(US$ million)

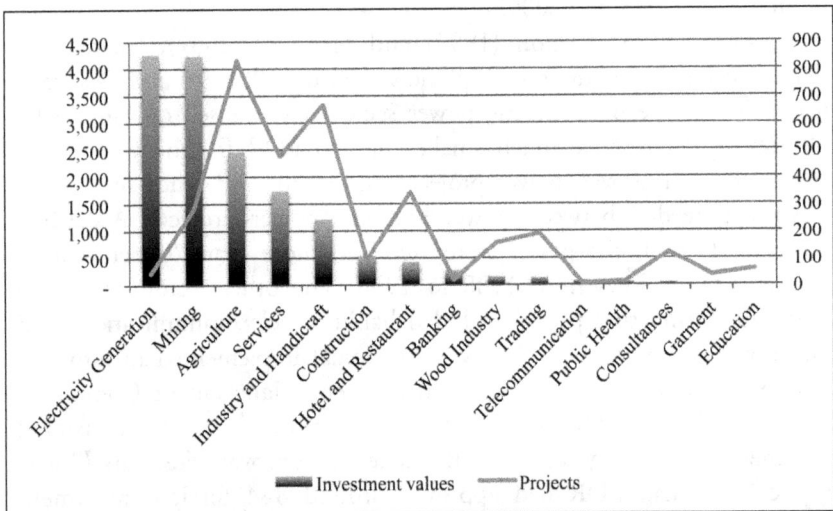

Source: IPD (2016b), IPD (2016c).

Table 10.3 shows the rankings of source countries for aggregate FDI inflows to Lao PDR from 1989 through to 2015, based on the approved investment values. During this period, there were foreign investments from fifty-two countries totalling 3,454 projects, which were worth about US$18 billion of licensed or approved investments. Although China still ranks the largest foreign investor in Lao PDR, Thailand and Vietnam are rising fast to close the gap.

TABLE 10.3
Top Ten FDI Inflows to Lao PDR, 1989–2015

Ranks	1989–2015			2011–15		
	Country or Origin	Number of Projects	Approved Values (US$ million)	Country or Origin	Number of Projects	Approved Values (US$ million)
1	China	834	5,484	China	185	2,536
2	Thailand	748	4,491	Vietnam	88	1,132
3	Vietnam	417	3,574	Thailand	95	1,038
4	Malaysia	103	812	Malaysia	12	569
5	South Korea	291	751	Netherlands	3	426
6	France	223	490	South Korea	30	222
7	Japan	102	438	United Kingdom	8	154
8	Netherlands	16	434	Japan	23	90
9	Norway	6	346	Australia	10	67
10	United Kingdom	54	201	Singapore	4	45

Source: IPD (2016*d*), IPD (2016*f*).

Table 10.4 clearly shows the strong presence of the big three investors (namely China, Thailand and Vietnam) in recent years as they together rank among the top five investors since 1989. These three top countries together account for roughly 76 per cent of total FDI inflows. The less diverse "spread" of investors by country implies that Laos' aggregate FDI inflow is more vulnerable to an economic downturn occurring in just one or two of these countries.

TABLE 10.4
Top Five Foreign Investors to Lao PDR by Period

Ranks	1	2	3	4	5
1989–2015	China	Thailand	Vietnam	Malaysia	South Korea
2005–10	China	Vietnam	Thailand	South Korea	Norway
2011–15	China	Vietnam	Thailand	Malaysia	Netherlands
2015	Vietnam	Malaysia	China	Hong Kong	United Kingdom

Source: IPD (2016*d*), IPD (2016*e*), IPD (2016*f*), IPD (2016*g*).

In terms of the distribution of investment inflows by sector, however, it has become relatively more diverse in 2000s. While the share of energy sector has declined, mining, services, agriculture, and industry and handicraft sectors have increased their shares.[9] In particular, the mining (e.g. copper and gold) sector and plantation agriculture have now become more attractive compared to the 1990s. Among the top three foreign investors, Vietnam, China and Thailand have been investing heavily in the mining sector, while the energy sector, in second position, attracted the largest investments from China and Thailand.

Investment in the services sector is mainly from Vietnam. The wood industry and garment sector has received less interest from investors in recent years. A decreasing inflow of FDI into wood industry is a result of the government's environment protection policy on sustainable development. For the garment sector, it has also become less attractive to foreign investors as the Generalised System of Preferences (GSP) privileges for exporting to the EU has been minimized since 2005. The sector also faced challenges in terms of gradual increase in wages. But as the services sector plays an increasingly important role in economic growth, the number of banks in the country has tripled since 2000. At the same time, hotel and restaurant businesses are also growing to meet the demands of tourists in the recent years. Logistics services also play an increasingly important role in distribution of goods across Lao PDR through nearby countries.

FDI and Policy Changes

Since the first law on foreign investment in Lao PDR was promulgated in 1988, it was revised in 1994, 2004, 2009, and again in 2016 (draft). The government proclaimed the law on foreign investment promotion and management in 1988, two years after the adoption of the economic reforms from centrally planned to a market-oriented system in 1986. It allowed 100 per cent foreign ownership of investments for selected sectors, since the beginning.[10] The investment terms of a foreign investment enterprise depends on the nature, size, and conditions of the business project but normally cannot exceed fifteen years for 100 per cent foreign ownership and twenty years for joint venture. In addition, in the 1988, 1994 and 2004 versions, it requires a minimum of foreign equity participation of at least 30 per cent for joint ventures. The profit tax differed largely by sectors and their reduction and exception measurements were ambiguous (see Table 10.5).

TABLE 10.5

Major Points of Law on Investment in Lao PDR, 1988–2016

Formal Name	Joint Venture	Values (US$)	Expiration	Profit Tax	Reduction & Exemption[a]
1988 Law on Foreign Investment Promotion and Management	30 per cent+	100,000+	15–20 years	20–50 per cent by sectors	By items
1994 Law on Foreign Investment Promotion and Management	30 per cent+	100,000+	15–20 years	All 20 per cent	None
2004 Law on Foreign Investment Promotion and Management	30 per cent+	100,000+	50–75 years	All 20 per cent	By zone
2009 Law on Investment Promotion	10 per cent+	Register Capital+	99 years or no limit	24–28 per cent	By zone and by level
2016 Law on Investment (draft)	10 per cent+	Register Capital+	50 years (can renew)	24–28 per cent	By level

Notes: [a] Concessions and tax preferences will be reduced and exempted by items, zones or levels. The mark '+' means the minimum share of foreign equity participation for joint ventures and registered capital requirement.

Sources: Law on Foreign Investment in Lao PDR 1988, 1994, 2004, 2009 and 2016 (draft).

The first revision to investment law was done in 1994 when the profit tax was simplified to 20 per cent for all sectors, whereas the expiration of investment term was retained at a relatively short period of fifteen to twenty years. It seems that although the government wanted to promote FDI, it used a cautious approach by keeping expiration date unchanged. In the second revision in 2004, the investment term of a foreign investment enterprise was extended to fifty years and under special circumstances, it could be further extended to seventy-five years with the approval of the government. The profit tax was maintained at 20 per cent for all sectors. Moreover, the reduction and exemption criteria were revised into three zones. These zones are demarcated based on social-economic conditions and geographical locations: zone 1 includes mountainous, plateau zones with no economic infrastructure to facilitate investments; zone 2 is similar to zone 1 with a moderate level of economic infrastructure to accommodate investments and finally zone 3 are plateau areas with good economic infrastructure available for investments. Based on Lao PDR's geography, zone 2 covers parts of provinces located along the Mekong River while zone 3 covers Vientiane Capital, parts of Savannakhet province, Pakse District[11] and Luang Prabang District.[12]

Lao PDR joined ASEAN in 1997 to promote regional integration. This is perhaps the reason for the removal of the word "management" from the official name of the law — to enable it to appear more open (Onphanhdala and Suruga 2010). Moreover, under the 2009 unified investment promotion law, the investment term allows no expiration dates for general projects, and a duration of ninety-nine years for large projects, subject to concessions from the government. The measures for profit tax reduction and exemptions are promoted with more incentives. However, the taxes on profit are between 24–28 per cent, which is higher than the 2004 version (National Assembly 2011). This 2009 revision may be similar to the 2004 version, but tax exemption is based on activities that are classified by three levels of promotion (see Table 10.6). These include activities with high level of promotion as level 1; level 2 is for activities with moderate level of promotion and level 3 is reserved for activities with a low level of promotion.[13]

TABLE 10.6
Incentive or Corporate Profit Tax of Investment Promotion Law 2009

Promoted Sectors	Zone	Level	Period of Exempt (years)
Agriculture, Industry, Handicraft, and Services	1	1	10
		2	6
		3	4
	2	1	8
		2	4
		3	2
	3	1	4
		2	2
		3	1

Source: Law on Investment Promotion no. 02/NA, 8 July 2009.

Table 10.6 shows four promoted sectors, which include agriculture, industry, handicraft and services. Profit tax exemption is used to attract more investments into the rural and undeveloped areas. The period of profit tax exemption given is between one to ten years. The longest period is for sectors where there is no infrastructure available. It seems the government is using FDI to reduce poverty and improve the living conditions by creating jobs and improving infrastructure, mostly in the rural area.

The latest draft revision of 2016 looks similar to the 2009 version, in terms of foreign equity participation, values and profit tax rates. However, this revision has limited the period of concession to fifty years. It appears that this may become less attractive to foreign investors compared to the former Law, but the amendments have provisions that permit renewal of concession period after the date of expiration, if necessary. In the 2016 draft, which has yet to be approved by the National Assembly, it classifies the tax and concession exemptions based on two levels of promoted sectors in the annex of Law on Investment Promotion 2016 draft. The promoted sectors include education, health, agricultural-forestry, manufacturing, advance technology industrial sector, eco-friendly production and eco-tourism, which are categorized into two levels (see Table 10.7). The period of tax exemption for promoted sectors is between three to seven years, after firms have made a profit. It will increase to five more years when investments are located in poor districts. The exemption period is up to ten years, especially for promoted sectors for both levels in poor districts, while these sectors are not mentioned in the previous version of the Law. This implies that the government is especially trying to attract investment in rural areas in order to generate employment and income.

TABLE 10.7

Incentive or Corporate Profit Tax in Investment Law 2016 (draft)

Sector by Levels[a]	Period of Profit Tax Exemption (years)		Period of Concession Exemption (years)	
	General	Poor District[b]	General	Poor District[c]
Level 1	7	+5	10	+10
Level 2	3	+5	5	+10

Notes: [a] Contents of levels 1 and 2 are included in the 2016 draft of Law on Investment.
[b] Add up five more years of tax exemption in levels 1 and 2, respectively, if the investment is in poor district.
[c] Add up ten more years of concession exemption in levels 1 and 2, respectively, if the investment is in poor district.
Source: "Draft of Law on Investment Promotion", 2016.

Logistics Business in Lao PDR

The Law on Land Transport no. 24 was officially issued on 12 December 2012 by Lao National Assembly, where logistics is viewed as a system management chain that plans, controls, stores, packs, loads, transports and provides efficient and effective service and information of moving goods between point of origin to destination in order to meet customers' requirement. It should be noted that although Lao PDR does not have any port and maritime transportation, it is part of the East–West Economic Corridor that connects Thailand, Laos and Vietnam through Savannakhet province (Lao PDR) by road no. 9 (R9). According to the Law on Land Transport no. 24, there is no specific restriction on trade in logistics services. It seems that there is no limitation in market access for foreign participation in this sector. However, according to MoPWT's report no. 12660 that was officially issued on 16 August 2011, joint ventures with local service provider(s) are required.

Table 10.8 shows the extent of restrictiveness in logistics services. For example, there is a restriction on foreign participation in domestic passenger transport as it only allows for local investors. Other logistics subsectors, however, may allow for foreign equity participation between 49 to 100 per cent.

TABLE 10.8
Domestic Restrictions in Logistics Services

Restrictiveness		Openness	
Domestic passenger transport	Local investors	Domestic freight transport	Foreign equity participation is 100 per cent.
		Rental of commercial vehicles with operator	Foreign equity participation is limited to 49 per cent.
Cross border passenger transport		Cross border freight transport	
		Domestic supporting services for freight	
Bus station		Cross border supporting services for freight	
		Freight agency services	

Source: Department of Transport, Ministry of Public Works and Transport.

RESEARCH FINDINGS

Liberalization Commitments on Logistics Service Sector under AFAS

The Schedules of Commitment under AFAS is expected to remove restrictions on trade in services by 2015 for the logistics sector by allowing foreign equity participation of up to 70 per cent. For Lao PDR, the MoIC is in-charge of the commitments in the roadmap for liberalization and facilitation of logistics services. But, the MoPWT is in-charge of air transport services liberalization commitments in the ninth package of commitment on air transports service under AFAS.

Table 10.9 shows that there is no limitation on market access and national treatment in modes 1, 2 and 3 on maritime, inland waterway and rail transport services, especially when Laos does not have any seaport. Laos has only one railway station in Thanaleng (Vientiane Capital). It should be noted that in this sense, Laos has achieved 100 per cent of its commitments in maritime, inland waterway and rail transport services. However, as mentioned above, there is restriction on road transportation services, as foreign equity participation is limited to 49 per cent for cross border freight transportation and 70 per cent for vehicles rental (CPC 7124) and transport supporting service (CPC 744) such as highway, bridge operation, parking and minor vehicles repair services (see Table 10.9). On the other hand, both the domestic restriction list and Laos AFAS commitment allows foreign equity participation up to 100 per cent for domestic freight transportation within Lao PDR, indicating some progress in the liberalization of some logistics sectors in order to comply with the country's commitments in AFAS.

Main Findings from KIIs

Since Lao PDR is a relatively open economy, it leads to both opportunities and challenges for local businesses, including the freight forwarders. The results from KIIs found that there are three main challenges of logistics services: lack of a comprehensive logistics system, too many procedures and high costs.

In Lao PDR, the Thanaleng storage does not have a comprehensive logistics system management as this place is only providing storage for goods. In addition, 80 per cent of entrepreneurs find it very difficult to distribute goods because there is a lack of warehouse management that can support a logistics system. This implies that the freight transport

TABLE 10.9

Lao PDR Schedule of Logistics Sector Commitments under AFAS 9

Sector or Subsector	Limitation on Market Access Status	Limitation on National Treatment Status
Maritime Transport Services • Passenger transportation (CPC 7211) • Freight transportation (CPC 7212) • Rental of vessels with crew (CPC 7213) • Pushing and towing services (CPC 7214) • Maintenance and repair of vessels (CPC 8868) • Vessels salvage and re-floating services: not applicable in harbour (CPC 7454)	None	None
Inland Waterway Transport Services[a] • Passenger transportation (CPC 7221) • Freight transportation (CPC 7222) • Rental of vessels with crew • Maintenance and repair of vessels (CPC 8868**)	None	None
Air Transport Services[b] • Aircraft repair and maintenance services (CPC 8868) • Aircraft leasing with crew (CPC 734) • Aircraft leasing without crew (CPC 83104) • Airfreight forwarding services (CPC 74800) • Aircraft catering services • Aircraft line maintenance • Refuelling services • Cargo handling services (CPC 741) • Selling and marketing of air transport services • Computer reservation system services (CPC 7532)	None in modes 1 and 2. 3) A joint venture company should have at least 10 per cent foreign equity. Moreover, 100 per cent of foreign equity participants are allowed to operate business in Lao PDR. 3) A joint venture company should have at least 30 per cent foreign equity. Moreover, 100 per cent of foreign equity participants are allowed to operate business in Lao PDR.	None in modes 1 and 2. 3) Foreign service suppliers are asked to provide improvements on land (when they lease land) and training opportunities to Lao PDR nationals. 3) Foreign service suppliers are asked to provide improvements on land (when they lease land) and training opportunities to Lao PDR nationals.

TABLE 10.9 (*continued*)

Sector or Subsector	Limitation on Market Access Status	Limitation on National Treatment Status
Rail Transport Services • Passenger transportation (CPC 7111) • Freight transportation (CPC 7112) • Pushing and towing services (CPC 7113) • Maintenance and repair of rail transport equipment (CPC 8868**) • Supporting services for rail transport services (CPC 743)	None	None
Road Transport Services[a, c] • Freight transportation (CPC 7123) • Rental of commercial vehicles with operator (CPC 7124) • Supporting services for road transport services (CPC 744) • Maintenance and repair of road transport equipment (CPC 6112+8867)	Domestic freight allows 100 per cent for foreign equity participation. Cross border freight limited to 49 per cent for foreign equity participation. Foreign equity participation is limited to 70 per cent. Unbound for mode 4	None, except mode 4 is in unbound status.
Services Auxiliary to All Modes of Transport • Storage and warehousing services (CPC 742)	None	None

Notes: [a] These two subsectors are included in the WTO list of article II (MSN) exemption, which are a preferential treatment for freight and passenger transportation between countries within the Greater Mekong Subregion.
[b] Lao PDR the Ninth Package of Commitments on Air Transport Service under ASEAN Framework Agreement on Services.
[c] The level of restriction of this subsector is similar to the information in Table 10.8.
Source: Lao PDR the Ninth Package of Commitments on Logistics Sector under ASEAN Framework Agreement on Services.

system works inefficiently, especially in the case of a large volume of cargo. LIFFA's chairman further mentioned that Lao PDR acts as a transit for trans-shipment of cargos between Thailand and Vietnam, in which case only Thai or Vietnamese trucks are used for cross border freight transportation instead of Lao trucks. This is a result of production network activities between Thailand and Vietnam. It also makes it difficult for Lao freight firms to increase their market share in the country. Freight firms often find it more profitable to focus only on transit custom clearance and reloading service instead of investing in trucks and dealing with complicated logistics management. For these reasons, freight-forwarding firms in Lao PDR serve mainly as local subcontractors and do not get into the real cross border freight transportation business.

Second, there are many procedures required to get permission to import/export goods especially in terms of documentation. It gets more challenging as each of these procedures pertain to different ministries. For example, agricultural goods are under Ministry of Agriculture and Forestry's authority. Matters related to medicine are under Ministry of Health's authority. This leads to more documentation and increases the time cost of logistics. On average, it takes more than forty-five days to complete all procedures, which directly affects the quality of goods, especially perishable goods, leading to high wastage that increases costs. Due to this complicated and long documentation process, it leads to long queues of freight vehicles at the border of Laos and Thailand, especially at the Lao–Thai Friendship Bridge I. On the government side, more documentation inspection with different authorities implies that the government does not provide good facilitation in the freight transportation business.

Third, according to the freight transportation firms, transportation cost is more expensive in Lao PDR, compared to Thailand and Vietnam. This is because, in Laos, they have to pay document fees of up to 30 per cent of total cost for a trip. While the extra charge for outbound trip is understandable, an extra fee for inbound trucks that are often empty makes it very difficult for Lao entrepreneurs to compete in the global market.

In addition, there is a duplication of tax collection for cross border transactions. First, value added taxes (VAT) are imposed for semi-produced imports when a freight transport vehicle crosses border. Second, a trader also has to pay a lump-sum tax for import/export every year. This duplication of tax collection pushes up the cost of doing business and prevents them from being able to compete in the region. It has been found that 99 per cent of freight forwarders in Laos, which are micro, small and medium enterprises (MSMEs)[14] face this problem and it is extremely difficult for them to strengthen their capacity to compete regionally.

Key Findings from Survey of Joint Venture Freight Companies

In Laos, the main goods transported are consumer goods, followed by agricultural products, garment and construction materials. Table 10.10 shows that almost 70 per cent of joint venture freight firms in the survey have an investment value less than US$375,000.[15] To start up an international freight business, firms generally need an investment of around US$375,000 or more.[16] Firms covered in the survey claim that the scale of investment in Laos, even though it is a joint venture firm, is too small compared to foreign investment elsewhere.

Trucks and relevant vehicles play an important role in the freight business. Besides good infrastructure, good quality trucks are needed for good quality logistics services. When trucks are able to carry more goods, firms can reap economies of scale and achieve higher profits. The survey results also reveal that there are insufficient trucks available for each firm. Also, 30 per cent of vehicles are older than ten years, while only 7 per cent are new trucks (see Table 10.10). Many freight forwarding

TABLE 10.10

Distribution of Freight Firms in Terms of Value of Investment, Staff Qualification and Vehicles Lifetime

	Frequency	Percentage
Investment Value (US$ thousand)		
Less than 62.5	1	7.1
Between 62.5 to 362.5	9	64.3
Between 375 to 625	2	14.3
More than 625	2	14.3
Logistics Specialist		
None	5	35.7
Less than 3 persons	2	14.3
3 to 5 persons	3	21.4
6 to 10 persons	2	14.3
More than 10 persons	2	14.3
Vehicle Lifetime		
Less than 2 years	1	7
2 to 5 years	5	37
5 to 10 years	4	26
More than 10 years	4	30

Source: Authors' calculation (2016).

firms in Laos focus only on transit custom clearance work due to lack of capital for improving their capacity and intense competition with the large firms. This prevents the local firms from expanding their freight transportation business.

Most of the staff in the freight forwarding business are not qualified. Training in logistics is essential to build up their skill and knowledge. In term of human resource development in logistics, there are only two major sources: a) Faculty of Engineering (National University of Laos) and b) Technical Vocational Education and Training (TVET) programme, which provide transportation engineering and freight forward training, respectively. At present, there is a lack of TVET graduates, as in many other sectors (Ministry of Education and Sports, 2015).

Survey result suggests that almost half of the freight forwarding firms have never conducted any training programmes for their staff. Figure 10.2 shows the types of training programmes provided by the firms for staff. On average, there are few firms that have conducted training programmes, and these are confined to mainly basic on-the-job training. Driving and repair training are for drivers, while marketing training is the least type of training that is provided, as firms are not aware of marketing strategies. The interviews also reveal that there are sufficient drivers. But there are some issues, like goods getting damaged by drivers or the drivers using firms' trucks for their own business or in the worst case, drivers stealing trucks' fuel. A possible reason for the lack of investment in human resource development is a general lack of capital in these freight forwarding firms.

Table 10.11 shows the types of facilitating equipment that are available in freight forwarding firms. It can be seen that only 20 per cent of them have all the necessary equipment such as cranes, forklifts, pallets and containers. This may be the result of the small-scale of investment. Since most of the firms are small family businesses, they do not invest enough to have all the equipment needed for their work.

The capacity to compete with international freight firms depends a lot on marketing. It is perceived that a firm can generate more profits, if it can preserve or expand its market share. In other words, while the existing freight firms have a share in the old freight transport market, to move into the new segments and enhance capability to compete internationally, it needs to do marketing. The results also show that a freight firm will generally directly approach the targeted customers to offer its services. This type of marketing meets the need of retail freight transportation where there is a constant volume of cargo. The outcome of the interview shows that 64 per cent of the surveyed firms have a marketing strategy.

FIGURE 10.2
Staff Training Programmes

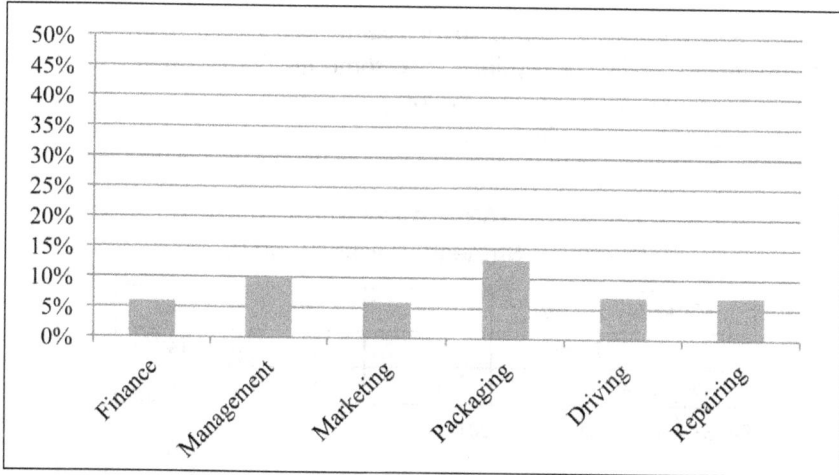

Source: Authors (2016).

TABLE 10.11
Freight Forwarders' Facilitating Equipment

Firm	Cranes	Forklifts	Pallets	Containers
A	✓	✗	✓	✓
B	✓	✓	✓	✓
C	✓	✓	✗	✓
D	✗	✗	✗	✓
E	✓	✓	✓	✓
F	✓	✓	✓	✗
G	✗	✓	✓	✗
H	✓	✗	✗	✓
I	✓	✓	✓	✗
J	✓	✓	✓	
K	✓	✓	✗	✗
L	✗	✓	✓	✗
M	✗	✗	✓	✓
N	✗	✗	✓	✗

Source: Authors (2016).

For those who do not have marketing strategy, they also indicate that it is not important for their business as the customers are already aware of them. Some of them further mentioned that marketing also increases their business cost, which leads to decreasing capacity to compete with other businesses. These perceptions raise some queries on the capacity of freight forwarding firms in Laos to compete internationally as it implies they are not willing to utilize any marketing strategies for expansion.

TABLE 10.12
Marketing Strategy of Freight Firms

Marketing Strategy	Yes	No	Total
Number of Firms	9	5	14
Percentage	35.7	54.3	100

Source: Authors' calculation (2016).

Figure 10.3 shows the obstacles of freight forwarding business in Lao PDR. The finding suggests three major obstacles in this business: a) trucks returning with empty load; b) road conditions; and c) changes in fuel price.

FIGURE 10.3
Obstacles of Freight Forwarding Business in Lao PDR

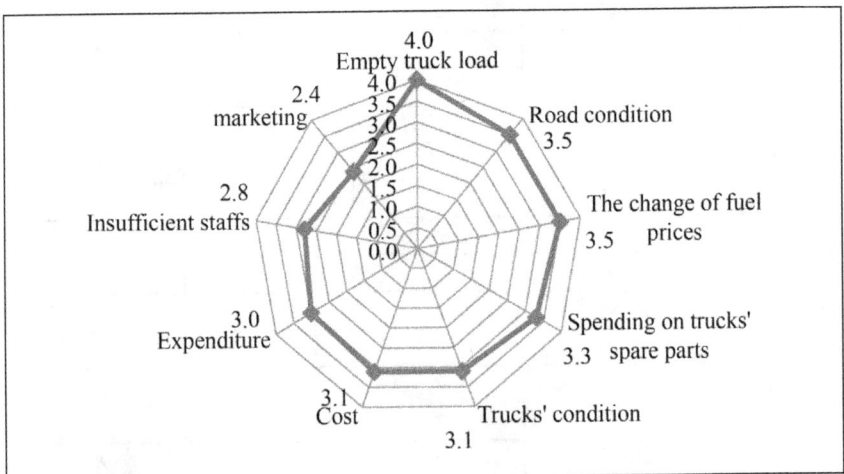

Source: Authors' calculation (2016).

Trucks usually carry goods from origin to destination with full truck load while they tend to return empty as the trucks are small and can carry a correspondingly smaller volume of cargo. However, customers have to pay transportation cost for a round trip. This implies that one way to reduce transportation costs is to collect goods from many points of origins to one location and thereafter distribute the goods to each destination. Based on the results from the survey, it reveals that nine out of ten trucks are facing this problem. For this reason, customers will choose foreign firms instead of Lao firms that can carry a larger volume of cargo due to larger trucks in order to find the lowest price offering.

Second, bad road conditions increase the business cost and time duration taken for transportation of goods. In the rainy season, it is difficult to transport goods especially in the northern part of Laos. Trucks will consume more fuel and will take a much longer time. Sometimes, it will lead to overtime payment for drivers and staff.

At the same time, an increase in fuel price can directly affect transportation cost. However, when fuel price goes down, it does not lead to rapid cost reduction. This is because firms have to frequently invest in truck repairs due to the use of secondhand spare parts as it is cheaper and easier to find, but it also leads to frequent truck breakdowns. Moreover, firms have to pay drivers' overtime wages when trucks break down during cargo transportation.

CASE STUDY: THE DEVELOPMENT OF DRY PORTS

A dry port can be defined as an inland amenity with cargo-handling facilities allowing several functions to be carried out, for example, consolidation and distribution, temporary storage, customs clearance, and the connection between transport modes (Jeevan et al. 2015). In Lao PDR, road infrastructure improvement is needed in the first stage of logistics hub development but this can be solved in the short term. In the long term, the major challenge for the Lao freight business is high cost due to the small volume of cargo. It can be seen that there is currently no place for goods consolidation and distribution that can support the increasing trade volume between the Greater Mekong Subregion (GMS) countries. For this reason, the government plans to develop dry ports as inland intermodal terminals that can connect directly roads and rail to seaports for transporting goods and people between Lao PDR and its immediate neighbouring countries in the GMS.

There are two crucial components for dry port operations: providing management of a logistics hub (including cross dock warehousing) and establishing a single custom declaration. The idea of a logistics hub is to bring everything to the hub by consolidated trucks, then sort the cargo by destination before sending the cargo to each of these destinations to avoid waiting time of full truck loading. This will reduce the number of empty truck loads to each destination, leading to more efficient freight transportation. Establishing a single custom declaration at the dry port will also save time as it is a single gateway for an inspection.

For Lao PDR, it is a priority of the government to transform a landlocked to a land-linked country in the GMS by providing efficient transport infrastructure and facilitating cross border transport (Phounsavath 2014). The Public Works and Transport Sector Five Years Plan (2016–20) aims to build dry ports by 2020. It also aims to develop logistics parks to provide logistics service in order to facilitate freight transportation. There are nine dry ports nominated under the Intergovernmental Agreement on Dry Port across the country as shown in Figure 10.4 (Phounsavath 2015). Four of them are located in central; the other four are located in northern part of Laos and only one is located in the south. The major dry ports are Seno in Savannakhet (SVK) and Thanaleng in Vientiane Capital (VTC), one of which have been operating in 2016, while the other is expected to operate in 2017, respectively.

Lao PDR has bilateral transport agreements with Cambodia, China, Thailand and Vietnam, but not as yet with Myanmar. This means that Lao trucks can go to these countries based on these bilateral agreements (Yoshida 2016). Developing dry ports therefore provides an opportunity for Lao PDR to transform itself from a landlocked country to a more integrated one to the region through the North–South Economic Corridor (NSEC) and the East–West Economic Corridor (EWEC).

FIGURE 10.4
Map of Dry Ports in Lao PDR

Source: Department of Transport, Ministry of Public Works and Transport, compiled by the authors (2016).

Figure 10.5 shows that Thanaleng dry port can be a centre of a
logistics hub for Lao PDR and its neighbouring countries. It has been
suggested that this location can be used to transport goods between
Laos and China. For instance, goods can move from Thanaleng through
Luang Prabang, Muangxai to Nateuy (Luang Namtha province) where
the border between Laos and China is 651 km, which will take less
than fifteen hours, based on current road condition (see Table 10.13).

FIGURE 10.5
Map of North–South Economic Corridor, Lao PDR

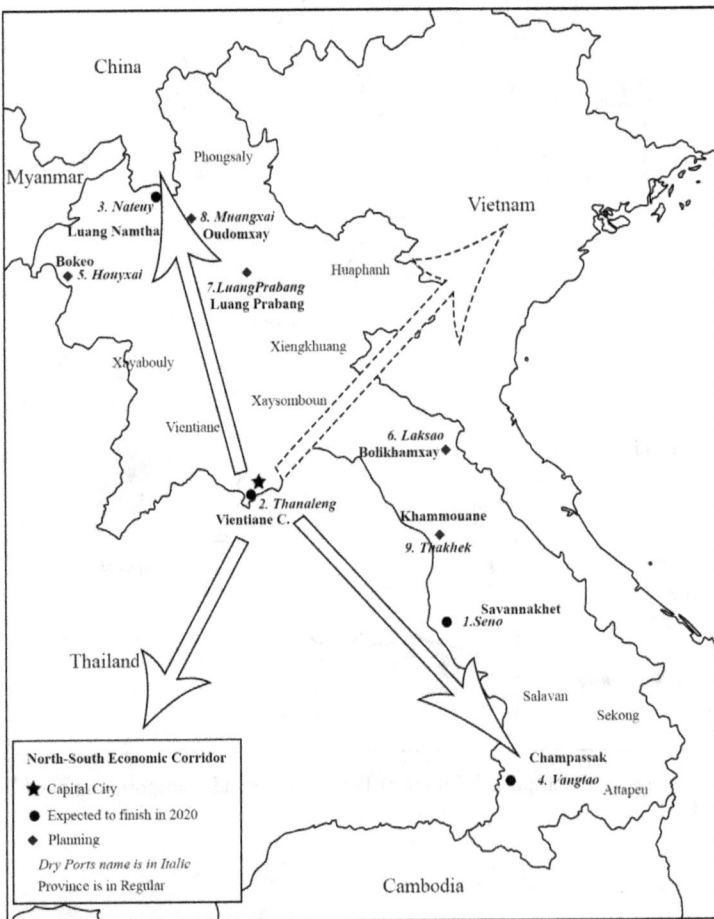

Source: Department of Transport, Ministry of Public Works and Transport,
compiled by the authors (2016).

TABLE 10.13

Distance Between Lao Main Dry Ports and Nearby Countries' Ports (km)

| Strategic Plan | Potential Hubs | Laos | | | Thailand | Vietnam | | | Cambodia | China | Myanmar |
		LNT	VTC	SNK	Laem Chabang (BKK)	Danang (HA)	Hai phong	Saigon (HCM)	Phnom Penh	Border	Mawlamyine
EWEC	Seno (SNK)	1,060	442	–	745	455	704	819	847	1,092	1,010
NSEC	Thanaleng (VTC)	673	–	442	734	895	794	1,261	1,274	651	813

Source: Google Maps (2017).

At present, most of agricultural products in the northern part of Laos are exported to China. This proves Laos has a potential to trade, at least in primary products, with China through logistics links that integrate the rural agricultural sector in this area with China.

Savannakhet province can be connected by EWEC and NSEC in this region as shown in Figure 10.6. All main cities in the Mekong area are within twenty-four hours of one-way truck distance to and from

FIGURE 10.6
Map of East–West Economic Corridor, Lao PDR

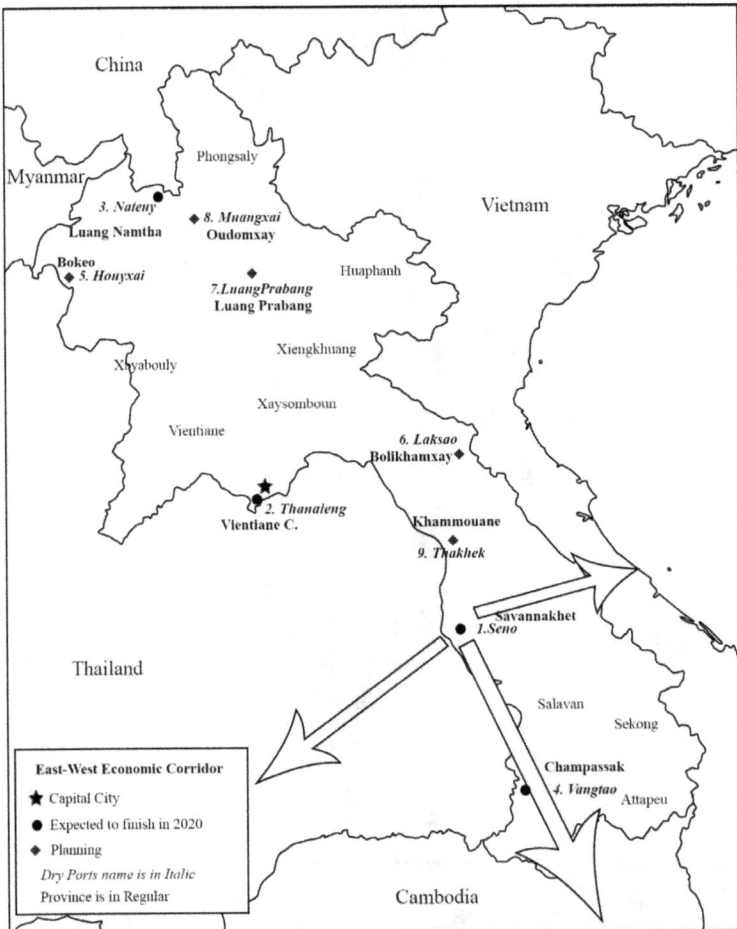

Source: Department of Transport, Ministry of Public Works and Transport, compiled by the authors (2016).

Savannakhet, which are mostly shorter than 1,000 km for each route. The Lao government has therefore seized this opportunity to develop Savannakhet as a logistics hub (Nissin 2016). The dry port in Savan-Seno Special Economic Zone is the result of a government pilot project to create a model dry port for a logistics hub in Lao PDR. The port was officially operationalized at the beginning of 2016. The capacity of loading cargo weighting is at least 300 kg. This means that the port can be used to dispatch goods from different sources into one container for transporting, thereby reducing the cost and time of transportation for businesses in Savannakhet and in Laos. For example, it currently takes two days, on average, compared to five days previously to ship goods from Laem Chabang (Thailand) to Savannakhet (Laos). This decreases the cost from US$4,320 to US$1,460 per forty-foot container (Lao Trade Portal 2016). Savannakhet logistics hub can also be used for the consolidation and distribution of goods mostly between Thailand and Vietnam and transported further to Japan through Vietnam. It assumes that this dry port will contribute to the successful economic integration within the region.

CONCLUSION

As a land-linked country with four AMS, the development of logistics sector of Lao PDR plays an important role in deepening its economic integration in the ASEAN region. Lao PDR is a latecomer in services liberalization in ASEAN. Despite this, the country has met its targets in market access and national treatment on maritime, inland waterway and rail transport services. These subsectors allow 100 per cent foreign equity participation as well as domestic freight transportation. But in the case of cross border freight, it is still limited to 49 per cent of foreign equity participation. It is worth noting that Laos is accelerating its speed for FDI liberalization in terms of the cap on foreign equity ownership.

The main findings suggest that there are three main challenges confronting freight forwarders in Lao PDR. First, there are insufficient logistics hubs and existing ones are inefficient. Second, there are too many bureaucratic procedures for importing goods. Third, transportation cost is relatively high compared to neighbouring countries. Higher cost and a longer time of transportation are the two major problems faced by Lao freight forwarding firms. These are caused by a lack of port infrastructure that can provide efficient logistics service. It is also difficult for small firms to invest more in freight equipment, human resource development and marketing. These are some significant obstacles that prevent local providers from competing successfully in the regional market.

Previous experience indicates that FDI can help to enhance the competitiveness of the logistics industry. In 2013, the government allowed Nissin Societe Mixte de Transport Limited Company to operate its logistics service in Savannakhet. As it is the first Lao international logistics service provider, it aimed to transport goods between Hanoi and Bangkok by single Lao trucks and driver without reloading and switching of trucks on the way. This causes no delay and no damages of goods along the way from origin to destination. To guarantee safety and security during transportation, drivers are monitored by Yazaki Digital Techograph in order to control driving behaviour. The entry of this firm has strengthened Laos' capacity to compete in the market. Nevertheless, this system requires investing heavily in technology, human resource and financial assistance from international development partners. Since the scale of investment of domestic Lao freight forwarding firms are generally still small, it is suggested that the government should progressively remove its restrictions on FDI and gradually encourage more FDI to flow into the country in terms of investment value and technology transfer. According to the current situation, it is not the right time to allow 100 per cent foreign equity participation because local providers will not be able to face the sudden competition. It is suggested that the liberalization should be gradual, in line with the economic growth of the country. Furthermore, in order to enhance efficiency of the logistics sector in Lao PDR, the country will require time to absorb technology transfer, especially in skills such as reloading the container by using mobile crane or reloading cargo between trucks, and not only driving skill for multimodal transportation.

In order to create more demand to overcome the challenge of imbalanced trade as a contributory factor towards the relatively high logistics cost, the government should take advantage of the relatively low wages of Lao labour compared to its neighbours to attract more foreign investment into the country. More investment will lead to a greater demand for more materials as inputs for its use in domestic semi-production. It will improve the balance between inbound and outbound logistics, thereby enabling domestic freight firms to enlarge their businesses and avoid an empty truck load problem.

The case study in this chapter demonstrates the benefits of dry port development. There are several recommendations to develop this further. First, the government should accelerate the development of dry ports in the country and increase their contribution to the economy by facilitating the development of logistics hubs, focusing on local providers, at each of these dry ports. Second, it is also suggested that the government should reduce import procedures by setting a single custom declaration at these dry ports. Third, in terms of human development, it needs to encourage freight firms to improve the skills of their workers, including logistics soft skills. It is also suggested that Lao PDR can learn from other AMS's development of their respective logistics sector, mainly from Singapore, Thailand and Vietnam, as well as the development of dry ports in landlocked countries. For institutional development, the Lao government should improve logistics service by improving linkages and coordination between relevant ministries by the central government in order to facilitate goods distribution among GMS countries. Finally, to enhance the competitiveness of the domestic industry, it is very important for the Lao government to impose VAT equally and tax exemptions of raw material that is imported for semi-production in Lao PDR in order to decrease costs, attract more investment and remain competitiveness in this business. For instance, VAT has been collected from some firms when importing cargo but not others, and sometimes the amount of VAT collection varies from firm to firm.

Furthermore, as a long term vision, it is essential to negotiate for a trilateral and/or multilateral agreement on the liberalization of land transportation, which will allow Lao trucks to enter multi-destinations without crossing Lao border. For instance, Lao truck may go to Malaysia from Thai border, or go to China from Vietnamese border. This implies that multilateral agreements on land transportation will allow Lao truck to go into third country. This will help to transform Lao PDR to a concrete unique land-linked country that operates transboundary transportation among the GMS countries.

Notes

1. Known as the former Foreign Investment Management Committee and former Department for Promotion and Management of Domestic and Foreign Investment. In present it is known as Investment Promotion Department.
2. Known as the former Committee of Planning and Cooperation and former Committee of Planning and Investment.
3. The FDI figures may be inaccurate due to: (1) joint venture projects by multiple foreign investors which are often attributed to the lead investor only and sometimes it is not clear the division of share ownership between

foreign investors and the local partners; and (2) the official FDI data may not cover many of the investments made by former Lao citizens now living overseas, typically in collaboration with families and friends. Likewise, small scale investments by foreigners may also be under-reported.

4. The authors observed significant differences in FDI data among sources in terms of project numbers, approved investment values, and investments by sectors and country of origin over 1988 to 1999 presented by Menon (1999), Freeman (2001), Gunawardana and Sisombat (2008a), Kyophilavong (2009) and Suzuki (2010).

5. The FDI data since 2000 are more relatively consistent as shown in Sihomvong (2010), U.S. Commercial Service (2010), and Suzuki (2010).

6. Freeman (2001) presents two different figures of the FDI data depending on whether they were based on FIMC or IMF sources in his paper.

7. Known as Investment Promotion Department under the Ministry of Planning and Investment, Lao PDR.

8. The authors found a number of discrepancies among the previous studies. For example, according to Gunawardana and Sisombat (2008b), during the same period, the top investors were Thailand, United States, Malaysia, France and South Korea, and the approved investment values differed significantly from Freeman (2001).

9. For an overview of the recent development of energy, mining and agriculture sectors, see Pholsena and Phonekeo (2004), Kyophilavong (2009) and Voladet (2009).

10. Law on Foreign Investment Promotion and Management in 1988 emphasized that foreign investors cannot invest in or operate enterprises which are detrimental to the national security, the natural environment, public health or the national culture, or which violate the laws and regulations of the Lao PDR.

11. Champassak province in the southern part of Laos.

12. Luang Prabang province in the northern part of Laos.

13. The promoted activities include prioritized activities of the government, activities related to poverty reduction, improving the living conditions of the people, infrastructure construction, human resource development and job creation, etc.

14. Micro, Small and Medium Enterprise based on the latest revised draft of Law on SMEs in 2016.

15. US$375,000 is roughly equal to 3 billions kip at exchange rate of 8,000 LAK/USD.

16. Ministry of Public Works and Transport's report, no. 24/PWT, officially issued on 12 December 2012.

References

Asian Development Bank (ADB). *Key Indicators for Lao PDR. Manila:* ADB, 2016.

Freeman, Nick. "The Rise and Fall of Foreign Direct Investment in Laos, 1988–2000". *Post- Communist Economies* 13, no. 1 (2001): 101–19.

Gunawardana, Pemasiri J. and Sinnaka Sisombat. "Trends and Patterns of Foreign Direct Investment in Lao PDR". *International Journal of Business and Management* 3, no. 1 (2008a): 41–57.

————. "An Overview of Foreign Investment Laws and Regulations of Lao PDR". *International Journal of Business and Management* 3, no. 5 (2008b): 31–43.

Investment Promotion Department (IPD). "Approved Foreign and Domestic Investment Projects by Sector, 1989 to 2015", 2016a. Available at <http://www.investlaos.gov.la/images/Statistics/rpt_Invest_Summary_Sector1A_1989-2015.pdf> (accessed 10 October 2016).

————. "Approved Foreign and Domestic Investment Projects by Sector, 2005 to 2010", 2016b. Available at <http://www.investlaos.gov.la/images/Statistics/rpt_Invest_Summary_Sector1A_2005-2010.pdf> (accessed 10 October 2016).

————. "Approved Foreign and Domestic Investment Projects by Sector, 2011 to 2015", 2016c. Available at <http://www.investlaos.gov.la/images/Statistics/rpt_Invest_Summary_Sector1A_2011-2015.pdf> (accessed 10 October 2016).

————. "All Approved Investment Projects by Country, 1989 to 2015", 2016d. Available at <http://www.investlaos.gov.la/images/Statistics/rpt_Invest_Summary_Country1A1989-2015.pdf> (accessed 10 October 2016).

————. "All Approved Investment Projects by Country, 2005 to 2010", 2016e. Available at <http://www.investlaos.gov.la/images/Statistics/rpt_Invest_Summary_Country1A_2005-2010.pdf> (accessed 10 October 2016).

————. "All Approved Investment Projects by Country, 2011 to 2015", 2016f. Available at <http://www.investlaos.gov.la/images/Statistics/rpt_Invest_Summary_Country1A_2011-2015.pdf> (accessed 10 October 2016).

————. "All Approved Investment Projects by Country, 2015", 2016g. Available at <http://www.investlaos.gov.la/images/Statistics/rpt_Invest_Summary_Country1A_2015.pdf> (accessed 10 October 2016).

Jeevan, Jagan, Shu-ling Chen and Eon-seong Lee. "The Challenges of Malaysian Dry Ports Development". *The Asian Journal of Shipping and Logistics* 31, no. 1 (2015): 109–34.

Kyophilavong, Phouphet. "Mining Sector in Laos". BRC Discussion Paper Series no. 18. Bangkok Research Center, IDE-JETRO, 2009.

Lao Trade Portal. "Dry Port to Slash Time and Cost of Goods Transport", 2016. Available at <http://www.laotradeportal.gov.la/index.php?r=site/display&id=1050#.WBXtcWC_K4l> (accessed 10 October 2016).

Menon, Jayant. "Lao PDR in the ASEAN Free Trade Area". *Journal of the Asia Pacific Economy* 4, no. 2 (1999): 340–64.

Ministry of Education and Sports (MoES). "Annex Matrix: School Year", 2015. Available at <http://www.moes.edu.la/moes/images/statistic/Annual-school-census-2014-2015.pdf> (accessed 6 September 2017).

Ministry of Planning and Investment (MPI). "Draft of Law on Investment Promotion". Unpublished. Vientiane: National Assembly of Lao PDR, 2016.

Ministry of Public Works and Transport (MoPWT). "Report no. 12660/PWT", 16 August 2011. Vientiane: MoPWT, 2011.

National Assembly. *Law on the Promotion and Management of Foreign Investment, no. 07/PSA, The People's Supreme Assembly.* Vientiane: National Assembly of Lao PDR, 1988.

———. *Law on the Promotion and Management of Foreign Investment (Amended) no. 01/NA.* Vientiane: National Assembly of Lao PDR, 1994.

———. *Law on the Promotion of Foreign Investment (Amended) no. 11/NA.* Vientiane: National Assembly of Lao PDR, 2004.

———. *Law on the Promotion of Investment (Amended) no. 02/NA.* Vientiane: National Assembly of Lao PDR, 2009.

———. *Law on Tax (Amended) no. 05/NA.* Vientiane: National Assembly of Lao PDR, 2011.

Nissin SMT. *Introduction of Mekong Landbridge: Thailand, Laos and Vietnam Door to Door by Direct Single Lao Truck in 45 feet HC Container,* 2016.

Onphanhdala, P., P. Sirisack, and L. Khantiyavong. "Challenges on Logistics Business Development in Lao PDR". *LJI Business Management Journal* 8 (2017): 35–47.

Onphanhdala, Phanhpakit and Terukazu Suruga. "FDI and the Investment Climate in Lao PDR". *Lao Trade Research Digest* 1 (2010): 31–58.

Pholsena, Sommano and Phonekeo Daovong. "Lao Hydropower Potential and Policy in the GMS Context". United Nation Symposium on Hydropower and Sustainable Development, China, 27–29 October 2004.

Phounsavath, Phanthaphap. "Policy and Preparatory Project on Dry Ports in Lao PDR". Seminar on Capacity Building for the Development and Operation of Dry Ports of International Importance, UNESCAP, Bangkok, 18–19 March 2014.

———. "Status on Dry Ports Development in Lao PDR". 1st Meeting of Working Group on Dry Ports of International Importance, UNESCAP, Bangkok, 25–26 November 2015.

Suzuki, Motoyoshi. "Transitions in Foreign Investment Policy of Lao PDR" (in Japanese). Paper presented at Seminar of Institute of Developing Economies, 13 August 2010. Mimeo.

United Nations Conference on Trade and Development (UNCTAD). UNCTADstat [online]. Geneva: UNCTAD, 2016. Available at <http://unctadstat.unctad.org/wds/TableViewer/tableView.aspx?ReportId=96740> (accessed 9 May 2016).

United Nations Economic and Social Commission for Asia and the Pacific (UNESCAP). *Asia-Pacific Trade and Investment Report*. Bangkok: UNESCAP, 2015.

U.S. Commercial Service. *Doing Business in Laos: 2010 Country Commercial Guide for U.S. Companies*. Department of Commerce, U.S., 2010.

Voladet, Saykham. *Sustainable Development in the Plantation Industry in Laos: An Examination of the Role of the Ministry of Planning and Investment*. Canada: International Institution for Sustainable Development, 2009.

Yoshida, Toshifumi. "Introduction of Mekong Landbridge Door to Door by Single Lao Truck between Laos with Thailand, Vietnam, China and Cambodia". Paper presented at the special seminar for National University of Laos, Vientiane, 9 November 2016.

11

FACILITATING FDI FOR THE LOGISTICS SECTOR IN MYANMAR: AGENCY, INCENTIVES, AND INSTITUTIONS

Min Ye Paing Hein and Ruth Banomyong[1]

INTRODUCTION

After a few decades of self-imposed economic isolation under the Burmese Socialist Programme Party, Myanmar began to embark upon a gradual and staggered journey to reintegrate with the global economy in the 1990s. In 2011, the government under President U Thein Sein introduced a series of liberalization measures in selected sectors. The recent transition from semi-military to democratic government and the concomitant removal of the US sanctions presented a strategic window to further facilitate Myanmar's integration into the regional and global economy. Myanmar also chaired the 2014 ASEAN Summit and was granted observer status in the 2014 G20 Summit.

Although successive governments have stressed the critical and central role of the development of infrastructure in Myanmar's economic development, the logistics sector has yet to receive dedicated policy attention. This chapter draws attention to the role of the logistics sector in overcoming some of more critical challenges in the formation of positive linkages between Myanmar's economy and the global value chains (GVCs). Facilitating foreign direct investment (FDI) in logistics infrastructure and services is a critical link for domestic enterprises to participate in GVCs. It will also help to create productivity gains through the use of new technology and generate positive spillovers through linkages with local service providers. In this chapter, we discuss two interlocking layers of challenges, namely, governance of FDI and governance of the services and logistic sector in Myanmar's development strategy.

The chapter examines various issues of agency in the governance of the services sector and posits that agency issue at the national level, manifests itself as an issue of coordination given the vast differences in information and incentives amongst multiple principals (focal agencies) and agents (implementing agencies) in terms of negotiation and implementation of agreements. However, at the local level, "thinness" of the presence of government agencies in regulating and monitoring economic activities at the border leads to limited agency of the state in the governance of the services and logistics sectors. Second, it is important to induce inflows of FDI into the logistic sector in the broader context of regulatory and institutional reforms in order to create an enabling ecosystem for logistics in Myanmar. We recommend the government to initiate key strategic reforms in certain sectors to ascertain cross-cutting issues in logistics that need to be addressed. We also recognize that by articulating Myanmar's economic reform agenda with the on-going initiatives in ASEAN and beyond, the new government can push for the emergence of a coherent and coordinated governance in logistics policies with robust feedback mechanisms from the private sector, which are essential in resolving the agency issues and maximizing the benefit from its commitments toward deeper regional economic integration.

In this chapter, we start with describing the country context where the Myanmar economy is developing from a low base and the limited impact of the recent robust economic growth on the country's economic structure. We then present the country's FDI regulatory regime and general investment climate and discuss the state of capacity and coordination in logistics issues across key government agencies. Finally, we present some policy recommendations in the conclusion of our chapter.

COUNTRY CONTEXT

With the military coup in 1988, Burma fell under the military-led government until the dissolution of the State Peace and Development Council in 2011. In 2012, the quasi-civilian government under President U Thein Sein rolled out an important political reform by holding a by-election in a small number of selected constituencies in which the opposition political party, the National League for Democracy (NLD), secured forty-two seats out of the forty-three contested constituencies. Within the menu of priorities depicted in the strategy document known as the Framework' for Economic and Social Reforms (FESR) by this government, transport and infrastructure sector featured prominently stressing its role in promoting agricultural productivity and enhancing connectivity and integration with regional economies, including ASEAN. In the general *election* of 8 November 2015, the NLD secured a landslide victory with approximately 77 per cent of the contested seats. Both the campaign manifesto of the NLD and new economic policy of the government stressed the role of basic economic infrastructure in generating economic growth.

Myanmar's economy grew at an average of 8.5 per cent for two consecutive years from 2013 and 2014. However, the economy suffered a slight downturn due to a severe supply shock from nation-wide floods and declining commodity prices in 2015. In terms of value-added, economic losses due to the flood was significant with an estimate of 2 per cent of the Gross Domestic Product (GDP) in 2014–15. It was expected that the economy would recover in 2016 with the projected real GDP growth of 7.8 per cent.

The share of agriculture value added has declined sharply from 60 per cent in 1995 to 27.9 per cent in 2014 while the shares of industry and services sectors have increased (see Figure 11.1). The share of the services sector has increased noticeably from 2011 to 2015, accounting for more than 37 per cent of the GDP in 2015. This is contributed in part by the liberalization of some services such as the telecom sector in 2013. Consequently, the mobile penetration rate catapulted from 7 per cent in 2013 to over 50 per cent in 2015.

However, it is interesting to note that within the services sector, the share of trade subsector in the GDP has declined from 23.2 per cent in 1995 to 18.7 per cent of the total GDP in 2014 while the share of transport subsector has increased sharply from 2.8 per cent to 11.5 per cent over the same period.

Despite robust economic growth and an increasing share of industry and services in GDP, the employment structure in Myanmar has not changed much between 2005 and 2015. Figure 11.2 shows that the relative share of employment by sector has been maintained, with the share of agricultural employment remaining constant at around 50 per cent from 2005 to 2015. The share of utilities and transport revolves around

FIGURE 11.1
Share of Sectors by GDP, 1995–2014

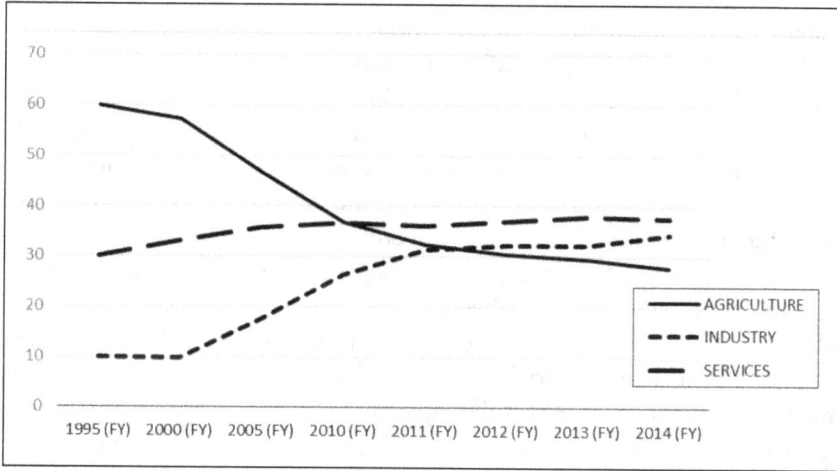

Source: Myanmar Statistical Information Service, Gross Domestic Product, available at <http://mmsis.gov.mm/statHtml/statHtml.do> (accessed 5 March 2017).

FIGURE 11.2
Share of Employment by Sector in Myanmar, 2005–14

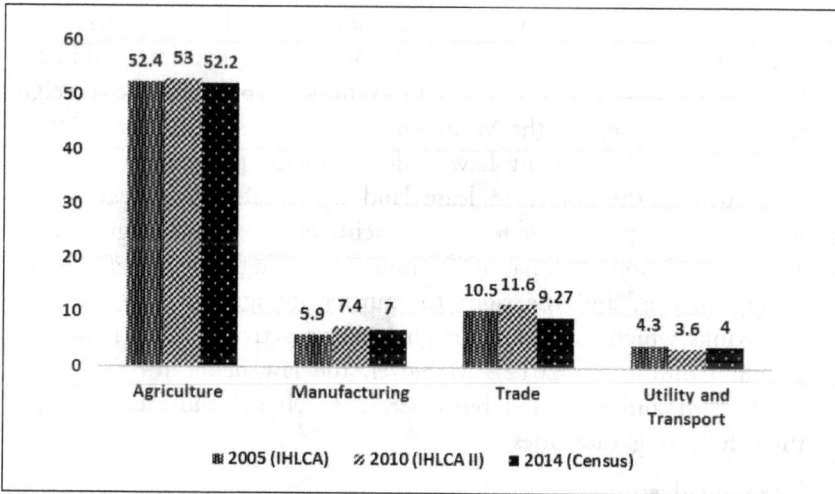

Source: Integrated Living Condition Survey Report (2005), Integrated Living Condition Survey Report (2010), Population Census of Myanmar in 2014, available at <www.themimu.info/census-data> (accessed 5 March 2017).

4 per cent for the same period. Similarly, the share of the manufacturing employment remains rather stable around 7 per cent. This trend indicates that the recent robust economic growth had a limited impact in inducing major structural economic transformation.

In July 2016, the new government under the leadership of the NLD announced four objectives and twelve points in Myanmar's new economic policy. In brief, the new economic policy is designed to support national reconciliation with a balanced and inclusive economic development across states and regions. Instead of setting specific sectoral priorities, the new economic policy espouses a multi-sectoral and holistic development approach, stressing a balanced growth in agricultural and industrial sectors as it recognizes the need to diversify the sources of growth. The new policy document explicitly addresses the need for rapid infrastructure development such as electricity, roads and ports. It also recognizes the strategic importance of ASEAN's regional framework and the use of a regional strategy for the emergence of a vibrant private sector. Furthermore, the development of the logistics sector is a necessary condition in the country's pursuit of a multi-sectoral and spatially inclusive development strategy.

OVERALL FDI LIBERALIZATION AND ENABLING ENVIRONMENT

A series of important legal reforms were introduced between 2012 and 2016 to enhance the attractiveness of Myanmar's investment climate for foreign investors. In 2012, the Government approved the Foreign Investment Law[2] to replace the Myanmar Foreign Investment Law of 1988. The new Foreign Investment Law endows certain privileges to foreign investors such as the ability to lease land up to fifty years (extendable by two additional periods of ten years each), tax exemptions, guarantees against expropriation and nationalization depending on the validity of investment permit, and the right to transfer foreign currency overseas through banks which carry out foreign banking activities, etc. (Myanmar Investment Commission 2012). Moreover, the law delineates a negative list (prohibited and restricted businesses), which are sub-classified into the three following categories:

(1) Prohibited economic activities
(2) Economic activities allowed in the form of a joint venture with Myanmar nationals
(3) Economic activities that comply with specific circumstances

The first category covers twenty-one economic activities that may pose a threat to national security, environment, domestic small and medium enterprises (SMEs) and the public sphere and the second category includes forty-two activities, which can be permitted if conducted as a joint venture with Myanmar nationals. Foreign investment in transport and infrastructure projects would fall under the ambit of the second category. The third category consists of 115 activities that require: (1) recommendation from relevant line ministries; (2) environmental assessment; and (3) other conditions. In July 2013, the government promulgated the new Myanmar Citizen's Investment Law to regulate investment of Myanmar citizens. This law mirrors the structure in the FIL in the sense that it also delineates a negative list for domestic investors, which covers seven restricted or prohibited activities.

Between 2013 and 2015, the government issued a number of amendments to the FIL. More specifically, the notification no. 11/2013[3] (foreign investment rules) (Myanmar Investment Commission 2013) and notification no. 49/2014, revised and expanded the scope of the activities in which 100 per cent foreign ownership is allowed, unless otherwise specified. With the issuance of these two notifications, the negative list for prohibited business has been reduced from twenty-one to eleven activities in the FIL. A new notification (no. 50/2014) was issued to specify economic activities which require Environmental Impact Assessment, such as heavy electricity production, construction of large scale infrastructure (highways, bridges, ports), construction of large scale hotels and resorts, operations in the vicinity of main public resources, etc. (Allen & Overy 2014).[4]

On 6 October 2016, the Parliament approved the Myanmar Investment Law,[5] which combines Foreign Investment Law (2012) and Citizen's Investment Law (2013). First, the provisions in this new investment law are now aligned with the economic policy on balanced regional development. In contrast with the previous policy regime with tax exemptions of five years given to all registered foreign investors, income tax exemptions, under this law, are only granted for strategic sectors (which will be delineated in future notifications) and based on the level of socio-economic development of the region in which the investment is made. Investment projects in the category 1 region or the "least developed region" would enjoy the benefit of income tax exemption for five years while investment projects in the category 3 region would only enjoy income tax exemptions for three years. Moreover, the law clearly expresses policy preferences for capacity building and subsidies for SMEs in Myanmar. The law also supports the pursuit of export-led growth for Myanmar with the exemption of customs duties for export-oriented enterprises and special treatment of domestic SMEs.

Although implementing rules and procedures have yet to be issued, the 2016 Investment Law is expected to be friendlier to foreign investors. Under the past regime, the registration with Myanmar Investment Commission (MIC) is needed for all foreign investors if they wish to enjoy benefits such as the ability to transfer funds, tax exemptions, the right to lease land and long-term business visas. Under the new regime, foreign investors can enjoy similar legal benefits with the endorsement from the Directorate of Investment and Company Administration (DICA) without having to apply for a permit in the MIC. Only strategic investments and large-scale capital-intensive projects with a large potential impact for environment and local community are required to submit a proposal to the MIC to receive a permit for operation.

Moreover, the law augurs a shorter version of negative list for prohibited and restrictive categories, thus further solidifying Myanmar's commitment to its liberalization agenda. Under the new Myanmar Investment Law, there are only six activities in the prohibited list. Prohibited list includes investments that would pose a threat to public health, cultural traditions, and natural environment as well as investments that may bring hazardous and untested materials into the country. Restricted list only covers four categories — public sector, excluded sectors for foreign investment, sectors for joint ventures and sectors that require approval from relevant line ministries. Finally, the law stipulates that the approval of the parliament would be needed for investment in special sectors, which have significant impact on security, economic condition, the environment and national interest. Detailed sectoral compositions for each list is not delineated in Myanmar's investment law and will be announced as implementing regulations of the Myanmar Investment Law, which is currently being drafted.

The main institution in the regulatory landscape of FDI had been the MIC.[6] After the new government came into power, the Commission was suspended for more than ten weeks and it was re-established with eleven members in June 2016. Under the current configuration, the Minister of Planning and Finance acts as the chair of the Commission with the Minister of Commerce acting as the vice-chair. Except for a single representative from the Union of Myanmar Federation of Chambers of Commerce and Industry (UMFCCI), the memberships hail exclusively from the high and middle echelons of the government — including two permanent secretaries, one director general, two former deputy director generals and one former director from the Ministry of Home Affairs. Under the MIC, the DICA acts as an agency for investment promotion and investment administration as well as the Secretariat of the MIC. In 2014, DICA has the strength of 225 staff in seven departments with a plan to boost its organizational manpower to 415 in 2016.[7]

Previous regulatory framework under the FIL entrusted the MIC with supreme discretionary power in dictating the terms of foreign investment in Myanmar. As per the FIL, the MIC can exercise discretionary power to allow the FDI even in prohibited sectors. Given that the criteria for such decisions have not been clearly specified in the legal framework, it will create ample space for rent-seeking, ambiguities and confusion. In the same spirit, the provisions in the FIL and subsequent notifications further broaden the scope of discretionary power for the government agencies and departments to allow FDI in restricted activities with unclear and non-transparent criteria. Under the new regime, the MIC does not have the discretionary power to dictate the terms of investment on a case-by-case basis although it does have the power to issue notifications to revise the list of restricted sectors.

Another important pillar in the enabling environment for FDI is the Competition Law, 2015 (Pyidaungsu Hluttaw Law no. 9). This law was enacted by the Parliament on 24 February 2015 and came into force in February 2017. The Competition Law covers measures against four categories of business practices that act to: (1) restrict competition; or (2) lead to monopolies; (3) promote unfair competition; and (4) promote business practices such as mergers that push for market dominance. The law sanctions the creation of two entities — the Competition Commission and the Enquiry Commission, for the regulation and enforcement of the law. The Competition Commission will serve as a regulatory body with responsibilities to determine regulatory boundaries of anti-competitive behaviours as well as establish arrangements and procedures to address infractions against the law. The Enquiry Commission is the investigative arm of the Commission with the mandate to conduct investigations and impose penalties against persons in breach of the act.

Approved FDI has been increasing steadily between 2011 and 2015. In the fiscal year ending in March 2016, approved FDI had reached US$9.4 billion with the approval of forty-eight projects (US$4 billion) in a single meeting on 25 March, the last MIC meeting under the previous government. Between March and June, 100 proposals (US$2.3 billion) were submitted to the MIC[8] (Myint 2016; Mclaughlin and Tun 2016), which has been meeting once a month regularly to clear the backlog since then. Although DICA collects quarterly data on actual investment, this self-reported data may not fully reflect the actual extent of FDI inflows. DICA has been planning a FDI survey to collect more reliable and robust data on actual inflows. However, according to the United States Conference on Trade and Development's (UNCTAD) annual data on FDI inflows, the numbers for reported FDI inflow is far lower than approved FDI figures. As shown in the Figure 11.3, the total combined actual investment for three consecutive years from 2011 to 2013 is around US$3 billion although the total combined approved FDI for the same period equalled US$13.54 billion. For the year 2015–16, the total FDI inflow is US$2.82 billion, which is a far lower figure than US$9.8 billion in approved FDI. Bissinger (2012) offers two potential explanations as to why there has been an acute discrepancy between actual and approved FDI figures over the years such as changing conditions on the ground and potential inflation of approved investment data. However, it is also possible that policy uncertainty due to political transition in the year 2015–16 may have played a role in this unusually large discrepancy for the same period.

FIGURE 11.3
Myanmar, Approved FDI, FDI Inflows, FDI Stock

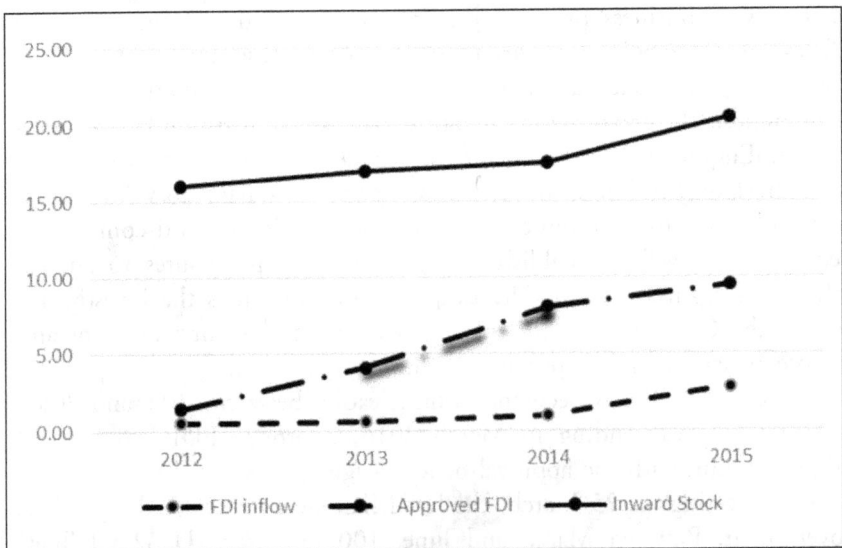

Source: UNCTAD Statistics, available at <unctadstat.uncctad.org> (accessed 5 March 2017); Directorate of Investment and Company Administration, Union of Myanmar, 2016.

Governance of Service and Logistics Sectors: Issues of Agency

There is no widely accepted official definition of logistics in Myanmar. In terms of FDI inflows, official data from DICA does not capture the information on approved FDI to the logistics sector. Both transport and communication are grouped together as one sector under the DICA's classification system. Infrastructure development has been one of the top policy priorities for successive governments since 2011. During the past government, the National Level Workshop on Economic Development through the integration of logistics services was held in Naypyidaw in 2008, with representatives from the public and private sectors and independent experts. Five consultative committees were established with the objective of developing a national logistics policy and roadmap (Myo 2012).[9] However, these committees did not make any progress towards the development and adoption of a national logistics policy.

During 2016, there is an initiative by the private sector to establish a National Logistics Association (NLA) with representatives from the transport industry. The objective of the NLA is to articulate the voice and concerns of the logistics service providers in Myanmar vis-à-vis the government. In this regard, the Myanmar International Freight Forwarders' Association (MIFFA) has become one of the important institutional players in the logistics sector. It was instrumental in the establishment of the NLA, while contributing to the emergence of regulatory and policy framework in the logistics and transport sector. International organizations such as the Japanese International Cooperation Agency (JICA) and the Asian Development Bank (ADB) have been active in the development of a sectoral strategy for the transport sector in the form of a Masterplan for the transport sector. According to an interview with the Ministry of Transport, the Ministry is now leading the country's efforts to formulate the National Logistics Master Plan, with the assistance of the JICA.

The issue of agency manifests itself in the structure of negotiations and representation of the services sector with ASEAN and other regional bodies. There is a distinct disconnect between negotiating and implementing agencies in logistics, in terms of information and incentive structures. For example, the Ministry of Planning and Finance (Department of Foreign Economic Relation Department) is the focal point for negotiations with ASEAN on trade-related agreements and the Minister of Planning and Finance represents Myanmar at the ASEAN Economic Minister's Meeting although the Ministry of Commerce (MoC) and Customs Department are implementing agencies. According to interviews, the focal agency has no institutional incentive to coordinate and there is a conspicuous absence of a mechanism for the focal agency to coordinate with the implementing agencies.

There is also information asymmetry between what the Ministry of Planning and other implementing ministries given that there is a very limited information flow on what the focal agency is supposed to do in terms of consultations and what is actually implemented by other agencies, after negotiations are conducted. As such, the incentives for both focal agencies and implementing agencies are not aligned since the first group of institutional actors are responsible for negotiating agreements and commitments which they would have no role in implementing whereas the second group of actors are responsible for implementing agreements and commitments which they had no role in negotiating.

To further complicate matters, depending on the nature of framework for regional cooperation, different ministries can assume the role of focal agencies at the negotiating tables. In the case of ASEAN and the Regional Comprehensive Economic Partnership (RCEP) agreement, the Ministry of Transport takes the lead while in the case of ASEAN–China Free Trade Agreement (ACFTA), the Ministry of Planning and Finance is the lead agency. Therefore, there is another layer of disconnect between multiple principals (multiple agencies that sit at the negotiation tables at the regional and ASEAN levels) and the implementing agencies. This creates coordination and implementation problems at all levels.

Similarly, the governance of transport and logistics sector in Myanmar is fragmented. City Development Committees or Municipal Councils in Yangon, Mandalay and Naypyidaw are responsible for the governance of urban transport systems in these three large metropolitan areas. The Ministry of Transport and Communications (MoTC) has the governing authority over four subsectors — air transport, inland water transport, railway and maritime transport, while the Ministry of Construction presides over construction and maintenance of national roads and bridges. However, the Ministry of Agriculture, Livestock and Irrigation is tasked with the construction and maintenance of roads and bridges in rural areas. Three other powerful ministries such as the Ministry of Border Affairs, the Ministry of Defense and the Ministry of Home Affairs are also responsible for transport systems in certain strategic areas in Myanmar. For example, the Ministry of Border Affairs exercises direct authority over the roads and bridges in the border areas. Given the diffused and fragmented governance structure over national transport systems, it has been difficult to identify and implement coherent and consistent national policy priorities.

Limited capacity and rigidity in bureaucratic practices coupled with multiple principals and multiple agents in the policy space are the major hurdles contributing to poor logistics performance in Myanmar. The sudden breakdown in logistics performance in 2016 because of an unprecedented large import volume of sugar through ports of Yangon is the most illustrative case of the policymakers' limited capacity to understand the root cause of the problem and to respond with appropriate policies. In 2016, China agreed to cap the quota of sugar import to 1.96 million metric tons with an import tariff rate of 15 per cent. Since sugar imports outside of the quota face a 50 per cent import duty, re-exporting sugar into China through informal channels has been a profitable business for the traders given high domestic sugar prices.[10] Myanmar has become a preferred transit route for sugar to be re-exported into China via the Mandalay-Muse Road.[11] It is estimated that 80,000–100,000 metric tons of sugar per month (approximately 100 cargo trucks per day) are making their way into China from Myanmar (including re-export from Thailand and India). Poor logistics infrastructure to handle the increase in cargo traffic was manifested in the form of severe congestion and roadblocks.

Port congestion at the Yangon port escalated in the months of April and May of 2016. During April and May, the average berth waiting time for the containers for cargo clearance jumped from an average of three to ten days, and occasionally more than two weeks. Poor port infrastructure and cargo clearance system at the Yangon Port, along with increased cargo, were the main contributing factors for the congestion. However, the extended holidays during the New Year festival in April further exacerbated the situation. Yangon Port is the major conduit of Myanmar's trading system since it handles more than 90 per cent of formal trade to and from Myanmar. The crisis continued unabated for a few weeks and near the end of May, the government responded to this crisis by organizing a high-level committee led by the Minister of Commerce. The committee implemented a number of stop-gap measures including the extension of operation hours to twenty-four hours per day and the development of procedures to clear the stockpile of empty containers.[12] Yangon regional government recently imposed a ban for container trucks to operate near the port during daytime to reduce congestion. Without addressing the core issues in cargo clearance and low storage fees at port, and the absence of options to clear cargo inland, such a measure so far has created more problems for logistics performance.[13] These measures offered a temporary reprieve from the congestion but none of them can be translated into sustainable solutions for the predicament at the systemic level. Since then, there is no coordinated effort to develop a sustainable strategy to address port congestion. More importantly, the congestion at Yangon Port is merely one of the symptoms of the structural malaise of the national logistics system as a whole.

Another incident of congestion took place on the Lashio-Muse Road, one of the main road arteries in cross-border trade between Myanmar and China. Traffic jams and accidents have been a rather frequent occurrence on the road. For example, due to an accident on one of the narrow and tortuous section of Lashio-Muse, the average travel time from Mandalay to Muse has seen a dramatic increase from seven–ten hours to two–three days. Although some stop-gap measures such as a separate timetable for cargo trunks have been implemented to restore the traffic flow, the passage of 1,500 trucks per day is imposing a severe strain on the two-lane asphalt highway. This capacity overload on the Mandalay-Muse Road is connected to the recent spike in sugar re-export smuggling to China via this route (in conjunction with extant convoluted domestic inspection and customs procedures at the border). The market value of sweeteners in China is markedly higher than its value in the global market. Recent rise in sugar prices is linked to recent steep drop in the domestic production in China due to 10 per cent shrinkage in average cane production as the sugar cane farmers have been shifting to other crops because of low government-mandated cane prices and higher production costs.[14]

These two cases of congestion are illustrative and emblematic of major stress and strain in the national logistics system to accommodate the increase in demand from Myanmar's integration into the regional and global economy. The constraints of an underdeveloped logistics infrastructure are further compounded and exacerbated by an underdeveloped policy framework and fragmented governance structure in the logistics sector. In other words, issues of agency in the logistics governance structure underpin the underdevelopment and overload of the national logistics system in Myanmar.

In the transport sector, there are six major state economic enterprises (SEEs) under the Ministry of Transport–Myanmar Railway, Myanmar Inland Water Transport, Myanmar Port Authority, Myanmar Shipyards and Myanmar National Airways. Except for Myanmar Railway, all the existing SEEs in the transport sector have gone through a corporatization process. The degree of competition varies greatly from subsector to subsector. For example, Myanmar Railway has a monopoly over the railway transport sector as the sole operator. Myanmar's railway network suffers from both poor infrastructure and poor maintenance and Myanmar Railway is equipped with antiquated locomotives with an average age of over thirty years (World Bank 2016). Out of 5,992 km of network, less than 12 per cent of the tracks are double-track. Myanmar Railway is one of the highest loss-making SEE with its losses accounting for 6 per cent of the total operating balance for all thirty-two SEEs in Myanmar (World Bank Staff Calculations). As shown in the Diagnostic Trade Integration Study (DTIS) report, railway cannot compete with road transport since it accounts for only 4 per cent of the total volume of freight transport in Myanmar (World Bank 2016).

In contrast, the road sector is the most important subsector for freight traffic. Road transport accounts for 93 per cent of freight traffic between Yangon and Mandalay, which are the two major growth hubs in Myanmar (World Bank 2016). According to the Ministry of Construction, Myanmar has 148,690 km of roads from which the ministry has jurisdiction over 26.3 per cent of total road. Private investors are allowed to enter into BOT (Build, Operate and Transfer) arrangement with the Ministry of Construction and currently, around thirty private companies have, as of 2015, established BOT arrangements on seventy different roads, accounting for around 17 per cent of all public roads under the Ministry of Construction.[15]

Given the specific geography of the country with 6,650 km of passable waterways along its major rivers, inland water transport is the second most important transport mode after trucking. In contrast with the rail sector, both private and public enterprises are free to enter and operate in this sector and Myanmar Inland Water Transport Enterprise is the main player from the public sector. However, the sector only accounts for about 10 per cent of the total freight and passenger transport in Myanmar as it suffers from an old and inefficient fleet, poor terminal infrastructure, and poor maintenance of navigable waterways.

Lastly, Myanmar airspace is liberalized with both private and public operators. Myanmar has eleven domestic airlines operating in the domestic airspace and only two of them are international carriers. According to the Center for Aviation (CAPA), there are twenty-four international airlines flying to and from Myanmar.[16] Myanmar National Airway is the flagship carrier of the government and it now presents a serious challenge to Myanmar International Airway (MAI), the only other domestic carrier with international routes. Most of the domestic carriers are facing intense competition and most of the airlines are in financial stress.

The Role of FDI in the Development of the Logistics Sector in Myanmar

Facilitating FDI in logistics is important in Myanmar for at least two reasons. First, the country has an underdeveloped domestic capital market and raising FDI is definitely needed to sustain high economic growth and for job creation. From 2012 to 2014, the average stock of FDI per GDP was estimated at about 25 per cent, which was lower than comparable high-growth developing countries in East Asia, such as Cambodia and Vietnam. In Figure 11.4, the stock of FDI per GDP in Cambodia was around 73 per cent during the same period and 43 per cent for Vietnam from 2006 to 2008 when its income per capita in current USD was comparable with Myanmar. Attracting more FDI can partially and temporarily address Myanmar's problems with access to finance for mobilizing domestic investments.

FIGURE 11.4
Stock of FDI to GDP
(%)

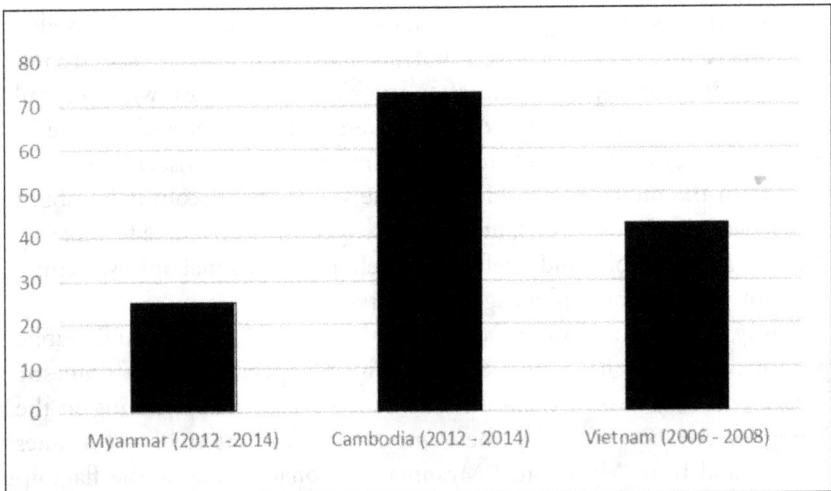

Source: Calculations based on UNCTAD Foreign Investment Database, available at <http://unctad.org/en/Pages/DIAE/FDI%20Statistics/FDI-Statistics.aspx> (accessed 5 March 2017); World Development Indicators, World Bank, available at <http://data.worldbank.org/data-catalog/world-development-indicators> (accessed 5 March 2017).

Second, FDI in logistics can have positive effect in improving competitiveness of Myanmar's trade sector. Services, particularly logistics, play a key role in internationalization of production activities by connecting different stages of production and distribution (Baldwin 2011). Indonesia's experience also suggest a positive impact of facilitating FDI in services on manufacturing productivity (Duggan et al. 2013).

In recent years, Myanmar has been attracting more investment proposals in manufacturing. However, more needs to be done to address constraints in accessing quality logistics services and competitive international shipping in Myanmar. According to 2016 World Bank Logistics Performance Index, Myanmar's logistics performance is ranked lower than its neighbouring ASEAN countries (see Figure 11.5). Facilitating more FDI in logistics can

FIGURE 11.5

Logistics Performance Index of Myanmar in 2016 Compared with ASEAN Countries (except Singapore)

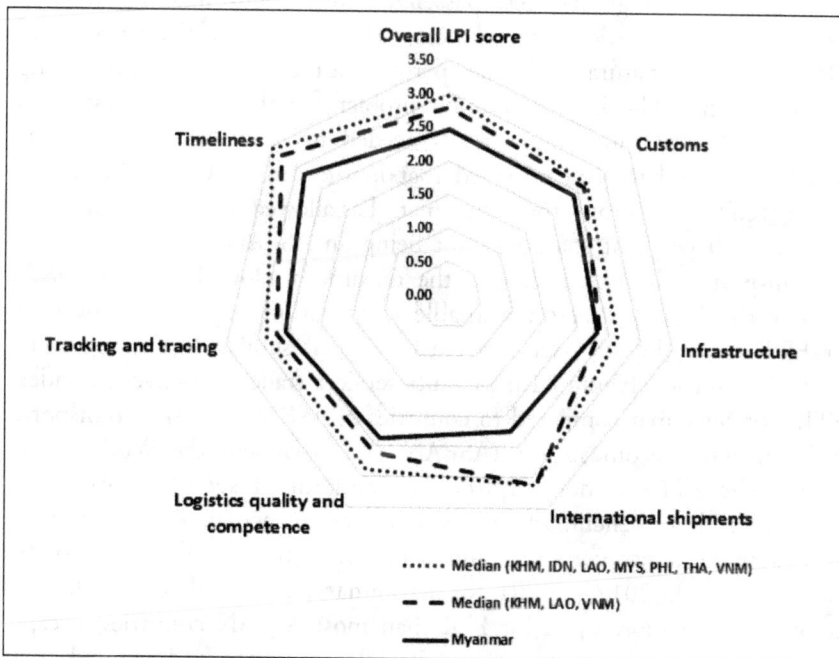

Note: KHM: Cambodia; LAO: Lao PDR; IDN: Indonesia; MYS: Malaysia; PHL: Philippines; THA: Thailand; VNM: Vietnam

Source: Logistics Performance Index, World Bank, available at <http://lpi.worldbank.org/> (accessed 5 March 2017).

have a positive effect in bringing up the quality of services, as foreign investments tend to bring technology and a global network of services that can further improve Myanmar's competitiveness as a production hub. For Myanmar, facilitating more FDI in logistics can have a significant and positive impact on its efforts in promoting deeper and faster integration with GVCs.

Liberalization of Logistics in AFAS and GATS

The Myanmar government is committed to fulfilling its obligation under the ASEAN priority integration sector roadmap for logistics services (see the introductory chapter of this volume). However, it has not been able to meet the timeline related to these commitments as in the case of the majority of other ASEAN countries. Nonetheless, from the government's perspective, further liberalization of the logistics sector needs to be done in a progressive manner even though there are a number of subsectors that are not acceptable as they relate to national security concerns such as customs brokerage services, passenger and freight inland waterway services. All of these logistics subsectors should have been opened since 2013 to ASEAN natural or juristic person with a maximum shareholding of 70 per cent. The implementation problems with these commitments are acknowledged but more time is needed to enable their progressive liberalization. It has been observed that in the case of Inland Container Depot (ICD) concessions, the government has allowed for foreign company to have a 70 per cent share without being an ASEAN national, whereas for transport, only 49 per cent is the maximum allowed to foreigners.[17]

For the logistics sector, available information suggests restrictions for FDI in key logistics services are in general similar to that of other ASEAN countries. Figure 11.6 presents services trade restrictiveness index (STRI) of Myanmar compared to countries in ASEAN, covering transport, retailing, and telecom sectors (ASEAN Secretariat and the World Bank 2015). The STRI is derived from a standardized set of information that would allow benchmarking restrictiveness of actual policies towards services trade across countries and across four modes of services trade (Borchert et al. 2012). STRI for Myanmar suggests that its telecom sector has been more open for FDI than most ASEAN countries, except Singapore. The government opened its telecom sector and granted two operating licenses for cellular services to foreign companies and it is also planning to auction off the fourth license. For transport services, STRI for Myanmar is similar to most countries in ASEAN where a cap on foreign ownership is commonly applied.

FIGURE 11.6
Services Trade Restrictiveness Index for Logistics Subsectors

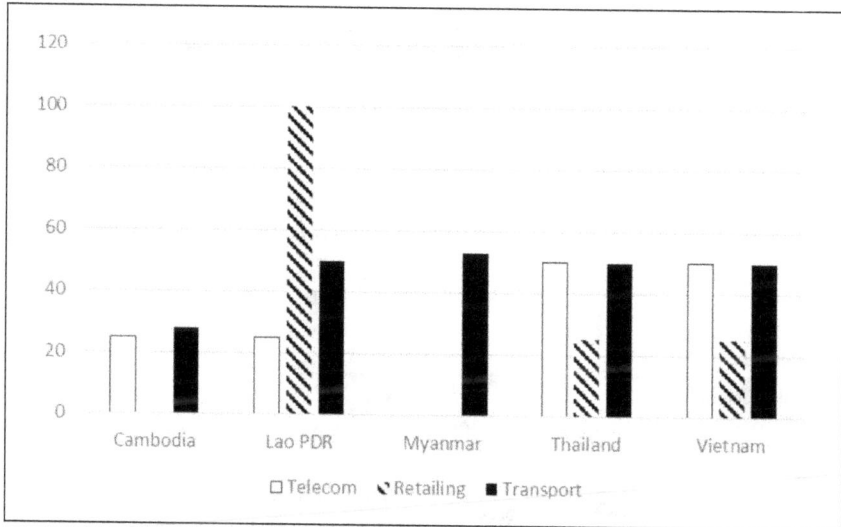

Note: Restrictions in retailing subsector in Myanmar is not yet reflected.
Source: Adapted from ASEAN Secretariat and the World Bank (2015) and Gootiz and Mattoo (2015).

Another set of regulations affecting entry and establishment of commercial presence for FDI in logistics services, including logistics, is the negative list in 2012 FIL. The list of sectors with conditions for FDI is presented in Notification no. 26/2016, which is an implementing regulation for the 2012 FIL. Table 11.1 shows important conditions for FDI in some logistics-related activities, which are mostly in transport services where a joint venture with Myanmar citizen is required. For multinational companies (MNCs) manufacturing food products and confectionaries, the restrictions suggest that MNCs should establish a joint venture with Myanmar citizen to engage in distribution. However, since there is no explicit threshold for joint venture, in practice this requirement may not be a serious constraint for foreign investment. In the case of freight transport services, a recommendation from MoTC is required for MIC's approval.

This restriction can be discriminatory against foreign operators, favouring incumbents or an implicit requirement to partner with incumbent operators. For fuel products, Myanmar requires foreign investors to establish a joint venture with the Ministry of Energy and Environment.

TABLE 11.1
Negative List (Restrictions) Affecting FDI in
Selected Logistics-related Activities

Restrictions	Activities
Requirement for joint venture with Myanmar citizen	Domestic and international transport services Manufacturing, sales and distribution of processed food (biscuits, noodles, cereal products) Manufacturing, sales and distribution of confectionary products
(1) and only by recommendations from Ministry of Transport and Communications	Domestic cargo vessels, inland water cargo transport Freight transport services
(1) and special conditions: Establish a joint venture with Ministry of Energy and Environment	Distribution and storage of fuels
Permission from Ministry of Transport and Communications	BOT or contract system with Myanmar Railway for passenger and cargo train services
Only for value-added products and up to 49 per cent foreign equity limit	Domestic distribution of crops cultivated using imported inputs
Compliance to WHO minimum standard	Distribution of vaccines

Source: Myanmar Investment Commission. Summarized from unofficial translation of Notification no. 26/2016 dated 18 October 2016.[18]

However, this negative list does not reflect all the barriers for FDI from establishing and operating logistics services in Myanmar. Other ministries may have rules that restrict foreign investment to operate in certain activities in logistics services. Except for the companies located in SEZs, the ability of foreign companies to engage in trade and distribution services are still strictly limited to the distribution and sales of motor vehicles. For other activities, the MoC requires foreign companies to utilize local companies to engage in trade and distribute goods to wholesalers or retailers. In 2015, the government relaxed some of the existing regulations allowing foreign companies to establish joint venture companies to import and distribute fertilizers and hospital equipment in Myanmar.[19] In addition, new businesses still have to go through long processes of registration and obtaining permits before they can fully operate. This also applies for logistics services whose operations require multiple permits from multiple departments. Approval for foreign investment in logistics services has been handled by MIC, which typically requires recommendations from relevant line ministries such as MoC and MoTC. To some extent, fragmented notification on rules in FDI by different line ministries and case-by-case approval process for FDI, have generated a web of uncertainty for FDI in logistics services.

Hence, given the incompleteness of the negative list governing FDI in logistics related sector in Myanmar, a potential foreign investor has two options. The first option is to go through the MIC. The MIC then checks with the concerned line agencies if there are any conditions or issues with the investment as it is the line agencies that will issue the necessary operating licenses. The other option is to go through the relevant authorities directly but then these authorities will still need to confer with MIC, although this might change with the passage of New Myanmar Investment Law and impending enactment of implementation regulations. According to the interviews with the private sector, the MIC is a better channel for investment in the logistics sector as there is more information available. Information related to liberalization in the logistics sector is not publicly available and the MoTC needs to upgrade its website in order to update information and data. The interviews further confirm the claim that FDI in the sector is important, as it will provide know-how, capital and capacity building for the country.

According to interviews with domestic logistics service providers (LSPs), the domestic private sector has expressed some concern about more foreign competition as foreign LSPs are already operating in the country. Some of these existing foreign logistics companies are operating under the umbrella of SEZ licensing while providing nation-wide logistics services and benefiting from duty exemptions and tax incentives. Some foreign companies may have registered as 100 per cent foreign owned firms under the Company Act while subcontracting all their logistics operations to local service providers. The MIFFA acknowledges that the government has already made commitments towards the liberalization of logistics services but they do not agree with 100 per cent foreign shareholding. Their position is that the foreign provider needs to form a joint venture company with local firms. Preference is given to 51 per cent to local and 49 per cent to foreigners and for certain cases, 70 per cent local and 30 per cent foreigners. To sum up, the preferred modality of FDI is a joint venture with at least 51 per cent local interest from the local industry's perspective. This approach seems to be quite successful especially if the local partner happens to be a state agency or organization.

For maritime liberalization, twenty subsectors have already been liberalized, with the exception of three subsectors as they are related to national security and operated by SEEs, such as pilotage as well as passenger and freight inland waterway transport. The liberalization of air transport is almost complete with twelve out of the thirteen subsectors liberalized. The only exception is for fuel refuelling service as it is under the Ministry of Energy and there are security concerns at the airports. The case of rail transport is uniquely interesting. Even though around 50 per cent of the subsectors have been liberalized, the main issue is the monopoly of the sector by Myanmar Railway Enterprise, a SEE. This SEE still needs to be subject to internal reforms and would require at least another two to three years before any foreign partners may be involved in rail transport. Road transport is under the Ministry of Construction and therefore the MoTC cannot provide detailed information. In addition, customs brokerage is not yet liberalized as it is considered a part of national interest. However, seaports can have 100 per cent foreign ownership while cruise shipping cannot have more than 49 per cent foreign ownership.

The local industry is fragmented and it is mostly composed of SMEs with limited access to finance, which can be very severe for SMEs in logistics as the Central Bank only allows immovable assets as collateral, while logistics providers have movable assets, e.g., transport vehicles. Therefore, it is difficult for them to provide end-to-end logistics services to large foreign investors who require not only full logistics capabilities but also financial guarantees in terms of logistics performance. These large foreign investors require a single entity capable of providing their required logistics services and therefore prefer to work with international LSPs who are already established in the country. International LSPs may not have the right to provide full services but they can still outsource the necessary logistics activities reserved to national firms on a subcontracting basis, such as in the case of customs brokerage. However, there is no need to subcontract if the local partner has more than 51 per cent equity with MIC licence. In most of the cases, outsourcing of activities does increase the cost of logistics and this can represent as much as 10 per cent in the case of domestic distribution.

In summary, logistics liberalization is not a difficult issue as foreign firms can come in and operate quite freely in the country. In certain cases, there is a need for a local partner. The selection of the right local partner is critical if the foreign firm wants to be successful. There is a gap between the actual commitments related to logistics service liberalization and its implementation but this does not affect logistics operations offered to customers. The only caveat is that customers still do not have access to integrated end-to-end logistics services and the current regulatory framework does increase logistics costs.

Currently, it is impossible to know exactly the number of foreign firms providing logistic services in Myanmar. If there is no such word as "logistics" attached to the company at the time of registration, it would be impossible to know what type of services they offer under the Company Act. The MIFFA see the need for some sort of registration/licensing related to the provision of logistics services. Another problem is that LSPs incorporated under the SEZ law are not only providing services within SEZ but also across the country. This is an unfair advantage as these firms accrue benefits from tax incentives and customs privileges. The biggest problem is the legal ambiguity related to the licensing of logistics operations followed by uncertainties related to the transport of dangerous goods. Last but not least, the logistics skill base in the country is still very low.

Local LSPs cannot compete with foreign providers when it comes to large contracts. As an example, for the transport of cement for the new Siam cement plant, there is a performance bond of US$4 million needed and another US$2 million to be put as a down payment for the building of cement barges. This issue is intimately linked to differential access to finance between local and international service providers. Compared to the foreign providers, local LSPs have a very circumscribed access to financial instruments offered by foreign financial institutions in Myanmar and international financial markets.

In short, the development of the logistics sector is hampered by a fragmented governance structure, weak policy environment and limited transport and logistics infrastructure in Myanmar. These factors are further compounded by the presence and ever-looming possibility of conflicts along some of the major trade routes. The following case study is emblematic how the interplay of these factors hampers the development of the logistics sector.

Case Study: A Cross-Border Perspective of the Challenges in Logistics

According to official records, one-fifth of Myanmar's international trade is across its overland borders. However, the magnitude of informal cross-border trade is deemed to be significantly higher than the official figures (Aung 2009). Border trade with China accounts for the majority of all border trade. The main exports to China are mostly agricultural products such as maize, rice and sugar. Imports from China are consumer goods, fertilizers and construction materials. In terms of logistics, the Chinese side has much better logistics infrastructure and facilities with adequate warehouse spaces as well as cranes to load/unload goods. This naturally attracts Myanmar traders to use the facilities in Ruili in China. As an example, Myanmar onions exporters utilize the Chinese warehouses as these Chinese service providers also clear the import duty when the onions are sold on the Chinese market.

Export clearance process to China is usually faster but the existing X-ray machine has to stop after fifty inspections for the unit to cool down. Therefore, the total time spent can be up to one day. Customs have implemented a risk management system which is not based on the risk profiles of the importers and exporters but more on a lottery type approach. Customs inspection is currently based on 60 per cent green lane; 30 per cent yellow lane; and 10 per cent red lane.[20] Most exports are single items while imports often have multiple items on one truckload, thus creating more complications during the import process.

The institutional environment is confusing and weak from the traders' perspective. Import clearance process does take longer at the border as there are limitations from both a procedural perspective as well as the number of documents needed. As an example, Customs declaration cannot have more than ten different items (three main items and seven attached in the annex of the Customs document). If there are more than ten different items, then the clearance requires an additional Custom form. It can take up to three to four hours just to pay for the duties charged. Imported goods will also need to pay additional 2 per cent tax to the revenue department and approval of the imports by the national bank, etc. The processing of documents takes place while the imported goods are held at the 105-mile border post near Muse.

All the efficient logistics facilities and services are on the Chinese side. It is easier for Myanmar traders to deliver their goods in Ruili and sell to the Chinese market from there. Myanmar goods are kept duty free in border bonded warehouses and duty is only paid when the goods are sold. Since there is no real incentive to use the limited storage facilities in Muse, most of the warehouses near the 105-mile border gate are largely unused. These are just run-of-the-mill warehouses without any value-added services. There are no bonded warehouses but there is a cold storage warehouse that receives frozen marine products from Yangon to be sold in Kunming and further afield. Commercial viability and quality of this cold storage facility is in question as there are no reefer trucks providing services and trucks use ice and blankets to control the temperature. The cold chain is not well maintained and there are large variations in temperature. Similar issues of logistics under-performance also emerge in the case of the transport for frozen marine products to China.

From an infrastructure perspective, the problem lies mostly with the road conditions and the number of tolls that needs to be crossed in order to link Muse to Lashio and even Mandalay. According to the local chamber of commerce, Muse represents around 70 per cent of border trade with China and it is a key border post for trade. Traffic management along the Muse-Mandalay corridor is critical. There are sixteen Build-Operate-Transfer (BOT) tolls from Mandalay to Muse with "Asia World" company being one of the main concessionaires. When questions about road safety were posed, there is apparently no agency in charge when accidents happen on these BOT roads. Currently, in order to ease congestion, a one-way truck traffic regime is being implemented with scheduled hours of operation such as from 6 a.m. (Lashio to Muse) to noon and 6 p.m. to midnight (Muse to Lashio). This is only a temporary solution to minimize the risk of traffic accidents which are known to induce tremendous delays. There is also a lack of insurance coverage and no roadside service in case of accidents. Freight rates are about one-third higher from Mandalay to Muse than from Muse to Mandalay due to imbalances in traffic flows. There is lack of transparency in the pricing as there is no reference freight price and this makes it difficult for traders to estimate their cost of delivery. Twenty-two wheeled trucks are considered as part of the problem with regards to road erosion and destruction but the quality of constructed roads are equally culpable. There are no truck stops, no truck terminals along the road. Transit time reliability is an issue and it can take from three to four hours (best case) to ten days (worse case) from Muse to Lashio. Low transit time reliability adds to the phenomenon of demand variability amplification between the origin of demand (consumer) and the suppliers along the supply chain. This phenomenon, otherwise known as the "bullwhip" effect[21] (Lee et al. 1997) has an impact on the traffic scheduling being put in place by the authorities.

Trade Logistics Governance at the Subnational Level: The 105-mile Border Gate

The MoC is the lead agency in the governance structure of all trading activities in this border gate. In the case of maritime borders such as ports and airports, clearance activities are led by the Department of Customs but for land border posts, the MoC is in charge of coordinating other related agencies with a "One Stop Service" approach basically meaning that all related agencies are physically co-located in the same building complex. There are six main agencies that are directly involved with the import/export process and eleven related additional agencies that may be involved in the procedure depending on the nature of the shipment. The primary rationale behind the MoC taking the lead is that the border posts are entrusted with the responsibility to meet trade targets.

The MoC has implemented a series of policy measures to facilitate cross-border trade such as temporary increase in traffic flow schedule from two to five times per day and extension of opening-closing time (5 a.m.–10.30 p.m.) for the delivery of Temporary Border Pass (TBP). Chinese cars are allowed to enter into Muse up to 9 p.m. Individual trading cap for small-scale traders has seen an increase from 30 lakhs (one lakh equals to 100,000 kyats) per day to 150 lakhs for five days. However, all these measures are not sufficient to reduce congestion at the 105-mile border post. In addition to the expansion of the road, the officials at the border post also speak of the need to increase the size of the resting area for the trucks from 48 acres to 100 acres.

At this border gate, there is a clear absence of Single Stop Inspection and Single Window Inspection. One of the respondents cited the problems at the border gate to be one of the reasons for the delay in finalization of the Cross-Border Transport Agreement (CBTA), although the agreement has already been signed and ratified by Myanmar. However, it is probably because the CBTA is under the MoTC and the MoC is not aware of this ratification. Myanmar trucks are free to go across the border but they may require a permit to go up to Kunming. Chinese trucks are only allowed to the 105-mile border gate. There is a Joint Border Trade Coordination Cooperation Committee with China. The meetings of this Joint Committee are held every six months in Kunming.

According to the MoC, their biggest challenge is related to the magnitude of illegal trade and undervaluation of traded goods. Smuggling needs to be curbed but the border is too porous and too immense for effective monitoring. It is estimated that there is around thirty to fifty trucks per day that are carrying smuggled goods. Another challenge is that some goods such as sugar, rice and maize can be legally exported from Myanmar but are considered illegal goods in China. This creates even more smuggling activities, which cannot be controlled on the Myanmar side as it is considered a legal activity. The MoC would like to see the establishment of new routes connecting to Muse combining more than one mode of transport so as not to be limited to just road transport.

More importantly, the border area along China is patrolled and governed by multiple ethnic arm groups and militia. Callahan (2007) speaks to the existence of multiple and overlapping areas of authority and jurisdiction in ethnic minority states. In the border areas, the authority and jurisdiction of the central government, especially at the Chinese border, is quite circumscribed and government agencies at the border simply do not have the wherewithal to effectively monitor and regulate multifarious trading activities involving ethnic army groups and militia. In other words, the government only has a limited agency in regulating trade and logistics in the border areas, especially in the vast tract of land outside of the border trade posts.

CONCLUSION AND POLICY RECOMMENDATIONS

In this chapter, we discuss two interlocking layers of challenges — governance of FDI and governance of the logistic sector in Myanmar's pursuit of developmental strategy. We bring our analytical attention to the spatial dimension in the issues of agency with multiplicity of principals and agents in the sector at the level of the union government and also the limited agency of the government in the border. This points to the need for a broader reform of public administration issues as well as conflict-sensitive development agenda. Therefore, we argue that the reform of governance and policy environment in FDI and general investment climate is the first priority in promoting the role of logistics and infrastructure in the national development agenda. Second, it is important to put facilitating FDI in logistics in the context of broader regulatory and policy reforms that can create an enabling ecosystem for the logistics sector. Then, policymakers can pilot reforms in specific sectors such as agriculture, to find out the crosscutting issues in logistics that need to be addressed. With the on-going initiatives in ASEAN, we further argue that clear coordination mechanisms in governance in logistics policies and feedback mechanism from the private sector within Myanmar is crucial for it to benefit from its commitments toward deeper regional economic integration. Facilitating FDI in logistics infrastructures and services can further link companies in Myanmar to GVCs, create productivity gains through the use of new technology, and can create positive spillover effect through linkages with local providers.

Implementing national logistics policies would require a coordinated effort to overcome the collective action problem induced by the presence of multiple principals and multiple agents in fragmented policy space. As discussed in this chapter, the government has launched a National Transport Masterplan and it is also in the process of developing a National Logistics Masterplan, with the MoTC as the lead agency. Yet, these Masterplans need to be coordinated and linked with the overall national strategic priorities. Here the government's role in improving competitiveness of supply chains is to provide LSPs with an institutional, regulatory, and operational environment that can stimulate and guarantee the level of service needed for the efficient movement and storage of goods, services, and information (Banomyong 2010).

Logistics is about managing supply chains and policies affecting logistics typically involve by many agencies/departments. As a first step, the government should examine the existing structure of governance in the service sector and logistics sector with a view to address the issues of agency in these sectors. Secondly, the government can further facilitate inter-departmental coordination by strengthening existing committees or working groups in the service sector. For example, the government can infuse life and vigour to the Special Task Force for Business and Trade Promotion chaired by MoC, by allowing MoTC and Myanmar Customs to co-chair "Transport and Trade Facilitation" working group and giving specific mandate to implement cross-cutting policy actions to facilitate trade logistics.

Rapid development of infrastructure is one of the foremost economic priorities of the new government. Furthermore, basic infrastructure has been mentioned as one of development assistance priorities for the government. Myanmar's development strategy is to prioritize basic infrastructure that will usher significant and fundamental changes in the performance and role of the logistics sector in the country's economic development. FDI in the logistics sector can play a definite role in transferring technical know-how and bringing much-needed physical capital in making Myanmar's economy competitive both regionally and globally.

It is also important for the government to forge a close and intimate feedback link with the private sector by facilitating a structured public–private dialogue on logistics issues.[22] The purpose of such a dialogue is to provide a structured forum for both local and international LSPs to express their views and concerns, with the view of contributing to the policy dialogue on the logistics sector. The pending formation of a national logistics association would also be helpful in shaping the tenor and texture of the dialogue. At the same time, Myanmar can use the ASEAN Framework Agreement on Services (AFAS) and on-going negotiations for the RCEP as reference points for dialogue on domestic policy reforms in logistics and identify actions that would allow domestic logistics providers to optimize benefits from openness and competition.

Notes

1. The authors would like to thank Dr Sjamsu Raharja of the World Bank office in Myanmar for his inputs in this chapter.
2. <http://www.moj.go.jp/content/000112674.pdf> (accessed 5 March 2017).
3. <http://www.burmalibrary.org/docs15/2013-FIL-Notification-1-2013-bu.pdf> (accessed 5 March 2017).
4. <http://www.allenovery.com/SiteCollectionDocuments/Myanmar%20-%20 Myanmar%20revises%20scope%20of%20prohibited%20and%20restricted%20 activities%20for%20foreign%20investment.pdf> (accessed 5 March 2017).
5. <http://www.dica.gov.mm/sites/dica.gov.mm/files/document-files/myanmar_ investment_law_draft_as_of_060716_translated_by_kcy_14_july_2016.pdf> (accessed 5 March 2017).
6. <http://www.dica.gov.mm/en/information-myanmar-investment-commission-mic> (accessed 5 March 2017).
7. <http://www.dica.gov.mm/sites/dica.gov.mm/files/document-files/fdipp.pdf> (accessed 5 March 2017).
8. <http://www.reuters.com/article/us-myanmar-investment-idUSKCN0YW13O> (accessed 5 March 2017); <http://frontiermyanmar.net/en/business/new-team-mic-faces-application-backlog> (accessed 5 March 2017).
9. <http://www.unescap.org/sites/default/files/10.2.Myanmar.pdf> (accessed 5 March 2017).
10. Ibid. <http://www.sugaronline.com/website_contents/view/1240345> (accessed 5 March 2017).
11. <http://www.mmtimes.com/index.php/business/18328-china-sucks-in-myanmar-sugar.html> (accessed 5 March 2017).
12. <http://www.mmtimes.com/index.php/business/20587-containers-pile-up-as-trade-backlog-clears-at-yangon-ports.html> (accessed 5 March 2017).
13. <http://www.mmtimes.com/index.php/national-news/yangon/24140-strand-road-backed-up-by-new-shipping-policy.html> (accessed 5 March 2017).
14. <http://www.agrimoney.com/news/china-sugar-import-curbs-may-prompt-rise-in-smuggling--8163.html> (accessed 5 March 2017).
15. <http://www.smedevelopmentcenter.gov.mm/sites/default/files/MOC1.pdf> (accessed 5 March 2017).
16. <http://centreforaviation.com/> (accessed 5 March 2017).
17. Interviews with the officials from the Ministry of Transport and Communications.

18. <http://www.dica.gov.mm/sites/dica.gov.mm/files/document-files/notification_26-2016_0.pdf?_ga=1.17940025.1803708208.1477828913> (accessed 5 March 2017).
19. Notification 96/2015, Union of Myanmar.
20. The green lane means that goods will not be subject to full physical inspections and can go through the border gate without stopping but post-audit may occur based on customs risk management practices. Yellow lane means that there will be a documentary inspection of the goods before a decision is made for full physical inspection and red means that the goods will have to be physically inspected every time.
21. The "bullwhip" effect is a common supply chain phenomenon where amplification occurs along the supply chain members when there is a change in consumer demand. The supply chain member that is the furthest from the end consumer will be the most affected by the "bullwhip" effect. The effect is akin to the impact of a tsunami on the shores where the waves maybe be just one metre high of the coast but when the waves arrives on the beach its height might be more than ten metres and destroy everything in its path.
22. For example, using Myanmar Business Forum as a platform for a structured public–private dialogue.

References

Allen & Overy. "Myanmar Revises Scope of Prohibited and Restricted Activities for Foreign Investment", September 2014. Available at <http://www.allenovery.com/SiteCollectionDocuments/Myanmar%20-%20Myanmar%20revises%20scope%20of%20prohibited%20and%20restricted%20activities%20for%20foreign%20investment.pdf> (accessed 7 March 2017).

ASEAN Secretariat and the World Bank. *ASEAN Services Integration Report*. Jakarta and Washington, D.C.: ASEAN Secretariat and the World Bank, 2015. Available at <https://openknowledge.worldbank.org/bitstream/handle/10986/22919/ASEAN0services0t0and0the0World0Bank.pdf?sequence=1&isAllowed=y> (accessed 7 March 2017).

Aung, Winston. "The Role of Informal Cross-border Trade in Myanmar". Asia Paper. Stockholm-Nacka: Institute of Security and Development Policy, 2009.

Baldwin, Richard. "Trade and Industrialisation After Globalisation's 2nd Unbundling: How Building and Joining a Supply Chain Are Different and Why It Matters". National Bureau of Economic Research, 2011. Available at <http://www.nber.org/papers/w17716.pdf> (accessed 7 March 2017).

Banomyong, Ruth. "Supply Chain Dynamics in Asia". ADBI Working Paper Series no. 184. Tokyo: Asian Development Bank Institute, 2010. Available at <https://www.adb.org/sites/default/files/publication/156039/adbi-wp184.pdf> (accessed 7 March 2017).

Bissinger, Jared. "Foreign Investment in Myanmar: A Resource Boom but a Development Bust?" *Contemporary Southeast Asia: A Journal of International and Strategic Affairs* 34, no. 1 (2012): 23–52.

Borchert, Ingo, Batshur Gootiiz and Aaditya Mattoo. "Guide to the Services Trade Restrictions Database". Policy Research Working Paper no. 6108. Washington, D.C.: World Bank, 2012. Available at <https://papers.ssrn.com/sol3/papers.cfm?abstract_id=2096025> (accessed 7 March 2017).

Callahan, Mary P. "Political Authority in Burma's Ethnic Minority States: Devolution, Occupation and Coexistence". *Policy Studies* 31 (Southeast Asia). Washington, D.C. and Singapore: East-West Center Washington and Institute of Southeast Asian Studies, 2007.

Duggan, Victor, Sjamsu Rahardja and Gonzalo J. Varela. "Service Sector Reform and Manufacturing Productivity: Evidence from Indonesia". Policy Research Working Paper Series no. 6349. Washington, D.C.: World Bank, 2013. Available at <https://papers.ssrn.com/sol3/papers.cfm?abstract_id=2210300> (accessed 7 March 2017).

Gootiz, Batshur and Aaditya Mattoo. "Regionalism in Services: A Study of ASEAN". Policy Research Working Paper no. 7498. Washington, D.C.: World Bank, 2015.

Integrated Household Living Conditions Survey Project Technical Unit (IHLCSPTU). *Integrated Household Living Conditions Survey in Myanmar (2004–2005).* Yangon: Ministry of National Planning and Economic Development, United Nations Development Programme, United Nations Children's Fund, Swedish International Development Cooperation Agency, 2006.

———. *Integrated Household Living Conditions Survey in Myanmar (2009–2010).* Yangon: Ministry of National Planning and Economic Development, United Nations Development Programme, United Nations Children's Fund, Swedish International Development Cooperation Agency, June 2011.

Lee, Hau L., V. Padmanabhan, and Seungjin Whang. "The Bullwhip Effect in Supply Chains". *Sloan Management Review* 38, no. 3 (1997): 93–102.

Mclaughlin, Timothy and Aung Hla Tun. "Myanmar's New Investment Commission to Tackle $2.3 Billion Backlog". *Reuters*, 10 June 2016.

Myanmar Investment Commission. *The Foreign Investment Law (The Pyidaungsu Hluttaw Law no 21/2012).* Nay Pyi Taw: Myanmar Investment Commission, 2 November 2012.

———. "Myanmar Investment Commission: Notification no. 1/2013". Nay Pyi Taw: Myanmar Investment Commission, 31 January 2013.

———. "Myanmar Investment Law (The Pyidaungsu Hluttaw Law no. 40/2016)". Nay Pyi Taw: Myanmar Investment Commission, 18 October 2016.

Myint, Than. "New Team at MIC Faces Application Backlog". *Frontier Myanmar*, 13 June 2016. Available at <http://frontiermyanmar.net/en/business/new-team-mic-faces-application-backlog> (accessed 7 March 2016).

Myo, Ei Ei. "Key Logistics and Transport System and Facilities Along the AH and TAR". United Nations Economic and Social Commission for Asia and the Pacific, 2012. Available at <http://www.unescap.org/sites/default/files/10.2.Myanmar.pdf> (accessed 7 March 2017).

World Bank. *Myanmar Diagnostic Trade Integration Study: Opening for Business*. Washington, D.C.: World Bank, 2016. Available at <http://www.worldbank.org/en/country/myanmar/publication/myanmar-diagnostic-trade-integration-study> (accessed 7 March 2017).

INDEX

www.ingramcontent.com/pod-product-compliance
Lightning Source LLC
Chambersburg PA
CBHW060133280326
41932CB00012B/1509